D1535261

THE JAPANESE BOND MARKETS

AN OVERVIEW & ANALYSIS

FRANK J. FABOZZI

EDITOR

PROBUS PUBLISHING COMPANY
Chicago, Illinois

© 1990, Frank J. Fabozzi

This publication is designed to provide accurate and authoritative information in regard to the subject matter covered. It is sold with the understanding that the publisher is not engaged in rendering legal, accounting or other professional service.

Library of Congress Cataloging in Publication Data Available

ISBN 1-55738-112-7

Printed in the United States of America

1   2   3   4   5   6   7   8   9   0

This book is dedicated to the memory of

Zenon S. Zannetos
Associate Dean and Professor of Management
Sloan School of Management, MIT

and

Leah G. Karp

Contents

PREFACE

The Japanese Bond Markets is designed to provide detailed information on the various sectors of the world's second largest bond market. The historical development, prevailing structure and market conventions are described for each bond sector—Japanese government bonds, Japanese government-related organization bonds, local government bonds, bank debentures, corporate bonds, convertible bonds, foreign bonds (including Samurai bonds, Daimyo bonds, Shibosai bonds, Shogun bonds and Geisha bonds), and Euroyen bonds. There is also coverage of repurchase agreements (gensaki), commercial paper and the Japanese government bond futures contract.

This book does *not* provide trading strategies or techniques for analyzing the various types of Japanese bonds. Nor does it attempt to convince the reader of the opportunities available in this market. No doubt there will be times when a combination of exchange rates and Japanese/non-Japanese yield spreads will present opportunities for non-Japanese institutional investors who have committed to global bond investing to enhance yield and for borrowers who seek financing in the global bond market to reduce their all-in-cost of funds.

This book is intended as a source of information for all those who currently participate or plan to participate in the Japanese bond market.

Acknowledgements

First, and foremost, I would like to express my appreciation to the contributors. This book is the product of a group thesis project that I supervised at MIT in the 1988–1989 academic year. With the exception of the appendix to Chapter 15, all contributors were graduate students at MIT's Alfred P. Sloan School of Management. Each student either had experience in the Japanese or U.S. bond market before attending MIT and/or had extensive training in financial markets at MIT as part of their coursework. The internationally diversified student body at MIT, coupled with the exceptional intellectual skills of students in the program, provided the ideal environment for this project.

I wish to thank the following individuals at the Sloan School for their assistance at various stages of this project: Arnoldo Hax (Deputy Dean of the Sloan School), David Weber (Associate Director of the Master's Program), Alan White (Associate Dean for Executive Education and Director, Sloan Fellows Program), Eleanor Chin (Administrative Assistant and Program Coordinator, Sloan Fellows Program) and Mary Marshall (Area Administrator of the Department of Applied Economics, Finance and Accounting). Thanks are also due to John Cox, Chi-fu Huang, Stewart Myers (Director, International Financial Services Center), Antonio Mello, and David Scharfstein for their comments on earlier drafts of some of the chapters. My secretary Jean Marie DeJordy and my administrative assistant Nate Weiss did a fine job coordinating various aspects of this project. Finally, I would like to thank the members of the editorial advisory board for their help.

Frank J. Fabozzi

EDITORIAL ADVISORY BOARD

CHAPTER 1

Overview

Frank J. Fabozzi
Visiting Professor of Finance
Sloan School of Management
Massachusetts Institute of Technology

The Japanese bond market is the second largest bond market in the world. As of December 1988, the total amount of publicly issued Japanese bonds outstanding was $2.161 trillion, compared to $4.517 trillion for the U.S. bond market. The Japanese bond market is almost three times the size of the West German bond market. Exhibit 1 compares the size of the Japanese bond market and its various sectors to that of other countries. Within the Japanese bond market, the largest sector is the Japanese government bond (JGB) market. While the Japanese bond market is slightly less than half the size of the U.S. bond market, the JGB sector is almost the same size as the U.S. Treasury market.

With the liberalization of Japanese financial markets in 1984 and the internationalization of the yen, certain sectors of the bond market have grown dramatically,[1] particularly the international bond sector which includes foreign bonds and Euroyen bonds. Moreover, the menu of permissible bond structures has been expanded as a result of relaxation of regulations. Permitting corporations to issue unsecuritized bonds (i.e., bonds not backed by specific collateral) is one example.

1

EXHIBIT 1: SIZE OF MAJOR BOND MARKETS AT YEAR-END 1988

(Nominal Value Outstanding; Billions of U.S. Dollars Equivalent[a])

Bond Market	Total Publicly Issued	As a % of Public Issues in All Markets	Central Govt.	Central Govt. Agency & Govt. Guar.	State & Local Govt.	Corp. (incl. Cvts.)	Other Domestic Publicly Issued	Intl. Bonds[b] Foreign Bonds	Intl. Bonds[b] Euro-bonds	Private Place. Unclass.
U.S. Dollar	$4,517.0	46.3%	$1,425.8	$1,116.9	$759.6	$715.8	$26.5	$59.9	$412.5	$496.2
Japanese Yen	2,161.0	22.1	1,227.5	152.6	55.2	184.0	433.3	38.0	70.4	335.0
Deutschemark	753.5	7.7	195.1	32.4	20.4	1.3	397.6		106.7	297.5[b]
Italian Lira	534.3	5.5	414.9	22.2	—	5.1	87.4	1.9	2.8	—
U.K. Sterling	344.4	3.5	247.6	—	0.2	2.3	—	6.5	67.1	—
French Franc	332.4	3.4	101.8	152.5	3.0	63.1	—	3.2	8.8	—
Canadian Dollar	245.3	2.5	94.6	—	79.3	37.0	0.9	0.8	32.7	—
Belgian Franc	187.8	1.9	109.6	43.9	—	5.4	22.9	5.6	0.4	—
Danish Krone	159.7	1.6	43.6	—	—	—	112.0	—	4.1	—
Swedish Krone	157.0	1.6	65.0	—	2.2	9.7	79.9	—	0.2	—
Swiss Franc	156.3	1.6	6.8	—	9.1	29.7	33.8	76.9	—	47.3
Dutch Guilder	133.5	1.4	80.3	—	3.2	33.4	—	9.5	7.1	86.2[c]
Australian Dollar	81.6	0.8	30.8	18.0	—	3.3	—	—	29.5	—
Total	$9,763.8[d]	100.0%	$4,043.4	$1,538.5	$932.2	$1,110.8	$1,194.3	$944.6[d]		$1,262.2[c]
Sector as a % of Public Issues in All Markets			41.4%	15.8%	9.5%	11.4%	12.2%	9.7%		

[a] Exchange rates prevailing as of December 31, 1988: ¥125.85/US$, DM1.7803/US$, Lit1,305.8/US$, £0.5526/US$, Ffr6.059/US$, C$1.1927/US$, Bfr37.345/US$, Dkr6.874/US$, Skr6.157/US$, Sfr1.504/US$, Dfl 1.9995/US$, A$1.689/US$, and ECU0.861/US$.
[b] Includes straight, convertible and floating-rate debt.
[c] In addition, there exists an unspecifiable amount of privately placed issues of the private sectors.
[d] In addition, $39.3 billion ECU-denominated Eurobonds were outstanding at year-end 1988.

Source: Rosario Benavides, "How Big is the World Bond Market?—1989 Update," Bond Market Research, International Bond Market Analysis, Salomon Brothers Inc (July 24, 1989), p.1.

The growth of satellite markets is also important to the functioning of the Japanese bond market. It would be difficult to conceive of a well-functioning U.S. bond market without the repurchase ("repo") agreement market. This market allows dealers to finance long positions and cover short positions; that is, it allows the buying and selling of collateral. The gensaki market is the Japanese repo market. The development of this market has provided dealers, as well as other market participants, with a mechanism for taking positions and thereby furnishing liquidity.

Other satellite markets include the market for derivative contracts: futures, options (on bonds and on futures), interest rate swaps, interest rate caps, etc. These contracts are employed by market participants to control interest rate risk. Their development is important for financial institutions seeking to accomplish asset/liability objectives, issuers wishing to protect against rising interest rates, and market participants attempting to arbitrage market inefficiencies. While the JGB futures contract was only introduced in October 1985, within a few years it had grown to the largest futures market in the world. In April 1989, an over-the-counter market for options on JGBs began; the trading of options on JGB futures contracts (i.e., futures options) is planned for mid-1990.

ROADMAP OF BOOK

Details of all key facets of the Japanese bond markets are presented in the 14 chapters that follow. Chapter 2 explains the historical development of the Japanese bond market, examining the roots of the present system and the key factors leading to liberalization and internationalization of the market. Participants in the Japanese bond market are explained in Chapter 3. For each participant their roles and investment behavior are explained. The Ministry of Finance is covered in this chapter.

Chapter 4 covers four important topics. First, conventions for calculating and quoting yields, remaining life or time to maturity under different circumstances, irregular first and final coupon payments, and accrued interest payments are explained. Second, several methods for calculating bond price volatility are explained. Third, pertinent tax provisions are reviewed. Finally, a brief review of the software for bond investing is provided.

Chapter 5 details the JGB market, followed by details of the gensaki market in Chapter 6. Japanese government-related organization bonds carry explicit guarantees on interest and principal from the Japanese government. They are described in Chapter 7. Local government bonds, which are debt instruments issued by various cities, prefectures, towns and villages of Japan, are the subject of Chapter 8. As of 1989, only six banks are permitted to issue bonds to support their ongoing business under Japanese law. The characteristics of these bonds, called bank debentures, are covered in Chapter 9.

Corporate securities are covered in Chapters 10, 11 and 12. Chapter 10 describes the commercial paper market—unsecured promissory notes issued by corporations to raise short-term funds. Chapter 11 reviews yen-denominated bonds that are issued in the Japanese domestic market by Japanese corporations. Because of the significant use of convertible bond financing by Japanese corporations in the 1980s, both domestically and overseas, a separate chapter, Chapter 12, is devoted to this bond structure.

The international bond market sector includes the foreign bond market and the Euroyen bond market. Foreign bonds may be yen-denominated or non-yen denominated. There are three types of foreign bonds that are yen-denominated: Samurai bonds, Daimyo bonds and Shibosai bonds. Shogun bonds and Geisha bonds, two other types of foreign bonds, are non-yen denominated. Foreign bonds are described in Chapter 13.

Eurobonds are those bonds underwritten and sold by an international syndicate in one or more international capital markets and, at issuance, are usually purchased by investors outside the governing country of the currency that denominates the cash flows. Issues denominated in yen are called Euroyen bonds. Chapter 14 describes the major innovations in the Euroyen bond market, as well as illustrating how interest rate and currency swaps have been employed.

The Japanese bond futures contract is covered in Chapter 15. This chapter highlights the differences and similarities in contract features and trading mechanics between these contracts and futures contracts on U.S. Treasury bonds. The appendix to Chapter 15 discusses the derivation of conversion factors for the contract and the role they play in the delivery mechanism.

ENDNOTES

[1] The growth of the various sectors of the bond market is shown in Exhibit 2 of Chapter 4.

CHAPTER 2

Historical Development of the Japanese Bond Market

Issen Sato
Tokyo, Japan

E.M. Kanovsky
Paris, France

In order to understand the present Japanese bond market, we must first examine the historical origins of the present system, and then the development of, and rationale behind, its internationalization and liberalization.

HISTORY OF THE JAPANESE FINANCIAL SYSTEM TO 1983

The Meiji Restoration until World War II

World War I and the interwar years saw the development of heavy industries, the consequential strengthening of the zaibatsu and the expansion of both the stock and bond markets.

Japan's two stock exchanges, at Tokyo and at Osaka, were established in 1878 (the Stock Exchange Ordinance), only ten years after the Meiji Restoration directly following the Tokugawa Shogunate. Government bond issues constituted the principal activity, with only slight trading in stocks. During this period, the predominant position

7

of the banks in loaning funds was established, particularly in relation with the zaibatsu companies, which were not active on the stock market until after World War I. The securities houses, on the other hand, dealt chiefly in national government bonds and in speculative stock transactions.

Since the 1921 recommendations by the then Minister of Finance, Korekiyo Takahashi, to amalgamate the small regional banks, and the 1924 decision by that Ministry in support of that recommendation, the Japanese government has played a major regulatory and policy-shaping role in Japan's financial system.

The Banking Law of 1927 provided the foundation for the banking system. (It was significantly revised only in 1981.) At that time, the banking system was divided into two sectors, national banks and small regional banks.

National banks had originally been set up after the Meiji restoration as partly government-owned institutions to finance basic industries on a long-term basis. They later became privatized as did commercial, trust, savings banks and the like. The big five banks that served the large industrial sectors and/or the zaibatsu, i.e., Mitsui, Mitsubishi, Yasuda, were national banks and dominated the loan market. The small regional banks lent funds mainly to small traditional industries, such as textiles.

Government control was, not surprisingly, enhanced during World War II, by the regulation of the securities industry for the war effort and the unification of the then 11 stock exchanges in the country into a single "Japan Securities Exchange."

World War II until 1955

Following World War II and until 1970–1971, the Japanese financial system, and its economy in general, were characterized by strict government control and objectives of growth and productivity through investment and exports. Japan's adherence to the fixed exchange-rate system of Bretton Woods of 1949 resulted in an institutionalized balance of payments deficit until the mid-1960s.

Japan responded to this exogenous factor by instituting foreign exchange controls, strict limitations to foreign investment, import quotas, tariffs, and tax incentives to promote exports. Until the end of the Bretton Woods system, Japan was a developing, semi-industrialized country, enjoying a high-growth period and continually improving terms of trade.

Postwar strategy was based on a "strong growth and productivity orientation of both government and business."[1] Both in Japan, and internationally, this was a period (1956–1971) of high growth and relative international stability.

The postwar environment was characterized chiefly by "export/investment-led high growth, the artificially low interest rate policy, and barriers to internationalization as well as predominance of indirect (bank) financing."[2]

Industrial policy formulation at this time (and until about 1965) was controlled by the Ministry of International Trade and Industry (MITI) and dominated by the pre-war generation of economists, which was "dedicated to the transformation of a defeated, underdeveloped nation into a modern, developed state through the creation of an industrial base hidden behind protective barriers."[3]

The Financial System—Regulation. One of the fundamental characteristics of the financial system, the separation between banks (for lending and borrowing) and the securities houses (for underwriting of securities), was introduced through the 1948 Securities and Exchange Law, modeled after the U.S. Securities Act of 1933.

Under this law, banks cannot underwrite securities except for public bonds and debentures. The law's Article 65 forbids banks from underwriting securities (but they can buy and sell them on behalf of their customers and can buy the new issues of government bonds directly through the syndicates).

The Ministry of Finance directed most activities of the financial sector (banks and securities houses) through ministerial ordinances and notifications, which could be enacted without seeking approval of the Japanese parliament, the Diet.

An example of the parallel powers is seen in the early control of interest rates. The Temporary Interest Rate Law of 1947 controlled maximum interest rates for bank deposits, which it maintained at a low level. It also set the maximum lending rate for all short-term (one year or less) bank loans with a principal amount of more than one million yen. But such loan rates could be set anywhere between the maximum rate and the prime rate, which was linked to the official discount rate determined by the Bank of Japan.

After World War II, trading was suspended on the Exchange on August 9, 1945. In 1947, the zaibatsu were liquidated and, through the "Securities Democratization Movement," a massive sale of stocks to individual investors was effected through the Securities Coordination Liquidation Committee. The character of the Japanese stock market was democratized and thereafter radically transformed.

An Anti-Monopoly Law based on U.S. antitrust laws was also introduced in 1947, but exemptions to this law were authorized on the basis of economic growth and productivity objectives.

Prior to the opening of a new stock exchange in 1949, the "Three Principles of Market Operation" were enacted, according to which "(1) transactions are to be recorded in the order that they take place, (2) transactions are to be concentrated on the exchanges, and (3) future transactions are not to be conducted."[4]

Two years later after the outbreak of the Korean War, margin transactions were introduced and the Securities Investment Trust Law instituted an investment trust system.

Other policies to promote growth and productivity included tax incentives to promote savings (including exemption of taxes on income from certain small savings accounts, both in the banking and postal services, and tax advantages to promote growth of companies and of exports). Certain developing target industries were also protected.

The Financial System—Operations. Since the end of World War II, the Japanese financial system used indirect financing, overloans, and overborrowing, among its practices.[5]

Indirect financing means raising funds through borrowing from banks (as opposed to raising funds through equity or debt issues). While banks remained the chief source of corporate financing, particularly for those in the keiretsu structures, other·institutions were created with more specialized objectives. The Export-Import Bank of Japan and the Japan Development Bank were established in 1950 and 1951 respectively to funnel funds to projects promoted by the government for development. The Japan Development Bank provided loans at lower interest rates and for longer terms than banks and did not impose any minimum balance requirements, but remained a "relatively insignificant" source of financing as a percentage of all loans.[6]

"Overloans" from city banks resulted from an almost exclusive corporate reliance on bank loans which led to a shortage of available capital. The government responded to the supplementary demand through loans directly from the Bank of Japan via the city banks. (It was not until 1963 that the government's Committee of Financial Systems Research recommended the "normalization" ("Seijhoka") of the relationship between the two institutions.[7]) The city banks were also active in an "overborrowing" relationship with the major corporations. The latter relied on the city banks for most of their financing, due in part to deliberate government restriction of development of the bond market.

There are two types of lending rates: the short-term lending rate (regulated) and the long-term lending rate (free rate set by consensus).

The Short-term Lending Rate. In 1959, the prime rate system related to short-term lending was formally introduced into Japan. This system was modeled on the U.S. prime rate system. At that time, the Banking Federation (composed of all banks in Japan), by a consensus procedure, set the prime rate as a minimum lending rate.

The high-growth period (until about 1965) was a lenders' market. As a result, the short-term prime rates were applied only to corporations with excellent performances. The oil crises and the economic slowdown that followed led to a borrowers' market, and the prime rate was applied on a wider basis.

As we have stated, the actual short-term lending rate is set between the prime rate and the maximum lending rate regulated by the Temporary Interest Rate Adjustment Law. (However, in practice, required compensation deposits made by borrowers make the effective rate much higher than the nominal rate.)

The Long-term Prime Rate. The long-term prime rate ("LTPR") was not regulated by the Temporary Interest Rate Adjustment Law, as was the short-term prime rate. Each bank could, at least theoretically, decide upon its own rate.

In practice, however, the long-term prime rate applied by the long-term credit banks and trust banks to their best clients is based on a consensus among the parties involved, including legislators. This LTPR has been the coupon rate of the five-year bank debenture plus 0.9%.[8]

Other financial institutions, such as city and regional banks and insurance companies, apply the long-term prime rate for long-term lending to their best clients.

Market Rates. Artificial control of interest rates at low levels, which applied to long- and short-term prime lending rates, as well as, on the asset side, to those held by private investors (such as rates on deposits or subscribers' yields on bonds), did not preclude the development of other financial markets in which the rates were market-determined and higher than the government-controlled rates. Such market rates were, for example, the call rate, CD rate, and yields on bonds in the secondary market.

An indirect effect of controlled rates, as Suzuki points out,[9] was—and is—protection of financial firms with growth potential.

The Economic Expansion after the Korean War until 1965

During this period of expansion, domestic demand and exports increased, leading to expansion in production and in investment and equipment. Japan's industries needed financing not only for capital investment, but also to import the needed raw materials and oil.

The government continued a policy of high growth through productivity and exports. Government investments in the economy and the expectations that the government's policy would succeed in expanding the Japanese economy were factors contributing to this high growth era.

The Financial System—Regulation. This period still saw the dominance of indirect (bank) financing. The economic boom as a result of the Korean War was accompanied by further organization of the financial system, through such legislation as the Mutual Financing Bank Law, the Credit Bank Law, the Long-Term Credit Bank Law, the Loan Trust Law, and others.

In 1951, the Export Import Bank of Japan was established, initially to provide funding for exports. In 1952, this mandate was widened to also provide funding for imports.

The Financial System—Operations in the Securities Market.   Following the two-year decline in economic activity directly after the Korean War, the five-year expansionary period after 1955 saw the growth of stock investment trusts, the modification—in August 1955—of the Securities and Exchange Law to provide for the formation of securities finance companies, and—in April 1956—the resumption of trading of bonds on the Tokyo and Osaka stock exchanges.

In February 1960, stock investment trusts were formally separated from securities houses, to which they had in general been subsidiaries. Public bond investment trusts were authorized at the beginning of the following year in order to widen the basis of savings. In October, a second section of the Tokyo Stock Exchange, as well as of the Osaka and Nagoya Exchanges, was authorized.

Over a two-year period starting in July 1961, a tight monetary policy led to a series of liquidations of stock holdings and of stock investment trusts, and to the enactment of temporary cooperative measures and long-term actions to stem the repercussions. For example:

(1) bond transactions were suspended in April 1962 on the Tokyo and Osaka exchanges,

(2) the Japan Joint Securities Corporation was set up at the beginning of 1964 (by banks and security houses), followed one year later by the establishment of the Japan Securities Holding Association (by the securities houses). Their purpose was to absorb the overflow of stocks and investment trusts that were being liquidated on the market. Their holdings were gradually sold off during the market recovery period. (They eventually made a profit and were dissolved in 1971 and 1969, respectively.)

(3) emergency loans were granted to Yamaichi Securities Company and to Ohi Securities Company in May and July of 1965 by the Bank of Japan.

The stock market recovered in July 1965, and the bond market reopened in February 1966 with the issuance of government bonds.

Following the upturn in the economy, revisions were made in the Securities and Exchange Law (substitution of licensing system for prior registration system) and in the investment trust system (to protect beneficiaries). Improvements were made in the system of margin transactions on the stock market (in August 1967) as well as to the disclosure system, including modification of the Certified Public Accountant Law in June 1966. Baikai transactions (simultaneous buying and selling of the same stock issue by the same exchange member) were also abolished.

The economy continued improving, due to among other factors an improvement in its balance of payments.

During this period of the mid-1960s, government control over the economy was loosened, but MITI (which lost control over foreign exchange allocations during this decade) and other agencies maintained great influence through an informal system of guidelines and directives.

The Start of Relaxation of Controls: 1971–1983

At the beginning of the new decade, the situation was exactly the same as in the periods previously described. The closed Japanese financial system was characterized by:

(1) corporate reliance on indirect financing (through banks and other financial institutions) rather than on direct financing (use of equity and debt issues). As a result, banks played a predominant role in the economy, as opposed to securities houses.

(2) two sets of interest rates, one regulated and inflexible—the other dependent on market forces.[10]

(3) continued indebtedness of the city banks to the Bank of Japan.

(4) isolation of the Japanese financial system from international markets, including strict limitations of capital inflows.

However, this highly-controlled economy received a series of shocks starting with the new decade.

Stock prices fell drastically in April 1970, following the news of the collapse of Bernard Cornfeld's IOS, which had marketed investment trusts (mutual funds) worldwide. This shock was followed in August 1971 with the Nixon announcement that the U.S. dollar was no longer pegged to gold. (By the end of the year, however, the major industrial nations had established a new currency realignment with percentage adjustments permitted above and below a fixed rate, e.g., ¥308/$ ± 2.5%.) In February and March of 1973, the major countries switched from fixed (adjustable) to floating exchange rates.

Following the collapse of Bretton Woods, yen-denominated assets were expected to appreciate and lead to increased buying by foreign investors. Therefore, the government imposed stern restrictions on currency inflows. These restrictions were relaxed only in 1974, when the government needed funds to finance budget deficits following the oil crisis.

The oil crisis also brought about a shift in the relative terms of trade, which now became less favorable to a Japan dependent both on imports of oil and of raw materials. From a country of high growth, Japan's GNP fell dramatically in 1974.

With the slowdown in economic growth, demand for goods and services declined, investments in plant and equipment declined, demand for borrowing declined, and tax revenues declined (but government expenditure increased). Exports, however, continued to rise. With government expenditure increasing, the government issued more bonds in the marketplace, and the price of government bonds fell.

The oil crises brought about a reorientation in Japan's industrial sector. Prior to the crises, industry was oriented towards capital-intensive heavy industry. Afterwards, industry was oriented to more skill-intensive industries.

The Financial System—Regulation. Following the end of the gold exchange standard and the end-of-year 1971 adjustment, Japan was the recipient of major international investments. During this same period, Samurai bonds were authorized (yen-denominated bonds issued by foreigners).[11] The Law on Foreign Securities Firms was passed in March 1971, and four months later the ban on investment by Japanese investors in foreign securities was cancelled. These measures were undertaken principally to control the Japanese capital surplus.

But deregulation at this time aimed also to insulate the regulated domestic sector from increasing international activities. (Only in 1984, with the policy of promoting the internationalization of the yen, were the controls relaxed.) For example, only government or supranational organizations such as the World Bank were allowed to issue in the Samurai bond market.

Prior to the first oil shock of 1973, inflationary pressures within Japan had resulted in contractionary policies by the government, including contraction of credit and increase in the official discount rate from 4.25% to 9.00%. Further measures were taken to curtail demand following the first oil crisis in the fall of 1973.

As a result, the volume of activities on the stock market was drastically reduced. In contrast, bond market yields increased so rapidly that terms of issue had to be revised five times in 1973 and 1974, and four times in 1975.[12]

Issues of yen-denominated foreign bonds (Samurai bonds) were suspended at the end of 1973 on the Tokyo market after the Brazilian government issued Samurai bonds for 10 billion yen. The market was reopened in July 1975, when the Finnish government issued Samurai bonds for the same amount.

After the oil crises, certain limited corporations were allowed to enter the Samurai market.

The Tokyo market became more active and more international, in both stock and bond trading. Corporations started issuing stocks and convertible bonds at market value (instead of the previous par value), and, as refers specifically to bonds, the terms of issue and maturities became more varied, and the size of issues increased.

This trend toward internationalization was reflected in the new Foreign Exchange Control Law of 1980, which eased international capital movements and established the principle of liberalization.

The Financial System—Operations. Following the 1973 oil crisis, a major shift also took place in the banking sector. First, let's look at the impact on borrowers. Prior to this period, corporations had been the major borrowers and corporate investment had been the major stimulus behind the rapid growth of the economy. However, the crisis resulted in huge government spending, which resulted in large government deficits that had to be funded. The government turned to massive issuances of long-term public bonds, which were underwritten chiefly by banks. These required that the secondary bond market and short-term money markets be more developed.

By mid-1974, public-sector deficits had replaced corporate deficits as the major sector of investments (until about 1978 when corporate investment started expanding). This period coincided with decreased corporate demand for financing (1974–1978), and the banks were thus able to transfer their surplus funds to the public sector. The decrease in corporate demand also led to a wider application of the prime rate, which in 1970 was established at the discount rate plus 0.25% (the discount rate was and is set by the Bank of Japan, as it is by the Central Banks in other nations).

In 1975, the Banking Federation's authority was replaced by the Leading Bank system, in which a leading bank determined the prime rate, and other banks followed suit. This change was introduced in response to antitrust regulations.

Since 1981, the prime rate has been the discount rate plus at least 0.50%, now announced by the leading bank. (The prime rate has been set at the discount rate - 2.5%, since February 1987, plus 0.875% = 3.375%. See Exhibits 1 and 2.) The discount rate was raised on May 31, 1989 to 3.25%, and a new prime rate system based on actual costs of funding is being gradually introduced.

Since 1983, more than 70% of the short-term loans have been offered at the prime rate or second tier prime rate (prime rate plus 0.25%).

Second, as for the impact on institutions, the share of deposits held by banks fell from 68.8% in 1970 to 54.5% in 1979, to the benefit of the government-run postal savings system, which increased from 19.0% in 1970 to 32.6% in 1979. These deposits then were used as sources of finance by the government through the Development Bank, Export-Import Bank, and others.

Third, the control of monetary policy exercised by the Bank of Japan was diminished as the city banks reduced the level of the "overloans" granted to them by the BOJ. During this period, there was little change in the determination of interest rates in the bank loan market (which were set with reference to the government discount rate by the leading bank—at the discount rate plus 0.5%—and which were below the free market level). There was also little change in the long-term bond market (where interest rates were set primarily or in conjunction with the Ministry of Finance in the issue market). In the Samurai bond market, the interest rates at issue were largely determined by reference to market rates, but the MOF intervened to maintain a balance with the domestic bond market.

The second oil crisis of 1979 saw the stock market remain relatively stable, but the bond market remained very slow due to the major issuances of government bonds and the continued tightening

EXHIBIT 1: OFFICIAL DISCOUNT RATE

As of Yearend

	Japan	US	UK	Germany	France	Italy	Canada	Swiss
1980	7.25	13.00	14.00	7.50	10.75	16.50	17.26	3.00
1981	5.50	12.00	14.38	7.50	15.13	19.00	14.66	6.00
1982	5.50	8.50	10.00	5.00	12.75	18.00	10.26	4.50
1983	5.00	8.50	9.00	4.00	12.00	17.00	10.04	4.00
1984	5.00	8.00	9.38	4.50	10.75	16.50	10.09	4.00
1985	5.00	7.50	11.31	4.00	8.75	15.00	9.49	4.00
1986	3.00	5.50	10.81	3.50	7.25	12.00	8.49	4.00
1987	2.50	6.00	8.38	2.50	7.75	12.00	8.66	2.50
1988	2.50							

Notes:
UK: Minimum Lending rate (1980); Market Intervention Rate (thereafter)
France: Market Intervention Rate in the call market
Canada: 3-month Treasury Bill Bid Rate

Source: Economic Statistics Monthly (the Bank of Japan).

EXHIBIT 2: THREE-MONTH TERM DEPOSIT RATE COMPARISON

	Japan	US	UK	Germany	France	Italy	Euro$	Prime
1980	5.00	18.65	11.75	8.20	5.25	NA	14.36	**7.500**
1981	4.25	12.49	12.38	9.32	5.25	NA	16.51	**6.000**
1982	3.75	8.66	6.81	5.35	5.25	NA	13.11	**5.500**
1983	3.50	9.69	5.50	5.02	5.00	NA	10.14	**5.500**
1984	3.50	8.60	6.25	4.87	4.50	NA	20.78	**5.500**
1985	3.50	7.80	7.86	3.95	3.50	NA	8.05	**3.750**
1986	1.76	6.04	6.92	3.86	4.50	NA	6.29	**3.750**
1987	1.76	7.66	3.58	3.03	4.50	NA	8.33	**3.375**
1988	1.76					NA		**3.375**

Note:
Prime: Short-term prime rate in Japan.

Source: Economic Statistics Monthly (the Bank of Japan).

of credit. A central depository system was set up for government bonds.

LIBERALIZATION AND INTERNATIONALIZATION: 1983 TO PRESENT

Although the economy remained slow due to the oil crises until about 1985, this period marked a quickening in the rate of internationalization and liberalization of the economy.

Internationalization of the yen and increases in capital outflows were due chiefly to the massive excess liquidity in the Japanese economy from its trade surpluses since the early 1980s. Demand for Japanese goods and services was stimulated not only by the products and services offered, but also due to the comparatively low value of the yen until its revaluation in September 1985, after the G5 meeting in New York.

Japanese corporations benefitted from the trade and current account surpluses and built up huge profits. Corporate excess reserves led to a decline in demand for loans from their traditional supplier, the banks. Banks, in turn, had to seek other clients and turned to foreign borrowers: first, subsidiaries of Japanese companies, then to foreign nationals.

At the same time, the high manufacturing costs in Japan and growing trade restrictions on Japanese goods abroad, combined with the effects of the oil crises, led to decreased investment in plant and equipment within the country, and to increased Japanese direct investment abroad. This, in turn, led to decreased borrowing within the country and increased activity on the international financial markets.

The threatened abolition of tax savings through the postal service savings accounts, as well as the access by consumers and by fund managers to new financial products yielding higher returns than controlled rate products, further stimulated the shift from the traditional banking sector to more lucrative investments such as the investment trusts, flexible interest rate insurance policies, the equity markets and foreign investments.

Most of the measures of deregulation of internal controls during and following this period have been aimed chiefly at increasing the outflow of yen, thereby controlling the further rise in value of that currency. The counterpart of the undervaluation of the yen was the overvaluation of the U.S. dollar. The counterpart of the Japanese current account and trade surpluses was, not surprisingly, a growing U.S. bilateral deficit.

U.S. pressure on Japan, particularly with the arrival of Reagan to the presidency in 1981, was focused on opening up the Japanese market to international suppliers and liberalization of the Japanese financial markets

The Japanese responded to the U.S. (and growing European) pressure on trade by reducing and eliminating some tariffs, by instituting import promotion campaigns, increasing industrial imports from developing countries, and improving and facilitating certain certification systems, among other responses. In 1983, the international economy started expanding, relieving some of the pressure on this issue.

But the U.S. blamed Japanese financial regulations for maintaining the yen at an artificially low exchange rate. The U.S. felt that freeing Japanese financial markets would lead to greater international use of the yen, thereby driving up its value. This policy would therefore, in turn, help resolve the U.S. trade deficit and give the U.S. trade and financial sectors greater access to the Japanese consumer and capital markets.

Economic and Financial Deregulation

Prior to 1984. The Ministry of Finance had already been slowly liberalizing the Japanese financial system since the 1970s. Already the question of internationalization of the Japanese economy had been addressed in a MITI report published in March 1980, which was followed by subsequent MITI reports in 1986. The Economic Planning Agency published studies in 1983, one of which listed four policy objectives of the government for the 1983–1990 period that were adopted by the government as guidelines.

In 1980, following the 1979 sudden depreciation of the yen, the Foreign Exchange and Trade Control Law was passed, which made foreign investment and foreign exchange activities free in principle. Other controls on capital inflows were also removed at this time, such as those prohibiting foreigners from investing in Japanese securities.

After 1984. U.S. and international pressure led to three key events in the reformulation of Japanese policies: the 1984 Yen/Dollar Accord, the 1985 Action Program, and the Maekawa Reports.

The Yen/Dollar Accord. Following pressure from the Business Roundtable, the U.S. decided to extend its pressure on the Japanese, not only to open up its consumer markets but also its capital markets. The November 1983 visit of President Reagan to Prime Minister Yasuhiro Nakasone resulted in a November 10th announcement by Treasury Secretary Donald Regan and Finance Minister Noboru Takeshita, by which the Japanese agreed to liberalize the Japanese financial market in several sectors including: liberalization of capital flows, foreign participation in the markets, further internationalization of the yen and deregulation of Japanese capital markets. Among U.S. measures agreed to were: continued U.S. commitment to reduction of the budget deficit; review of the system of worldwide unitary taxation, applicable in a number of states; and issuance of Japanese government guaranteed bonds in the U.S. capital market.

In order to monitor the implementation of the announced measures, and develop and implement other measures, an ad hoc Yen/Dollar Working Committee was set up. Its report was submitted on May 29, 1984.

Among the specific modifications was the elimination of the designated company system, which restricted the level of foreign control in 11 specified companies despite the 1980 Foreign Exchange and Trade Control liberalization. Another modification provided for the creation of a bond futures market. (Not coincidentally, the massive government bond issues of 1975 were coming due, and a bond futures market was under preparation in Singapore.)

Other measures included liberalization of domestic interest rate regulations, establishment of a yen-denominated bankers' acceptance market, deregulation of the Euroyen market and authorization of foreign banks to participate in domestic trust banking activities.[13]

The Action Program. Increased pressure led to the development of the Action Program, which served as a reaffirmation of the principles of the 1984 accord, as concerns the financial sector.

The Action Program, announced on April 9, 1985, provided for the opening of the Japanese market in six areas (tariff schedules, import quotas, standards and certification of imports, government procurement, financial and capital markets, and services and import promotion measures).

The importance of this program for our purposes is that it made official a process of liberalization that had already been developing in the financial sector. Among measures provided for in this sector included: relaxation (and later abolition) of interest rate ceilings on large deposits by spring 1987, liberalization of interest rate ceilings on small deposits (coupled with protective measures for small depositors), authorization of nine foreign banks to participate in the trust banking sector, and deregulation of the issuance of floating rate Euroyen notes.

Maekawa Reports. While the general results of the hastily-implemented Action Program were not concrete, the second Maekawa Commission Report, released on April 7, 1986, addressed directly the issue of internationalization of the economy.

The Maekawa Commission, composed of 17 members of Japan's business, government and academic elite, discussed, during a background of increasing trade disputes with the U.S., the annual economic summit to be held in Tokyo in May 1986.

Its six general recommendations focused on domestic economic growth, changes in the trade and industrial system, Japan's exchange rate and the need for stability, international cooperation, the liberalization and internationalization of the financial markets, and the review by the government of the preferential tax treatment of savings.

Specific recommendations included encouraging imports, which implied relaxation of government regulations, and expansion of private demand through, for example, tax incentives.

Following the Report, the government approved a series of guidelines on May 1, 1986, based on the Maekawa recommendations and spirit.

Implementation of Deregulation. As a result of the above-mentioned accords and reports, as well as from growing international economic (and other) pressures, deregulation was initiated in both the domestic and the international markets, and most importantly in the separation between the banks and securities houses.

Separation of Banks and Securities Businesses. It is widely recognized that Article 65 will not be abolished unless the U.S. Glass-Steagall Act is similarly amended or abolished. In addition to the Securities Act, the "Three Bureaux Agreement," reached among the Ministry of Finance's banking, securities and international finance bureaux in 1975, also delimited the barrier between the banks and securities houses even overseas. By this Agreement, the overseas branches of domestic banks are prohibited from becoming lead managers in underwriting bonds issued overseas by Japanese corporations.[14] This Agreement will most likely be abolished before Article 65 is abolished.

The commercial banks have seen the decrease in corporate borrowing in the indirect market and the increase in corporate borrowing on the securities markets. Article 65 prevents the banks from benefitting from this shift. But at the same time, the variety of deposits that are subject to interest rate control has decreased, providing a potential new source of funds for banks.

The separation between banks and securities houses has started to narrow, both through acquisitions or creation of entities exercising the activities not permitted to the banks or securities houses, and through broadening of the activities permitted, respectively, to banks and to securities houses.

First, in terms of creation or acquisition of entities, banks have shifted into securities activities, both abroad and even in Japan. Outside Japan, certain Japanese banks have acquired interest or control in, or created, foreign securities houses. For example, Sumitomo acquired 12.5% of Goldman Sachs in 1986. (But this was a pure portfolio investment, and Sumitomo was not permitted representation on the Board of Directors nor, even more important, participation in training programs.) Dai-Ichi Kangyo Bank has established securities subsidiaries in London, New York, the Netherlands, Switzerland, Frankfurt, and other financial centers.

Within Japan, securities subsidiaries of foreign banks have been allowed to open branches. For example, Citicorp purchased a majority share in Vickers da Costa's Far Eastern Operations in 1983, without the bank's license being revoked. Deutsche Bank's (50%) subsidiary, DB Capital Markets, was authorized in 1985, and in 1986, other securities subsidiaries of foreign banks were permitted to operate.[15]

Within Japan, a U.S. primary dealer (securities) affiliate of the Industrial Bank of Japan, one of Japan's long-term credit banks, opened a representative office in Tokyo in early 1987. The Ministry of Finance ultimately granted approval, and with it, the first indication that modifications to Article 65 might be considered.

Also within Japan, the Tokyo representative office of Sumitomo's partly controlled Swiss subsidiary, Banca del Gottardo, has become involved in domestic underwriting activities, since it is considered by the Minister of Finance as a foreign bank. (Sumitomo controls 42% of total shares and 52.7% of voting shares in this Swiss bank.)

Tokyo representative offices of English subsidiaries of Japanese banks have started selling Euroyen bonds to domestic investors.

Second, securities houses have shifted into the banking business, both within Japan and abroad. Within Japan, major U.S. securities houses such as Merrill Lynch, Goldman Sachs, Salomon Brothers, and Morgan Stanley are expected to be authorized to open their Tokyo banking branches of their European (in London or Frankfurt) banking subsidiaries.

Outside Japan, securities houses have successfully evaded Japanese restrictions by setting up banking operations. For example, Nomura acquired a license in 1986 to set up banking operations in England. Daiwa acquired deposit-taking rights in London for its subsidiary in 1987. All the major securities houses have banking operations in Luxembourg and/or Amsterdam.

In terms of widening the scope of activities, following a 1981 revision of the Banking Act and Securities and Exchange Act, 34 banks were allowed to make bond dealings for their own account as of June 1984, but only for those bonds with a maturity of less than two years. In June 1985, this restriction was eliminated, and full dealing by banks was permitted.

Increasingly, therefore, Japanese commercial banks take part in trading in both the Japanese government bond markets as well as foreign exchange markets. Many have informal affiliations with securities houses, and particularly regional banks have entered into close relationships with securities houses, allowing the latter to transform their medium-term government securities into money management instruments.

Other Deregulation within Japan. In 1981, a new Banking Law had already been promulgated. On the bond market, the 10-year public bonds, which had financed the huge government deficits in 1975, were coming due. In order to maintain the market for government securities, including rollover debt, the Ministry of Finance approved the creation of a short-term government securities market in 1981 and a government bond futures market in 1985.

During 1984, bond trading (both government and convertible issues) as well as new issuing of convertibles and Samurai bonds increased, and there was an explosion of over-the-counter activity of publicly offered bonds in the secondary market in 1985 (see Exhibit 3). Regulations for issuing unsecured bonds were also eased.

At this time, Japanese companies increased their debt issues on overseas markets.

Following the 1984 Yen/Dollar Accord, the government abolished the "real demand" rule on forward exchange transactions. (The "real demand" rule limited foreign exchange dealings to those specifically covering another underlying transaction in order to avoid speculative transactions.)

Towards the end of 1985, a bond futures market was set up, as equity futures contract started trading, and a year later, banks were authorized to participate in the currency futures markets.

Following the Japan US Yen/Dollar Accord, interest rate controls were removed on deposits of more than 1 billion yen in October 1985, then on those of more than 500 million yen in April 1986 and of more than 300 million yen in September 1986. There was an important shift of funds, particularly to money market certificates.

EXHIBIT 3: PUBLICLY OFFERED BOND SECONDARY TRADING

(Yen billion)

Year	Over-the-Counter		Exchange-Traded		Total	
1976	64,897	97%	2,291	3%	67,188	100%
1977	113,164	97%	3,789	3%	116,953	100%
1978	193,199	95%	10,278	5%	203,477	100%
1979	204,235	97%	5,419	3%	209,654	100%
1980	272,503	97%	8,813	3%	281,316	100%
1981	288,429	96%	13,000	4%	301,429	100%
1982	327,108	95%	15,724	5%	342,832	100%
1983	385,097	92%	34,880	8%	419,977	100%
1984	692,470	90%	74,690	10%	767,160	100%
1985	2,164,670	94%	133,870	6%	2,298,540	100%
1986	2,619,876	92%	224,231	8%	2,844,107	100%

(table continues)

EXHIBIT 3: (continued)

Publicly Offered Bond Trading by Category

Category	1984		1985 (Yen billion)		1986	
GBDs	628,763	82%	2,155,773	94%	2,592,586	91%
GGBDs	25,140	3%	23,641	1%	35,836	1%
Local GBDs	29,203	4%	21,302	1%	23,825	1%
BK Debenture	32,714	4%	25,862	1%	43,349	2%
Corp. Bonds	6,790	1%	6,076	0%	9,000	0%
CBs	26,359	3%	50,408	2%	121,169	4%
Others	18,191	2%	15,478	1%	18,342	1%
Total	767,160	100%	2,298,540	100%	2,844,107	100%

Notes:
GBDs: Government bonds
GGBDs: Government guaranteed bonds
Local GBDs: Local government bonds
Corp. Bonds: Corporate bonds
CBs: Convertible bonds
Others: Samurai, warrant bonds, etc.

Source: *Japanese Bond Market (Nihon no Shoken Shijo).*

Interest rates on large deposits were gradually removed by spring 1987. Interest rates were totally liberated on residents' foreign currency deposits.

One of the major problems for liberalization of interest rates is the Postal System's savings institutions, through which much government spending on public works and funding for the Export Import Bank of Japan and the Japan Development Bank is financed. The postal system offers slightly higher rates than the banks.

The discount rate was decreased several times since early 1986 in order to stimulate domestic demand, but has gradually been liberalized to reflect actual funding costs.

Liberalization occurred also in the money market sector. Authorization was given for the sale in Japan of:

- negotiable certificates of deposit (which had been authorized in April 1979 with a minimum issue amount of 500 million yen, decreasing to 300 million yen in January 1984, with a term of 3 to 6 months. The issue amount was later decreased to 100 million yen, with a term of 1 to 6 months).

- money market certificates (introduced in March 1985).

- commercial paper (foreign currency issued by foreigners was authorized for sale in Japan in 1984; yen-denominated C.P.s issued by foreigners were authorized for sale in the Euromarkets in 1987; Japanese corporations were authorized in 1988 in Japan).

- yen-denominated bankers' acceptances (introduced in June 1985).

Such measures resulted, among others, in the increased liquidity in the money markets in Japan. In 1987, issuance by banks of certificates of deposit and money market certificates was eased.

Deregulation of International Markets. Offshore banking began on December 1, 1986, free of national taxation and of certain domestic government regulations. The aim was to promote Tokyo as an international financial and 24-hour trading center, and to promote the yen as an international trading currency.

____ , __panese offshore market (JOM) provided freedom from certain Japanese regulations, such as those restricting interest rates on deposits, and those governing insurance and reserve requirements on deposits. JOM also provided freedom from withholding tax on interest payments and from corporate tax.

However, restrictions such as insulation of offshore accounts from domestic accounts, prohibition from issuing domestic certificates of deposits and from holding foreign securities, as well as the imposition of certain local taxes, greatly deterred the international financial community.

As of December 1987, 87 banks were authorized for operations by the MOF.

Activity in all currencies increased in the JOM, from 93.7 billion yen at the end of December 1986 to 294.2 billion yen at the end of May 1988. The yen portion of JOM activity increased from 21.8% at end of December 1986 to 42.8% at the end of May 1988.[16]

In the international markets, the following occurred. First, yen futures and currency options on the yen were developed outside the country, while the swap market using yen on the forward market expanded. Foreign corporations were allowed to issue bonds in the Euroyen market in late 1984, but the Ministry of Finance required that Japanese investors wait six months after issue in order to reduce the impact on the domestic market.

Second, efforts were undertaken to increase the international use of the yen as a trading currency. With the establishment of the bankers' acceptance market in Japan, Japanese importers could find domestic trade credits. In addition, most limits as to the size of foreign lending by Japanese banks as well as to the countries involved were lifted.

Third, foreign entities also gained greater access to Japanese financial markets. Nine foreign banks were allowed to participate in trust banking and, in addition to certain foreign securities houses, in the syndicate that underwrites new government bond issues. Foreign banks are permitted to trade in the government bond secondary market. Vickers da Costa (in 1978) and Bache, Halsey Stuart Shields Inc. (in 1979) were granted branch licenses.[17] By the end of 1986, 34 securities firms had acquired such authorization.[18]

In February 1, 1986, six foreign firms were granted seats on the Tokyo Stock Exchange (TSE). As of September 1, 1986, 30 more foreign firms were listed on the TSE. Certain foreign securities houses are authorized to participate in the securities futures market in Osaka.

Finally, the Euroyen money market expanded with both domestic and foreign banks issuing and trading in short-term negotiable yen-denominated certificates of deposit outside Japan. But the maximum maturity allowed by the Ministry of Finance was six months, as opposed to five years maximum for London-based transactions on the Eurodollar market. The yen maximum maturity was extended to one year in April 1986, and to two years in April 1988. The two-year limit reflected the same limit on commercial bank deposits in Japan.

In the first quarter of 1987, the value of Euroyen issues was greater than for Eurodollars issues. The yen became second only to the U.S. dollar in type of issuing currency in 1986. The expansion of the Euroyen market was due, not to the desire of foreign corporations for yen, but to the development of the swap market in which the yen was swapped for dollars (or other currencies).

Japanese recipients of the yen were basically commercial banks. City banks were limited to receiving deposits of up to two years, but were permitted by the MOF to acquire liabilities on a long-term basis to match their long-term lending through the Euroyen swaps.

In 1984, foreign private corporations were authorized to issue Euroyen bonds without limits as to number or size, and, at the same time, certain domestic corporations were allowed to participate in the Euroyen market.

The year 1986 also saw the massive development of new Euroyen innovations developed for the interests of specific Japanese investors.[19] However, activity in these new instruments has been limited. The Ministry of Finance has been pressuring for the institutions developing and purchasing these instruments to limit their activities.[20]

Foreign banks were permitted by the MOF and the Bank of Japan in 1986 to market yen/yen swaps to Japanese financial institutions.

SUMMARY

The liberalization of the Japanese financial markets has accompanied the transformation of the Japanese economy from that of a deficit economy based on heavy industry with a relatively undervalued yen to that of a surplus economy based on skills with the yen greatly appreciated in relation to other currencies.

The period from the Meiji Restoration to the mid-1960s was, broadly speaking, characterized by strong government controls and organization to promote exports and productivity. Since banks were the chief source of funding for industries, they predominated in activity over the securities houses. During this period, the separation between banks (for borrowing and lending) and securities houses (for underwriting securities) was formalized in the 1948 Securities and Exchange Law.

During the mid-1960s, the economy improved and direct government control was loosened.

With the collapse of Bretton Woods and the oil crises of 1973 and 1979, Japan's rapid economic growth took a downturn. Demand for loan funding from banks by corporations was replaced by government borrowing through bond issues underwritten chiefly by banks. Government expenses increased while tax revenues decreased.

Exports, however, continued to rise, due in part to the relatively low value of the yen. Deregulation of internal controls in the financial and other markets at this time was due in part to increased Japanese investment abroad, to promotion of yen outflows to control its rise in value, and to increasing U.S. pressure. In 1980, the old Foreign Exchange and Foreign Trade Control Law (1933) and its piecemeal modifications were replaced by the new 1980 law which consecrated the principle of liberalization. Following the 1984 Yen/Dollar Accord, the 1985 Action Program, and the Maekawa Reports, the Japanese government implemented deregulation on both the internal and international economic and financial markets. Such liberalization is clearly seen in the steady erosion of the separation between banks and securities houses.

ENDNOTES

[1] Chikara Higashi and G. Peter Lauter, *The Internationalization of the Japanese Economy* (Boston: Kluwer Academic Publishers, 1987), p. 8.

[2] Yoshio Suzuki, *Money, Finance and Macroeconomic Performance in Japan* (New Haven: Yale University Press, 1986), p. 3.

[3] Higashi and Lauter, *The Internationalization of the Japanese Economy*, p.11.

[4] Japan Securities Research Institute, *Securities Market in Japan* (Tokyo: Japan Securities Research Institute, 1988), pp. 15-16.

[5] For a more detailed analysis using these concepts, see James Horne, *Japan's Financial Markets* (Sydney & Boston: G. Allen & Unwin in asssociation with the Australia-Japan Research Centre, Australian National University, 1985), starting from page 26.

[6] Higashi and Lauter, *The Internationalization of the Japanese Economy*, p. 13.

[7] See Horne, *Japan's Financial Markets*, p. 237, footnote explanation.

[8] Bank debentures are discussed in Chapter 9.

[9] Suzuki, *Money, Finance and Macroeconomic Performance in Japan*, p. 8.

[10] For their interaction, see Suzuki, *Money, Finance and Macroeconomic Performance in Japan*, p. 429.

[11] Samurai bonds are the subject of Chapter 13.

[12] Japan Securities Research Institute, *Securities Market in Japan*, p. 21.

[13] From the *Report by the Working Group of Joint Japan-U.S. Ad Hoc Group on Yen/Dollar Exchange Rate, Financial and Capital Market Issues to Japanese Minister of Finance Noboru Takeshita, U.S. Secretary of the Treasury Donald T. Regan* (mimeographed copy), May 1984. See also: Jeffrey A. Frankel, *The Yen/Dollar Agreement: Liberalizing Japanese Capital Markets* (Washington, D.C.: Institute for International Economics, 1984, distributed by M.I.T. Press, Cambridge).

[14] Aron Viner, *Inside Japanese Financial Markets* (Homewood, Ill.: Dow Jones-Irwin, 1988), p. 266.

[15] In Germany, a "universal banking" system permits a bank to participate in both banking and securities (underwriting) activities. As of December, 1986, 11 universal banks were allowed to operate in the securities business in Japan.

[16] Ministry of Finance, *Okurasho Kinyukyoku Nenpo.* (International Finance Bureau Annual Report) (Tokyo: Zaisei Jijho Kenkyu Kai, 1988).

[17] The four licenses (required for Japanese and foreigners alike) cover: dealing for the firm's account, taking clients' orders, underwriting primary issues, and trading in securities). Securities firms can also have representative offices, but are not legally permitted to participate in securities activities.

[18] Thirty-six branches of thirty-four subsidiaries were authorized as of December 1986, of which, 24 subsidiaries with 25 branches were opened between 1985 and 1986. Source: Kimiaki Nakajima, *Nihon no Shoken Shijo (Japanese Securities Market)* (Tokyo: Zaikei Shohosha, 1988), p. 246.

[19] These developments are discussed in Chapter 14.

[20] Brian Robins, *Tokyo, A World Financial Centre* (London: Euromoney Publications, 1987), p. 30.

CHAPTER 3

Participants in the Japanese Bond Market

Noboru Honjo
The Sumitomo Trust and Banking Company, Ltd.

Lisa J. Turbessi
Business Development Manager
Guinness Flight Global Asset Management Limited

INTRODUCTION

This chapter will focus on the participants in the Japanese bond market: who they are, what their roles are, and their investment behavior. The main players within the Japanese bond market are as follows (the numbers shown in parentheses are the numbers of institutions as of the end of September 1987):

- Ministry of Finance
- Bank of Japan
- City Banks (13)
- Local Banks (64)
- Long-Term Credit Banks (3)
- Trust Banks (7)
- Mutual Banks (68)

35

- Institutions for Agriculture and Forestry
  - Norinchukin Bank
  - Credit Federations (82)
  - Cooperatives (5,934)
- Credit Associations
  - Zenshinren Bank
  - Credit Associations (445)
- Life Insurance Companies (24)
- Property Insurance Companies (23)
- Investment Trusts
- Business Corporations
- Foreign Investors
- Individual Investors
- Other Investors
  - Trust Fund Bureau
  - National Debt Consolidation Fund
  - Local Governments
- Securities Companies

Though many of these players perform many of the same functions within the Japanese bond market, each of them has a specific role within the primary and/or secondary markets. The Ministry of Finance oversees all activities within the Japanese bond market and, hence, influences the roles of each participant.

Before discussing each market participant, we will provide an overview of the primary and secondary markets and the securities business by banks. We then begin our discussion of market participants with the Ministry of Finance.

THE PRIMARY MARKET

Two methods exist for issuing bonds in the primary market, underwriting and auction. Regardless of the issuing method, the Ministry of Finance (MOF) approves all bond issues approximately one month in advance of the actual issue.

Underwriting Structure of Public Bonds

Government bond issues (for long-term government bonds and 5-year discount government bonds) are implemented by the Bank of Japan (BOJ) for the MOF. The syndicate for public bonds consists of city banks, long-term credit banks, local banks, trust banks, mutual banks, credit associations, Norinchukin Bank, Shoko Chukin Bank, insurance companies, and securities companies. The syndicate is committed to buying the entire issue. Exhibit 1a outlines the structure of underwriting of long-term government bonds and discount government bonds. As shown in Exhibit 1b, the mechanism for underwriting government-guaranteed bonds is very similar. The primary differences are that government guaranteed bonds do not go through the BOJ and the members of the underwriting syndicates are slightly different.

Underwriting Structure of Corporate Bonds

Eighty percent of all corporate issues are underwritten by the "Big Four" securities houses (Nomura, Daiwa, Yamaichi and Nikko). The bond flotation committee (called "Kisaikai"), made up of major underwriters and lead commissioned banks, decides on the volume of corporate issues coming to market one month in advance.

The primary bank of an issuing company acts as the lead commissioned bank which negotiates the deal with an appointed securities house. This designated securities house then forms a syndicate of 10 to 30 other securities houses which underwrite the issue. In Japan, the issuing corporation has a substantial influence on the members of the underwriting syndicate and on the buyers of the issue. Banks absorb most of the new corporate issues based on the large size of their financial assets and their longstanding business ties with corporations. Exhibit 2 outlines the structure of underwriting of corporate bonds.

Auctions

Auctions are used for 20-year government bonds, medium-term coupon bonds, Treasury bills, and some 10-year government bonds. As

EXHIBIT 1a: UNDERWRITING MECHANISM OF LONG-TERM INTEREST BEARING GOVERNMENT BONDS AND DISCOUNT GOVERNMENT BONDS

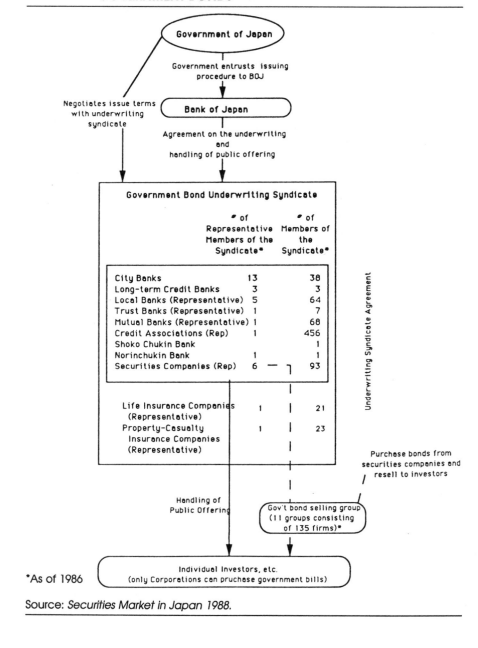

*As of 1986

Source: *Securities Market in Japan 1988.*

EXHIBIT 1b: UNDERWRITING MECHANISM OF GOVERNMENT GUARANTEED BONDS

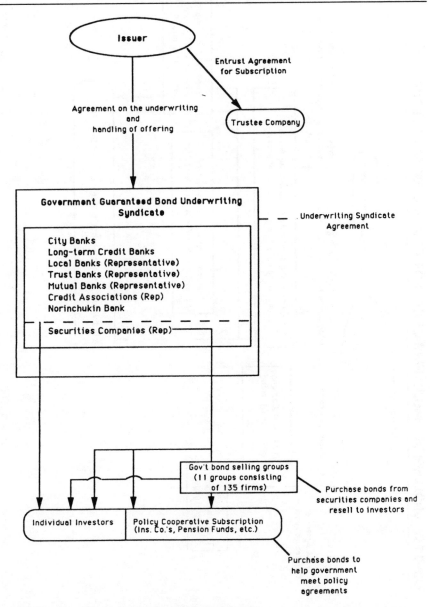

Source: The Bond Underwriters Association of Japan.

EXHIBIT 2: UNDERWRITING MECHANISM OF CORPORATE AND CONVERTIBLE BONDS

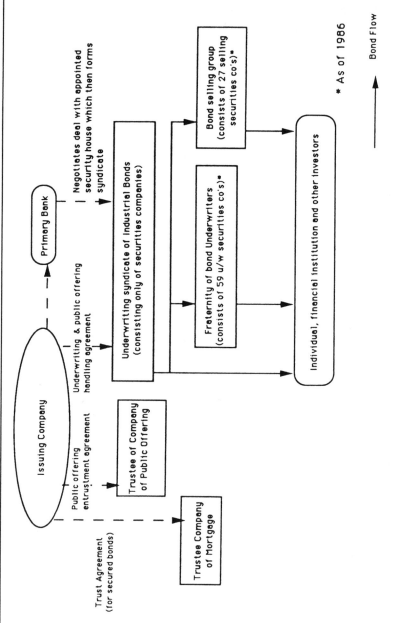

Source: *Securities Market in Japan 1988.*

of 1987, two types of auctions exist, straight and hybrid. In straight auctions the maturity date and coupons are announced by the MOF. Securities companies, banks, and other bidders then submit secret bids. On the day after the submission deadline, the MOF decides issuing terms and amount. All bids which meet the issuing terms are filled.

Hybrid auctions are used only for 10-year government bonds and were created to allow greater participation by foreign securities houses. Eighty percent of an issue goes through a normal syndicate and 20% to a hybrid auction. In a hybrid auction, investors bid for up to 1% of any announced issue without knowing the price. The price of the issue is then negotiated by the syndicate. If the bids received total more than 20% of the issue, all bids are scaled down proportionally and distributed. If bids total less than 20% of an issue, the remainder goes to the syndicate. Prices are nonnegotiable by the bidders on an issue. They must accept the price negotiated by the syndicate and they must purchase the full amount of their bid. Exhibit 3 outlines the structure of auctions.

Subscription of Bonds by Investor Type

Financial institutions are, by far, the largest purchasers of all types of bonds other than medium-term government bonds, corporate bonds, and bank debentures. Out of all of the financial institutions, city banks and long-term credit banks purchase the highest percentage of bonds. Local banks are the only other financial institution that purchase significant percentages of bonds. Of the nonfinancial participants in the market, individual investors and business corporations purchase the most bonds, concentrating their purchases in medium-term government bonds, corporate bonds, and bank debentures (see Exhibit 4).

THE SECONDARY MARKETS

Two types of secondary markets exist: over-the-counter and exchanges. The over-the-counter (OTC) market is by far the largest, encompassing over 90% of all secondary market activity in 1987, though this figure has been decreasing. Of this activity, over 95% of

EXHIBIT 3:   AUCTION MECHANISM

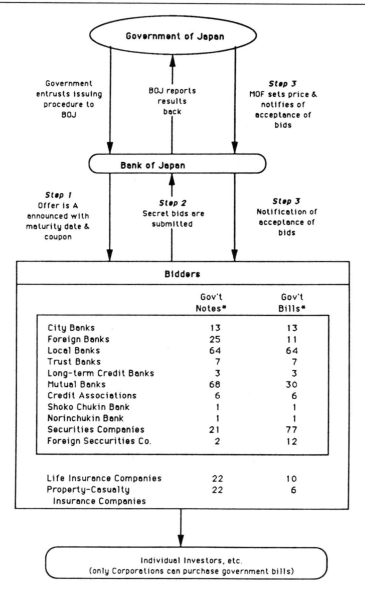

*As of 1986

Source: *Securities Market in Japan 1988.*

(Unit: 100 million yen)

	LTGBs	MTGBs	Discount GBs	Gov't Agency Bonds	GGBs	Pub. Offered Muni. Bonds	Priv. Placed Muni. Bonds	Corporate Bonds	Bank Debentures	Total
City Banks and LTC Banks	33,905 39.27%	3,797 12.65%	1,400 21.94%	12,618 26.88%	6,318 22.57%	3,375 38.85%	9,037 38.38%	1,485 15.15%	5,366 1.96%	77,301 16.41%
Local Banks	12,579 14.57%	2,040 6.80%	497 7.79%	5,585 11.90%	3,833 13.69%	416 4.79%	9,652 40.99%	537 5.48%	7,700 2.81%	42,839 9.10%
Trust Banks	4,193 4.86%	2,786 9.28%	160 2.51%	1,620 3.45%	1,995 7.13%	264 3.04%	575 2.44%	308 3.14%	435 0.16%	12,336 2.62%
Insurance Companies	3,911 4.53%	187 0.62%	0 0.00%	1,576 3.36%	1,410 5.04%	64 0.74%	304 1.29%	97 0.99%	4,480 1.64%	12,029 2.55%
Inst. for Agriculture and Forestry	2,797 3.24%	1,615 5.38%	147 2.30%	4,020 8.56%	2,589 9.25%	459 5.28%	1,151 4.89%	283 2.89%	356 0.13%	13,417 2.85%
Shoko Chukin Bank & Credit Associations	3,494 4.05%	164 0.55%	142 2.23%	1,970 4.20%	1,677 5.99%	232 2.67%	596 2.53%	354 3.61%	3,705 1.35%	12,334 2.62%
Mutual Banks	3,004 3.48%	501 1.67%	121 1.90%	1,723 3.67%	1,268 4.53%	173 1.99%	663 2.82%	144 1.47%	4,644 1.70%	12,241 2.60%
Subtotal (Fin'l Inst.)	63,883 74.00%	11,090 36.95%	2,467 38.66%	29,112 62.02%	19,090 68.18%	4,983 57.35%	21,978 93.34%	3,208 32.73%	26,686 9.75%	182,497 38.75%
Individual Investors	22,450 26.00%	18,927 63.05%	3,470 54.37%	344 0.73%	12 0.04%	189 2.18%	1,532 6.51%	3,616 36.90%	247,096 90.25%	288,575 61.25%
Others			445 6.97%	17,485 37.25%	8,897 31.78%	3,516 40.47%	36 0.15%	2,976 30.37%		
Total	86,333	30,017	6,382	46,941	27,999	8,688	23,546	9,800	273,782	470,971

Source: Nomura Research Institute, Bond Handbook (Koushasai Youran).

the transactions involve government bonds (see Exhibit 5). Serving as bond dealers, securities houses are most active in the OTC market with the Big Four dominating.

Approximately 5-10% of secondary market activity occurred on the eight formal stock exchanges in Tokyo, Osaka, Nagoya, Kyoto, Hiroshima, Fukuoka, Niigata, and Sapporo. The Tokyo Stock Exchange is by far the most active, with over 80% of all trading volume done on the exchanges. Most of the transactions on the exchanges involve large-lot government bonds (over 10 million yen) and convertible bonds.

Trading Volume in Secondary Market

Total trading volume (total bond purchases plus bond sales) for almost all participants increased during 1984 and 1985 when full dealing by banks began. The most notable are the bond dealers, whose total volume increased by 500% from 264 trillion yen in FY 1984 to 1,480 trillion yen in FY 1985 (see Exhibit 6).[1] Between FY 1984 and 1985, the relative presence of bond dealers in the secondary market increased from 41% to over 70% of the overall trading volume (see Exhibit 7). In contrast, the relative presence of nonfinancial institutions in the secondary market decreased from over 50% in FY 1978 to only 10% in FY 1987. This reflects the increasing role bond dealers played in facilitating the dealing done by banks in the secondary market.

SECURITIES BUSINESS BY BANKS

Transition in Banking Laws

After working on the amendment of the Banking Law and the Securities and Exchange Law for over two years, the MOF submitted revisions of these laws to the Diet in April 1981 and they were passed in May of the same year. The new laws, in essence, said that banks were allowed to deal in, and only in, public bonds in their business. However, new Article 65-2 of the Securities and Exchange Law required that the banks obtain permission from the MOF in order to deal in public bonds. Regulations and supervisions applicable to se-

EXHIBIT 5: OTC TRADING BY BOND DEALERS (FY 1987)

(Unit: 100 million yen, %)

	Trading Volume (a)	a/d	Securities Companies Trading Volume (b)	b/d	b/a	Bank Dealers Trading Volume (c)	c/d	c/a
Government Bonds	49,547,734	97.3	35,012,335	96.6	70.7	14,535,399	98.9	29.3
Super Long-term GB	695,263	1.4	533,417	1.5	76.7	161,846	1.1	23.3
Long-term GB	36,881,323	72.4	26,218,460	72.4	71.1	10,662,863	72.5	28.9
Medium-term GB	185,557	0.4	151,379	0.4	81.6	34,178	0.2	18.4
Discount GB	52,911	0.1	32,176	0.1	60/8	20,736	0.1	39.2
Treasury Bills	5,089,749	10.0	3,975,399	11.0	78.1	1,114,350	7.6	21.9
Financing Bills	6,642,931	13.0	4,101,504	11.3	61.7	2,541,427	17.3	38.3
Municipal Bonds	254,847	0.5	193,773	0.5	76.0	61,074	0.4	24.0
GGB	359,671	0.7	239,419	0.7	66.6	120,252	0.8	33.4
Others	780,672	1.5	780,672	2.2	100.0	0	0.0	0.0
Total Volume (d)	50,942,924	100.0	36,226,199	100.0	71.1	14,716,725	100.0	28.9

Source: The Securities Bureau, MOF.

EXHIBIT 6:   TOTAL TRADING VOLUME BY INVESTOR TYPE

(Units: 100 million yen)

FY	City Banks	Local Banks	LTC Banks	Trust Banks	Inst. for Agr. & Forestry
1981	140,045	128,300	35,501	105,924	143,393
1982	159,934	129,143	41,351	157,818	133,459
1983	242,552	152,341	88,478	248,153	176,025
1984	344,459	223,917	124,963	485,403	224,870
1985	326,934	302,918	140,462	980,002	458,779
1986	602,931	207,761	242,225	1,292,739	298,968
1987	944,675	213,695	415,900	1,920,623	300,807

FY	Mutual Banks	Credit Associations	Other Fin. Institutions	Insurance Companies	Investment Trusts
1981	46,492	84,213	54,648	44,723	69,437
1982	47,673	69,012	71,016	48,763	85,692
1983	38,883	80,262	76,663	45,889	124,439
1984	57,000	190,490	264,372	53,604	170,390
1985	113,204	193,881	355,026	154,254	150,786
1986	116,627	119,199	163,908	189,560	210,739
1987	152,245	141,985	196,451	337,669	323,496

FY	MAS of GE, etc.	Business Corporations	Other Corporations	Foreign Investors	Individual Investors
1981	25,520	135,103	25,929	93,787	50,395
1982	32,464	166,366	24,922	137,338	55,006
1983	32,835	205,062	26,196	317,249	54,386
1984	40,711	427,330	48,130	995,264	67,048
1985	53,341	611,258	71,928	1,113,183	98,609
1986	41,648	568,813	66,392	731,442	101,252
1987	45,110	494,380	64,666	715,505	101,952

FY	Others	Bond Dealers	Total
1981	57,714	377,842	1,618,966
1982	80,345	479,118	1,919,420
1983	77,319	843,805	2,830,537
1984	94,516	2,649,485	6,461,952
1985	100,507	14,804,278	20,029,350
1986	150,451	16,544,597	21,649,252
1987	152,593	20,030,849	26,552,601

Source: The Bond Underwriters Association of Japan.

EXHIBIT 7: SHARE OF INVESTORS IN TRADING VOLUME

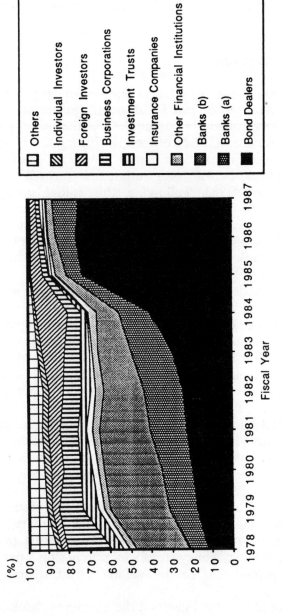

Fiscal Year

Legend:
- ⊞ Others
- ▨ Individual Investors
- ▨ Foreign Investors
- ▥ Business Corporations
- ▤ Investment Trusts
- ☐ Insurance Companies
- ▨ Other Financial Institutions
- ▨ Banks (b)
- ▨ Banks (a)
- ■ Bond Dealers

Banks (a) include City Banks, Long-Term Credit Banks and Trust Banks.
Banks (b) include Local Banks, Mutual Banks, Credit Associations and Institutions for Agriculture and Forestry.

Source: The Bond Underwriters Association of Japan.

curities companies under the Securities and Exchange Law were to be applied correspondingly to banks. The new laws became effective in April 1982.[2]

Resale of Bonds to the Public

Resale of bonds ("mado-han") by banks started for long-term government bonds in April 1983, and for discount government bonds and medium-term government bonds in October that same year. As an initial group, 158 banks (13,521 offices), including the Norinchukin Bank and all the city banks, local banks, long-term credit banks, trust banks, and mutual banks, were authorized to resell bonds to the public in January 1983. Following this initial group, the Zenshinren Bank and 54 credit associations were permitted to resell bonds in March that year. By January 1986, 630 banks (13 city banks, 64 local banks, 3 long-term credit banks, 7 trust banks, 69 mutual banks, Norinchukin Bank, Shoko Chukin Bank, and 452 credit associations) were authorized.[3]

The amount of bonds resold by banks in FY 1983 was about 1.5 trillion yen in total, which accounted for 33.5% of the amount they underwrote.[4] Their sales exceeded those of securities companies by more than 400 billion yen. In FY 1985, the amount of bonds resold by banks increased to 3.9 trillion yen. The ratio of their sales in mado-han to the amount of their underwriting jumped to 63.2%, while city banks and trust banks resold as much as 77% of the amount they underwrote.

The original intention of the MOF in establishing the resale market of bonds was to give individual investors access to the bond market. However, the major portion of resale by banks was actually made to business corporations. It was because business corporations scrambled for arbitrage deals which were called "one-touch-through." Profits could be made from these deals as a result of the discrepancy between the subscriber's yield in the primary market and the market yield in the secondary market. These deals gave corporations a chance to make money simply by purchasing a new issue from banks in the primary market and selling it immediately in the secondary market.

The resale of public bonds lightened the burden on banks of underwriting government bonds. Since 1983, when the sales began, institutions like city banks, local banks, and long-term credit banks had reduced their chronic overselling of bonds, sometimes even turning into net buyers as shown in Exhibit 8. The share of 10-year government bonds purchased by city banks, long-term credit banks and local banks dropped in FY 1983, improving the demand-supply situation in the secondary market.[5]

Bank Dealing

In May 1983, the MOF announced that bond dealing by banks (called "bank dealing") would start in June 1984. An initial group of 34 banks (consisting of 13 city banks, 10 local banks, 3 long-term credit banks, 7 trust banks, and the Norinchukin Bank) were licensed to trade bonds as dealers. Three additional foreign banks were licensed in September of 1984. By June 1988, 210 banks were authorized as bond dealers.

There were certain restrictions placed on the banks in their dealing activities. The largest of these were: (1) for the first year, the bonds for dealing were limited to government bonds, government guaranteed bonds and local government bonds due in less than two years; and (2) bonds for dealing and bonds for investments were to be maintained in separate accounts: a dealing account and a portfolio account. For the initial group of authorized banks, the first condition was removed in June 1985 and so-called "full dealing" started.

Bank dealing took place chiefly among bond dealers since it took too long for banks to develop clients for bond deals ("deal" means transaction by a dealer in a dealing account). In favorable circumstances, specifically, when the interest rate was going down right after bank dealing started, banks preferred the short-term profits (capital gain) taken from dealer-to-dealer trading. In FY 1984, bank dealers did 82.1% of their transactions with bond dealers, compared to securities companies which did only 36.2% of their transactions with bond dealers.[6] In FY 1985, as much as 92.5% of the transactions done by bank dealers took place among bond dealers.[7]

When full dealing started in June 1985, total monthly volume of dealer-to-dealer trading reached 35 trillion yen, almost triple the volume of the previous month. By January 1987, the monthly volume had grown to 109 trillion yen in 45,700 deals.[8]

EXHIBIT 8:   NET POSITION BY INVESTOR IN SECONDARY MARKET*

(Units: 100 million yen)

FY	City Banks	Local Banks	LTC Banks	Trust Banks	Inst. for Agr. & Forestry
1981	37,733	8,634	7,519	-14,908	-4,553
1982	43,096	23,465	7,377	-24,458	-14,595
1983	26,026	16,635	2,334	-16,311	-7,921
1984	12,779	8,433	-681	-22,221	-11,160
1985	-1,628	2,568	4,558	-17,794	-13,515
1986	-27,361	-5,965	4,443	1,349	-2,568
1987	-49,385	-20,029	7,018	-16,563	7,283

FY	Mutual Banks	Credit Associations	Other Fin. Institutions	Insurance Companies	Investment Trusts
1981	8	-7,171	5,092	233	-16,231
1982	5,861	-4,028	21,110	-617	-27,304
1983	7,277	7,088	13,401	2,059	-44,649
1984	3,164	2,264	80,700	2,544	-30,416
1985	4,068	4,851	93,524	-882	-13,112
1986	-3,333	1,859	-27,134	-20,372	-53,539
1987	-12,505	-2,251	-40,187	-1,061	-44,814

FY	MAS of GE, etc.	Business Corporations	Other Corporations	Foreign Investors	Individual Investors
1981	-4,704	-12,577	-1,035	-7,267	-10,239
1982	-5,014	-18,470	-4,728	-19,706	-8,636
1983	-3,701	2,216	-3,844	-9,355	-4,418
1984	-4,551	2,708	-4,556	-9,038	-9,730
1985	-7,209	10,318	-1,726	-15,207	-15,755
1986	-4,464	21,429	-5,990	10,746	10,260
1987	-3,940	14,984	-4,274	-867	16,216

FY	Others	Bond Dealers	Total
1981	18,628	4,160	3,322
1982	31,635	2,430	7,418
1983	21,531	11,045	19,413
1984	10,810	18,239	49,288
1985	31,383	46,522	110,964
1986	45,535	102,703	47,598
1987	53,095	144,151	46,871

*Positive net position=net seller (overseller), negative net position=net buyer (overbuyer)
Source: The Bond Underwriters Association of Japan.

The percentage of the total trading volume done by bond dealers jumped from 20-30% prior to FY 1983, to 41% in FY 1984, and
then to 74% in FY 1985, largely due to the increase in the number of
authorized dealers. Although their primary business was meant to
intermediate among investors, since 1985 bond dealers have dominated the bond market, trading as much as three-fourths of the total
market volume.

MINISTRY OF FINANCE

Overview and Organization

The MOF is important to the securities market because of the
amount of power it controls, both directly and indirectly. It exerts
direct power over the market through its policy-making responsibilities, tax collection duties, budgeting responsibilities, and administration of foreign financial activities. In addition to this direct power,
the MOF is able to exert strong indirect power, referred to as "administrative guidance (gyousei shidou)." This guidance is given via
the MOF's regular meetings and contacts with all financial institutions. Another source of this indirect power is the audits the MOF
does on all securities houses which are members of the Tokyo Stock
Exchange (including foreign firms).

The Law for Foundation of the MOF ("Okura-sho Secchi Hou")
outlines and governs the activities of the MOF. The MOF is organized into seven bureaus, each of which is further split into divisions.
The divisions having the most impact on the securities markets are
the International Finance Bureau, the Finance Bureau, and the Securities Bureau. In addition to these divisions, additional local organizations exist to facilitate the administration of MOF policies. Exhibit 9
outlines the organization of the MOF in further detail.

MOF Organizations for Securities Administration

The International Finance Bureau. The International Finance Bureau
is responsible for all Japanese financial activities with the rest of the
world. This includes monitoring the day-to-day operations of Japan-

EXHIBIT 9: ORGANIZATION OF THE MINISTRY OF FINANCE

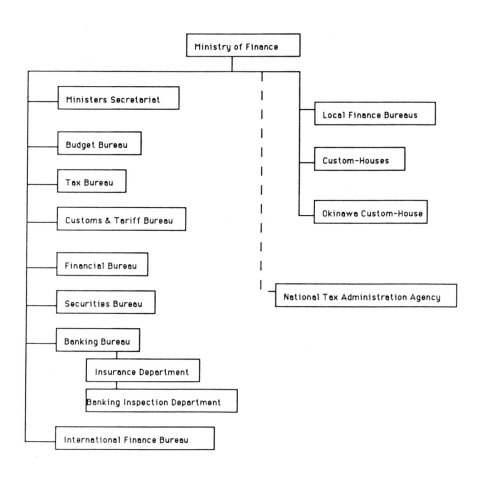

ese banks overseas and regulating portfolio investment by both foreign investors in Japan and Japanese investors overseas.[9]

The Finance Bureau. The Finance Bureau is the administrator for all
of the central government's borrowing activities. This involves over-
seeing the issue of government bonds and short-term government

bills. In addition to other activities involving fiscal investment and currency activities, the Finance Bureau oversees the Trust Fund Bureau, the industrial investment special account, National Debt Consolidation Fund Special Account, and other special government accounts. The Trust Fund Bureau and the National Debt Consolidation Fund Special Account enable the MOF to participate directly in the secondary market.[10]

The Securities Bureau. The Securities Bureau is in charge of the administration of all matters involving securities. The Bureau consists of six sections as shown in Exhibit 10. In addition to these sections, two deputy director generals and three special staffs for research and planning are in charge of supervision of the Bureau. There are three auxiliary bodies related to the Bureau: the Securities Exchange Council, the Business Accounting Deliberation Council, and the Certified Public Accountant (CPA) Examination Commission.

Local Organizations for Securities Administration. Local finance bureaus and the financial sections of their branch offices are local organizations in charge of securities administration. There are nine finance bureaus, one branch (Fukuoka Branch), 40 finance sections, and one finance department (Finance Department of the General Bureau of Okinawa Developing Agency) located throughout Japan. These local organizations take part in securities administration activities including the supervision of securities companies, inspection of securities activities, the examination of CPAs, and the maintenance of corporate statistics. Since November 1986, these organizations have also guided and supervised securities investment advisors under the Law Concerning the Regulation of Securities Investment Advisory Business.

In the eight cities where stock exchanges operate, stock exchange comptrollers under the directors of the local finance bureaus supervise the transactions in, and operations of, the exchanges.[11]

Securities Administration

The Securities Bureau is responsible for six major laws related to securities administration. These laws are: (1) the Securities and Exchange Law, (2) the Law Concerning Foreign Securities Firms, (3) the

EXHIBIT 10: ORGANIZATION OF SECURITIES ADMINISTRATION

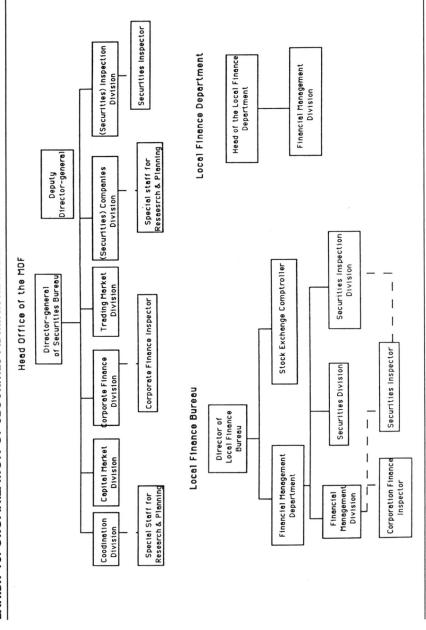

Head Office of the MOF

Director-general of Securities Bureau

Deputy Director-general

- Coodination Division
- Capital Market Division
- Corporate Finance Division
- Trading Market Division
- (Securities) Companies Division
- (Securities) Inspection Division

- Special Staff for Research & Planning
- Corporate Finance Inspector
- Special staff for Research & Planning
- Securities Inspector

Local Finance Bureau

Director of Local Finance Bureau

- Financial Management Department
- Stock Exchange Comptroller

- Financial Management Division
- Securities Division
- Securities Inspection Division

- Corporation Finance Inspector
- Securities Inspector

Local Finance Department

Head of the Local Finance Department

- Financial Management Division

Securities Investment Trust Law, (4) the Certified Public Accountant Law, (5) the Law Concerning Depository and Book-Entry for Share Certificates, Etc., and (6) the Law Concerning the Regulation of Securities Investment Advisory Business. All securities-related policy is planned and implemented in accordance with these laws.

Policies of the MOF are concerned with two primary areas of activity: (1) the supervision and guidance of the securities industry and (2) the provision of administrative assistance for the securities markets. Exhibit 11 shows the major lines of operation conducted in

EXHIBIT 11: SECURITIES ADMINISTRATION

Market administration	Research, planning and drafting of securities policy at large
	Drafting of policies concerning the trading market
	To ensure the formation of fair prices on the trading market
	Corporate financial disclosure system (acceptance of securities reports, etc., and their examination)
	The certified public accountant system
Supervisory function	Licensing and supervising securities companies
	Licensing and supervising branches of foreign securities companies
	Licensing and supervising investment trust management companies
	Licensing of securities business to banking institutions and their supervision
	Registration and supervision of investment advisers
	Licensing and supervision of securities exchanges and securities finance companies
	Designation and supervision of central depository agencies
	Inspection of securities companies
	Supervision of securities-related judicial persons for public benefit

Source: Japan Securities Research Institute, *Securities Market in Japan 1988.*

enacting MOF policies. The Law for Foundation of the MOF governs these, and other, activities of the MOF.

The main objectives of securities administration are: (1) to manage the national economy properly and (2) to protect securities investors. These two objectives are stated in the Securities and Exchange Law.

To manage the national economy properly, the MOF tries to facilitate the efficient operation of the securities markets as places for public and private entities to raise and invest their funds. To this end, the MOF focuses on the achievement of fair pricing of securities, because a fair (that is, competitive) pricing mechanism is the primary condition for efficient markets. Accordingly, its policies are meant to eliminate factors which can result in unfair pricing, such as excessive dealer to dealer trading, undesirable levels of speculation, and the abuse of insider information.

To protect securities investors, the MOF attempts to make available enough information so investors can make educated investment decisions. The MOF tries to ensure the disclosure of issuer information by the publication of securities reports. The MOF also encourages the securities industry to provide fair and correct information. The Securities and Exchange Law prohibits securities professionals from providing any biased or decisive advice to their clients, or making promises regarding investment performance.[12]

THE BANK OF JAPAN

Primary Business

The Bank of Japan (BOJ) is not a part of the government, though the government owns 55% of the BOJ. The BOJ serves as Japan's central bank and is the largest bank in Japan. It exists mainly to implement government policy usually under direction of the MOF.

The BOJ is organized much like city banks. The primary difference is that the BOJ tends to be "top heavy" with additional executives and decision making boards. The most important of these additional boards is the policy board which meets every week to set the official discount rate, establish reserve deposit ratios and maximum deposit interest rate ceilings, and determine availability of credit to the private sector.[13]

The two main goals of the BOJ are to serve as guardian of the yen, that is to safeguard the yen from devaluation by inflation and to shape monetary policy for the stimulation of economic growth. To facilitate these goals, the BOJ is: (1) the sole issuer of bank notes in Japan, (2) the government's bank, (3) the lender of last resort to commercial banks, and (4) the arbiter of monetary policy.

BOJ in Securities Markets

Two important divisions exist within the BOJ which directly concern the securities markets, the Foreign Department's Foreign Exchange Division and the Banking Division of the Banking Department. The Foreign Exchange Division monitors international transactions by all banks in Japan, ensures banks are within swap and position limits established by the MOF, and monitors business conditions for foreign banks within Japan and developments within international banking. The Banking Division negotiates bank-to-bank lending quotas and monitors developments in call and bill discount markets.

The BOJ has traditionally held vast amounts of power in the interbank market. This has changed in large part due to the partial deregulation of the Japanese securities markets. Deregulation has occurred in open markets, but not in the interbank market where BOJ regulations and low rates have all but destroyed the market. Historically, the BOJ has held extreme power over Japanese banks by virtue of its longstanding relationships with the banks. As such, the BOJ dictated their foreign exchange activities and monitored the activities of the banks' clients. However, with the increasing presence in the markets of foreign banks and non-bank Japanese financial institutions, the power of the BOJ over banks has been decreasing.

Currently, the BOJ intervenes in the open markets (through so-called "open market operations") primarily when the interbank and open market interest rates get too far out of line. Due to unattractive rates, the BOJ is also saddled with the responsibility of buying all of the financing bills issued by the MOF. The BOJ then sells them to dealers at rates closer to the market rates on a repurchase basis.[14]

CITY BANKS

Primary Business

City banks are among the most powerful financial institutions in Japan. Their total assets as of March 1988 were 270.3 trillion yen. The 13 city banks hold approximately 20% of all deposits within financial institutions.[15] Headquartered in major metropolitan areas (hence the name, "city banks"), the banks have branches throughout Japan, making them easily accessible to depositors. The primary function of city banks is to accept deposits from corporations and individuals and invest these funds by making loans or purchasing securities. City banks provide about 20% of all loans to the private sector. In addition, as commercial banks, city banks are authorized to provide the function of settlement of payments.

In the course of these functions, city banks serve as "primary" banks for private companies. As a primary bank of a company, a city bank is responsible for providing many of the funds and financial services required by the company. Most of these services involve holding short-term deposits and providing loans, however these services can extend to offering strategic business advice. It is not unusual for city banks to hold shares of these private companies, though they are prevented by law from owning more than 5% of the outstanding shares of any company.

Investment Behavior

Increasing Net Sales In the Predealing Period. The three largest sellers of bonds in FY 1981 were city banks, local banks, and long-term credit banks. These institutions were running short of funds as a result of the large amount of government bonds they had under-written during the 1970s. To compensate for this, these banks resorted to selling off much of their bond holdings, becoming over-sellers[16] as early as 1973. This overselling escalated in 1975 when the government began issuing massive amounts of public bonds. In FY 1973, city banks oversold only 250 billion yen. Due to the government bonds issued in FY 1975, this figure jumped to approximately 2 trillion yen.

City banks were, by far, the largest net sellers of bonds in FY 1981 having oversold by 4.1 trillion yen. This was more than four times the amount oversold by long-term credit banks, which were the second largest net sellers behind the city banks.

The primary reason for this overselling behavior by city banks was because they were chronically short of funds. As the primary lenders to large, private companies, they were unable to obtain enough funds for corporate loans merely through savings deposits. In addition, the city banks were required to underwrite over 30% of all long-term bonds issued by the government, further compounding their funding problem.

During the early 1980s, city banks experienced a significant decline in deposits. In FY 1982, individual investors began shifting their funds from savings deposits to newly developed financial assets of trust banks, long-term credit banks, and investment trusts, all of which paid higher interest than deposits. Corporate clients began placing funds in open markets rather than deposits. These outflows of deposits forced city banks to increase their net bond sales in order to improve their fund position.[17]

The weight of the underwriting requirements on city banks was large relative to other financial institutions in Japan. In the early 1980s, city banks controlled approximately 30% of the assets within financial institutions in the underwriting syndicate (excluding securities companies) in Japan, but they were responsible for underwriting as much as 42% of the 10-year government bonds issued. The relative positions of the members of the underwriting syndicate of government bonds have changed. With the large increases in government bond issuances, which began in 1975, city banks were forced to oversell amounts equal to their increased underwriting activities.[18] The heavy burden of underwriting on city banks only exacerbated their overselling positions during the early 1980s.

As long as city banks held massive quantities of government bonds they had underwritten, they suffered from increasing interest rate risk (i.e., price risk). This occurred in two ways. First, from the "mismatch" of funding costs and investment revenue that occurred because government bonds had fixed rates while rates on deposits floated. Second, restrictions on the types of bonds city banks could sell resulted in huge book losses when bond prices fell.

City banks were limited as to the types of bonds they were permitted to sell to meet their funding shortfalls. In April 1977, city banks were permitted to sell deficit-financing government bonds which were more than one year old. In October of 1977, this was expanded to other one year old government bonds.[19] Even so, city banks continued their huge overselling activities until 1985, when they were allowed to start full bond dealing.

Another problem was caused when a deviation occurred between subscriber's yield and market yield. When interest rates were on an uptrend, subscriber's yield usually went lower than the market yield because bond issue terms were not promptly adjusted to the upward shift of the market yield.[20] It meant that when interest rates were going up, the banks immediately suffered book losses when they underwrote government bonds.

Investment Activities In the Predealing Period. The trading volume of city banks increased from 3.6 trillion in 1978 to 14.2 trillion yen in 1981. This increased activity can be attributed to two factors: (1) flatness in commercial banking activities, and (2) anticipation of changes in market regulations which would allow them to become involved in bond dealing activities.

Commercial banking activities flattened during the late 1970s and early 1980s due to decreasing spreads between funding costs and lending rates. Interest rates for deposits stayed high due to the increasing sensitivity of their clients to interest rates. Low demand for loans by borrowers kept lending rates low. Consequently, in the half year ending September 1981, the spread between the funding rate and the lending rate had become negative for every city bank. In an attempt to make up for these losses, the city banks turned to the bond market in order to generate profits.[21]

City Banks In the Bank Dealing Era. When full dealing started in 1985, some of the top, actively trading, city banks held more than 100 billion yen in their dealing accounts.[22] City banks, which had previously been the largest net sellers in the bond market, became net buyers for the first time in FY 1985. They overbought by 163 billion yen that fiscal year and the volume has increased every year since. In FY 1986, their amount of overbuying jumped to 2.7 trillion yen. In FY 1987, this figure had jumped again to 4.9 trillion yen, because their fund positions improved due to increased sales of certificates of deposits and money-market certificates and increased large-lot deposits. City banks are now among the largest net buyers of bonds, signaling that, for city banks, the bond market has changed from a place for fund raising to a place for investment.

In the first fiscal year of the full dealing era (FY 1985) every bank realized a large profit from bond dealing. City banks made total profits of 105 billion yen from bond dealing, which was more than four times the profits of the previous year. Some banks had caught up with securities companies in terms of profits from bond dealing. The profit structure of the city banks became less dependent on their commercial banking activities as their profits from bond dealing increased. For 13 city banks, the share of income from bond dealing, to total recurring profits (keijou rieki), increased from 2.2% in FY 1984 to 12% in FY 1986.[23]

Portfolio of Investments. In looking at Panel A in the appendix, we can see several trends in the investment portfolios of city banks. Over the period from 1983 to 1988, the percentage of foreign securities within their securities portfolios increased (from 6.5% to 11.2%) as the percentage of government bonds, local government bonds, and corporate bonds decreased. The overall percentage of securities within the total assets remained stable at around 12%. When compared to other financial institutions, city banks held a relatively large percentage of stocks (30.2% in March 1988) in their securities portfolios.

LOCAL BANKS

Primary Business

After city banks, local banks are among the largest private financial institutions in Japan. The total assets within local banks were 136.9 trillion yen in March 1988. There are 64 local banks which have over 5,000 branches throughout Japan. There is no legal separation between city and local banks; the classification is based on size and business focus. City banks concentrate their lending and deposit taking activities in the wholesale market and target large industrial companies. Local banks, on the other hand, are stronger in the retail market and provide loans primarily to locally based, medium-sized companies (capital below 100 million yen) throughout Japan. The major portion of their deposits are from individual clients, of which, approximately 80% are time deposits. As such, the banks' deposits are relatively stable.

Investment Behavior

Local banks were the third largest net sellers of bonds in 1981, over-selling by 700 billion yen. The investment activity in the local banks fluctuated on a seasonal basis. Most of their sales occurred in the second half of the fiscal year, while most buying activity occurred during the first half of the year when they had surplus funds. This behavior was typical, especially before the resale of bonds by banks started. After the banks started the resale of bonds, the seasonality of their investment behavior diminished since the resale activity im-proved the fund position of local banks.

This seasonality occurs because the fund operation of local banks is highly dependent on the financial status of local govern-ments. Most local banks are appointed by the relevant local govern-ments, such as prefectures and cities, to exclusively hold their public deposits. These public deposits cause local banks to have surplus funds during the first half of the fiscal year when local governments receive distribution of local allocation tax from the national govern-ment. However, in the second half of the year, the banks run short of funds because they lose funds from the public deposits and, due to an increased need for funds by local governments, they underwrite local government bonds.[24]

As major, allied banks of local governments, local banks are the largest underwriters of local government bonds. In many prefec-tures, local banks are the exclusive underwriter of the bonds issued by the local government. In FY 1980, the amount of government bonds underwritten by local banks was 1.2 trillion yen, just half of that underwritten by city banks. However, local banks underwrote 1.1 trillion yen of privately-placed local government bonds, which was almost twice as much as the volume underwritten by city banks. This underwriting activity caused local banks to be large oversellers of bonds.[25]

Impact of Bank Dealing. With the advent of bank dealing in FY 1984, the investment behavior of local banks followed that of city banks. In March 1984, 10 local banks were permitted to deal in public bonds and started bond dealing in June that year. The remainder of the local banks were authorized to participate in bond dealing in 1985 and 1986, and by June 1987 all 64 of the local banks had started full dealing (see Exhibit 11).

In FY 1982, local banks were the second largest seller of bonds next to city banks, having oversold by 2.3 trillion yen. The amount of their overselling has decreased each year since resale by banks started in 1983. They turned into net buyers in FY 1986, overbuying 597 billion yen. In FY 1987, their net purchases jumped to 2 trillion yen due to the increased sales of certificates of deposits and money-market certificates (see Exhibit 9). However, unlike institutions such as city banks, long-term credit banks, and trust banks, which have been increasing their trading volumes of bonds, local banks have been decreasing their trading volume since FY 1987.

Portfolio of Investments. In looking at Panel B in the appendix, we can see several trends in the investment portfolios of local banks. Over the period from 1983 to 1988, the percentage of foreign securities within their securities portfolios increased (from 2.3% to 10.4%) as the percentage of local government bonds decreased (from 18.3% to 11.7%). The overall percentage of securities remained stable at around 18% of the total assets. When compared to other financial institutions, local banks still held a relatively large percentage of local government bonds (11.7% in March 1988) in their securities portfolios.

LONG-TERM CREDIT BANKS

Primary Business

Three long-term credit banks exist, each of which has branches nationwide. Their total assets, as of March 1988, were 56 trillion yen. Long-term credit banks were established under the Long-term Credit Bank Law of 1952 to provide long-term financing for Japanese industry. This was done in order to ease the pressure on city banks and local banks to provide long-term loans. These long-term loans are used primarily for working capital and capital investment needs. Long-term credit banks are able to issue bank debentures[26] in order to raise funds for loans, but are limited in where and how they may accept deposits. In addition to providing long-term loans, long-term credit banks are required to underwrite large portions of government bond issues similar to city banks.

Investment Behavior

Long-term credit banks were as strong in lending activities as the city banks. In 1981, their sales of bank debentures declined. In the half year ending September 1981, the outstanding balance of their bank debentures increased by only 410 billion yen, compared to a 720 billion yen increase for the same period the previous year. The poor placement of their debentures caused a severe shortage of funds for lending. As a result, long-term credit banks became significant sellers of bonds in 1981. In that year, the amount of their over-selling totalled 1 trillion yen, more than ten times that of the previous year.[27]

The flatness in the bank debentures market was caused by the massive issuance of government bonds during the late 1970's. In 1979, a total of 3 trillion yen of coupon debentures was issued, 54% of which were purchased by individual investors. The remaining debentures went primarily to financial institutions like city banks, local banks, trust banks, and so on. However, the large increase in government bond issues required huge underwriting activities by all of these institutions, thus limiting their ability to purchase bank debentures from the long-term credit banks. By 1981, this resulted in the radical shift in the debenture market mentioned above. As long as the government continued to issue massive quantities of bonds, the long-term credit banks had to oversell bonds in order to meet their lending requirements.

In addition, strong competitors to bank debentures appeared in 1980. Bank debentures, which had a maturity of 5 years, started to compete with long-term government bonds due in 4-6 years. For instance, in December 1980, bank debentures with a coupon rate of 7.9% were issued at par value, while 8% government bonds due in 4-6 years sold under par in the market. Another competitor was the medium-term government bond with maturities of 2-4 years. The coupon rate of the medium-term bonds began to reflect market rates around 1980. Accordingly the bonds became more attractive to individual investors, taking the place of bank debentures as an investment alternative.[28]

In 1984, the turnover of bonds by long-term credit banks sharply increased with decreasing net sales. In FY 1984, when the bank dealing started, long-term credit banks, which used to be one of the largest sellers of government bonds, overbought by 68 billion yen.

Portfolio of Investments. In looking at Panel C in the appendix, we can see several trends in the investment portfolios of long-term credit banks. Over the period from 1983 to 1988, the percentage of their investments in foreign securities increased (from 7.5% to 14.8%) as the percentage of government bonds decreased (from 41.0% to 33.9%). The overall percentage of securities within the total assets remained stable at approximately 20%. When compared to other financial institutions, long-term credit banks held a relatively large percentage of corporate bonds (18.2% in March 1988) in their securities portfolios.

TRUST BANKS

Primary Business

There are seven trust banks in Japan all of which have branches throughout Japan. In addition to these seven trust banks, one city bank (Daiwa Bank) and two local banks (Ryukyu and Okinawa) are allowed to engage in some trust bank activities. Trust banks are long-term financing institutions much like long-term credit banks and are regulated under the Banking Law, the Trust Law, and the Law Concerning Concurrent Operation, Etc. of Savings Bank Business or Trust Business by Ordinary Banks, Etc.

Trust banks conduct both banking business and trust business. However, they are required to operate the two businesses out of two separate accounts, a bank account and a trust account. The major business of the trust banks is the trust business. This business is in three areas: (1) savings, (2) investment management, and (3) custodial. The primary sources of funds for these activities are: loan trusts (savings), money trusts (savings and custodial), pension trusts, and fund trusts (investment management). The portfolios are invested differently depending on the nature of the trust. For example, there are government restrictions on the make-up of the portfolios of loan trusts and pension trusts.

With the recent expansion of trust funds, trust banks have become one of the top institutional investors in the Japanese securities markets both in terms of the size of securities assets held and trading volume. In March 1988, the total assets of trust banks were 187.9 trillion yen, of which, 42.3 trillion yen were from bank accounts and 145.6 trillion yen were from trust accounts.

Investment Behavior

Pension Trust Funds. The total pension funds in eight banks (that is, seven trust banks and Daiwa Bank) increased nearly three times from 2.3 trillion yen in FY 1976 to 6.5 trillion yen in FY 1981. Most of this growth was due to the tax advantages of pension funds relative to retirement allowances and the increase in the percentage of elderly people in the population.

The shift in the portfolio of pension funds can be seen from the following.[29] At the end of March 1975, the major portion (52.5%) of their pension trust funds were in loans, reflecting the commercial nature of the business of trust banks. However, during the period 1975-1985, higher yielding bonds were replacing loans as an investment vehicle for their pension funds. In March 1985, bond investments accounted for approximately 41% of the pension assets of trust banks; this was up from 1975, when the figure was only 17%. In addition, the actual investment in bonds was twenty times the investment ten years earlier.

This increase in bond investment activity was caused by a number of factors. First, the flatness in the loan market made it difficult to place all of the money from the pension trusts into loans. Second, the trust banks preferred to fulfill loan demands primarily through funds from loan trusts and deposits. Third, the costs of pension trust funds were expensive relative to the costs for loan trusts and deposits.

In March 1987, the pension funds in the eight banks had reached 14.1 trillion yen, which was more than twice the amount in 1982. With the yields of new government bond issues as low as 4%, trust banks invested huge amounts of money in the bond market in order to try to generate capital gains from bond trading, since it was not possible to achieve their target performance (8-9%) only through coupon income. As such, they began operating in huge lots of bonds.[30]

During the early 1980s the trust banks began investing more of their funds in riskier assets, such as stocks and foreign securities with high potential yields. By March 1987, investments in foreign securities accounted for as much as 15% of the assets in pension trust funds. The actual investment amount in foreign securities had increased by as much as 90% from 1986 to 1987. Thus, the weight of government bonds in their portfolios was declining.

Fund Management Trusts. Fund management trusts are another source of funds for trust banks. Among these trusts, specified money trusts (called "Tokkin") and fund trusts have expanded significantly in the 1980s. The funds in Tokkin and fund trusts are invested mostly in securities such as domestic bonds and stocks and foreign securities.

Tokkin and fund trusts are slightly different. Tokkin is a trust of custodial nature. With Tokkin, the investors (that is, trustors) place their funds with the trust banks, but the investors retain discretionary power over the portfolios in the funds. On the other hand, a fund trust is a trust of investment management nature. With fund trusts, the trust banks hold discretion over the management of funds.

Business corporations, insurance companies, and financial institutions have actively invested in securities through these fund management trusts since 1984, mainly because of the accounting benefits. The seven trust banks held total assets of 2.4 trillion yen in Tokkin and fund trusts in March 1984. This figure increased to 10 trillion yen in 1986, and to 29 trillion yen by September 1987. Since Black Monday in October 1987, its growth has slowed. In September 1988, the amount invested in these trusts totalled 32.5 trillion yen.

Exhibit 12 shows the portfolios of these fund management trusts. In both Tokkin and fund trusts, the weight of stocks within

EXHIBIT 12: PORTFOLIO OF FUND MANAGEMENT TRUSTS

(Unit: 100 million yen, %)

End of March	1985		1986		1987		1988	
(i)Specified Money Trusts (Tokkin)								
Domestic Bonds	20,816	63.3	n/a	n/a	39,884	31.1	34,289	24.4
Foreign Securities	3,067	9.3	n/a	n/a	15,431	12.0	15,804	11.2
Stocks	6,264	19.0	n/a	n/a	42,999	33.5	54,646	38.9
Others	2,758	8.4	n/a	n/a	30,069	23.4	35,904	25.5
Total	32,905	100.0	61,394	100.0	128,383	100.0	140,643	100.0
(ii)Fund Trusts								
Domestic Bonds	8,314	49.7	16,298	35.9	31,315	30.6	39,604	26.2
Foreign Securities	2,417	14.5	10,077	22.2	17,238	16.9	16,534	11.0
Stocks	3,916	23.4	8,969	19.7	28,030	27.4	48,271	32.0
Others	2,069	12.4	10,092	22.2	25,664	25.1	46,478	30.8
Total	16,716	100.0	45,436	100.0	102,247	100.0	150,887	100.0
(i) + (ii)								
Total	49,621		106,830		230,630		291,530	

Source: Nomura Research Institute, *Bond Handbook (Koushasai Youran)*.

the portfolios has increased over the past four years, while that of domestic bonds has sharply decreased.

Portfolio of Investments. Panel D in the appendix indicates several trends in the investment portfolios of trust banks. Over the period from 1983 to 1988, the percentage of stocks and foreign securities within their securities portfolio dramatically increased as the percentage of government bonds and local government bonds decreased. The overall percentage of securities within the total assets increased from 25.0% to 30.4%, primarily due to the expansion of pension and fund management trusts. When compared to other financial institutions, trust banks held a relatively large percentage of stocks (33.2% in March 1988) in their securities portfolios.

MUTUAL BANKS

Primary Business

Mutual banks are located throughout Japan in rural and urban areas. Though generally much smaller than local and city banks, some of the mutual banks near metropolitan areas are approaching the smaller city banks in size. Like commercial banks, mutual banks accept deposits (primarily from individuals) and make loans (generally to small businesses). Mutual banks are the only financial institutions in Japan authorized to participate in the mutual installment savings business. This allows depositors to make deposits in installments and, after a certain period of time, take out loans.

Investment Behavior

In 1980 the weakness of the loan market hit mutual banks particularly hard since their loans were expensive relative to other banks' and financial institutions'. The total outstanding balance of loans of 71 mutual banks had increased 5-6% every half year since 1976. However, in the half year ending September 1980, the increase declined to only 3.4%, which was the lowest in history after World War II.

Suffering from declining profits, the banks entered the bond market. They started trying to earn profits from bond trading instead of purely from interest earned on loans. The ratio of the balance of their securities investment to their total deposits increased from 12.9% in September 1978 to 15.4% in September 1981.[31]

Up until the mid-1980s, it was common for mutual banks to hold a new issue of government bonds or bank debentures until maturity, simply to receive the coupon income. However, with the necessity to increase profits via the bond market, mutual banks began investing in corporate bonds with high coupons and selling the government bonds and bank debentures they underwrote. They bought corporate bonds because of their higher yields, but they had to watch the market to ensure they sold these corporate bonds before their prices dropped. This enabled mutual banks to secure a yield higher than what they had earned on their government bonds.[32]

Portfolio of Investments. In looking at Panel E in the appendix, we can see several trends in the investment portfolios of mutual banks. Over the period from 1983 to 1988, the percentage of foreign securities within their securities portfolio increased (from 1.9% to 9.6%) as the percentage of corporate bonds and bank debentures decreased. The overall percentage of securities to total assets steadily increased from 12.9% to 15.4%.

INSTITUTIONS FOR AGRICULTURE, FISHERY, AND FORESTRY

Primary Business

The financial institutions for agriculture, forestry, and fishery have a three-tier network system. At the top, the Central Cooperative Bank of Agriculture and Forestry (the Norinchukin Bank) acts as the central bank for the whole system. The middle tier consists of credit federations for individual cooperatives. Cooperative societies are the lowest level organizations and have the actual contact with individual members. Within this system, the lower institutions can put their excess funds in deposits held by upper organizations. Centralizing the funds in the upper organizations enables the entire system to invest its funds more efficiently. Exhibit 13 shows the investment activity within the network.

EXHIBIT 13: FUND OPERATION WITHIN AGRICULTURAL INSTITUTIONS (END OF SEPTEMBER 1986)

(Unit: 100 million yen, %)

	Cooperatives	(%)*		Federations	(%)*		Norinchukin Bank	(%)*
Deposits	392,197		→ Deposits	297,234		→ Deposits	181,117	
						Debentures	38,982	
System Savings	271,966	69.3	System Savings	156,511	52.7			
Securities	19,361	4.9	Securities	113,007	38.0	Securities	106,307	48.3
Loans	127,832	32.6	Loans	40,010	13.5	Loans	97,676	44.4

*Ratio to Deposits and Debentures

Source: Nihon Keizai Shinbun, Inc., *Bond Secondary Market (Koushasai Ruytsu Shijou)*.

The Norinchukin Bank was founded under the Norinchukin Bank Law as a government-related organization. It was converted to a private organization in 1986. A revision to the Banking Law in 1981 modified the Norinchukin Bank Law and thus, enabled the Norinchukin Bank to deal in public bonds.

The Norinchukin Bank oversees the distribution of financial services throughout rural Japan. The primary method for accomplishing this is via a nationwide network of private cooperative institutions. The two largest networks are the agricultural cooperatives and the fishery cooperatives, followed by the forestry cooperatives. Each network of cooperatives is regulated by its own separate set of laws.

The agricultural cooperatives provide a wide variety of services to the agricultural sector. In addition to offering financial services, they sell seeds, equipment, and fertilizer, and buy crops at the end of the growing season. As financial institutions, agricultural and fishery cooperatives accept deposits and make loans. Though similarly structured, forestry cooperatives cannot accept deposits. All of these cooperatives make both short-term loans to provide money for items such as seeds, bait, and fertilizer; and they offer long-term loans to enable farmers, fisheries and foresters to expand their operations. Unlike other financial institutions, agricultural cooperatives can accept this year's crop as collateral for loans, enabling many farmers to continue their operations from year to year. By providing much needed financing services to the rural sector, these cooperatives play a vital role in the Japanese economy.

Investment Behavior

Early Investment Behavior. Prior to 1981, among the investors, financial institutions for agriculture and forestry (including the cooperatives, credit federations and Norinchukin Bank) were regarded as the largest buyers in the bond market. In 1979, they had the largest trading volume among all the investors in the market, with a share of 14.7%. In 1981, the institutions bought 7.9 trillion yen and sold 7.2 trillion yen in total, resulting in 680 billion yen of overbuying. In addition, through investment trusts, they bought 6.1% of coupon government bonds in the same year, which effectively raised their level of overbuying to more than one trillion yen.[33]

The assets of these institutions at the end of September 1981 were about 39 trillion yen in total, consisting of 33 trillion yen of deposits and 6 trillion yen of insurance funds. Though rather small when compared to city banks (with assets of 94 trillion yen) or local banks (with assets of 64 trillion yen), the agricultural institutions were the largest buyers in the market primarily due to an excess of funds stemming from a relatively low demand for lending or underwriting services.

Borrowers from these institutions were chiefly involved in industries such as agriculture, forestry, and fishery, which require much less capital investment than companies in manufacturing and service industries. Consequently, the institutions did little lending and structurally had excess funds to invest in the bond market.[34]

Impact on Overall Market. Though relatively small, these financial institutions could have a huge effect on the overall bond market due to its rigid structure. In that structure, major net sellers were city banks and local banks short of funds for lending while major net buyers were the agriculture and forestry institutions having excess funds. As a result of this somewhat rigid structure, if any of the major participants in the market suffered from a poor year, the entire market was affected. An example serves as the best illustration.

In 1980, a poor crop due to cold weather resulted in a depression of the entire Japanese bond market. In the summer of that year, the deposits to the institutions for agriculture and forestry declined as a result of the poor crop. This decline in deposits put them in such a tight fund position that the institutions, previously the largest buyer in the market, turned into an overseller in August. This situation resulted in a bearish bond market until the end of the year.[35]

Recent Investment Behavior. By FY 1985, the balance of the securities investment by the Norinchukin Bank had increased from 5.4 trillion yen (including 1.9 trillion yen of government bonds) at the end of FY 1980 to 10.3 trillion yen (including 5.2 trillion yen of government bonds), accounting for as much as 41% of its assets in FY 1985. At the end of September 1986, the total assets of the institutions were 44.2 trillion yen, of which, 23.8 trillion yen was invested in securities.[36] Although their investment in government bonds had increased, the influence of these institutions on the bond market was comparatively reduced, as bond dealers and other investors rapidly expanded their trading volumes.

The institutions typically bought government bonds when the yield of those bonds exceeded their target yield, and then held them to maturity. For instance, they bought bonds from October to December 1985 when the bond market declined because of the high short-term interest rates maintained by the BOJ. Since 1986, however, they have had to actively seek capital gain in order to achieve their target yields due to the declining coupon income from government bonds. Consequently they have gone into the dealing of highly liquid, long-term government bonds.[37]

Portfolio of Investments. Several trends in the investment portfolio of the Norinchukin Bank can be seen in Panel F in the appendix. Over the period from 1983 to 1988, the percentage of foreign securities within its securities portfolio increased (from 4.8% to 18.1%) as the percentage of corporate bonds and bank debentures decreased. The overall percentage of securities to total assets remained stable at approximately 44%. When compared to other financial institutions, the Norinchukin Bank held a relatively large percentage of government bonds (45.1% in March 1988) in its securities portfolio.

CREDIT ASSOCIATIONS

Primary Business

Credit associations were converted from credit cooperatives under the Credit Association Law of 1951. The primary business of credit associations is to take deposits and make loans, similar to commercial banking. The main difference between ordinary banks (city banks and local banks) and credit associations is that the latter have a membership system. Loans, as a rule, are made only to members though the associations will accept deposits from nonmembers. Like local banks and mutual banks, the associations are locally based throughout the country, and carry on most of their business in certain limited regions. The associations have developed as regional institutions financing small to medium-sized firms.

The Zenshinren Bank acts as the central bank of the credit associations, based on the Credit Association Law. Like the Norinchukin Bank for the agricultural cooperatives, the Zenshinren Bank has a membership system. Within the system, individual associations, as members, can put their excess funds in deposits with the Zenshinren Bank in order to invest the funds more efficiently as a whole. The Zenshinren Bank is authorized to deal in public bonds to invest in securities.

Investment Behavior

In the 1980's, the lending activities of credit associations declined as a result of increased competition from larger banks, such as city banks, which were focusing on loans to small and medium-sized companies. The ratio of balance of loans to total deposits for credit associations dropped 4% from 1981 to 1986. This flatness in the loan business for credit associations made them more active in securities investments.

In 1986, some credit associations invested short-term in so-called "benchmark"[38] issues of government bonds seeking to earn capital gains from frequent turnover. They also invested in bonds through fund trusts and Tokkin.[39]

Portfolio of Investments. As seen in Panel G in the appendix, the percentage of stocks within the securities portfolios of credit associations increased form 2.4% to 9.1% during the period 1983 to 1988. At the same time, the percentages of government bonds and local government bonds decreased. When compared to other financial institutions, the credit associations consistently held a relatively large percentage of corporate bonds (31.7% in March 1988) in their securities portfolios.

However, different trends existed in the investment portfolio of the Zenshinren Bank (see Panel H in the appendix). Over the same period (1983 to 1988), the percentage of its investments in corporate bonds dropped sharply from 47.1% to 17.4% as the percentage of government bonds increased (from 29.8% to 46.4%).

LIFE INSURANCE COMPANIES

Primary Business

There are 24 life insurance companies in Japan, all licensed under the Insurance Business Law. Life insurance companies are authorized to sell only life insurance. The Japanese are the largest purchasers of life insurance in the world, with over 90% of all households subscribing to some type of life insurance.[40] The popularity of life insurance is a direct result of the Japanese propensity to save. At the end of March 1985, the deposited assets from insurance contractors totalled 41 trillion yen, which accounted for 8% of the balance of financial assets of the household sector.[41]

The BOJ has kept interest rates low to stimulate economic growth and, as a result, insurance policies with endowments or annuities offer yields which are competitive with bank rates. This, combined with the tax advantages offered by the MOF to purchasers of life insurance, helps contribute to the enormous popularity of life insurance as an investment.

In addition to providing financial assets for households, the companies play an important role as institutional investors in the securities market and in the long-term financing of Japanese industry by providing loans to heavy industry such as the electric power, steel, and chemical industries. However, insurance companies are regulated by the government as to the composition of their financial portfolios.

Investment Behavior

Due to the flat loan market of the late 1970s, insurance companies were forced to become more active in the bond market in order to make money from their surplus funds. Examining 21 major insurance companies over several years, we found that the ratio of additional loans to additional assets dropped from 82% in 1970 to below 50% in 1981. In 1978, when the demand for loans hit bottom, the ratio was as low as 35%. In that year, 54% of the additional financial assets of these companies were invested in securities, two thirds of which were bonds.[42]

Investments by life insurance companies typically are oriented towards high-coupon securities. It is characteristic for life insurance companies to prefer coupon income to capital gain, since they are not allowed to pay dividends out of their capital gains. As a result, they prefer high coupon bonds even if those bonds are rather expensive (i.e., offer a lower yield). With high interest rates in Europe and the U.S. forcing the yields of foreign bonds as high as 15%, some insurance companies began to invest heavily in foreign bonds around 1979. Their assets in foreign bonds increased more than ten times, increasing from 56 billion yen in FY 1977 to 640 billion yen in FY 1980.[43]

Since 1986, domestic interest rates have been lower than ever. Since new issues of bonds have had low coupons, life insurance companies no longer were able to achieve high coupon income from the long-term investment in new issues. Consequently, they have bought high-coupon bonds in the secondary market, although these bonds, since they sell at a premium to par, can result in capital losses at their maturity. In addition, life insurance companies have increasingly invested in bonds through specified money trusts (called "Tokkin"), since they are permitted to pay dividends out of capital gains from these trusts.

Portfolio of Investments. Several trends in the investment portfolios of life insurance companies can be seen in Panel I in the appendix. Over the period from 1983 to 1988, the percentage of foreign securities within their securities portfolios increased (19.5% to 28.1%) as the percentage of local government bonds decreased (7.7% to 2.4%). The overall percentage of securities to total assets increased from 32.7% to 44.1%. When compared to other financial institutions, life insurance companies held a relatively large percentage of stocks (44.6% in March 1988) in their securities portfolios.

PROPERTY INSURANCE COMPANIES

Primary Function

Twenty-three property insurance companies are licensed to operate in Japan under the Insurance Business Law. In addition to their primary activity of providing insurance, the companies play a role in financing Japanese industry and as institutional investors in the market. Their presence in the loan and securities markets is smaller than life insurance companies. Because of the uncertain nature of their business, property insurance companies must invest in highly-liquid assets. As such, property insurance companies function primarily as short-term financing institutions. Like life insurance companies, property insurance companies are regulated as to the composition of their investment portfolios.

Investment Behavior

Due to the relatively frequent turnover of their funds and unpredictability of their insurance payments, property insurance companies generally used to invest in highly-liquid assets such as bank deposits. As a result of the increasing demand for savings-oriented insurance, property insurance companies began selling this type of insurance in the early 1980s. Since the weight of savings-oriented insurance in their funds was increasing during the mid-1980s, property insurance companies began investing in medium to long-term assets as well. Similar to life insurance companies, property insurance companies sought high coupon income by investing in higher yielding bonds such as local government bonds, government-guaranteed bonds, and foreign securities. However, since FY 1986, they have been rather pessimistic about foreign securities due to the appreciation of the yen.

Portfolio of Investments. Panel J in the appendix shows several trends in the investment portfolios of property insurance companies. Over the period from 1983 to 1988, the percentage of foreign securities within their securities portfolios increased (9.8% to 19.6%) as the percentage of stocks sharply decreased (52.0% to 33.7%). The overall percentage of securities to total assets steadily increased from 40.6% to 48.2%.

INVESTMENT TRUSTS

Primary Business

Investment trusts are among the biggest institutional investors in Japan. They provide the important function of directing the savings of individuals into the purchase of securities. Because of both their size and their investment behavior (generally buying as market declines and selling as market rises), the investment trusts have a large influence on the performance of the markets in Japan. By law, investment trusts can only invest in listed stocks, bonds, and convertible bonds, or extend call loans. In addition, the trusts are limited as to the percentage of money which may be invested in any one company or any one issue.

Investment Behavior

Investment trust funds began investing heavily in bonds during the late 1960s. Their low price volatility, relative to stocks, and the fixed income of the coupon payments made them secure investments for the investment trusts which were shifting to more conservative investment practices. In 1967, the percentage of the investment trust funds invested in bonds reached 50% for the first time. This figure increased steadily through 1981. By 1981, the total assets in investment trusts were over 7 trillion yen, of which, 1.5 trillion yen were invested in stocks and 4.3 trillion yen were invested in bonds.[44]

In January 1980, investment trusts began selling shares of medium-term government bond funds ("Chu-koku funds"). These funds invested primarily in medium-term government bonds and, since they had many of the properties of money market funds in the U.S., they performed much better than deposits in banks. The funds were popular not only with individual investors, but also with corporations and local governments. Within two years of the first sale, more than 600 billion yen was being invested in Chu-koku funds. As such, the focus of investment by these trusts had shifted from long-term to medium and short-term government bonds.

Following the success of these medium-term government bond funds, Daiwa Securities introduced a "new government bond fund (shin kokusai fund)" in October 1981. These funds bore as much as 8.8% annual interest, incorporating the moderately priced, 6.1-6.8% coupon government bonds. Within two months total sales reached 870 billion yen, making the funds the most popular in the history of investment trusts.[45] As the popularity of these funds increased, the net purchases by the investment trusts increased.

With the commanding success of these government bond funds, investment trusts became the largest overbuyers in the bond market for the first time in FY 1981. Between April 1983 and January 1986 the total assets invested in investment trusts rose from 10 trillion to 20 trillion yen, and by March 1987 this number had jumped to 35 trillion yen. As the total assets invested in these funds expanded, the trusts increasingly invested in bonds for their investment funds in order to secure a certain yield. Bonds were even incorporated into stock investment funds with as much as 46% of these funds invested in bonds.[46]

Composition of Investment Trusts Portfolios. The chief investment vehicle for investment trusts is the domestic bond. In 1980, 2% of all domestic bonds outstanding were held by investment trusts so the funds could seek capital gain from short-term trading. This figure had grown to 5% by the end of 1986. Of these investments, an increasing amount of convertible bonds were being purchased by the trusts. By 1986, over 24% (2 trillion yen) of the outstanding convertible bonds on the exchanges in Japan were held by investment trusts.[47] Though the majority of their investments remained in domestic bonds, investment trusts shifted some of their assets into foreign bonds between 1984 and 1986 as the yields became favorable relative to the domestic bonds available.

BUSINESS CORPORATIONS[48]

Prior to the oil crisis of 1972–1973, business corporations in Japan used the bond market primarily to raise funds and did very little investing of any surplus operating funds. Most investments were in the form of fixed-rate bank deposits. With the sharp increase in interest rates that occurred following the oil crisis, corporations began looking to the bond market as a place to invest surplus funds. There was a shift of corporate investments from bank deposits to other market-oriented assets. The contribution to the increase in their financial assets, of assets with regulated interest rates, dropped from 59% during 1970–1974 to 5.6% during 1980–1984.[49]

Investment Behavior

Business corporations typically invested their surplus funds in short-term instruments which they turned over frequently. Since their funds were temporarily invested, and not in long-term investments, the repo market was suitable because repurchase agreements had terms ranging from several days to a few months. Until FY 1984, business corporations had been by far the largest buyers in the repo market, having a 55-65% share of the balance of repo purchases.

As business corporations became more experienced in fund management, their investments became more diversified. The balance of their investments in the repo market declined from 3.5 trillion yen at the end of FY 1980 to 1.9 trillion yen in FY 1984. This was largely due to the availability of new types of financial assets like certificates of deposits and foreign currency deposits which could be used for short-term investments. At the same time, corporations also began to invest in long-term bonds to diversify their investment portfolios.

With the exception of financial institutions, in FY 1986, one-third of all corporations listed on the stock exchanges made profits from their financial activities (including investment, borrowing, and lending activities).[50] This was an increase from 1981 when only one-fifth of these corporations made profits. This activity helped compensate for the recession caused by the appreciation of the yen which had started in September 1985. Business corporations had attempted to earn through their cash management activities by using highly sophisticated financial techniques called "Zai-tech activities."[51]

Business corporations typically had invested their surplus funds in relatively short-term operations, being primarily concerned about the price stability of their investments. However, in the Zai-tech boom, they highly leveraged their operations, as their operating funds expanded and their financial skills developed. Specifically, they increasingly invested in securities through specified money trusts and foreign securities. They also invested in convertible bonds and Treasury bills, seeking capital gain, because bank deposits and repo operations were no longer profitable due to low interest rates. In terms of their net position, business corporations have been net sellers since FY 1983, because of their participation in the popular "one-touch-through" deals.

FOREIGN INVESTORS

Since foreign investors are exposed to foreign exchange risk in bond trading, the level of their activity in the bond market is dependent on expectations about foreign exchange rates. Although they were traditionally overbuyers, in FY 1979, the amount of overbuying by foreign investors dropped sharply due to the depreciation of the yen. When the yen soared from 250 yen/dollar to 190 yen/dollar in 1980, foreign investors became the largest overbuyers for FY 1980. Since 1985, foreign investors have invested heavily in short-term bonds hoping to realize exchange rate profits from the appreciation of the yen.

Investment Behavior

Exhibit 14 shows the remarkable growth in the presence of foreign investors in the Japanese bond market. They became major players almost immediately upon beginning to participate in the market. In fact, it was the foreign investors and individual investors in Japan that supported the market during its depression in 1980. From April

EXHIBIT 14: BOND TRADING BY FOREIGN INVESTORS IN JAPAN*

(Unit: 100 million yen, %)

FY	Sales	Purchases	Net Position	Trading Volume	Market Share
1980	28,005	38,662	10,657	66,667	5.7
1981	43,260	50,527	7,267	93,787	5.8
1982	58,816	78,522	19,706	137,338	7.2
1983	153,947	163,302	9,355	317,249	11.2
1984	493,113	502,151	9,038	995,264	15.4
1985	548,988	564,195	15,207	1,113,183	5.6
1986	371,094	360,348	-10,746	731,442	3.4
1987	357,319	358,186	867	715,505	2.7

*Excluding repo transactions

Source: The Bond Underwriters Association of Japan.

to July that year, foreign investors overbought more than 100 billion yen each month, investing over 5.3 billion dollars over the course of the year.[52]

The trading volume of foreign investors in the bond market expanded more than ten times from FY 1981 to FY 1985. One factor in this expansion was the increasing volume of bond trading by overseas affiliates of Japanese financial institutions, which was counted as part of the trading volume of foreign investors. Another factor was the appearance of foreign financial institutions in the Tokyo market, most notably in the primary market of medium-term government bonds.[53]

In 1986, foreign investors became net sellers in order to realize exchange rate profits. Since FY 1986, foreign investors have refrained from overbuying partly because they do not expect further significant appreciation of the yen.

Most of the increase in the trading volume of foreign investors can be attributed to the deregulation of foreign exchange in Japan. All restrictions on the acquisition of certain types of bonds (including Treasury bills) by foreign investors were removed in August 1974. In 1977, foreign exchange and overseas transfer of proceeds from bond trading were liberalized. With the deregulation of the repo market in May 1979, no special restrictions remained on bond trading by foreign investors. This was followed by the inauguration of a new foreign exchange law (the Foreign Exchange and Foreign Trade Control Law) in December 1980.

INDIVIDUAL INVESTORS

The total financial assets of individuals increased to about 570 trillion yen in 1985, more than 18.3 times the assets at the end of 1965. This growth was higher than the growth of disposable income.[54] In addition to this remarkable growth, the composition of these assets changed dramatically over the period.

Several things occurred which caused this growth and shift in assets. First, from 1975 on, the growth rate of cash and demand deposits rapidly declined. The share of those assets among the total financial assets of individuals decreased from 18% in 1965 to less than 10% in 1985. Second, the relative share of securities in investment funds decreased slightly from 1976 through 1980, as investment funds shifted from stocks to government bonds. Third, investment trusts expanded faster than other assets from 1981 to 1985 with the successful development of government bond investment trusts. These shifts reflected the increasing demand of households for higher yielding, yet safer, investments.

In the spring of 1980, a shift occurred in the behavior of individual investors due to a crash of the bond market. It was one of the worst bond market crashes in Japanese market history. During the resulting depression in the bond market, many securities companies shifted their marketing focus to the individual investors. As a result, individual investors began purchasing government bonds, but in lots of only one million yen. These lots were considered quite small from the standpoint of bond traders who had previously only sold lots greater than 10 million yen. This shift in focus by the securities houses enabled individual investors to become more active in the secondary market.

Before this occurrence, the securities companies had regarded individual investors as purchasers of new issues, but never as investors in the secondary market. As a result of the bond market crash, however, the securities companies started to pay keen attention to individual investors, despite the small lots, since institutional investors had cut back their investment activity because they held pessimistic views of the market. As a result, in April and May 1980, individual investors overbought by more than 100 billion yen, more than any other investor category. Even though the trading volume of individual investors remained small (less than 3-4% of the total trading volume) when compared to those of financial institutions, it is believed that the participation of individual investors supported the market through this depression.[55]

Investment Behavior

Several factors existed which encouraged individual investors to become active in the secondary market. In 1981, the financial assets per household reached 5 million yen for the first time. As their financial assets grew each year, investors became more sensitive to the yields on their investments. Compounding this factor was the market crash mentioned above. The crash resulted in the emergence of bonds offering a higher yield. Government bonds having coupons of 6.1%, yielding more than 10%, became popular among individual investors.

Another factor was the massive issuance of medium-term government bonds which began in FY 1978. The medium-term bonds were originally meant to be sold mainly to institutional investors. However, since the yields of the bonds were intentionally set lower than the market rates under the control of the MOF, institutional investors did not find these bonds attractive. Consequently, securities companies switched their marketing focus and sold these bonds primarily to individual investors.[56]

The medium-term bonds, newly purchased by individual investors in the primary market, were officially counted in bonds traded. As a result, the overbuying volume of individual investors has increased every year since 1980. In 1986, individual investors overbought by 1.14 trillion yen, which placed them third behind investment trusts and business corporations.

Securities Portfolios. From March 1983 to March 1988, the investment in government bonds by individual investors decreased from 26% to 17.9%. Instead, individuals invested more heavily in investment trusts whose share increased from 16.4% to over 34% during the same period. The percentage of funds invested in securities remained stable at approximately 13% (see Panel K in the appendix).

OTHER PARTICIPANTS

Among other investors are public entities such as the Trust Fund Bureau, the National Debt Consolidation Fund, and local governments. Their activities are outlined below.

Trust Fund Bureau

Primary Function. The primary function of the Trust Fund Bureau is to receive postal savings deposits and deposits of excess funds of various special accounts of the government and use these funds to finance special corporations such as public bodies, government financial institutions, and local government bodies.[57]

There are several sources of deposits for the Trust Fund Bureau. Over 60% of the Bureau's deposits come from postal savings.[58] Other sources include accumulated funds of special accounts of government, investment portions of surpluses of special accounts, Treasury surplus, surplus funds and accumulations from the Bureau's special accounts, and proceeds from the redemption funds from earlier investments.

By the end of March 1987, the Bureau was the world's largest financial institution, with assets of 181 trillion yen. Funds are invested under the supervision of the MOF.

Investment Behavior. Unlike many other market participants, the Bureau is required to invest funds in ways that will be profitable and will guarantee a return. In addition, the Trust Fund Bureau must invest "in activities that will contribute to the improvement of public welfare."[59] The major investment vehicles for the Bureau are: (1) Japanese government bonds, (2) local government bonds, (3) government-agency bonds, (4) debentures of electric power resources development companies, and (5) bank debentures.

Each year the Bureau underwrites a certain portion of government bonds (4 trillion yen in FY 1987). As such, a major portion of the long-term bonds in its portfolio consists of the bonds it has underwritten. In addition, the Bureau trades bonds with the excess temporary funds available until the Bureau makes loans (typically occurring in March of each year). Because of the seasonality of its funds, the Bureau often buys bonds with repurchase agreements. The Bureau buys in such large lots, that going directly to the market would result in extreme market shifts. To avoid this, the Bureau buys from the BOJ. For example, in FY 1980, from April through December, the Bureau bought government bonds totaling 4.5 trillion yen from the BOJ and then sold them back to the BOJ from January until March of 1981. The Bureau sometimes made these repo deals with the National Consolidation Fund Special Account. However, in November 1980, the Bureau began buying bonds with repurchase agreements from the private sector (called "operational intervention") in order to prepare for the lowering of interest rates.[60]

The Bureau did not always buy bonds. In November 1981, it sold 300 billion yen of medium-term government bonds to the market which were due in one year. This was a result of a shortage of working funds due to the decline in postal savings, the major source of funds for the Bureau.

Long-term government bonds and loans to government-related financial institutions provided the largest portion of the Bureau's investment portfolio. Over the period from 1983 to 1987, the percentage of its investment in long-term government bonds increased (from 15.6% to 26.5%) as the percentage of loans to governmental institutions decreased.

National Debt Consolidation Fund Special Account

The massive issuance of government bonds which began in FY 1975 meant massive redemption of them beginning in FY 1985. The National Debt Consolidation Fund Special Account was used for the repayment of these government bonds. This special account was created by the central government and operated by the MOF. The funds expanded from 480 billion yen in FY 1975 to 3.5 trillion yen in FY 1981 as the outstanding balance of government bonds expanded.

Investment Behavior. Under MOF regulations, the funds were restricted to investments in either government bonds or Treasury bills. Because of their higher yields, the funds tended to invest more heavily in government bonds.

There were three ways for the funds to buy government bonds: (1) from the BOJ or the Trust Fund Bureau, (2) directly from banks and securities companies through a bidding procedure in which the fund requested bids from these institutions, and (3) over-the-counter from bond dealers. When they began buying bonds in FY 1976, the funds bought primarily from the BOJ. However, since FY 1979, the funds have bought from the private sector either through the bid procedure or over-the-counter.

The primary reason the funds bought government bonds from the private sector was to support the bond market rather than to operate the funds efficiently. The bond market was flat in 1979 due to increasing interest rates, however, the funds provided support for the market by buying about 800 billion yen of government bonds in FY 1979. They continued their buying trends in FY 1980 since the MOF intended to lower the long-term interest rate even though open market interest rates were going up. These special account funds bought as much as 1.5 trillion yen in FY 1980, more than either foreign investors or the institutions for agriculture and forestry.[61]

Local Governments

Local governments were allowed to invest for the long term over a fiscal year, but they built in systems of reserve funds for future expenses, such as sinking funds and financial adjustment funds. At the end of March 1981, their accumulated reserve funds amounted to 1.2 trillion yen just from prefecture governments, and over 3 trillion yen from all local governments. The funds increased to over 5 trillion yen from all local governments in March 1985. Consequently, they invested heavily in higher yielding bonds for the long-term, with special concern for the security of the bonds.

SECURITIES COMPANIES

Primary Business

Securities companies were founded under the Securities and Exchange Law. Article 65 of the law prohibits non-securities companies from dealing in any securities except government bonds, local government bonds, and government-guaranteed bonds. The resulting monopoly of the securities companies in the securities market allows them to play a central role in the marketplace. As of September 1987, 221 securities companies operated in Japan. Of these, the "Big Four" (Nomura, Daiwa, Yamaichi, and Nikko) dominate the market.

The primary business of securities companies is regulated by Article 28-2 of the Securities and Exchange Law. There are four types of businesses the securities companies engage in: (1) dealing, (2) brokering, (3) underwriting, and (4) the sale of securities. The MOF provides individual licenses for each of these types of businesses. With the expansion of the bond market in the 1980's, bond-related business has grown to be the main business of these companies. The bond-related business of the securities companies involves both the underwriting and distribution of new issues and dealing of outstanding issues.

Bond Dealing

The securities companies serve as intermediaries among the sellers and buyers of bonds by dealing in bonds for their own accounts. In order to meet their clients' requests, the companies need to carry a certain amount of inventory in their dealing accounts. The companies increase their inventories when they expect a bullish market, and they decrease them when they expect a bearish market. The level of inventory held by each of the Big Four securities companies, on average, is considered to be about 200 to 400 billion yen.[62]

Exhibit 15 shows the amounts and types of bonds dealt by the securities companies in the OTC market. Two significant trends occurred over the period from FY 1984 to FY 1987. First, their trading volume increased dramatically from 1,746 trillion yen in FY 1985 to 3,622 trillion yen in FY 1987. Second, government bonds (especially, 10-year bonds) were traded more heavily than before. These trends can be attributed to increased dealer-to-dealer trading and the concentrated trading on specific issues of long-term government bonds (called "benchmark" issues).

CONCLUSION

The Japanese bond market has undergone significant changes during the period from the mid-1970s to 1988. The market size has increased dramatically in terms of both volume of new issues and overall trading volume. Along with this growth have come changes in the relative positions of existing participants and the emergence of new participants in the market. Shifts have also occurred in the net positions of investors. Some investors who were previously net sellers are now net buyers and vice versa. These changes can be attributed to the increasing deregulation of the market by the Japanese government, the growing presence of Japanese non-bank financial institutions and foreign investors, and to the increasing sophistication of the participants within the Japanese bond market.

EXHIBIT 15: BONDS DEALT BY SECURITIES COMPANIES

(Unit: 100 million yen, %)

FY	1984*		1985		1986		1987	
Government Bonds	514,230	86.4	16,424,054	94.0	24,470,391	95.1	35,012,335	96.6
Super Long-term GB	0	0.0	0	0.0	157,154	0.6	533,417	1.5
Long-term GB	314,871	52.9	12,311,058	70.5	19,866,726	77.2	26,218,460	72.4
Medium-term GB	29,342	4.9	205,556	1.2	145,489	0.6	151,379	0.4
Discount GB	1,227	0.2	19,442	0.1	30,217	0.1	32,176	0.1
Treasury Bills	0	0.0	82,684	0.5	2,089,919	8.1	3,975,399	11.0
Financing Bills	168,790	28.4	3,805,314	21.8	2,180,886	8.5	4,101,504	11.3
Municipal Bonds	19,256	3.2	213,771	1.2	211,931	0.8	193,773	0.5
GGB	18,320	3.1	262,032	1.5	276,833	1.1	239,419	0.7
Other Bonds	43,390	7.3	566,118	3.2	764,920	3.0	780,672	2.2
Total Trading Volume	595,196	100.0	17,465,975	100.0	25,724,075	100.0	36,226,199	100.0

*For FY 1984, figures are monthly trading volumes

Source: The Securities Bureau, MOF.

Total volume of new issues almost doubled from 38.4 trillion yen in FY 1981 to 75.9 trillion yen in FY 1987. The outstanding balance of bonds in the market increased approximately 1.7 times during the same period, from 173.3 trillion yen to 296.3 trillion yen. The most dramatic increase occurred in the overall trading volume, which ballooned from 161.8 trillion yen in FY 1981 to 2,655.2 trillion yen in FY 1987.

The major factor contributing to the growth in overall trading volume is the increase in the amount of government bonds traded among dealers, especially long-term government bonds. Two factors contributed to the increased trading in government bonds. First was the concentrated trading of particular "benchmark" issues. Over 90% of all long-term government bond trading has been concentrated on these benchmark issues. Second, an increase in the amount of short-term investments being made by investors has increased government bond turnover and, hence, overall trading volume.

During the pre-bank dealing era, city banks, local banks, and long-term credit banks were the primary net sellers in the market, reflecting the large amounts of government bonds they underwrote and then resold. The primary net buyers during this period were the investment trusts, trust banks, business corporations, and the institutions for agriculture and forestry. However, since bank dealing began, the picture has changed, with the largest net sellers being bond dealers, business corporations, and individual investors. As of March 1988, the primary net buyers were city banks, investment trusts, and local banks.

Though it is impossible to summarize the changes in the investment portfolios of the market participants, two major trends are common to almost all of the participants. First, overall investment in securities has increased dramatically during the 1980's. Second, their investments in foreign securities have increased reflecting the extremely low domestic interest rates.

These changes have led to a conformity of market participants, with over 90% of all trading being done by banks and securities companies. The concentrated trading of benchmark issues has resulted in the deviation of benchmark yields from the yields of other bonds traded in the market. The overall result is a more volatile market.

ENDNOTES

[1] The Japanese securities markets are operated on a fiscal year which runs from April 1 to March 31.

[2] Kaichi Shimura, *Gendai Nihon no Koushasai Shijou [Bond Market of Modern Japan]*, Tokyo: Tokyo Daigaku Shuppan Kai, 1987, pp. 72–73.

[3] Ibid., p. 74.

[4] Ibid.

[5] Ibid., p. 75.

[6] *Annual Report of Securities Bureau 1985 edition*, Tokyo: Ministry of Finance, 1985, p. 25.

[7] *Annual Report of Securities Bureau 1986 edition*, Tokyo: Ministry of Finance, 1986, p. 32.

[8] Nihon Keizai Shinbun, Inc., *Koushasai Ryutsu Shijou [Bond Secondary Market]*, Tokyo: Nihon Keizai Shinbun, Inc., 1987, p. 52.

[9] Stephen Bronte, *Japanese Finance: Markets and Institutions*, London: Euromoney Publications, 1982, pp. 127–128.

[10] Ibid., p. 128.

[11] Kimiaki Nakajima, *Zusetsu, Nihon no Shouken Shijou [Securities Market in Japan]*, Tokyo: Zaikei Shoho Sha, 1988, pp. 278–279.

[12] Ibid., p. 273.

[13] Bronte, pp. 139–140

[14] Henny Sender, "The Bank of Japan Under Siege," *Institutional Investor* (November 1988), pp. 146–151.

[15] The Bank of Japan, *Waga Kuni no Kinyu Seido [The Financial System of Japan]*, Tokyo: The Bank of Japan, 1986, p. 246.

[16] The term overseller means net seller, similarly, the term overbuyer means net buyer.

[17] Kaichi Shimura, pp. 190–192.

[18] The Sanwa Bank, Ltd., *Ginkou no Shouken Senryaku [Securities-Related Strategy of Banks]*, Tokyo: Toyo Keizai Shinposha, 1988, p. 14.

[19] Mitsui Research Institute, *Kinvu Shihyou wo Yomikonasu [Interpretation of Financial Indices]*, Tokyo: Koudansha, 1988, pp. 224–225

[20] The Sanwa Bank, Ltd., p. 14.

[21] Nihon Keizai Shinbun, Inc., *Madohan ni Yureru, Koushasai Ryutsu Shijou [Bond Secondary Market]*, Tokyo: Nihon Keizai Shinbun, Inc., 1985, pp. 54–55.

[22] *Koushasai Ryutsu Shijou [Bond Secondary Market]*, p. 49.

[23] Masao Shimizu, *Gekihen Suru Mane Maketto [Changing Money Market]*, Tokyo: Jiji Tsushin Sha, 1988, p. 109.

[24] *Koushasai Ryutsu Shijou [Bond Secondary Market]*, p. 84.

[25] *Madohan ni Yureru, Koushasai Ryutsu Shijou [Bond Secondary Market]*, p. 59.

[26] Bank debentures are discussed in Chapter 9.

[27] *Madohan ni Yureru, Koushasai Ryutsu Shijou [Bond Secondary Market]*, p. 58.

[28] Ibid, p. 57.

[29] *Koushasai Ryutsu Shijou [Bond Secondary Market]*.

[30] Ibid., p. 66.

[31] *Madohan ni Yureru, Koushasai Ryutsu Shijou [Bond Secondary Market]*, p. 49.

[32] *Koushasai Ryutsu Shijou [Bond Secondary Market]*, p. 69.

[33] *Madohan ni Yureru, Koushasai Ryutsu Shijou [Bond Secondary Market]*, p. 35.

[34] Ibid., pp. 36–37.

[35] Ibid., pp. 35–36.

[36] *Koushasai Ryutsu Shijou [Bond Secondary Market]*, p. 27.

[37] Ibid., p. 27.

[38] Benchmark issues are relatively large issues of long-term government bonds. An issue becomes a "benchmark" issue because of the expectation by bond dealers that the issue will be actively traded and, hence, be extremely liquid.

[39] *Koushasai Ryutsu Shijou [Bond Secondary Market]*, pp. 68–69.

[40] Bronte, p. 102

[41] The Bank of Japan, p. 349.

[42] *Madohan ni Yureru, Koushasai Ryutsu Shijou [Bond Secondary Market]*, p. 48.

[43] Ibid., p. 48.

[44] Ibid., pp. 49–50

[45] Ibid., pp. 50–51.

[46] *Koushasai Ryutsu Shijou [Bond Secondary Market]*, p. 64.

[47] Ibid., p. 64.

[48] Business corporations refers to nonfinancial corporations.

[49] Yoshio Suzuki (ed.), *Financial System and Banks of Japan (Jissen Zeminaru, Nihon no Kinyu to Ginkou)*.

[50] *Koushasai Ryutsu Shijou [Bond Secondary Market]*, p. 76.

[51] Zai-tech activities refer to securitites trading or fund management unrelated to a company's basic business. Companies borrow/raise funds inexpensively by (1) taking advantage of their strong credit ratings, (2) utilizing financial agreements such as swaps, or (3) issuing equity-related corporate bonds (most often using Euromarkets). They then invest these funds to yield an incremental amount over the cost of their borrowed funds. The amount of funds they raise are much greater than their funding needs for business operations.

[52] *Madohan ni Yureru, Koushasai Ryutsu Shijou [Bond Secondary Market]*, pp. 43–44.

[53] *Koushasai Ryutsu Shijou [Bond Secondary Market]*, p. 78.

[54] Suzuki, *Fianacial System and Banks of Japan*.

[55] *Madohan ni Yureru, Koushasai Ryutsu Shijou [Bond Secondary Market]*, pp. 41–42.

[56] Ibid., pp. 42–43

[57] Yoshio Suzuki (ed.), *The Japanese Financial System*. New York: Oxford University Press, 1987, pp. 281–283.

[58] Ibid., p. 280.

[59] Ibid., p. 281.

[60] *Madohan ni Yureru, Koushasai Ryutsu Shijou [Bond Secondary Market]*, p. 63.

[61] Ibid., p. 61.

[62] *Koushasai Ryutsu Shijou [Bond Secondary Market]*, p. 98.

APPENDIX

PORTFOLIO COMPOSITION: END OF 1983, 1986 AND 1988

(unit: 100 million yen, %)

A. Portfolio of City Banks

	1983		1986		1988	
Securities	189,375	100.00	231,861	100.0	324,241	100.0
Government Bonds	63,773	33.7	61,206	26.4	84,254	26.0
Municipal Bonds	19,402	10.2	16,027	6.9	17,061	5.3
Corporate Bonds	29,138	15.4	30,529	13.2	38,877	12.0
Bank Debentures	13,949	7.4	24,677	10.6	38,020	11.7
Stocks	49,032	25.9	67,465	29.1	97,876	30.2
Foreign Securities	12,210	6.4	28,672	12.4	36,357	11.2
Other Securities	1,871	1.0	3,285	1.4	11,796	3.6
Total Assets	1,506,140		2,089,826		2,703,925	
Securities/Total Assets		12.6		11.1		12.0
Bonds in Dealing a/c	0		16,336		11,532	
GB in Dealing a/c	0		13,902		9,590	

B. Portfolio of Local Banks

	1983		1986		1988	
Securities	168,663	100.00	198,494	100.0	245,435	100.0
Government Bonds	59,871	35.5	65,936	33.2	82,355	33.6
Municipal Bonds	30,803	18.3	28,276	14.2	28,674	11.7
Corporate Bonds	31,263	18.5	33,360	16.8	39,236	16.0
Bank Debentures	25,723	15.3	28,299	14.3	32,866	13.4
Stocks	11,877	7.0	17,130	8.6	24,166	9.8
Foreign Securities	3,934	2.3	18,054	9.1	25,624	10.4
Other Securities	5,192	3.1	7,439	3.7	12,514	5.1
Total Assets	859,192		1,131,330		1,369,181	
Securities/Total Assets		19.6		17.5		17.9
Bonds in Dealing a/c	0		6,908		7,143	
GB in Dealing a/c	0		6,171		6,083	

C. Portfolio of Long-Term Credit Banks

	1983		1986		1988	
Securities	62,722	100.00	88,247	100.0	112,579	100.0
Government Bonds	25,741	41.0	26,050	29.5	38,201	33.9
Municipal Bonds	6,020	9.6	8,455	9.6	7,013	6.2
Corporate Bonds	12,581	20.1	22,666	25.7	20,511	18.2
Bank Debentures	101	0.2	22	0.0	488	0.4
Stocks	13,021	20.8	16,998	19.3	25,432	22.6
Foreign Securities	4,731	7.5	12,822	14.5	16,695	14.8
Other Securities	527	0.8	1,234	1.4	4,239	3.8
Total Assets	327,612		456,470		560,436	
Securities/Total Assets		19.1		19.3		20.1
Bonds in Dealing a/c	0		3,498		1,888	
GB in Dealing a/c	0		3,053		1,706	

D. Portfolio of Trust Banks*

	1983		1986		1988	
Securities	174,621	100.00	346,662	100.0	570,696	100.0
Government Bonds	84,156	48.2	125,427	36.2	152,730	26.8
Municipal Bonds	18,520	10.6	19,435	5.6	14,098	2.5
Corporate Bonds**	35,892	20.6	70,810	20.4	94,455	16.6
Stocks	21,354	12.2	64,700	18.7	189,562	33.2
Foreign Securities	8,757	5.0	54,327	15.7	97,706	17.1
Other Securities	5,942	3.4	11,963	3.5	22,147	3.9
Total Assets	697,460		1,203,885		1,879,586	
Securities/Total Assets		25.0		28.8		30.4
Bonds in Dealing a/c	0		5,500		2,208	
GB in Dealing a/c	0		4,508		1,973	

*Total of Bank a/c and Trust a/c
**Including Bank Debentures

E. Portfolio of Mutual Banks

	1983		1986		1988	
Securities	50,088	100.00	61,802	100.0	81,465	100.0
Government Bonds	13,543	27.0	15,007	24.3	22,326	27.4
Municipal Bonds	6,420	12.8	5,679	9.2	6,536	8.0
Corporate Bonds	14,184	28.3	15,406	24.9	17,790	21.8
Bank Debentures	10,351	20.7	12,044	19.5	12,151	14.9
Stocks	3,142	6.3	4,819	7.8	9,406	11.5
Foreign Securities	937	1.9	6,125	9.9	7,854	9.6
Other Securities	1,511	3.0	2,722	4.4	5,402	6.6
Total Assets	387,500		452,480		527,722	
Securities/Total Assets		12.9		13.7		15.4

F. Portfolio of Norinchukin Bank

	1983		1986		1988	
Securities	62,257	100.00	99,631	100.0	113,670	100.0
Government Bonds	29,089	46.7	52,206	52.4	51,265	45.1
Municipal Bonds	6,804	10.9	4,155	4.2	1,799	1.6
Corporate Bonds	10,597	17.0	14,158	14.2	12,341	10.9
Bank Debentures	8,876	14.3	8,330	8.4	11,991	10.5
Stocks	1,608	2.6	3,471	3.5	7,587	6.7
Foreign Securities	2,960	4.8	15,109	15.2	20,519	18.1
Other Securities	2,323	3.7	2,202	2.2	8,168	7.2
Bonds in Dealing a/c	0		2,127		1,227	
Total Deposits*	145,808		217,983		256,875	
Securities/Total Deposits		42.7		45.7		44.3

*Total Deposits = Deposits + CDs + Securities in Liability

G. Portfolio of Credit Associations

	1983		1986		1988	
Securities	76,239	100.00	83,458	100.0	97,711	100.0
Government Bonds	18,586	24.4	18,507	22.2	18,730	19.2
Municipal Bonds	13,661	17.9	11,316	13.6	11,818	12.1
Corporate Bonds	27,084	35.5	27,617	33.1	30,973	31.7
Bank Debentures	9,931	13.0	10,227	12.3	9,283	9.5
Stocks	1,809	2.4	3,264	3.9	8,917	9.1
Foreign Securities	2,977	3.9	7,441	8.9	7,064	7.2
Other Securities	2,191	2.9	5,086	6.1	10,926	11.2
Total Assets	482,309		596,923		707,200	
Securities/Total Assets		15.8		14.0		13.8

H. Portfolio of Zenshinren Bank

	1983		1986		1988	
Securities	19,903	100.00	26,367	100.0	37,325	100.0
Government Bonds	5,932	29.8	13,125	49.8	17,303	46.4
Municipal Bonds	3,066	15.4	2,591	9.8	2,292	6.1
Corporate Bonds	9,368	47.1	7,422	28.1	6,507	17.4
Bank Debentures	894	4.5	1,630	6.2	3,090	8.3
Stocks	68	0.3	269	1.0	438	1.2
Foreign Securities	396	2.0	419	1.6	3,150	8.4
Other Securities	179	0.9	911	3.5	4,545	12.2
Deposits	39,701		65,462		92,876	
Securities/Deposits		50.1		40.3		40.2

I. Portfolio of Life Insurance Companies

	1983		1986		1988	
Securities	113,278	100.00	189,813	100.0	349,337	100.0
Government Bonds	9,565	8.4	26,967	14.2	44,959	12.9
Municipal Bonds	8,760	7.7	7,168	3.8	8,525	2.4
Corporate Bonds	16,945	15.0	26,648	14.0	35,970	10.3
Stocks	55,847	49.3	81,138	42.7	155,777	44.6
Foreign Securities	21,693	19.2	46,681	24.6	98,030	28.1
Other Securities	468	0.4	1,211	0.6	6,076	1.7
Total Investments	341,886		529,451		776,117	
Total Assets	346,137		538,705		792,584	
Securities/Total Assets		32.7		35.2		44.1

J. Portfolio of Property Insurance Companies

	1983		1986		1988	
Securities	35,749	100.00	54,711	100.0	84,407	100.0
Government Bonds	4,249	11.9	7,500	13.7	10,795	12.8
Municipal Bonds	1,576	4.4	2,057	3.8	3,766	4.5
Corporate Bonds	7,369	20.6	11,224	20.5	17,001	20.1
Stocks	18,601	52.0	22,079	40.4	28,476	33.7
Foreign Securities	3,496	9.8	10,125	18.5	16,508	19.6
Other Securities	458	1.3	1,726	3.2	7,861	9.3
Total Investments	75,177		106,284		158,128	
Total Assets	88,141		121,734		175,242	
Securities/Total Assets		40.6		44.9		48.2

K. Portfolio of Individual Investors

	1983		1986		1988	
Securities	505,957	100.00	696,176	100.0	743,554	100.0
Government Bonds	132,123	26.1	160,887	23.1	133,269	17.9
Municipal Bonds	6,265	1.2	6,916	1.0	6,920	0.9
Corporate Bonds	18,655	3.7	33,074	4.8	28,775	3.9
Bank Debentures	155,199	30.7	204,665	29.4	203,264	27.3
Stocks (book value)	69,805	13.8	74,558	10.7	76,044	10.2
Investment Trusts	83,193	16.4	180,973	26.0	255,223	34.3
Other Securities	40,717	8.0	35,103	5.0	40,059	5.4
Total Financial Assets	4,118,563		5,399,185		5,876,265	
Share of Securities		12.3		12.9		12.7

Source: Nomura Research Institute, *Bond Handbook (Koushasai Youran)* 1988 ed.

CHAPTER 4

Yield Measures, Volatility Measures and Tax Treatment

Lisze Lee
Associate
Merrill Lynch Capital Markets

Yoshiki Kaneko
Associate
The Sanwa Bank Ltd

Rodolphe Gobe
Associate
Citibank, N.A.

The purpose of this chapter is fourfold. First, we explain the conventions employed in the Japanese bond market to calculate and quote yields. No attempt is made, however, to explain yield measures that should be used to assess the relative value of bonds. Second, we review measures of bond price volatility. We then explain the tax treatment pertaining to bond investments. Finally, we provide a brief review of software for bond investing in Japan. The various types of bonds referred to in this chapter are explained in later chapters.

YIELD MEASURES

Coupon Bonds

For coupon-bearing bonds, it is a common Japanese practice to use *simple yield to maturity* (or simple yield) in calculating their return. The formula for simple yield is as follows:

$$r = \frac{C + \frac{R - P}{Y}}{P} \times 100$$

where
C = coupon (in yen)
R = redemption value[1]
P = bond price
Y = number of years to maturity
r = simple yield to maturity (in %)

The redemption profit (or loss) is assumed to accrue at an equal rate per year throughout the bond's life. The coupon is then added to the redemption gain or loss to determine the total payout rate from the bond. The payout rate per ¥ of bond price is the (simple) yield of the bond.

By rearranging the simple yield equation, it is possible to calculate the bond price, given the simple yield, by the following equation:

$$P = \frac{R + (C \times Y)}{1 + \frac{r \times Y}{100}}$$

The simple yield measure does not take into account the reinvestment of interest payments. In contrast, the yield to maturity measure, which is used in the U.S. and Europe, does, but implicitly assumes that these payments are reinvested at the same yield. The yield to maturity is the interest rate that will equate the present value of the cash flows from the bond to its price. Thus, unlike the simple yield measure, the yield to maturity takes into consideration the time value of money, and is, essentially, a *compound yield* measure.

Although the yield to maturity takes into account the time value of money, it may not give a realistic estimate of the actual yield from a bond since it assumes a reinvestment rate equal to the yield to maturity. If the actual reinvestment rate is known, or can be estimated, it is possible to calculate the realized compound yield, which gives the total return on a bond, including the actual reinvestment income based on the assumed rate.

In comparison with the compound yield formulas used in the U.S. and Europe, the Japanese simple yield formula neglects the interest-on-interest component of the total return. Yields calculated by the different methods (for the same bond) are not as different as they may appear, and the Japanese method really stands out because of its simplicity. Moreover, unlike the yield to maturity, the simple yield does not make any assumptions about the reinvestment rate.

As an example, a comparison of the different methods is made in Exhibit 1 using an 8%, 10-year bond with a redemption value of ¥100. Exhibit 2 shows the yields at different bond prices, calculated under three methods: Japanese simple yield, U.S. and AIBD compound yields. Exhibit 2, in a plot of the yields versus bond prices, illustrates the following facts:

- When priced below par, a bond's simple yield is higher than its compound (U.S. or AIBD) yield.

EXHIBIT 1: COMPARISON OF SIMPLE (JAPAN) AND COMPOUND (U.S. & AIBD) YIELDS ON AN 8%, 10-YEAR BOND WITH A PAR (REDEMPTION) VALUE OF ¥100

Price (¥)	Simple Yield (Japan)	Compound Yield (U.S.)	Compound Yield (AIBD)
85	11.18	10.45	10.72
90	10.00	9.58	9.81
95	8.95	8.76	8.95
100	8.00	8.00	8.16
105	7.14	7.29	7.42
110	6.36	6.62	6.73
115	5.65	5.99	6.08

EXHIBIT 2:   COMPARISON OF SIMPLE (JAPAN) AND COMPOUND (U.S. & AIBD) YIELDS

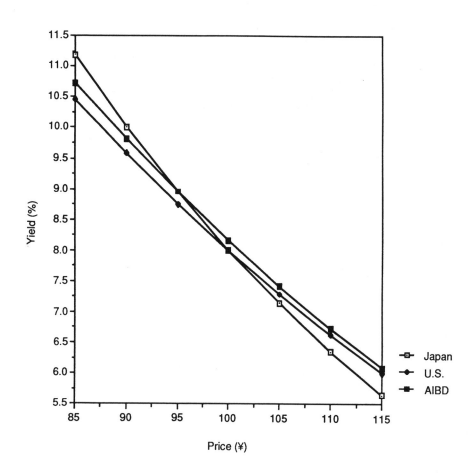

- When priced at par, a bond's simple yield is equal to its compound yield.
- When priced above par, a bond's simple yield is lower than its compound yield.

Overall, a change in the simple yield has a smaller effect on the selling price of a bond than a change in compound yield.

The Early Redemption Feature. Corporate and public bonds are redeemed at par value at maturity. However, in most cases, an issuer can retire part or all of the outstanding bonds before their maturity dates. There are essentially three possible ways by which an issuer can retire an outstanding issue before its maturity: (1) open market repurchase, (2) optional redemption, and (3) compulsory periodic redemption.

(1) In an *open market repurchase*, the issuer can retire outstanding bonds at any time by repurchasing them from the market at the prevailing market price.

(2) An *optional redemption* provision can be written into the terms of the issue. This provision is similar to the embedded call option in a callable bond. Under the optional redemption provision, the issuer has the option to call back part or all of an issue at pre-specified premium prices, but can only do so after a certain number of years, known as the grace period, has elapsed from the issue date. The grace period is usually five years for 12-year bonds and three years for 10-year bonds. Redemption prices are scaled down over time. For example, a 10-year issue, with a grace period of five years, can have a call price of ¥104 for the sixth year, ¥103 for the seventh year, ¥102 for the eighth year, ¥101 for the ninth year and ¥100 for the year of maturity. Partial redemption of the issue is typically exercised by lots.

The yield due to optional redemption is calculated as:

$$r_o = \frac{C + \dfrac{R' - P}{t}}{P} \times 100$$

where

r_o = yield due to optional redemption (in %)
C = coupon
R' = nearest redemption price at time t
P = bond price
t = time to redemption

(3) Under the *compulsory periodic redemption* provision, the issuer has the right, and is obliged, to redeem at par, in semiannual or annual installments, a specified amount of an issue. A grace period usually applies to compulsory periodic redemption the same way it does for optional redemption. For example, in the case of 10-year government- guaranteed and local government bonds, 3% of the initial issue is retired after a grace period of three years. For samurai bonds, the length of the grace period and amount to be redeemed varies from issue to issue.

Retirement of the issue is made by periodically drawing the bonds by lot, or by purchasing from the open market. While the latter is more acceptable to bondholders, drawing bonds by lot is common for most convertible bonds, and for some corporate bonds. This method requires the issuer to deposit, after the initial grace period, a certain amount of reserves in a trustee bank. In the case of a 10-year convertible, the amount is typically between 15% to 20% of the issue, while that for a 6-year convertible is around 30%. Subsequently, approximately equal amounts are selected (again by lottery) to be retired at intervals of half or one year, with the remaining balance retired at maturity. Also, the amount of reserves to be deposited depends on the balance of the issue outstanding in the market, which varies over time due to the exercise of the conversion of the bonds into stocks.

Government bonds are usually redeemed through a sinking fund schedule legislated by law, while nonpublic local government bonds are required to use a different form of compulsory periodic retirement. This form of compulsory periodic redemption requires the issuer to equally retire all bonds under a schedule which is already fixed and specified at issuance. Like early redemption by lot for convertible and corporate bonds, this equal amount redemption provision also redeems bonds periodically after an initial grace period.

The average outstanding yield due to compulsory periodic redemption is calculated as:

$$r_c = \frac{C + \dfrac{R - P}{Y_c}}{P} \times 100$$

where
R   =   total face value
P   =   bond price
Y_C =   average outstanding years (weighted average life of bond due to compulsory periodic redemption)
r_C =   average outstanding yield (due to compulsory periodic redemption) (in %)

where
Y_C is the average outstanding years as calculated by:

$$Y_c = \sum_{t = t_1}^{t_n} \frac{(R_t \times t)}{R}$$

where
R_t =   face value of bonds redeemed at time t (total of n redemptions)
t   =   number of years to redemption (earliest/first redemption at t_1, last at t_n)
R   =   total face value of bond at issuance.

Discount Bonds

Discount bonds are those in which no periodic interest is paid. Instead, the investor purchases the bond below par. The interest earned is then the difference between the maturity (par) value and the purchase price.

For discount bonds, the simple yield measure is used in the following cases:

1. Short-term (discount) government bonds and discount bank debentures with an initial life of not more than one year.
2. Medium-term discount government bonds and NTT telephone subscriber bonds with an initial life of more than one year, but residual life of less than one year, which are traded over-the-counter.

Simple yield is calculated as follows:

$$r = \frac{F-P}{P \times \dfrac{D}{365}} \times 100$$

where
r   =   simple yield (%)
F   =   face value of bond
P   =   bond price
D   =   number of days to maturity

The compound yield measure is used for discount bonds in the following cases:

1. Medium-term discount government bonds with an initial life of more than one year.
2. NTT telephone subscriber bonds with an initial life of more than one year.

The compound yield measure is calculated as follows:

$$r^* = \left[\left(\frac{F}{P} \right)^{\frac{1}{Y}} - 1 \right] \times 100$$

where

r*	=	compound yield
F	=	face value of bond
P	=	bond price
Y	=	number of years to maturity

Special Features of Japanese Bonds

The topics to be discussed here include the measurement of the remaining life or time to maturity of bonds under different circumstances, the calculation of irregular first and final coupon payments, and accrued interest payments.

Measurement of Time to Maturity. The measurement of the remaining time to maturity of a bond depends on the type of bond, and whether price or yield is being calculated. Under most circumstances, the first or starting day (of the transaction) is excluded, while in special cases it is included. For bonds with a periodic redemption feature, the time (usually measured in years) to maturity is calculated using a weighted average of the times to redemption over the life of the bond.

1. The remaining number of days to maturity of a straight bond, starting from the day of transaction, is measured by one of two methods, namely:

    - the "one-sided" or Kataha method, where the starting day is excluded, or
    - the "two-sided" or Ryoha method, where the starting day is included.

For example, the period between May 20 and August 15 of the same year will be measured as 87 days (=11+30+31+15) by the one-sided method, and 88 days (=12+30+31+15) by the two-sided method.

The selection of which method to use in measuring the remaining time to maturity depends on the nature of the bond, and on whether price or yield is being calculated. First, bonds can be classified into the following categories:

a. Discount bonds with an initial life of not more than one year.
b. Discount bonds with an initial life of more than one year.
c. Coupon bonds.

In the case of (a), the method is either:

• the two-sided method, in the calculation of price based on discount rate, or
• the one-sided method, in the calculation of yield (discount) based on price.

In cases (b) and (c), the one-sided method is used under all circumstances. Therefore, except for bonds with an initial life of not more than one year, the one-sided method is always used.

The inclusion of that extra day during a leap year applies only to bonds with an initial or residual life of less than one year. In longer term bonds (more than one year), the extra day is ignored. To convert the number of days to years, division by 365 is carried out, regardless of whether the year is a leap year or not.

2. For bonds with a periodic redemption feature, the effect of early partial redemption must be taken into account when measuring the (average) number of years to maturity. The use of the average outstanding years measure in the calculation of the average outstanding yield of a bond (with a compulsory periodic redemption feature) was discussed earlier. The formula for calculating the average outstanding years to maturity was presented earlier in this chapter.

Calculation of Interest Payments. There are special situations pertaining to interest payments; these occur when:

1. the time interval between the issue date and the first coupon payment does not correspond to an interval between consecutive (regular) coupon payments, or the last coupon payment date does not coincide with the redemption date, or

2. the trading or transfer of coupon bonds is effected between coupon payment dates.

When (1) occurs, the amount of interest payment due is referred to as irregular interest, while in (2), the amount due is the accrued interest.

1. In the calculation of irregular interest payments, the closest coupon date (or redemption date, when appropriate) is usually chosen to be the irregular interest payment date. As mentioned, these irregular intervals over which interest is earned are either:

   a. the time interval between issue date and the first coupon payment date, or

   b. the time interval between the last scheduled interest payment date prior to redemption and the redemption date.

The selection of the irregular interest payment dates and the calculation of the corresponding irregular interest payments will be discussed below for different scenarios.

Case 1:

In this case, the irregular interest is paid at the nearest next coupon payment date (or at redemption, in the case of the last interest payment), such that the period between the previous coupon payment (or issue date, in the case of the first interest payment) and the irregular interest payment is shorter than the regular interval between coupon payments. The calculation of irregular interest payments is as follows:

- In (a), the irregular interest to be paid on the first coupon payment date is calculated for the period between the issue date and the first coupon payment.
- In (b), the irregular interest to be paid on the redemption date is calculated for the period between the penultimate coupon payment date and the redemption date.

Case 2:

In this case, the irregular interest is paid, not at the next coupon payment date following, but at the second next coupon payment date (or at redemption, in the case of the last interest payment). The irregular interest payment due on this date is thus slightly higher than regular coupon payments, as it accrues over a longer interval. The calculation of irregular interest payments is thus performed as follows:

- In (a), the "scheduled first coupon payment date" is skipped over, and the "scheduled second coupon payment date" is now designated to be the actual first coupon payment date on which the irregular interest will be paid. The irregular interest will cover the period between the issue date and this designated payment date.
- In (b), the "scheduled penultimate coupon payment date" is skipped over, and irregular interest is paid on the redemption date. The irregular interest payment will cover interest earned during the period between the date on which the last coupon payment was made and the redemption date.

Both cases are illustrated in Exhibit 3. In the calculation of irregular interest payments, the one-sided method is used in almost all cases to measure the length of the interval over which the irregular interest is earned. The exception occurs in the case of government bonds when the irregular interest payment on the first coupon payment date is calculated, whereby the two-sided method is used. The methods used in the calculation of irregular interest for different types of bonds are presented below.

- Government bonds:

$$\text{Irregular Interest} = C + \frac{d}{365} \times A$$

where
C = regular coupon
A = annual interest/coupon

EXHIBIT 3:   IRREGULAR INTEREST PAYMENT DATES

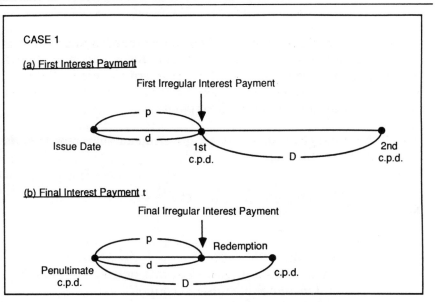

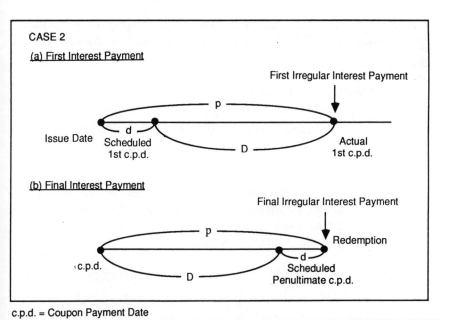

c.p.d. = Coupon Payment Date

$$d \quad = \quad \text{interval used in the calculation of irregular interest}$$

$\qquad\qquad$ payment not included in coupon.[2]

In Case 1 mentioned above (where no coupon payment date is skipped over), the coupon C is excluded from the equation. It should also be recalled that in calculating the first interest payment the two-sided method is used in measuring the interval d. The one-sided method is used in calculating the final payment.

- Public local government issues, government guaranteed bonds and corporate bonds:

$$\text{Irregular Interest} = C + \frac{d}{D} \times C$$

where
C = coupon
d = interval used in the calculation of irregular interest payment not included in coupon
D = regular interval between coupon payments

Again, in Case 1 mentioned above, the coupon C is excluded from the equation. The one-sided method is used in measuring the interval d.

- NTT and Samurai bonds:

$$\text{Irregular Interest} = \frac{p}{365} \times C$$

where
p = d + D, which equals the total interval over which irregular interest and coupon interest, if any, accumulate
A = annual interest/coupon.

The one-sided method is again used in measuring p.

- Bank debentures:

$$\text{First Irregular Interest} = C + \frac{d}{365} \times A$$

$$\text{Final Irregular Interest} = C$$

where
C = regular coupon
d = interval used in the calculation of irregular interest payment not included in coupon
A = annual interest/coupon.

Note that in the case of bank debentures, the irregular interest amount in excess of the regular coupon payment, i.e., $d/365 \times A$, is always paid when the bond is sold, and the remaining regular coupon amount is paid on the first coupon payment day. Also, the final payment is always equal to the regular coupon payment.

Examples:
The following are examples illustrating how irregular interests for different types of bonds are calculated. The two bond types considered are government and corporate bonds.
In the first example, consider the following government bond:

- Issue date: January 20, 1985
- Annual Coupon Rate: 6%
- Coupon Payment Dates: February 20, August 20.

This case corresponds to a Case 2 scenario, where the "scheduled first coupon payment date," February 20, 1985, is skipped over, making the designated or actual first payment date August 20, 1985. Using the two-sided method, which applies under these circumstances, the interval between the scheduled first payment date and the actual date on which the irregular interest will be paid (d) is equal to 32 days (January 20, 1985 to February 20, 1985, inclusive of January 20). Using the equation given above for government bonds, the first irregular interest payment, inclusive of coupon payment, is calculated as follows:

First Irregular Interest (%) = $6.0/2 + 32/365 \times 6.0 = 3.5260^3$

In the second example, consider the following corporate bond issued by Hokkaido Electric Company:

- Issue date: December 22, 1984
- Annual Coupon Rate: 6.2%
- Coupon Payment Dates: June 25, December 25
- First Payment Date: June 25, 1985
- Maturity: December 22, 1997.

Recall that the one-sided method will be used here. The interval between the issue date and the first scheduled coupon date is 3 days (December 22, 1984 to December 25, 1984), while that between the penultimate coupon payment date and the redemption date is 180 days (June 25, 1997 to December 22, 1997). The regular interval between coupon payments is 183 days. Using the equation given above for corporate bonds, the first and last irregular interest payments are calculated as follows:

First Irregular Interest Payment (%)
$= 6.2/2 + 3/183 \times 6.2/2 = 3.1508$
Final Irregular Interest Payment (%)
$= 180/183 \times 6.2/2 = 3.0492$

2. When a coupon bond is traded in between coupon payment dates, the accrued interest over the time elapsed from the last coupon date is paid by the seller to the buyer. The calculation of the accrued interest payment is as follows:

- Tax-free trade:

Accrued Interest (%) = $C \times E/365$

Accrued Interest on Face Value = Accrued Interest $\times \dfrac{\text{Face Value}}{100}$

where
C = regular coupon
E = number of days elapsed from the last coupon
payment[4]

- Taxable trade:[5]

$$\text{Accrued Interest } (\%) = C \times \left(1 - \frac{w}{100}\right) \times \frac{E}{365}$$

Accrued Interest on Face Value = Accrued Interest × Face Value/100

where
w = withholding tax rate (%) of buyer

BOND PRICE VOLATILITY

There are several methods for calculating bond price volatility in Japan. The most often used methods are:

(1) price volatility based on price sensitivity to changes in simple yield,

(2) price volatility based on simple yield to maturity, and

(3) duration.

Price Volatility Based on Price Sensitivity to Changes in Simple Yield

This convenient measure is based on the average of the corresponding price changes of a bond if the simple yield is changed by plus or minus 10 basis points (0.10%). The calculation of this volatility measure is as follows:

Price Volatility Based on Price Sensitivity to Changes in Yield (%)

$$= \frac{C_u + C_d}{2P} \times 100$$

where
C_u = price change due to –0.10% change in simple yield
C_d = price change due to +0.10% change in simple yield
P = current bond price

Price Volatility Based on Simple Yield

This measure of price volatility is based on the formula for the calculation of simple interest on a bond. Recall that the price of a bond based on its simple yield is calculated as follows:

$$P = \frac{R + (C \times Y)}{1 + \dfrac{r \times Y}{100}}$$

where
P = bond price
R = redemption value
C = coupon
Y = number of years to maturity
r = simple yield to maturity.

The price volatility based on simple yield is derived from the above equation by differentiating price (P) with respect to simple yield (r). After rearranging the resulting equation, the expression for dP/P, the price volatility based on simple yield, is obtained. This expression is as follows:

$$\frac{1}{P} \times \left(\frac{dP}{dr} \right) = -\frac{Y}{100 + r \times Y}$$

The term, $Y/(100 + r \times Y)$, is known as the *coefficient of price volatility based on simple yield*. Note that the equation for the price volatility based on simple yield does not include the coupon term. This indicates that the coefficient of price volatility, as defined, is not sensitive to changes in coupon. This result is explained by the fact that implicit in the calculation of simple yield to maturity is the assumption that coupons are reinvested at the same yield. Exhibit 4 shows the values of the coefficient of price volatility based on simple yield corresponding to different yield levels and years to maturity. The exhibit highlights the fact that price volatility increases with time to maturity, but decreases with yield.

Duration

A popular measure of bond price volatility is one that is related to the weighted average term-to-maturity of a bond's cash flow. The weighted average term-to-maturity measure was first suggested by Frederick Macaulay in 1938 as a proxy for the length of time a bond investment will be outstanding,[6] and is therefore popularly referred to as Macaulay duration. The formula to calculate Macaulay duration for a noncallable, semiannual pay bond on a coupon anniversary date is given below:

EXHIBIT 4: COEFFICIENT OF PRICE VOLATILITY CORRESPONDING TO DIFFERENT VALUES OF SIMPLE YIELD AND MATURITY

	Simple Yield (%)					
Years to Maturity	5	6	7	8	9	10
1	0.95	0.94	0.93	0.93	0.92	0.91
2	1.82	1.79	1.75	1.72	1.69	1.67
3	2.61	2.54	2.48	2.42	2.36	2.31
4	3.33	3.23	3.13	3.03	2.94	2.86
5	4.00	3.85	3.70	3.57	3.45	3.33
6	4.62	4.41	4.23	4.05	3.90	3.75
7	5.19	4.93	4.70	4.49	4.29	4.12
8	5.71	5.41	5.13	4.88	4.65	4.44
9	6.21	5.84	5.52	5.23	4.97	4.74
10	6.67	6.25	5.88	5.56	5.26	5.00

Note:
Values in the table correspond to values of the coefficient of price volatility multiplied by 100.

$$\text{Duration} = \frac{\displaystyle\sum_t \frac{t \times C_t}{(1 + r_m/2)^t}}{\displaystyle\sum_t \frac{C_t}{(1 + r_m/2)^t}}$$

where
C_t = cash flow at time t
t   = time until receipt of the cash flow
r_m = yield to maturity

Macaulay duration is related to bond price volatility as follows:

change in price (in %) =

$$-\frac{1}{(1 + r_m/2)} \times \text{Macaulay duration} \times \text{yield change}$$

When the first two terms are combined, the resulting number is called *modified duration;* that is,

$$\text{modified duration} = \frac{\text{Macaulay duration}}{(1 + r_m/2)}$$

The change in price (in %) can then be rewritten as:

$$-\text{modified duration} \times \text{yield change}$$

As can be seen from the above formula, modified duration measures the percentage price change for a 100 basis point change in yield. However, it should be noted that it is only an (linear) approximation.[7]

Oftentimes the term duration is used to refer to Macaulay duration or modified duration. At low yield levels, the two numbers will not differ significantly.

TAX TREATMENT

Investors of corporate and public bonds realize returns from three sources (ignoring reinvestment income):

- coupon payments (for coupon-bearing bonds)
- redemption gains (gains realized when a bond is redeemed), and
- capital gains (gains realized when a bond is sold prior to its maturity date).

For Japanese investors, different tax treatments apply to these three different components of a bond's return. In addition, a transfer tax is imposed when bonds are sold.

For nonresident investors, however, the tax imposed on coupon payments and redemption gains may be reduced to a large extent by certain tax treaties established between the investor's home country and Japan. Certain foreign investors like government organizations and central banks, as well as other entities which satisfy certain criteria established by the Japanese authorities, may be completely exempt from taxes on bond income.

Taxation on Coupon Payments

In general, coupon payments are subject to a 20% withholding tax for all investors: resident as well as nonresident, individual as well as corporate. However, subsequent tax treatments for resident investors depend on whether the investors are individuals or corporations. Non-resident investors will be subject to special tax treatments different from those imposed on resident investors. In the case of Samurai and yen-denominated bonds issued by foreign entities, some bonds are free from a withholding tax. The taxation of coupon payments for different classes of investors will be more fully discussed below.

Resident Individual Investors. The current tax treatment of coupon payments for resident individual investors is called "separate taxation at source." Under this tax system, a 20% withholding tax is imposed on coupon payments for all corporate and public bonds. No other tax payments, reports to tax authorities, etc., are needed later. The tax-exempt system for coupon payments was abolished in April, 1988.

Resident Corporate Investors. Under the current tax system, which is called the "taxation on total income," a 20% withholding tax is levied on coupon payments for corporate investors. When they close their accounts, corporations have to report these coupon payments as revenues to tax authorities and must pay a corporate tax which is imposed on their total revenues. However, the 20% withholding tax is deductible from this corporate tax.

The amount of the withholding tax, which is deductible from the corporate tax, applies for the length of the holding period of the bonds by the corporate investors. There are two methods of calculating this deductible amount.

Method 1:

Deductible withholding tax

$$= \text{withholding tax} \times \frac{\text{length of holding period}}{\text{length of interval between coupon payments}}$$

Method 2:

Deductible withholding tax = withholding tax

$$\times \frac{\text{beginning balance} + \frac{\text{ending balance} - \text{beginning balance}}{2}}{\text{ending balance}}$$

In Method 2, the amount of deductible withholding tax is measured separately for each type of bond. The beginning and ending balances refer to the total par value of each type of bond held at the beginning and end of the accounting period. The total deduction for all bonds in the portfolio is obtained by summing up the individual deductions for each bond type.

There are two exceptional cases in which corporate investors are not subject to the 20% withholding tax under the current tax system. As specified in the Special Tax Treatment Act, when certain designated financial institutions hold registered bonds, they are not required to pay any withholding tax incurred during their holding period of these registered bonds.

Another case in which investors may be exempt from the 20% withholding tax for coupon payments is that of tax-exempt corporations, such as schools, religious entities, social wealth entities, etc. All of these entities are classified in the current income tax law.

Resident Investors of Samurai Bonds. There are two types of tax treatments for Samurai bonds. The type of treatment depends on the characteristics of issuers:

- In the first case, withholding tax is not levied on samurai bonds issued by certain international institutions. These institutions include the World Bank, Asian Development bank, etc. However, the coupon payments of these bonds are subsequently subject to taxation on total income.
- All other samurai bonds are subject to the 20% withholding tax.

Nonresident Investors. Coupons payable to nonresident investors are also subject to the 20% withholding tax. However, Japan has various tax treaties with different countries to avoid double taxation, so foreign investors can arrange with the Japanese tax authorities to have their tax rates reduced.

In the case of yen-denominated bonds issued by foreign entities, no tax is levied on the coupon payments if the owner is a nonresident who has no permanent domicile or permanent establishment in Japan.

Taxation on Redemption Gains from Discount Bonds

An 18% withholding tax is imposed at bond issuance on the expected redemption gain of discount bonds. This gain is the difference between the issuing price and redemption price, usually face value.

A corporate investor can deduct this withholding tax from its corporate tax. The amount of the deductible tax applies for the length of the holding period over which the discount bonds are held (the calculations are the same as those discussed above). Tax-exempt corporations are eligible for a refund of the withholding tax at the maturity of the bonds. For foreign investors living in a country with a tax rate below 18%, a tax reduction may be claimed, provided the discount bond was bought in the primary market and held until maturity.

Taxation on Capital Gains

Except for convertible and warrant bonds, the current Japanese tax system imposes no taxes on capital gains from corporate and public bonds.

The taxation rule on convertible and warrant bonds is based on the concept of "declared separate taxation." Under this rule, investors separate these capital gains from other components of bond income, and then declare the former to the tax authorities at the next tax payment period. The tax rate on this form of taxation is 26% of the realized capital gains.

Under special situations,[8] as stipulated by the Japanese tax authorities, the taxpayer has the option to request for taxation at source. Using this alternative, the investor pays 0.5% withholding tax on the principal of all the convertible and warrant bonds he sells, and, thereafter, is not liable for any further tax payments on actual capital gains.

For nonresidents with no permanent domicile or business establishment in Japan, there is no capital gains tax on straight corporate and public bonds. However, the same rule of taxation applies to capital gains on convertible and warrant bonds for nonresident and resident investors alike.

Taxation on Transfers

A transfer tax will be levied on the seller of a security. The tax rate depends on the type of security sold. For convertible and warrant bonds, the transfer tax is 0.26% of the principal, while for other bonds it is 0.03% of the principal. The same transfer tax rates apply when nonresident investors sell Japanese domestic bonds, including samurai bonds, to a Japanese resident.

Tax Exemption

As previously mentioned, tax treaties between certain foreign countries and Japan contain tax exemption clauses for governmental and central bank investments in Japanese bonds.

For government organizations and central banks of countries having no tax treaty with Japan, exemption from Japanese tax on their bond investments may be granted by submitting to the Japanese Tax Administration Agency a statement that the acquisition of Japanese securities is not for commercial purposes. To be tax exempt, the investment funds must be part of the foreign reserves of the country concerned. It is an established practice to grant tax exemption on income from investments made by foreign diplomats based in Japan.

COMPUTER SOFTWARE FOR BOND ANALYSIS

The appearance of bond-related computer software in Japan goes back to the late 1950s, when securities companies felt the need for tools that would improve the efficiency of clerical work in their business. These tools had mainly back-office applications and ran on machines which, at that time, were extremely costly. Also, their computation power was modest. For this reason, the use of computers was limited to data processing jobs, which required much less computation power than analytical jobs.

Since the 1960s, financial markets became more complex, liquid and global, increasing the need for timely delivery of market information. It also became important that this information be more accurate and readily available. Securities companies, in critical need of that information, were the first to develop the tools that would ensure them permanent access to it. To lower their cost of development, they decided to make these tools accessible to other investors and charge them for the service. This was made possible by the availability of cheaper and more powerful hardware. The availability of financial information, combined with the availability of more powerful hardware, expanded the use of computers to the development of new financial products that could take advantage of new opportunities created by financial deregulation and the evolution of the markets.

By 1970, the use of computers had taken root in the securities companies. Firms expanded the use of machines from inventory management and information services to investment and market analyses that use timely market information. At the same time, the development of desktop machines and of telecommunications made it easier for small investors to access the on-line financial information provided by the large securities companies. Some institutional investors have been developing their own in-house analytical software too.

Individual investors were the big winners of the personal computer boom. It allowed them inexpensive access to financial information. Recent technological innovations have also made it possible for TV game terminals to be used to access the information even more cheaply. Individual investors can now trade from remote terminals in their homes or offices. At this time, such systems are developed primarily for stocks, and it seems likely that a bond trading system will also soon be developed. Also, the development of "home trading" will possibly bring about some deregulation in the legislation regarding these terminals.

Today, the cost of hardware is so low that the cost of development and maintenance of the software is more relevant. Also, the appearance of new financial products, and very sophisticated theoretical models to describe the behavior of those products, makes it more and more complex—and costly—to develop appropriate software. Most of the models developed recently in Japan focus on stock analysis (the most recent models for bonds seem to be much more complex than their equivalent for equities). Large Japanese securities companies concede that U.S. firms are several years ahead in the field of analytical software for the bond market.

Only a small number of companies can develop sophisticated bond analysis software in-house, and this will primarily become the task of either very large players, or of dedicated software companies, or, even more likely, of joint ventures between the two. This is why Japanese firms have teamed up with American experts (finance academic leaders and software companies) to develop Japanese versions of very sophisticated packages. Some of the difficulties they encounter are translating the language into kanji (Japanese characters) and adapting the software to the not yet completely standardized Japanese computer market.

Some companies have decided to take the lead in the area. For these companies, getting the information and stuffing it into the best models has become a priority. The big four—Nomura, Daiwa, Nikko and Yamaichi—all have quantitative analysis departments. Sanyo, a smaller but very progressive security house in Tokyo, deliberately bases its strategy on information technology and invests heavily, not only in hardware and networking, but also in artificial intelligence.

The new Japanese equity models merge Japanese accounting standards and transaction costs; they also allow money managers to stipulate market capitalization conditions and to screen for capital liquidity. The models focus on risk management and portfolio analysis.

An example of a joint venture to develop financial analysis software is the cooperation between Yamaichi and GAT, a U.S. financial software company. One of their major products, the Integrated Bond System (IBS), is used by U.S. institutions, mainly life insurance companies and money managers. A Japanese version of IBS, adapted for the bond market in Japan, is currently in development.

An example of a system providing on-line financial information and market analysis is Daiwa Securities Co. Ltd's Portfolio Management System (Daiwa has a 100% stake in a software subsidiary, and has developed in-house its "Bond Management Information System").

Currently, major players in delivering financial information like Reuters and Telerate, are about to provide on-line analysis to their customers, including those in Japan. Reuters has also made available Reuters Bond Equation, a PC software that deals only with Japanese government bonds.

CONCLUSION

Many of the analytical techniques and models used in the Japanese bond market are tailored closely to traditional conventions used in the U.S. and internationally. Methods and conventions peculiar to the Japanese markets were discussed in this chapter, and direct comparisons were made with U.S. and international standards to highlight their differences and to suggest means of compensating for them in assessing Japanese securities.

The Japanese bond software market has recently undergone many innovations. Many Japanese investment firms have formed joint ventures with leading U.S. academic and investment consultants to develop high-technology software products that quantify risk and assess trends in Japanese bond markets. Japanese technologists have created state-of-the-art software products tailored to the unique financial, political, and cultural nuances of the Japanese securities markets. Major players in the arena are the big four securities companies—Yamaichi, Daiwa, Nikko and Nomura—and international suppliers of financial information and services, like Reuters and Telerate.

Further deregulation and increased activity and globalization of the Japanese financial markets will bring about greater liquidity and efficiency, with a greater emphasis placed on the use of more sophisticated analytical methods and tools for assessing the markets.

ENDNOTES

[1] Typically, the redemption value of a bond is ¥100.

[2] Total time over which interest is earned = p. In Case 1, p = d, whereas in Case 2, p = D + d. Thus, d is either the interval between the issue date and the first scheduled coupon payment date, or that between the last scheduled coupon payment date and the redemption date. Refer to Exhibit 3 for an illustration.

[3] This implies that for a par value of ¥100,000, the odd interest payment amount will be ¥3,526.

[4] The two-sided method is used only in the case of first interest payments on government bonds; the one-sided method is used otherwise. Also, in a leap year, February 29 is counted as an extra day, though the total number of days per year stays at 365.

[5] Later in this chapter, information on taxation of interest payments will be presented.

[6] Frederick Macaulay, *Some Theoretical Problems Suggested by the Movements of Interest Rates, Bond Yields and Stock Prices in the United States Since 1865* (National Bureau of Economic Research, 1938).

[7] For a more detailed discussion of duration, see Frank J. Fabozzi, *Fixed Income Mathematics* (Chicago: Probus Publishing, 1988), Chapters 9–11.

[8] An elaboration on the types of situations would be too complicated and is beyond the scope of this chapter. Information regarding recent changes to the tax laws (since April 1989) is obtained from the *Japanese Economic Newspaper*.

CHAPTER 5

The Japanese Government Bond Market

Christopher Argyrople
Financial Analyst
The Ford Motor Company

Thomas C. Rutledge
Associate
Merrill Lynch Capital Markets

The Japanese government bond (JGB) market is the most important bond market in what is arguably the most important national economy in the world. Japan's economic prosperity in the 1980s has focused the world's attention on Japan's financial activities. Japan's trade surplus and high savings rate have contributed to a huge capital base that influences financial markets around the world. The largest, most liquid credit market in Japan—and therefore the bellwether of Japanese investment trends—is the JGB market. Measured in terms of trading volume and value of bonds outstanding, the JGB market is second only to the U.S. government bond market.

Much of the information in this chapter comes from interviews with several market professionals, including: John Clark and Don Boughrum, Merrill Lynch Capital Markets; Mariko Tanabe, Goldman Sachs; Simon Maru, Daiwa Securities America; Kazuo Ono, The Sanwa Bank Limited; and Shinsuke Kataoka, Nikko Securities. The authors also benefited from the comments of Andrew Gordon of First Boston.

The JGB market plays a role in the Japanese domestic economy similar to that of the U.S. Treasury bond market in the U.S. economy. The market grows and, in Japan's case, shrinks with the expansion and contraction of the government's budget deficit. Yields on the most liquid JGBs, like those on Treasuries, are a standard by which interest rates nationwide are measured. Many Japanese investors use trading and investment strategies that center on the use of JGBs, either alone or in relation to other instruments. JGBs are the focus of the intense speculation that dominates activity in trading rooms of the largest securities houses.

Yet the JGB market is not what a U.S. investor familiar with the U.S. government bond market would consider a free market indicating "true" risk-free interest rates. There are many market inefficiencies, and no meaningful JGB yield curve can be constructed. Traditions, customs, and specific laws applicable to the JGB market distort interest rates implied by the bonds to create a misshapen and kinked "yield curve." No investors would consider this curve an accurate representation of relative preferences for short-term and long-term funds.

Nevertheless, the most popular JGB issue—the "benchmark" bond—is the most liquid yen-denominated fixed-income instrument in the world, and is, consequently, the subject of considerable overseas attention. This attention has become even more intense with the trend toward global financial markets and the ever growing importance of Japan to the world economy. Purchasing JGBs is a popular way to speculate on the appreciation of the yen, and U.S. dollar-based investors have seen handsome returns on such investments; although a dramatic sell-off in the JGB market accompanied the yen's decline in early 1990, yen appreciation has more than compensated for the lower yields on Japanese bonds in previous years.

Moreover, fixed-income investors are beginning to see the advantages of diversifying into other countries' interest-rate markets. Dollar-based investors, for example, can reduce the volatility of their portfolios without incurring currency exposure by purchasing instruments that are not strictly correlated with U.S. interest rates and hedging away currency exposure in forward currency markets. Increasing numbers of portfolio managers are also employing explicitly global strategies in fixed-income money management, tracking global bond indexes such as the Salomon Brothers World Government Bond Index. Both of these trends have led to increased purchases of nondollar bonds generally, with JGBs prominently among them.

THE STATE OF THE JGB MARKET

The Japanese government issues bonds to finance its annual budget deficit and to finance specific construction projects. The first modern issuance, in 1966, was of seven-year coupon bonds used to finance construction projects. Since Japan's net oil imports are among the largest in the world, the government found itself running budget deficits in 1973 for the first time since World War II. In 1975, it issued its first deficit finance bonds. It was in the mid-1970s that Japanese government bond issuance first reached levels comparable to U.S. government debt. JGBs still fall into the two categories of construction finance bonds and deficit finance bonds.[1]

Two major trends have marked the evolution of the JGB market since its inception. First, the structures of the bonds have expanded since the first construction bond was issued as a seven-year coupon bond. Now, the Ministry of Finance offers both zero-coupon bonds—known as discount bonds—and coupon bonds, in maturities ranging from two to twenty years. Discount bonds are issued only with maturity of five years; coupon bonds are issued with maturities of two to four years, ten years and twenty years. All issues are fixed-coupon instruments, although the government has also privately placed fifteen-year floating rate notes. Within the past few years, the government also began issuing 60-day and 180-day Treasury bills for money-management purposes. These bills have no coupons and trade at a discount to par, like U.S. T-bills.[2] Seeking a more liquid short-term market, foreign firms have pressured the Japanese government to issue more short-term paper. In response to this pressure, Japan's Ministry of Finance announced plans in March 1989 to issue three-month T-bills in the fall of 1989.[3] (The types of bonds issued by the Japanese government are summarized in Exhibit 1.)

Second, the JGB market has progressed from being a highly regulated enterprise that restricted participation to certain Japanese financial institutions to a more open marketplace that has increasingly included foreign institutions. The Japanese government's willingness

EXHIBIT 1: TYPES OF GOVERNMENT BOND ISSUES

Long-Term Government Bond (plain vanilla JGB)

Maturity: 10 years on the coupon date
Coupon: Semiannual, payable on the 20th of the month
Issue Volume: 500 to 1,000 billion Yen
Issue Frequency: Monthly
Par Value: 100,000 Yen
Issue Mechanism: 60% Underwriting synd. 40% market auction
Form: Registered (about 97%) or bearer

Medium-Term Government Bonds (two types)

Maturity: 5 years
Coupon: Discount Bond
Issue Volume: 100 billion Yen, depends on financing needs
Issue Frequency: Bimonthly (Jan., March...Sept., Nov.)
Par Value: 100,000 Yen
Issue Mechanism: Negotiated underwriting.

Maturity: 2, 3, and 4 years
Coupon: Semiannual Coupon Bond
Par Value: 100,000 Yen
Issue Mechanism: Auction.

Treasury Bills

Maturity: 180 days
Coupon: Discount Bond
Par Value: 100,000 Yen
Issue Mechanism: Market auction

Super-Long Term Government Bond

Maturity: 20 years on the coupon date
Coupon: Semiannual, payable on the 20th of the month
Issue Frequency: 4 or 5 times per year
Par Value: 100,000 Yen
Issue Mechanism: Market Auction

Source: *Introduction to Japanese Bonds*, Daiwa Securities Co. Ltd., Fourth Edition, 1985.

to combine the traditional syndicate underwriting with a bond auction proves that the JGB market is becoming more competitive. While this reform falls short of the standard for efficiency set by the U.S. market, and while continued progress is uncertain, considerable changes have taken place.

One short-term trend of the late 1980s may also turn out to have a long-term effect on the JGB market: the declining growth of the JGB market as the Japanese government moves closer to a balanced budget. (See Exhibit 2.) Domestic and foreign investors rely on Japanese government bonds as a tool for use in their investment strategies. JGB shortages (especially for high coupon bonds) hamper these strategies. This demand for JGBs has been one component of the rise of activity in interest rate derivatives in Japan's financial markets; the derivatives have served as JGB surrogates. Some observers believe the demand for high-quality, yen-denominated bonds will lead to

EXHIBIT 2:   THE SHRINKING JGB MARKET

Nominal Amount of JGBs Issued, Outstanding (Trillions of Yen)

Fiscal Year	Amount Issued	Amount Outstanding
84	18.24	109.70
85	18.20	121.69
86	23.00	134.43
87	25.90	145.13
88	27.27	151.81
89	23.35*	154.55#
90	22.14*	

*—Estimated

#—As of October 1988

The Fiscal Year starts April 1 and ends the following March 31. FY89, for example, started on April 1, 1988 and ended on March 31, 1989.

Source: Marcus W. Brauchli, "Not All Applaud Japan's Cutback In Debt It Issues," *The Wall Street Journal*, January 4, 1989, p. C1.

other governments (especially the U.S.) issuing yen-denominated debt in Japan.

STRUCTURE OF BONDS AND TRADING CONVENTIONS

The Nature of the Bond

Both varieties of Japanese government bonds, construction finance and deficit finance, are direct obligations of the Japanese government. Although they are not rated, bonds issued by the Japanese government are considered to have the highest credit quality in Japan.[4] Construction bonds and deficit bonds are indistinguishable as far as cash flow is concerned. If construction bonds and deficit bonds were issued in the same month with the same terms, however, they would be considered different bonds and labeled with different trading numbers. Therefore, if one issue was more numerous or more commonly traded, there might be a price and yield difference between the two issues based on liquidity.

Ninety-seven percent of JGBs are held in registered form; the remaining bonds are held in bearer form. The Bank of Japan, Japan's central bank, keeps the register for registered bonds. Transferring a bond from one form to another takes about two days; the government does not permit such a transfer twenty days (or less) prior to a coupon date, due to the mechanism used for paying the coupon. Transfer from registered to bearer form used to be more popular, when only bearer bonds were listed on public stock exchanges. Now, however, registered bonds can also be traded on exchanges. As a result, and because of the costs and risks of dealing in them, bearer bonds are less popular and, consequently, less liquid than registered bonds—a fact reflected in dealer's prices for bearer bonds. They tend to yield (on a simple yield basis) 5 basis points more than comparable registered bonds.[5]

Each Japanese government bond (including medium-term, long, super-long and 5-year discount) is issued with a distinct trading number that distinguishes it from other issues of its kind. For example, the number 100 ten-year refers to a ten-year, 4.0% coupon bond maturing on June 20, 1997. Each new bond issue is given the next number in sequence; investors usually refer to a specific security by referring to its number. As of April 1989, there were over 100 of the most common type of bond (the ten-year long bond) in the marketplace.

A complete listing of 10- and 20-year coupon JGBs outstanding as of April 1989, with their trading numbers, dates of issuance and redemption and coupons, is provided in the appendix to this chapter.

Cash Flow and Maturity

The cash flow characteristics of JGBs are for the most part similar to those of U.S. government bonds, but important differences exist. As with Treasuries, JGBs come in both discount and coupon-paying form and coupons are paid on a semiannual basis in arrears. For JGBs, however, coupons are paid only on the 20th of the month (or the next business day if the 20th is not a business day).[6]

JGBs also differ from Treasuries in the maturities available, and the type (coupon or discount) available in those maturities. Maturities include 60-day T-bills, 180-day T-bills, two-year, three-year and four-year (medium-term) coupon bonds, five-year discount bonds, the dominant ten-year (long) coupon bond (constituting 86% of all JGBs), and the twenty-year (super-long) bond.[7]

Simple Yield—Coupon Bonds. The Japanese convention of simple yield reflects a general Japanese discomfort with compound interest calculations, and is an effort to simplify the complex cash flows of bonds that trade at premiums or discounts to their par values. In the simple yield calculation, the premiums or discounts are taken as adjustments to the coupon payments, allowing the adjusted coupon payments to be considered as simple interest payments on the principal invested.

The simple yield calculation for JGB coupon bonds is:

$$\text{Simple yield} = \frac{\text{Coupon} + \dfrac{(\text{Par} - \text{Price})}{\text{Years to maturity}}}{\text{Price}}$$

This convention assumes that yield equals the coupon plus (or minus) a share of the discount (or premium) proportional to the number of years to maturity. Fractional years to maturity are calculated by taking the actual number of days and dividing by 365 (in market parlance, this is the "actual/365" convention).

To calculate yield in this way is to act as if the investor in a discount bond were receiving a portion of the discount as a cash flow with the coupon every six months, instead of with the principal at maturity. For the investor in a premium bond, it is as if the coupon were reduced by a portion of the premium every six months, instead of the principal payment at maturity being less than the original bond price.[8]

Simple Yield—Discount Bonds. Yield quotations of discount bonds are less important than those of coupon bonds, because discount bonds do not trade as frequently as coupon bonds. This reflects two elements of the Japanese market: 1) again, the discomfort Japanese investors have with pricing fixed-income instruments on the basis of compound interest; and 2) the predominance of individual investors in the discount market due to a tax advantage they enjoy on discount instruments over taxable institutions.

Discount bonds of less than one year maturity are priced like U.S. T-bills. The calculation is as follows:

$$\text{Discount bond yield} = \frac{100 - \text{Price}}{\text{Price}} \times \frac{365}{\text{Days to maturity}} \times 100$$

This calculation takes the percentage appreciation between investment and maturity and scales that figure to an annual percentage rate by multiplying it by the ratio of days in the year to days to maturity.

Yields on discount bonds of more than one year maturity are simply the annually compounded interest. The computation based on price and years to maturity is:

$$\text{Discount bond yield} = \left[\left(\frac{100}{\text{Price}} \right)^{\left(\frac{1}{\text{Years to maturity}} \right)} - 1 \right] \times 100$$

Callability. Although the Japanese government reserves the right to call any outstanding bond at par, it has never done so and the market presumes the government can be trusted never to do so. In theory, the call option investors have written the government would reduce the price of the bond. But, as in so many other aspects of the Japanese markets, strict economic logic takes a backseat to traditions and gentlemen's agreements when it comes to JGB pricing. As a result, many bonds trade at a huge premium to par.

A case in point: even though the government had an obvious economic incentive to call the #58 long bond, a 7.5% coupon issue maturing in December 1993 (in April 1989 it was trading at a price of 111.43 to yield 4.728%), that bond is still outstanding. The same goes for the many other high-coupon bonds issued during the high interest-rate periods of the 1970s and early 1980s. Clearly, yields on government bonds are not inflated by the fact that investors have written the government a call option. In fact, as we will see, yields tend to be lower on high coupon bonds than other bonds of comparable maturity due to the unique Japanese phenomenon known as the *reverse coupon effect*.

Trading Conventions

Those JGBs that are traded regularly are quoted by dealers in terms of their yield on a simple yield basis. So, if you were talking to a dealer and asked him or her to quote the current benchmark bond, the dealer would say something like "24-23." This quote would imply a bid of 5.24% simple yield and an offer of 5.23% simple yield (the 5% "handle" would be understood by market participants abreast of the market's current level). In other words, you could sell the benchmark to the dealer at a price that worked out to 5.24% simple yield, or you could buy the benchmark from the dealer at a price that worked out to 5.23% simple yield.

Although it is not customary to do so, spreads can also be quoted in terms of price. The term Japanese dealers use when quoting in price terms is called the "sen." One yen is equivalent to 100 sen.

Information About JGB Trading. Exchange-traded JGBs are easily tracked with market prices listed on accessible computerized terminals. Over-the-counter trading in JGB securities is tougher to monitor because it is comprised by interdealer and broker trading (which consists of transactions made by institutions that normally like to keep their intentions secret). Since OTC trading makes up much more of total JGB trading volume than Tokyo Stock Exchange trading, the Securities Dealers' Association of Japan periodically publishes two bond quotation lists that provide information about over-the-counter JGB activity to those without access to the information large market players have.

The *Representative Bond Quotation List* is a daily listing of prices and yields of 24 bond issues that provide a reasonable gauge of OTC market action. Fifteen large securities firms furnish bid and ask prices on these bonds for large-lot trades (over 100 million yen). The list is released daily at 10:00 a.m., and the association also releases information on daily highs and lows at 1:30 p.m. This list consists of JGB and other relevant Japanese bond issues including government guaranteed and corporate issues.

The *Standard Bond Quotation List* is a weekly listing of about 200 securities that are not included on the *Representative Bond Quotation List*. Each Thursday, this list provides average prices and high/low information to individual investors who have no other method of obtaining this information. The list encompasses a wider range of issues that may appeal to individual investors including discount and medium-term JGBs.

The *OTC Market Quotation List* is a daily newspaper listing that covers a select group of bonds taken from the *Representative Bond Quotation List*. This list is also aimed at informing individual investors on OTC market action. The quotations are submitted by 29 banks and brokerage firms that are government bond dealers. The quotes provide large-lot bid and ask prices in addition to the name of the quoting dealer.

The Benchmark. In the United States and many other fixed-income markets, the most recent government bond issue is the liquid issue with the highest trading volume. This is not the case in Japan. The benchmark bond, a ten-year maturity long bond, is the most liquid security, and it does not necessarily have to be the most recent issue.

The benchmark bond is characterized by huge trading volume compared to the volume of similar nonbenchmark issues. Daily turnover for the benchmark can be many times the total number of benchmark bonds outstanding.

The benchmark is important for several reasons. It is the only Japanese bond that trades with a liquidity similar to that of U.S. Treasury bonds. It is the target of huge daily speculation by Japanese securities firms. The benchmark is expensive relative to other JGBs because of the premium the market pays for its liquidity, causing a kink in the already distorted Japanese yield curve. The benchmark is also watched around the world as an indicator of Japanese interest rates. Although yields on other yen-denominated bonds are not priced in relation to JGBs (as dollar-denominated bonds are priced in relation to the U.S. Treasury yield curve), yen bond investors do keep an eye on the benchmark yield to determine interest rate levels and credit and maturity spreads.

Accrued Interest. The accrued interest paid on coupon bonds traded between coupon dates is calculated by figuring the fraction of a year between coupon and settlement on an actual/365 basis. Interest accrues according to the following formula:

Accrued Interest = Par Value × Coupon Rate
× Fraction of Year from Last Coupon to Settlement.

No withholding tax is paid on accrued interest, unless a bond is delivered in settlement of a JGB futures contract. In that case, a taxable investor would pay according to the rate that the investor normally paid.

Settlement. Strict delivery and settlement dates are set according to a calendar determined by the Brokers' Broker (a dealers' market-making intermediary in Tokyo) and the Ministry of Finance. Each trading day is assigned a "value date" (i.e., settlement date) that normally falls about twelve days after the trade date. The value date changes every three to eight days. For example, if a trade took place between April 6 and April 10, it would settle on April 20; if it took place between April 11 and April 13, it would settle on April 25, and so on. There are normally five or six value dates each month (see Exhibit 3).

EXHIBIT 3:   SETTLEMENT

Trade Date	Value Date
Feb. 1–3	Feb. 15
Feb. 6–9	Feb. 20
Feb. 10–17	Feb. 28
Feb. 20–23	Mar. 6
Feb. 24–28	Mar. 10
Mar. 1–3	Mar. 15
Mar. 6–9	Mar. 20
Mar. 10–15	Mar. 27
Mar. 16–20	Mar. 31
Mar. 22–24	Apr. 5
Mar. 27–30	Apr. 10
Mar. 31–Apr. 5	Apr. 17
Apr. 6–10	Apr. 20
Apr. 11–13	Apr. 25
Apr. 14–18	Apr. 28
Apr. 19–25	May 10
Apr. 26–May 1	May 15

Trading Patterns

Designation of the Benchmark. There is no systematic method for determining which issue will become the benchmark. Since the benchmark is frequently traded by the four dominant securities firms (Nomura, Daiwa, Nikko and Yamaichi), a security must have the trading support of these four primary market-makers to become the benchmark. When the current benchmark begins to lose support (that is, its trading volume falls and the premium paid for its liquidity declines), the Big Four securities firms will begin to speculate (both in the rumor mill and in their trading activities) on which issue will be the next benchmark. Since there is a large liquidity premium for the benchmark, the transition between benchmarks can be costly. Many transitions take place over a period of months, and two candidates often end up "competing" with each other to become the benchmark.

In general, the benchmark security must be a high coupon issue with Nomura's backing. Lower coupon issues are expensive to hold in inventory. All else equal, Japanese investors prefer to buy high coupon issues, and the benchmark issue must have yield support to satisfy customers and market makers. The benchmark must also be a recent long bond issue that is large enough to satisfy heavy demand; 1.5 trillion yen is considered adequate.

Ultimately, a sort of implied consensus emerges and a new benchmark is anointed. Once a security is designated as the benchmark, it can remain the focus of the bond market for over a year until another satisfactory issue takes its place as the benchmark. Typical benchmarks last about nine months (see Exhibit 4).[9]

The Yield Curve and Its Irregularities. Most investors familiar with the variety and liquidity of U.S. Treasury issues would say that there is no real yield curve in Japan. The benchmark is the only bond with liquidity comparable to that found in the U.S. market, and only former benchmarks are liquid enough that dealers regularly make markets in them. These issues are mostly in the seven-to-ten year range of maturities, so other portions of the yield curve are made up of bonds that are either illiquid or have been held by investors so long that they simply do not trade. In addition to its problems with liquidity, the yield curve is also distorted by certain unique characteris-

EXHIBIT 4: HISTORY OF THE BENCHMARK

No.	Maturity	Coupon	Tenure as Benchmark
#22	Nov. 1989	7.7	Jan. 82–Sep. 83
45	Jun. 1992	7.5	Oct. 83–Dec. 83
53	Jan. 1993	7.5	Jan. 84–Sep. 84
59	Dec. 1993	7.3	Oct. 84–Jul. 85
68	Dec. 1994	6.8	Aug. 85–Dec. 85
78	Jul. 1995	6.2	Jan. 86–Oct. 87
89	Jun. 1996	5.1	Nov. 86–Nov. 87
105	Dec. 1997	5.0	Dec. 87–Dec. 88
111	Jun. 1998	4.6	Jan. 89–Nov. 89
119	Jun. 1999	4.8	Dec. 89–present

tics of the Japanese market—the reverse coupon effect, the benchmark's liquidity premium, and various tax considerations—to the point that yields on Japanese government bonds do not accurately describe a continuous term structure of risk-free yen interest-rates.

A few general statements can be made about the tendencies of the JGB yield curve, or what there is of it. Typically, the JGB yield curve will slope upward, as the Treasury yield curve does in the United States. An inverted yield curve exists when shorter term Japanese yields rise above the 10-year government yield. As in the United States, inverted yield curves in Japan occur infrequently. High Japanese inflation due to the oil price shock in 1974 caused the yield curve to invert for a year and a half. The Japanese rate of inflation doubled in 1980 (rising from 4% to 8%) and the yield curve inverted again.[10]

The most dramatic distortions of the yield curve are created by Japanese investors' preference for high-coupon issues—a characteristic of the JGB market known as the reverse coupon effect.

Because of Japanese laws and accounting rules, Japanese institutional investors, especially insurance companies and banks, prefer high-coupon bonds. This preference has a strong effect on the shape of the Japanese yield curve because investors bid up the price of high coupon bonds, forcing down their yields below the yields of other securities with similar maturities.

Japanese regulations force insurance companies to make their benefit payments fall in line with their earnings. Their earnings, in turn, are determined on the basis of coupon income only—not capital gains. Therefore, in order to make their policies competitive, insurance companies pay up for the high coupons that place their earnings at a competitive level.

Banks are also dominant investors in government bonds, and they have been subject to accounting laws which favor coupon income over capital gains. Japanese accounting allows banks to claim coupon or interest revenue as income, but banks must declare capital gains and losses as extraordinary items. Thus, Japanese banks prefer coupon income because capital gains from bond trading cannot be considered as ordinary income. In 1990, this accounting policy will change and banks will be allowed to treat income and capital gains identically.[11]

Insurance firms typically hold high-coupon securities to maturity because this practice allows them to maximize their coupon income. The preponderance of insurance firms holding high-coupon securities to maturity has created limited liquidity in the high-coupon sector of the JGB market.

The yield curve in the JGB market reflects the high-coupon preference of Japanese investors. To fully understand the structure of the yield curve, one must look back at the level of interest rates in the early 1980s. At that time, long bond rates in Japan were hovering between 8% and 9%. But in early 1989, with long bond rates in the 4% to 5% range, Japanese investors preferred to buy the high coupon bonds of the early eighties.

As a result, high demand for the older bonds put downward pressure on the yield for these older bonds. Since these bonds were ten-year issues, they made up the bulk of issues with remaining lives of under six years. The strong demand for the shorter maturities has pushed down yields at the short end of the yield curve. This is a unique characteristic of the yield curve in the Japanese bond market.

In Fiscal 1990 (i.e., as of April 1, 1989), the Federation of Bankers Associations of Japan transformed bank accounting rules in a way that included capital gains from bond trading in the key measure of bank profitability. This decision would appear to reduce the incentive to hold high-coupon bonds and mitigate the reverse coupon effect. Indeed, the JGB market reacted to bring prices of high and low-coupon bonds more in line with each other when discussions about such an accounting change first began. Between January 19, 1989 and March 1, 1989, amid public speculation about an accounting change, the spread between the high-yielding, low-coupon 4% No. 100 bond and the low-yielding, high-coupon 6.8% No. 68 narrowed from about 140 basis points to less than 90 basis points (on a simple yield basis). This spread subsequently increased again, so the eventual fate of the reverse coupon effect is difficult to forecast.[12]

The unique attention commanded by the benchmark also accounts for yield-curve irregularities. Most of the massive speculation that takes place in the JGB market is focused on the benchmark. Since the market is characterized by large swings, active investors (especially the securities firms and the large Tokyo banks) prefer to deal in liquid issues to avoid large transactions costs, and the most liquid issue is the benchmark. And, since investors seek that liquidity, they bid up the price of the benchmark to the point that it trades at a premium to similar side (i.e., non-benchmark) issues. This liquidity premium creates an incentive for buy and hold investors to avoid the benchmark. Given the financial power of Japan's banks and securities houses, their demand for the benchmark can bid down yields to as much as 100 basis points below similar side JGBs.

Liquidity and Bid-Offer Spreads. Spreads between dealers' bid prices and offer prices for an issue are a good indication of the issue's liquidity. A dealer demands a wider spread on a less liquid issue to compensate it for the risk it takes in making a market; conversely, spreads are narrow for more liquid issues.

The most liquid issue, the current benchmark, trades at spreads of one basis point (again, JGBs are quoted on a yield basis). Former benchmarks are the second-most active issues, with spreads at brokers of 2 basis points and 3 basis points for dealers. The market in former benchmarks is broad compared to that for other JGBs, so traders are more likely to execute large block trades in those issues without suffering large adverse price movements. Non-benchmark long bonds trade at 4 basis point spreads. Dealers will not make a standing market in inactive issues such as T-bills, medium-term coupon bonds, and the five-year discount bonds since they trade so infrequently and are so illiquid. For such issues, dealers will often only trade by appointment, executing an order only if a counterparty can be found.

Market conditions are the second factor that determines spreads. Bid-offer spreads will be tighter in a buyer's market where an abundance of supply exists. On the other hand, when the supply of JGBs decreases, spreads will widen to compensate for the adverse market conditions.

Exhibit 5 highlights spreads on March 24, 1989 on representative JGB issues. These are closing quotes, so the spreads are wider than they would be during the day's most active trading. Notice that the spread for the benchmark 111 issue is the tightest at 2.6 basis points. Issue #105, the benchmark before #111, is clearly the second-most liquid issue in the JGB market with a 3.5 basis point spread. The rest of the higher coupon issues traded at least 0.3 basis points higher than issue #105 at the close on March 24th. This higher spread reflects the relative illiquidity of these issues versus #111 and #105. March 24th,

1989 is a typical example of an average day in the JGB market, but spreads and liquidity will vary depending on market supply and demand.

Trading Volume. Average daily trading turnover in the JGB market is over 10 trillion yen. This is a sharp increase over the volume of the 1970s and early 1980s, before Japanese banks received the June 1984 go-ahead to join securities firms as JGB dealers.[13] Trading is highly concentrated in the benchmark. An extreme example of the market's fixation on the benchmark occurred on one day in 1987, when broker trades in the benchmark outnumbered by 23-to-1 trades in the second-most active issue—a bond that had the same coupon and a maturity difference of one month. The benchmark accounts for 60% of all JGB trading, compared to 5-to-10% for the most active issue in the U.S. Treasury market, the 30-year long bond.[14]

Volume can vary widely, depending on market sentiment—a bull market stirs up interest and trading volume. The transition from one benchmark to another can also generate considerable speculative interest. In April 1987, during an unprecedented period of extreme

EXHIBIT 5:   REPRESENTATIVE SPREADS IN THE JGB MARKET

Bond Number	Ask	Bid	Spread
	Closing Quotes, 3/24/89		
34	4.624	4.673	4.9
43	4.568	4.607	3.9
53	4.526	4.565	3.9
59	4.526	4.565	3.9
68	4.516	4.556	4
78	4.544	4.582	3.8
89	4.698	4.736	3.8
105	4.773	4.808	3.5 (previous benchmark)
111	5.109	5.135	2.6 (benchmark in April, 1989)

Source: Nikkei Telecom, Japan News & Retrieval Database, Nihon Keizai Shimbun Inc.

volatility, daily JGB trading volume increased to about 50 trillion yen.[15] Overseas JGB trading makes up a small portion of total trading (less than 1 trillion yen on average) but is active enough to ensure liquid markets for JGBs when the Tokyo market is closed.

Volatility. The benchmark JGB can be expected to move five-eighths of a point (or about 20 basis points in simple yield) on any given day; on particularly volatile days, the benchmark will move as much as a full point (or about 35 basis points in yield).

Over the past ten years, JGBs have lost the reputation of being one of the most stable bond markets in the world; JGBs are now considered among the world's most volatile government bonds. This volatility change took place in 1984–85, as a result of the admission of Japanese banks as market makers, the Plaza Accord and subsequent decline of the dollar, and the advent of the JGB futures contract. In 1987, 20-day yield volatility (i.e., the average daily yield movements as a percentage of yield over a 20-day period) at one point reached 60%, compared to an average volatility of around 15% for widely traded government bonds of other countries.[16] It is worth noting, however, that since Japanese interest rates are so low, a given move in yield constitutes a much higher percentage change than the same move in a higher-yield instrument (such as U.S. or UK government bonds).

The Difficulty of Shorting. The Japanese bond market is not organized to facilitate selling bonds short. Although the Ministry of Finance has promised to put an efficient repurchase (repo) market in place to facilitate short sales, and although selling the benchmark short is relatively easy, significant practical obstacles remain. In addition, a great deal of prejudice against selling bonds short lingers in the market. Many market participants believe it is unpatriotic to sell JGBs short, since in the extreme case a soft bond market would cause debt finance problems for the government.

To see the problems of shorting, let us go step-by-step through the procedure of selling a bond short and consider the obstacles that would be faced by a trader short JGBs. After one party (the short) agreed to sell a bond to another, that party would have the choice of either delivering the bond or making restitution for the coupon payments the second party (the long) would receive if the bond had been delivered. In the U.S., the short party has an incentive to deliver because the cost of restitution for the coupon usually exceeds the cost of borrowing the bond to deliver. However, the short does have the choice. In Japan, the short party must deliver the bond. To fail to deliver would be to violate an important taboo and result in a severe loss of reputation in the business community.

So, a trader who was short a JGB would have to borrow the bond from the time the bond was sold short until the bond was bought back. First, however, that would mean finding a party who owned the bond and was willing to lend it. In New York, investment firms have finance or funding desks that seek out bonds to borrow to cover their short positions and lend out their bonds as collateral for borrowing cash. In Japan, on the other hand, no such structured repo market exists and short sellers must seek out bond owners directly. (Although a market in which securities are used for collateral against short-term loans does exist—the gensaki market—it is designed for financing purposes, not borrowing specific issues to deliver against a short position.[17]) Many bond holders, in turn, are suspicious about the repo arrangement and are unwilling to take part, even though lending their bonds out would provide a low-cost source of funds.

The lack of liquidity in many issues presents yet another obstacle to finding bonds to borrow. Nonbenchmark issues are illiquid and thus cannot be borrowed in large enough volume for shorting, if at all. Regardless of whether specific securities are available, the lack of supply of bonds for collateral, relative to demand, makes repo expensive (i.e., the interest paid on funds lent in exchange for collateral is low).

Finally, once a trader borrows a bond, the bond must be borrowed until the trader buys the bond back. If the trader borrows the bond for a long period, he or she is locked into that commitment, restricting the trader's flexibility. The alternative is to borrow on a short-term basis and roll over the short-term repo until the short is covered. The market's strict delivery rules (see the discussion of "Settlement" above) dictate that one must use gensakis to roll over short positions. A transaction tax of 0.01% on every gensaki transaction makes gensaki financing a costly aspect of shorting bonds.

When it is difficult to short a bond, its price is not held tightly in check by arbitrage conditions. For example, if JGBs become undervalued relative to JGB futures,[18] one can arbitrage the price inefficiency by purchasing the cash bond and selling the corresponding futures contract. This arbitrage transaction creates price boundaries in which the bonds and futures must trade to prevent riskless arbitrage. Because shorting in large volume is difficult, the reverse arbitrage trade is difficult to execute. As a result, arbitrage conditions do not provide a strict lower boundary for the futures price or upper boundary for the cash bonds, but investors will sell bonds and buy futures if the futures contracts become cheap enough relative to the cash bonds. The exact spread at which this happens depends on many factors, and this spread may vary considerably depending on market conditions.[19]

Determinants of Fundamental Value.   Ultimately,   interest   rate movements are the main determinant of JGB prices. When interest rates rise, JGB prices fall, and bond prices rise in response to falling interest rates. An inverted price-yield relationship exists in all bond markets, but it is an extremely strong relationship in the JGB because government bonds are never called. When required yields fall, non-callable bond prices rise. Callable bonds, on the other hand, display "negative convexity" when market yields drop; that is, interest rate declines are not fully reflected in appreciating bond prices. JGBs, though callable in theory, have never been called in practice. Given the government's stake in keeping interest costs low, there is no indication that any JGB issues will be called in the near future.

Interest rates, in turn, depend on both the economy's demand for credit and government economic policy. Japan's central bank, the Bank of Japan (BOJ), performs a function similar to that of the Federal Reserve Bank (the Fed) in the United States. Like the Fed, the BOJ controls monetary and interest rate conditions in Japan. It can alter the Japanese money supply and domestic interest rate levels by purchasing or selling JGBs in the public markets, in other words, performing open market operations. If the BOJ purchases government bonds (in exchange for money), it is increasing the money supply; on the other hand, an open market bond sale decreases the money supply.

Increases in the money supply create downward pressure on interest rates and decreases in the money supply create upward pressure on rates. Thus, the government bond market is sensitive to the

BOJ's policies, just as the U.S. Treasury market is sensitive to moves by the Federal Reserve.[20]

The BOJ also sets the discount rate in Japan, and a revision in the discount rate generally has a significant effect on the entire Japanese interest rate structure. Government bonds are very sensitive to discount rate changes, but such changes are infrequent.

Although Japanese interest rates are the major determinant of JGB prices, the market reacts to many other factors. Inflation exerts a strong influence on bond prices due to the relationship between inflation and interest rates. Import prices are a major determinant of the Japanese inflation rate. Since Japan is a nation with relatively scarce natural resources, the Japanese economy is sensitive to prices of imports. Japan imports almost all of its energy; its large consumer and industrial base requires enormous annual shipments of oil, gas, and coal. Rising energy prices can exert inflationary pressures in the Japanese economy. Traders and economists incorporate inflation expectations into their interest rate forecasts, and this has a direct influence on government bond prices.[21]

Currency factors also influence the government bond market. When the yen rises, imported goods and services become cheaper in Japan. If the yen falls, Japanese goods become more competitive on world markets at the expense of foreign products. In general, a weak yen has a negative impact on the government bond market because of inflationary expectations. When the yen falls, prices of imported goods rise and fuel expectations of higher domestic inflation. Expected inflation due to a weak yen is immediately embodied in lower prices for fixed-income instruments. On the other hand, bond prices react positively to a strong yen because it is an indication of stable domestic inflation. Currency markets are dynamic and open 24 hours a day; therefore, the currency factor is a continuous influence on the JGB market.

International investors often view foreign fixed-income investments as a legitimate method of currency speculation. Empirical evidence lends substance to this claim. A Salomon Brothers study on foreign equities, bonds, and money market instruments showed currency plays a major factor in the return on an international investment. Exhibit 6 shows coefficients of determination (R-squareds) between the local investments and exchange rates.

EXHIBIT 6: CORRELATION BETWEEN CURRENCY AND TOTAL RETURN

Currency Factor as a Determinant of Total Returns Measured in U.S. Dollars
(R-squareds from monthly data, Jan. 1982 to March 1985)

	Equity Market Return in U. S. Dollars versus Exchange Rate	Govt. Bond Return in U.S. Dollars versus Exchange Rate	3 mo. Eurodeposit Return in U.S. Dollars versus Exchange Rate
Canada	39.0%	67.4%	97.6%
Japan	69.8	95.3	99.9
U.K.	42.0	65.1	99.8
Germany	40.0	93.0	99.8
Netherlands	12.2	89.2	99.8
Switzerland	60.9	93.2	99.5
France	31.7	89.0	99.2
Average	42.2%	84.6%	99.4%

Source: Salomon Brothers Inc.

It is hard to dispute the fact that foreign money-market instruments are anything but a pure currency play. The average R-squared between currency and Eurodeposit returns was 99.4% for the seven countries analyzed. This analysis suggests that short-term Japanese government instruments are excellent instruments for short-term currency speculators. For government bonds, the pattern is similar. Eighty-four percent of the dollar return on foreign government bonds can be explained by currency movements, suggesting that currency speculators may provide a strong demand for JGBs and T-bills in the future.

JGBs are also influenced by fixed-income markets in the United States. Until recently, the yield spread between JGBs and U.S. Treasury securities has been large. In the fourth quarter of 1988, the spread (on a simple yield basis) between U.S. and Japanese government 10-year issues was as high as 475 basis points.[22] Large differentials like this provide incentives to sell JGBs and buy U.S.

government bonds. Although U.S. government securities are backed by the full faith and credit of the U.S. government, there is no free lunch for Japanese investors seeking a higher yield. Why? The currency risk involved exposes the Japanese investor to a significant amount of risk. If the dollar depreciated 5% versus the yen, the 4.75% yield pickup would be wiped out and the JGB investor would have been better off by 25 basis points holding JGBs.

Expected currency movements affect the JGB market as investors choose between JGBs and non-yen-denominated securities. If the dollar is expected to appreciate versus the yen, Japanese investors will sell JGBs and invest the money in U.S. government securities. The strong dollar of the early 1980s provided windfall gains for Japanese investors who owned U.S. government debt. They received two sources of return: the high yield on U.S. securities and the currency gain. Sentiment in currency markets has an effect on JGBs through supply and demand factors. If Japanese investors believe that the dollar will appreciate, they will sell JGBs to buy U.S. government bonds. This will have an adverse effect on the JGB market. On the other hand, Japanese investors own a substantial amount of American debt, and an expected yen appreciation can create demand for Japanese government bonds.

Determinants of Day-to-Day Value. Active participants in the Japanese government bond market make their day-to-day buy or sell decisions less on the basis of fundamental value or economic analysis than by taking the cue of certain key indicators of bond value. Day-to-day news events that may not have a long-term effect on the fixed-income market can exert significant short-term influence. In other words, traders often do not care about the same things long-term investors care about.

Because of the Big Four securities houses inclination toward massive speculation, the biggest influence on the market in the short run is what traders describe as sentiment. Rumors and participants' general mood can move the market as quickly and dramatically as a significant economic statistic.

Ranking next in importance is the performance of the yen in international currency markets. The economic reality of Japan's status as a net importer of primary goods and the awareness on the part of the Japanese of their vulnerability to imported inflation focus attention on the yen as an indicator of imported inflation. The yen-dollar rate and the yen-deutschemark rate hold particular importance.

As the most liquid and efficient interest-rate market in the world, the U.S. bond market often leads bond markets elsewhere in the world. This is even truer for the Japanese market because of Japan's close economic relationship with the U.S. and its earlier history of dependence on the United States. U.S. Treasury bonds and the bond futures contracts are actively traded in Tokyo, and trends in U.S. trading often spill over into the JGB market.

Since the U.S. market closely follows the release of U.S. government economic statistics (normally done at 8:30 Eastern Time), the JGB market has learned to watch for "a big number" as a clue to which direction the market will follow. Interestingly, the Japanese market cares much more about U.S. economic statistics than statistics released by the Japanese government. West German statistics are also probably more important to the JGB market than Japanese numbers.

The annual fiscal year-end book closing at the end of March can have a concrete effect on the JGB market. Japanese corporations close their annual books each year at the end of March, and, like their American counterparts, Japanese institutional investors "dress up" their portfolio holdings in an interesting manner. Just as in the United States, where "no one ever got fired for owning IBM," Japanese portfolio managers buy certain reliable securities to help their investors rest easier when annual reports are released detailing the portfolio's holdings. Specifically, Japanese investment managers generally want to buy conservative instruments like government bonds for their fiscal year-end portfolios. Immediately after the fiscal year end, the managers have a tendency to increase their risk profile and invest more in stocks during the April to June quarter.[23]

In the past, this window dressing has led to a predictable year-end rally in the JGB market, although in 1989, this did not take place because of the market's general bearish trend.

INSTITUTIONAL ISSUES

Issuance

The Bank of Japan conducts primary market issues of Japanese government bonds under mandate from the Ministry of Finance.[24]

The Bank of Japan issues JGBs in two ways: through an under-writing syndicate and through auctions of various types. Over the years, the syndicate has been the predominant means of issuance, fostering close ties between the Ministry of Finance and the financial institutions that make up the syndicate. More recently, however, the government has faced pressure from foreign governments and finan-cial institutions to introduce a more competitive mechanism for issu-ing bonds. In response, and in step with the general trend toward liberalization of the Japanese financial market, the government has gradually displaced syndicate underwritings with auctions of vari-ous forms.

Although the changes in JGB issuance have largely followed American prescriptions for change—that is, to move toward the 100% auction system in place in the U.S.—Japanese officials warn that the current trend may not ultimately consummate in a com-pletely competitive issuance mechanism. Toyoo Gyohten, the Minis-try of Finance's vice minister in charge of the international division, told *Institutional Investor* in November 1988 that "if the aim is simply to reproduce the U.S. market in Japan, Americans will be disap-pointed."[25]

How Different Bonds Are Issued. During the last fifteen years of vi-brant activity in the Japanese government bond market, five-year discount bonds, long (10-year) bonds and super-long (20-year) bonds have mostly been issued at prices and coupons fixed by the govern-ment through offerings to a syndicate of financial institutions that underwrites JGBs. Medium-term (2-, 3-, and 4-year) coupon bonds and 180-day T-bills have been issued primarily by auction. Recently, however, auction systems have crept into use for issues where the syndicate has traditionally made up the primary market (except for the five-year discount, which is still offered at a fixed price and cou-pon).[26]

The government has gradually moved toward auction issuance, introducing auctions to one issue at a time. The first government bond auction took place in June 1979 for the issuance of the government's medium-term bonds (2-, 3-, and 4-year maturity). In September 1987, the super-long bond (20-year maturity) was first auctioned. Auctions for both these issues are similar to U.S. Treasury auctions: bidders submit sealed bids for issues of set maturity and coupon, and all bids above a certain "stop" price, which is set to match the amount the government wants to issue, are filled.[27]

The first long-bond auction, held in November 1987, was of a different form. While 80% of the long bonds issued were handled in the usual way by the underwriting syndicate, 20% were set aside for a so-called "share auction" or "volume auction." In this form of auction, the price, coupon and maturity of an issue are set, but a bidder may indicate how much of the issue it is willing to take, up to 1% of the whole issue. If the issue is oversubscribed, shares are allocated on a pro rata basis. For example, if bids outnumbered bonds issued ten-to-one, each bidder would receive one-tenth of its bid.[28]

Foreign firms were dissatisfied with the share auction system because they felt that it kept too many bonds in the hands of the syndicate and it still allowed the government to issue at non-market interest rates. In response, the Ministry of Finance instituted an auction system for long bonds that much more closely resembles the U.S. Treasury's auction system.

The New Long-Bond Auction System. The Ministry of Finance conducted its first long bond auction under the new system on April 5, 1989. Under the system, 60% of an issue is issued as before, with syndicate members receiving fixed allocations at a set price, and with the coupon being negotiated by the syndicate board, the Bank of Japan and the Ministry of Finance in the month prior to the issue. The remaining 40% is auctioned in the manner of medium-term and super-long bonds. That is, the government accepts bids specifying both quantity and price.[29] The price of the 60% issued via syndicate is set at the average price paid for bonds at the competitive auction.[30]

Many of these changes in the issuance procedure arose because of pressure from U.S. securities firms and U.S. Treasury officials, especially during 1988. U.S. participation in the Japanese bond market was a prominent topic in U.S. trade talks with Japan that year. Many observers believe the U.S. Treasury delayed the designation of Yamaichi Securities as a primary dealer of U.S. government securities until the Ministry of Finance made some gesture of liberalization in its JGB issuance procedure. In the U.S.'s 1988 Omnibus Trade Bill, a provision sponsored by Representative Charles Schumer (D-New York) permitted the U.S. Treasury to revoke Japanese securities firms' status as primary dealers of U.S. government bonds unless

J.S. firms were given access to the Japanese primary market beyond heir portion of the 2.5% of issues then allotted to foreign syndicate members. In September of 1988, the Ministry of Finance capitulated by expanding foreigners' syndicate share to 8% and announcing the price auction system's launch in 1989.[31] In a largely symbolic gesture, the Ministry also granted certain foreign firms co-manager status in the underwriting syndicate.[32]

The pressure for liberalization has not only come from abroad, however. The large Japanese securities houses have also lobbied for expanded auctions, believing they have the capital and know-how to compete successfully with their domestic and foreign competitors.[33]

The Syndicate. About 800 banks, securities firms and insurance companies—and, since 1984, foreign securities firms—make up the syndicate that underwrites Japanese government bonds. Membership allows a firm to have direct access to new issues of Japanese government bonds—a valuable right generally considered necessary for full participation in the Japanese financial community. Syndicate members also receive a commission on the new issue. For long-bond issuances, the commission is 0.6375% of the face value of the new issue— lower now that auctions, rather than negotiations, are used to set the new issue's price. Before the auction system began, underwriters received 0.90% commission.

This right to primary access to JGBs does not come without a price, however. Syndicate members must accept bonds at the price and coupon assigned. The quantity of bonds a syndicate member purchases is proportional to the firm's capital assets—an accounting measure based on a firm's shareholders' equity and, for securities firms, brokerage deposits held on behalf of the firm's brokerage customers.[34] Thus, the government has issued bonds at above-market prices and below-market coupons in order to assure interest costs in line with the amount allocated for debt service in the government's annual budget.[35] Although fixing below-market interest rates is impossible in an auction system, the Ministry of Finance likes having a guaranteed market for its debt and will try to preserve this feature of the issuance process, even in the face of U.S. pressure to move toward the open auction system of issuance. "The issuers always want stable sales of the obligations at the lowest possible price (i.e., cost)," says Ministry of Finance Vice Chairman Toyoo Gyohten. "But underwriters have different interests that may conflict with that. So I think the ultimate answer should be a compromise."[36]

Syndicate members have some say in the terms of issuance. A board of syndicate members that represents the different types of financial institutions in the syndicate negotiates with the Bank of Japan and the Ministry of Finance at the end of each month over the coupon rate and quantity of the following month's issue. (The Bank of Japan acts as the Ministry of Finance's administrative arm, and, consequently, takes a small role in syndicate negotiations; the negotiations are primarily a two-sided matter, between the Ministry and the syndicate members.) In July 1983 and in June and July 1984, the syndicate went so far as to refuse the terms of new issues; as a consequence, ten-year long bonds were not issued in those months.[37] Although the Ministry of Finance still holds considerable power in the syndicate negotiations, the financial institutions participating in the syndicate—especially the Big Four securities firms of Nomura, Daiwa, Nikko and Yamaichi—have squared the balance of power as the size and quality of their financial assets has grown. Many observers believe that, since 1987, the negotiations have taken place on fairly even footing.

One serious drawback to the traditional issuance procedure was that syndicate members possessed sensitive inside information on MOF and BOJ policy. Syndicate members obtained inside valuable knowledge through the negotiating process, and the MOF has admitted that information has leaked from the syndicate. There is pressure to keep retail clients informed on market developments, and securities firms had incentives to use this inside information to improve customer service and their own profits. The auction procedure of issuance is expected to solve this problem to some extent, but on the advice of the U.S. Federal Reserve, the MOF is going one step further. It is developing its own "dealing room" to monitor the auctions of the 10-year benchmark bonds. The dealing room will be similar to the trading rooms at major securities firms in that traders will have several computer screens and telephones to inform them on the latest economic, currency, and bond market conditions. They will not, however, be trading inventory as do their counterparts at securities firms. Rather, they will monitor market information and dispense it via fax and modem transmissions to all market participants in a timely manner.[38]

As of the April 1989 long-bond auction, once syndicate members possessed the new bonds, they were required to wait three days before they could resell bonds in the secondary market. This waiting period was greatly reduced from the more restrictive rules that governed previous issuances.

The Future. Will these free market-oriented reforms continue? If they do, they will likely continue at a slower pace. As previously mentioned, the Ministry of Finance is not eager to emulate the U.S. bond market. Moreover, U.S. firms are likely to be less insistent about further liberalizations. Deryck Maughan, chairman and CEO of Salomon Brothers Asia Limited, told *The Wall Street Journal* in 1988, "We don't wish to take a position as complaining foreigners." Such a reputation would hurt foreign firms' ability to maintain business contacts in Japan, many believe.[39]

Some questions also remain about how well foreign firms can compete in a less regulated environment. Domestic firms bring certain expertise, knowledge and resources to the JGB business that foreign firms have difficulty matching. Considering that Japanese banks and securities houses are the largest financial institutions in the world, they enjoy unique economies of scale and scope on their home turf. They aggressively demonstrated their muscle in the first long-bond price auction, taking the lion's share of the bonds open to competition at a yield 14 basis points below the usually expensive benchmark. As the JGB business becomes more competitive, it may become less profitable, following the trend of the U.S. Treasury market and its narrowing profit margins. This may spell defeat for less competitive foreign firms. "It was a mistake for the foreign firms to call for the price-auction system," says Isao Teranishi, general manager of the treasury and bond dealing department of Nomura Securities.[40] The Japanese believe that the competitive auctions will reduce the profitability of bond dealing just as it has in the U.S. market.[41]

Dealers and Exchange Trading

Government bonds are traded on the Tokyo Stock Exchange and the over-the-counter (OTC) market. OTC trading comprises approximately 90% of volume.[42]

The vast majority of JGB trading conducted in Tokyo, and all of the trading around the world, is done over-the-counter. Trading on the Japanese stock exchanges—the Tokyo, Nagoya and Osaka stock exchanges—is conducted by floor brokers matching buy and sell orders, primarily for the benefit of small investors.

Banks and securities firms around the word—including, since June, 1984, Japanese city banks—conduct their trading both by dealing directly with one another and by dealing with brokers. The brokers accept standing bids and offers from dealers, posting the most competitive current prices on on-line computer screens viewed by all market participants. A dealer wishing to buy at an offered price or sell at a bid price calls the broker, executes the trade and pays a negligible commission.

In Tokyo, the broker that serves all market participants is the Broker's Broker, commonly referred to as "BB." BB was established by the Big Four securities houses and the Ministry of Finance. In Tokyo, securities firms do not talk directly to each other, making BB especially important. Firms trade through BB to conceal their identities when conducting trades, or to manipulate the prices indicated on the screen in the hope of moving the market. Trades between securities houses and banks are usually conducted directly. Direct trades outnumber broker trades in the Tokyo market by about two-to-one.

In New York, the broker "FBI" has a near monopoly on broker trading, but broker trading is less common. The New York offices of Japanese trading houses have abandoned their taboo about talking to one another (after some bad initial experiences making prices well out of line with one another). Consequently, intra-dealer communications are more common and the dealer-to-dealer market is much more active.

Taxes

Two key taxes have a direct effect on JGB trading: transfer tax and withholding tax.

For Japanese residents, there is a transaction tax of 3 basis points (0.03%) when a bond changes hands. Nonresident investors are not subject to any transaction tax, making the bonds slightly more attractive for foreigners. The Japanese government cannot accurately keep

rack of exactly who owns bearer bonds, so it may have trouble levy-
ng the transaction tax on sellers of bearer bonds.[43]
    The standard withholding tax on JGBs is 20%, and this rate must
be paid by both Japanese and foreign investors. Lower rates (see Exhibit 7) are available to investors from nations that have a double tax
treaty with Japan. Investors must file a tax relief application with
Japan's tax authorities to reduce the withholding tax on their bonds.
Supranational organizations (World Bank, IFC, etc.) and foreign governments are not subject to withholding taxes on Japanese government bonds.
    Investors in the countries that have tax treaties with Japan can
recover the lost coupons in part through their own tax system. For
example, an American investor in a JGB is entitled to take a U.S. tax
write-off for the withholding tax on his or her JGB. This write-off
prevents the double taxation of coupon payments by Japan and the
United States.
    The most important exemption from withholding taxes, how-
ever, is the exemption for organizations considered "Designated Fi-

EXHIBIT 7: WITHHOLDING TAXES

Withholding taxes on coupons payable to foreign bondholders are 10% in
the following countries:

Australia	Austria	China	Denmark
Finland	France	Germany	Ireland
Italy	Malaysia	Netherlands	Norway
Philippines	Spain	Sweden	
Switzerland	U.K.	United States	

Countries with withholding taxes higher than 10% on JGBs:

Belgium	15%		
Canada	15%	Korea	12%
Singapore	15%	Brazil	12.5%

nancial Institutions" (DFIs) by the government. These institutions pay no withholding tax, and they include most Japanese financial institutions and most overseas institutions with Japanese subsidiaries. This benefit was granted to institutions as an incentive to hold government debt in the mid-1970s, when the Japanese government was running large deficits due to the OPEC oil shock and rising inflation in primary products.

This distinction between bonds held by DFIs and those not held by DFIs is very important in Japanese capital markets. Bonds held by DFIs are considered "clean-registered" and are liquid; when market observers discuss the activity or conventions in the market, they mean the market for clean-registered bonds. Bonds not held by DFIs, by contrast, are considered "dirty-registered" and are not liquid. Dealers are not willing to provide reasonable price quotes for dirty-registered bonds.

The "clean vs. dirty" distinction provides obvious incentives for tax evasion, but there is no method of measuring how large this practice is. In one scheme, a brokerage house will hold a bond on behalf of a brokerage client, permitting the client to receive the full coupon thanks to the brokerage's status as a DFI.

Discount government bonds are subject to a 16% tax at issuance. This is a one-time-only tax, and is calculated by subtracting the issue price of the bond from the par value. Thus, the buyer must pay an immediate tax of 16% on the bond's future income stream. Of course, once the bond begins to trade in the secondary market, it is not subject to the 20% withholding tax on coupon income. Consequently, discount government bonds are priced accordingly to take the tax difference into account.[44]

Tax-exempt institutions (including U.S. and foreign pension funds) are among the largest potential investors in Japanese bonds. Withholding taxes make foreign bonds appear less attractive than comparable domestic issues. When an international tax-exempt investor compares equity to bond purchases, the witholding tax becomes a major issue. Since coupon income is a major source of a bondholder's return, a withholding tax is a substantial deterrent to purchasing a foreign bond. On the other hand, dividend yields on equities are considerably lower, and the withholding tax on dividends is not a major obstacle to international equity investing. Dividend yields on Japanese stocks are currently about 0.5%. The 10%

witholding tax on a 5% JGB is equal to the dividend yield on a typical Japanese stock.

Individual investors are subject to an 18% tax on five-year discount bonds, compared to 20% for other JGBs. This gives them a marginal advantage over institutional investors, so the market for discount bonds tends to be concentrated in individuals.

Delivery

It is illegal to deliver a JGB outside of Japan. Overseas investors typically have custodian accounts with a bank in Japan that holds the bonds in the investor's behalf.

CONCLUSION

The Japanese government bond market begs comparison with the U.S. government bond market. It is second in size to, and in large part modeled after, the market for U.S. Treasuries. The U.S. and Japan are two of the most important economies in the world, and each country's government bond market is a bellwether indicator for worldwide interest rates and economic trends.

Yet observers familiar with the efficient, laissez-faire U.S. Treasury market can see obvious differences in the more regulated, less liquid and often inefficient JGB arena. No meaningful JGB yield curve exists, due to several factors: the accounting standards that produce the reverse coupon effect, the liquidity premium included in the benchmark long-bond's price, and the scant trading of so many JGB issues. Massive speculation in the uniquely liquid benchmark bond often creates considerable volatility. Moreover, the obstacles to short-selling JGBs cause considerable inefficiencies, especially the common discrepancy between JGB futures prices and prices in the cash market for JGBs.

In recent years, however, the byword for the JGB market has been liberalization. The globalization of financial markets and, in particular, pressure from U.S. institutions, have forced the Japanese to conform to international standards and deregulate markets. The most dramatic example of this trend has been the transformation of the all-important long-bond issuance procedure. It has changed from, as recently as 1987, a negotiated syndicate- underwriting that cultivated a partnership between influential Japanese institutions and the Japanese Ministry of Finance to, today, an auction system that almost imitates the blind auctions used to issue U.S. government bonds.

The logical extention of these reforms would be a Tokyo-based, yen-demoninated imitation of the U.S. Treasury market, but such a result seems unlikely in the near future. The pace of change is slowing. This is partly because the amount of Japanese government debt outstanding is shrinking, a trend that will tend to make the JGB market less efficient. In addition, the Ministry of Finance seems unlikely to reform its issuance procedure further, since it believes the current system provides some assurance that the market will supply the government with funds at a reasonable borrowing rate. Japanese financial institutions, acclimated to the bond market's unique features, also have little incentive to press for change in a market that has brought them considerable profits, unless they stand to profit from a particular change (as was the case with auctioning rather than underwriting JGBs).

Foreign governments and financial institutions will surely continue to urge change in the JGB market, and some change will come. But the changes will not be as rapid as some foreigners would hope. The dominant voice in the debate about the Japanese government bond market's ultimate character will probably be a powerful participant that is quite comfortable with the status quo: Japan itself.

ENDNOTES

[1] *The CSFB Guide to the Yen Bond Markets*, Probus Publishing Company, Chicago, Illinois, 1988, p. 45.

[2] "Bond Market in Japan, 1988," Economic Planning and Research Division, Bond Underwriters Association of Japan, 1988, p. 11.

[3] Article from Nikkei Telecom, Japan News & Retrieval Database, Nihon Keizai Shimbun Inc., March 25, 1989.

[4] Sally J. Staley, *International Bond Manual, Japanese Yen*, Second Edition, Salomon Brothers Inc, p. 12.

[5] *The CSFB Guide to the Yen Bond Markets*, op. cit., p. 51.

[6] Ibid., p. 50.

[7] Ibid., p. 49.

[8] For a further discussion of simple yield and a comparison to the yield-to-maturity measure used in the U.S., see Chapter 4.

[9] *The CSFB Guide to the Yen Bond Markets*, op. cit.

[10] *World Financial Markets*, Morgan Guaranty Trust, NY, NY.

[11] Kermit Schoenholtz and Tomoko Fuji, *Portfolio Preferences of Japanese Banks: The Potential Impact of Proposed Accounting Changes*, Salomon Brothers Inc, February 2, 1989.

[12] Richard H. Woodworth, *Yen Money and Bond Markets; A Monthly Review*, Merrill Lynch Capital Markets, March, 1989, p. 5.

[13] Nicholas Sargen, Kermit Schoenholz and Bernadette Alcamo, *Japanese Bond Market Volatility and International Capital Flows*, Salomon Brothers Inc, August, 1987, p. 2.

[14] Michael Sesit, "Futures on Japanese Government Bonds are Matching Cash Market in Volatility," *The Wall Street Journal*, July 14, 1987, p. 39.

[15] Sargen, et al., op. cit., p. 5.

[16] Ibid.

[17] The gensaki market is discussed in Chapter 6.

[18] JGB futures contracts are the subject of Chapter 15.

[19] *The CSFB Guide to the Yen Bond Markets*, op. cit.

[20] *Note on the Japanese Public Debt Markets*, Harvard Business School Case, 1986, p. 2.

[21] Nikkei Telecom, Japan News & Retrieval Database, Nihon Keizai Shimbun Inc.

[22] Ibid.

[23] Ibid.

[24] "Bond Market in Japan," op. cit., p. 24.

[25] Henny Sender, "The View from the Ministry of Finance," *Institutional Investor*, November 1988, p. 154.

[26] *The CSFB Guide to the Yen Bond Markets,* op. cit., p. 51-2.

[27] Tomio Shida, "Foreigners May Rue Auction for National Bonds," *Japan Economic Journal,* Nihon Keizai Shimbun Inc., March 18, 1989, p. 1.

[28] "Japan's Change in Bond Auctions Appears Delayed," *The Wall Street Journal,* September 28, 1987, p. 51.

[29] Michael R. Sesit and Terence J. Gallagher, "Japan Unveils New Measures to Widen Foreign Role in Government Bond Mart," *The Wall Street Journal,* September 7, 1988, p. 3.

[30] Shida, op. cit.

[31] Sesit and Gallagher, "Japan Unveils New Measures to Widen Foreign Role in Government Bond Mart," op. cit.

[32] Henny Sender, "Good—and Bad—News About Japan's Incredible Shrinking Government Bond Market," *Institutional Investor,* October, 1988, p. 26.

[33] Michael R. Sesit, "Japanese Plan Auction Sales of Some Bonds," *The Wall Street Journal,* May 12, 1987, p. 29.

[34] Kathryn Graven, "Trade Bill's Proposal on Primary Dealers Causes Concern at U.S. Firms in Japan," *The Wall Street Journal,* April 21, 1988, p. 41.

[35] Ibid.

[36] Sender, "The View from the Ministry of Finance," op. cit.

[37] Staley, op. cit., p. 8.

[38] Seth Sulkin, "MOF's 'Dealing Room' Trade in Transparency," *Institutional Investor,* March 1989, p. 172.

[39] Graven, op. cit.

[40] Shida, op. cit.

[41] Nikkei Telecom, Japan News & Retrieval Database, op. cit.

[42] *The CSFB Guide to the Yen Bond Markets,* op. cit., p. 54.

[43] Staley, op. cit.

[44] *The CSFB Guide to the Yen Bond Markets,* op. cit.

APPENDIX

JAPANESE GOVERNMENT BOND ISSUES OUTSTANDING AS OF APRIL, 1989

Name	Number	Date of Issuance	Redemption Date	(%) Coupon
10 year Govt	18th	1979/04/27	1989/05/20	7.20
10 year Govt.	19th	1979/06/20	1989/05/20	7.20
10 year Govt.	20th	1979/07/20	1989/08/21	7.20
10 year Govt.	21st	1979/09/20	1989/08/21	7.70
10 year Govt.	22nd	1979/12/20	1989/11/20	7.70
10 year Govt.	23rd	1980/02/20	1990/02/20	7.70
10 year Govt.	24th	1980/02/20	1990/02/20	7.70
10 year Govt.	25th	1980/03/21	1990/02/20	8.00
10 year Govt.	26th	1980/03/21	1990/02/20	8.00
10 year Govt.	27th	1980/05/20	1990/05/21	8.70
10 year Govt.	28th	1980/06/20	1990/05/21	8.70
10 year Govt.	29th	1980/09/20	1990/08/20	8.50
10 year Govt.	31st	1980/11/20	1990/11/20	8.50
10 year Govt.	32nd	1980/12/20	1990/11/20	8.00
10 year Govt.	33rd	1981/03/20	1991/02/20	8.00
10 year Govt.	34th	1981/03/20	1991/02/20	8.00
10 year Govt.	37th	1981/06/25	1991/02/20	7.60
10 year Govt.	35th	1981/04/20	1991/05/20	8.00
10 year Govt.	36th	1981/05/22	1991/05/20	7.60
10 year Govt.	41st	1981/09/30	1991/08/20	8.00
10 year Govt.	42nd	1981/12/21	1991/11/20	8.00
10 year Govt.	43rd	1982/02/20	1992/02/20	7.70
10 year Govt.	44th	1982/03/20	1992/02/20	7.70
10 year Govt.	45th	1982/04/26	1992/06/20	7.50
10 year Govt.	46th	1982/05/20	1992/07/20	7.50
10 year Govt.	47th	1982/06/21	1992/07/20	7.50
10 year Govt.	49th	1982/09/20	1992/07/20	8.00
10 year Govt.	50th	1982/11/30	1992/12/21	8.00
10 year Govt.	51st	1982/11/30	1992/12/21	8.00
10 year Govt.	52nd	1983/01/07	1992/12/21	7.70
10 year Govt.	53rd	1983/03/28	1993/01/20	7.50
10 year Govt.	55th	1983/05/25	1993/06/21	7.50
10 year Govt.	57th	1983/09/20	1993/07/20	7.50
10 year Govt.	58th	1983/10/20	1993/12/20	7.50
10 year Govt.	59th	1984/01/20	1993/12/20	7.30
10 year Govt.	61st	1984/02/20	1994/01/20	7.30
10 year Govt.	62nd	1984/03/29	1994/01/20	7.30

Name	Number	Date of Issuance	Redemption Date	(%) Coupon
10 year Govt.	63rd	1984/05/21	1994/06/20	7.00
10 year Govt.	64th	1984/08/20	1994/07/20	7.30
10 year Govt.	65th	1984/09/20	1994/07/20	7.10
10 year Govt.	66th	1984/10/20	1994/12/20	7.10
10 year Govt.	68th	1984/12/20	1994/12/20	6.80
10 year Govt.	69th	1985/01/21	1995/01/20	6.50
10 year Govt.	70th	1985/06/20	1995/01/20	6.50
10 year Govt.	71st	1985/05/20	1995/01/20	6.80
10 year Govt.	73rd	1985/05/20	1995/06/20	6.80
10 year Govt.	75th	1985/06/20	1995/06/20	6.50
10 year Govt.	77th	1985/07/20	1995/07/20	6.50
10 year Govt.	78th	1985/09/20	1995/07/20	6.20
10 year Govt.	79th	1985/10/21	1995/12/20	6.00
10 year Govt.	80th	1985/12/20	1995/12/20	6.50
10 year Govt.	81st	1986/01/20	1996/01/20	6.10
10 year Govt.	82nd	1986/01/20	1996/01/20	6.10
10 year Govt.	87th	1986/03/20	1996/01/20	5.70
10 year Govt.	83rd	1986/01/20	1996/06/20	6.10
10 year Govt.	84th	1986/02/20	1996/06/20	6.00
10 year Govt.	88th	1986/03/20	1996/06/20	5.70
10 year Govt.	89th	1986/06/20	1996/06/20	5.10
10 year Govt.	90th	1986/09/22	1996/07/22	5.10
10 year Govt.	91st	1986/10/20	1996/12/20	5.10
10 year Govt.	92nd	1986/11/22	1996/12/20	5.40
20 year Govt.	2nd	1987/02/20	2007/03/20	5.70
20 year Govt.	3rd	1987/05/20	2007/09/20	4.80
20 year Govt.	4th	1987/09/21	2007/09/20	5.60
20 year Govt.	5th	1987/12/21	2008/03/20	5.70
20 year Govt.	6th	1988/03/22	2008/03/20	5.30
20 year Govt.	9th Nov.	1988/11/21	2009/03/20	5.00
20 year Govt.	7th	1988/05/20	2008/09/22	4.90
20 year Govt.	8th	1988/08/22	2008/09/22	5.30
10 year Govt.	93rd	1986/12/22	1996/12/20	5.30
10 year Govt.	94th	1986/12/22	1996/12/20	5.30
10 year Govt.	98th	1987/03/20	1997/01/20	5.00
10 year Govt.	95th	1987/01/21	1997/06/20	5.30
10 year Govt.	97th	1987/03/20	1997/06/20	5.00
10 year Govt.	99th	1987/04/20	1997/06/20	4.70
10 year Govt.	100th	1987/05/20	1997/06/20	4.00
10 year Govt.	101st	1987/06/22	1997/06/20	3.90
10 year Govt.	102nd	1987/07/20	1997/09/22	4.30
10 year Govt.	103rd	1987/08/20	1997/09/22	4.60
10 year Govt.	104th	1987/09/21	1997/09/22	4.90

Name	Number	Date of Issuance	Redemption Date	(%) Coupon
10 year Govt.	105th	1987/12/21	1997/12/22	5.00
10 year Govt.	106th	1988/01/20	1998/03/20	4.90
10 year Govt.	109th	1988/03/22	1998/03/20	4.80
10 year Govt.	113th Oct.	1988/10/20	1998/12/21	5.00
10 year Govt.	108th	1988/06/20	1998/06/22	4.80
10 year Govt.	111th	1988/05/20	1998/06/22	4.60
10 year Govt.	114th Nov.	1988/11/21	1998/12/21	4.80
10 year Govt.	115th Dec.	1988/12/20	1998/12/21	4.70
10 year Govt.	116th Jan.	1989/01/20	1999/03/22	4.70
10 year Govt.	112th	1988/09/20	1998/09/21	5.00

CHAPTER 6

The Gensaki Market

Jeffrey L. Dickson
Associate Investment Manager
Prudential Capital Corporation

Hiroaki Fuchida
Vice President
The Mitsubishi Bank, Ltd.

Yutaka Nishizawa
Senior Vice President
The Mitsubishi Bank, Ltd.

Gensaki refers to a repurchase agreement under which a seller of bonds will buy back the bonds from the buyer at a predetermined date and price. The agreement, in essence, is a short-term financing for the seller and a lending opportunity for the buyer. The bond traded is used as collateral, and the difference between the selling price and the repurchase cost is the interest on the financing. Transactions range from a few days to a maximum period of twelve months. The majority of transactions are between three days and three months. A gensaki transaction is usually for over ¥100 million, with many transactions over ¥10 billion.

The gensaki market is important because it is an "open market" with rates determined by the supply and demand for funds. Partici-

171

pants include both financial and nonfinancial institutions. Prior to the establishment of the gensaki market, the only short-term markets were the call and bill discount markets, which are limited to only financial institutions. These markets generally had below-market rates that were set with the guidance of the Bank of Japan. The gensaki market has been the driving force in the liberalization of Japanese interest rates.

Gensaki accounted for over 50% of the bond market volume in the last half of the 1970s. From 1981 to 1984, however, gensaki volume decreased annually to a low of ¥148 trillion or 19.4% of the total bond market volume in 1984[1] (see Exhibit 1). The main reason for the decline in volume was the diversification of financing vehicles that became available, not only to financial institutions and securities companies, but also to corporations. These vehicles included certificates of deposit, foreign-currency deposit accounts, and Treasury bills. Another reason for the decline in gensaki volume was the imposition of a securities transaction tax on gensaki contracts. This tax increased the net financing costs of gensaki compared to other vehicles. However, since 1984, volume has risen due to the increase in tax-exempt gensaki contracts. That is, gensaki selling of Treasury bills and other tax-exempt target securities.

It should not be inferred from the decline in volume of taxable gensaki contracts that the market is no longer an important one in Japan. Gensaki will continue to serve as a major financing vehicle due to many of its characteristics that will be discussed in this chapter. Further, because of the expansion of "open markets," such as the gensaki market and the CD market, arbitrage opportunities exist between the open markets and the call and bill discount markets.

The gensaki yields now seem to serve as an indicator reflecting the liquidity position of corporations. The arbitrage efforts continue to bring various segments of the short-term money markets increasingly close to one another. In an effort to disseminate information about rate movement in the gensaki market, the Securities Dealers Association now publishes standard yields and trading volume of gensaki transactions.[2] The gensaki market serves as a benchmark in the liberalization of the short-term money market.

EXHIBIT 1: TRADING VOLUME AND OUTSTANDING BALANCE OF BOND TRANSACTIONS WITH REPURCHASE AGREEMENT

(Yen billion)

Year	Total Trading Volume of Bonds (A)	Of which, Total Trading Volume of Bond Transactions with Repurchase Agreements (B)	(B)/(A)	Balance of Bond Transactions with Repurchase Agreement (Year End)			Balance of Call Loans (Year End)	Balance of Bills Discounted (Year End)	Balance of CDs (Year End)
				Members' Account	Customers' Account	Total			
1976	¥ 67,187.8	¥ 37,224.0	55.4%	(¥ 822.9)	(¥1,122.9)	(¥1,945.8)	¥ 2,567.1	¥ 5,091.0	—
1977	116,953.0	60,781.9	52.0	2,180.9	955.3	3,136.2	2,616.4	6,084.0	—
1978	203,476.4	106,264.8	52.2	2,755.2	1,451.7	4,206.9	2,326.0	6,590.2	—
1979	209,653.9	116,781.6	55.7	1,784.2	2,176.2	3,960.4	3,472.5	6,326.8	¥1,819.9
1980	281,316.0	156,006.5	55.5	2,496.1	2,010.7	4,506.8	4,133.2	5,738.1	2,357.6
1981	301,429.4	141,530.6	47.0	2,816.3	1,664.7	4,481.0	4,698.6	4,015.5	3,290.9
1982	342,832.3	135,274.2	39.5	2,762.6	1,540.9	4,303.5	4,493.5	5,412.8	4,341.5
1983	419,976.8	137,206.0	32.7	2,650.1	1,637.7	4,287.8	4,455.5	6,763.4	5,664.5
1984	767,160.2	148,702.8	19.4	2,647.4	914.4	3,561.8	5,037.2	7,997.7	8,460.6
1985	2,298,539.8	251,577.3	10.9	3,556.2	1,085.7	4,641.9	5,110.4	14,655.8	9,657.2
1986	2,844,107.4	590,802.6	20.8	4,853.2	2,263.7	7,116.9	10,226.2	13,544.4	9,926.3

Note: Balance of bond transactions with repurchase agreement at the end of 1976 represents the total of those of 22 major securities companies, and those for 1977 and after represent the total of those of securities companies that had a balance of bond transactions with repurchase agreements.

Source: Securities Market in Japan 1988, Japan Securities Research Institute.

HISTORY OF THE GENSAKI MARKET

The development of the gensaki market can be traced over several time periods from about 1949 to the present (see Exhibit 2).

EXHIBIT 2: DEVELOPMENT OF THE SAIKEN-GENSAKI MARKET

1949   Creation of conditional sales (Repo) market.

1955   Increase in retained bonds because the secondary market was poor.

1961   Creation of open-end bond investment trust, after the contract cancellation increased.

1972   During the period of easy monetary policy, number of participants increased.

1974   Voluntary rules for conditional sales.

1976   Ministry of Finance report on gensaki transactions. First official recognition of gensaki.

1978   Yen-denominated foreign bonds included as target securities.

1979   Liberation of nonresident gensaki transactions and creation of domestic certificates of deposits (CDs).

1980   Trust Fund Bureau begins kai-gensaki operations.

1981   Liberalization of uri-gensaki by city banks. Open market sales of short-term government securities retained by Bank of Japan.

1984   Permission given to deal foreign CDs and commercial paper (CP). Foreign bonds included as target securities.

1985   Securities companies begin to deal domestic CDs in the secondary market. Yen-denominated bankers acceptances (BA) was created.

1986   Open market sales of government short-term securities by gensaki method.

The Creation of the Issue Market

The saiken-gensaki (bond gensaki) market, developed around 1949, is historically the oldest short-term market in Japan. During this time period, Japan was trying to restore its economy mainly through an allocation system controlled by the government and the Bank of Japan.[3] Corporations had a need to issue bonds because of a lack of investment capital, while the government's main policy goal was to prevent inflation. These aims were conflicting in that the government created an issuing market for bonds but then regulated the amount and rate of issuance in order to insure that interest rates did not rise rapidly.

The bonds that were issued were mainly purchased by financial institutions and securities companies. Banks held the issues until maturity and securities companies tried to sell the issues to investors. However, interest rates were held low by the government so that there was very little interest on the part of investors. Inevitably, the securities companies were left holding excess inventory, which disrupted their flow of funds. In order to improve the flow of funds, securities companies sold the excess bonds to agriculture and forestry financial institutions under the condition that they buy back the bonds at a repurchase price that included a higher interest rate than the controlled interest rate. These transactions represented the first conditional sale of bonds in Japan.

Expansion

After 1955, the issuing market became active. However, the secondary market remained stagnant. For this reason, investors still hesitated to invest in bonds and new issues did not sell well. In order to improve the situation, an open-end bond trust was created in 1961 to absorb newly issued bonds that could not be sold to investors.[4] However, due to tight monetary policy, cancellation of planned issues increased and the flow of funds at securities companies deteriorated again. Bonds that were bought back from open-end bond investment trusts could not be resold due to the lack of a secondary market. Therefore, the bonds continued to be disposed of by means of conditional sales.

Market Formation

The formation of a secondary market began in 1965 with the creation of itaku-gensaki (gensaki transactions where dealers intermediated between buyers and sellers). During the period of tight monetary policy around 1965, financial institutions, particularly city banks and corporations, joined securities companies as sellers of gensaki. In 1966, the secondary market developed and the government began to issue bonds in earnest. Most of the original issues were purchased by financial institutions so that they became large sellers of bonds in the secondary market. However, in order to avoid losses in a bear market, financial institutions began to actively raise funds through the securities companies by means of the saiken gensaki market.

During the period of tight monetary policy, corporations had difficulty raising funds through financial institutions. Therefore, they too tried to raise funds in the saiken gensaki market by using itaku-gensaki. The main buyers were agriculture and forestry financial institutions, governmental mutual aid associations, and a few corporations that had excess funds.

After 1971, a loose monetary policy made corporate financing easier and corporations quickly became the best buyers in the saiken gensaki market. On the other hand, the agriculture and forestry financial institutions became active sellers during this period of easing monetary policy. These institutions raised funds in the gensaki market (sell gensaki) and invested the proceeds in other bank investments that had systematic interest rates much higher than the gensaki rate.[5] That is, they arbitraged the spread between the open market gensaki rate and the more controlled bank rates.

Recognition by the Ministry of Finance (MOF)

In March 1976, the chief of the Securities Bureau of the MOF presented a report to the Japanese Securities Dealers Association regarding the dealing of conditional sales of bond gensaki. The report endorsed the voluntary rules that were established by the securities industry in February 1974 to promote the orderly expansion of the bond gensaki market.[6] The report was the first formal recognition of the gensaki market at the administrative level of Japan. The two main points of the report were to limit the amount of gensaki sales relative to the asset size of the securities companies and to ensure that the contract price of gensaki reflected the market price of the underlying collateral.

These rules were established after the oil shock and a period of tight monetary policy, between 1973 and the beginning of 1975, which caused gensaki rates to increase to 20%. The rates increased so dramatically because of the demand for funds by financial institutions as well as corporations. The vast expansion of the market, with little administrative guidance, led to problems in the market order system. As a result, the MOF forced the securities industry to develop voluntary rules in 1974, which then became administrative policies after the MOF report in 1976.

Diversification of the Open Markets

Gensaki transactions accounted for more than 50% of the total bond market volume in the second half of the 1970s. From 1981 to 1984, however, the gensaki volume declined significantly. By the end of 1984, gensaki volume was down to 19.4% of bond market volume.[7] The reason for the decline in volume is that the short-term market became liberalized, allowing for new open market investments. In May 1979, the CD market was established after financial institutions clamored for a vehicle to compete with gensaki. Conditional sales of CDs (CD gensaki) were also allowed at this time. In December 1980, foreign currency deposits by residents became liberalized. In May 1981, the government began to issue short-term Treasury bills (T-bills) at market rates in the public market. In 1984, foreign CDs and foreign commercial paper (CP) started trading in Japan, and, in 1985, the rate on large amount time deposits was liberalized and money market certificates (MMC) were introduced. Finally, in November 1987, the domestic CP market was established.

The introduction of these competitive short-term money market investments caused the ratio of bond gensaki to total open market investments to decline substantially throughout the 1980s. However, the flow of bonds has increased since 1984 when banks were allowed to deal bonds. Therefore the role of gensaki in terms of general bond sales has increased dramatically, particularly due to the growth of tax-exempt gensaki contracts.

GENSAKI TRANSACTIONS

The two methods of bond sales in Japan are *general sales* and *gensaki transactions*. General sales refer to the normal purchase of and sale of bonds in the market. Gensaki transactions are bond transactions that require a sale (purchase) of a bond with a promise to buy back (sell back) the bond after a certain period and at a specified price. The word "gensaki" most likely originates from the words "Genbutsu" meaning "real good" and "sakimono" meaning "future goods." Gensaki is the sale or purchase of real goods and the promise to buy back or sell back future goods. The word "uri" in Japan means "sale" and "kai" means purchase. Therefore, "uri-gensaki" is the sale of bonds (or other collateral) with the promise to buy them back after a certain period and at a specified price. Similarly, "kai-gensaki" is the purchase of bonds (or other collateral) with a promise to sell them back after a certain period and at a specified price. In Japan, these transactions are also known as "conditional bond sales." In fact, gensaki trades are money transactions between lenders (appearing as buyers) and borrowers (appearing as sellers).

The Gensaki Rate

The gensaki rate is determined by the difference between the original selling price of the gensaki transaction and the eventual repurchase price. For the seller of gensaki, the difference is equivalent to interest paid on money borrowed. For the buyer of gensaki, the difference is equivalent to interest earned on money invested. The gensaki rate is shown as either an annual interest rate on a 365-day basis or as a per diem rate for ¥100 (see Exhibit 3).

Itaku-Gensaki—"Commissioned Gensaki"

Securities houses often act as intermediaries for their clients. The broker buys the gensaki from clients who desire short-term funding. That is, the clients raise funds using uri-gensaki. The broker will then find a buyer who wishes to invest funds at the conditions established by the original seller of the gensaki contract. In effect, the broker finds counterparties on either side of the transaction. However,

EXHIBIT 3:   GENSAKI RATE CALCULATION

a = starting price of gensaki
b = repurchase price of gensaki
i = interest rate of bond
n = term (in days)
R = annual rate of gensaki (%)
r = Hibu (interest per diem for 100 yen)
    1 sen = 1/100 of 1 yen

$$a + i = b$$

$$i = a \times \frac{r}{100} \times n$$

$$r = \frac{b - a}{a \times n} \times 100 \text{ (sen units)}$$

$$R \text{ (annual rate)} = r \times \frac{365}{100} \text{ (%)}$$

the clients actually sell and buy from the securities firm. By the security firm acting as intermediary, confidentiality is assured for clients and, more importantly, credibility of the contracts is standardized in the name of the securities house. The security for the gensaki buyer is in the credit of the securities firm, not the original seller. This type of transaction is known as itaku-gensaki, or commissioned gensaki.[8]

The largest securities firms publish daily rates for one- to three-month periods. An interested client negotiates with the securities firm, specifying the amount of funds, the desired terms, the commencement date, and other particulars. Once the transaction is completed, it is generally accepted that the securities firm will keep custody of the bonds purchased under a gensaki transaction (see Exhibit 4).

Due to the liberalization of the short-term money market over the past few years, fewer companies use itaku-gensaki as a means of fund-raising. In addition to the liberalization, the decline in the use of itaku-gensaki has also been caused by balance restrictions imposed on securities firms. The restrictions were established due to the price risk of the collateral in an itaku-gensaki transaction. The contract price of a gensaki is usually the effective price of the collateral (the underlying price of the bond). If the original seller of gensaki failed in its obligation to repurchase the bond, and the price

EXHIBIT 4:   ITAKU-GENSAKI FLOW DIAGRAM

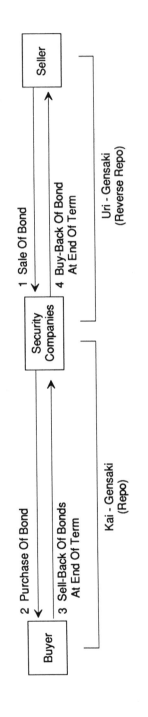

of the bond declined during the gensaki term, then the security firm would face potential losses when it closed out the other side of the transaction. Itaku-gensaki balance restrictions were established in 1974 to minimize this risk. The restrictions have been revised several times, with the latest revision having taken place in 1988 (see Exhibit 5).

Jiko-Gensaki — Financing Dealer Inventory

Securities houses have huge funding needs as a result of their securities positions and new issue underwriting. Under jiko-gensaki transactions, the securities firms sells bonds or other target securities to their clients in order to satisfy their funding needs rather than acting as an intermediary in the case of itaku-gensaki (see Exhibit 6). Kaigensaki sold by securities houses are termed "regular" gensaki and are very common in the market since securities firms need funds to run their operations.[9] The bonds or other target securities are owned by the securities companies themselves.

EXHIBIT 5: ITAKU GENSAKI BALANCE RESTRICTIONS

March 1976

Total balance restrictions per company:
Largest 4 securities companies — net assets x 1.5
Other securities companies   — net assets x 2

Balance restriction per customer:
No more than 10% of net assets with any one customer.

.
.
.   Several revisions throughout period
.   between 1976-1988
.
.

January 1988

Total balance restrictions per company:
All companies — net assets x 1.0

Balance restrictions per customer:
No more than 30% of net assets with any one customer.

EXHIBIT 6: JIKO-GENSAKI FLOW DIAGRAM

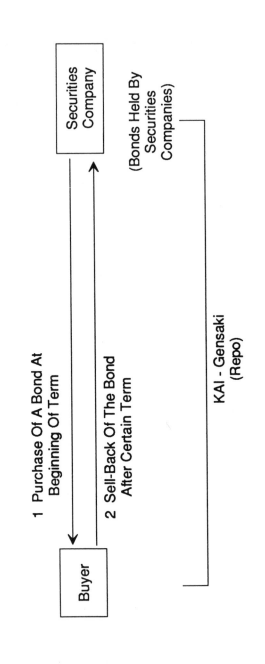

In contrast, securities houses sometimes lend money to financial institutions, such as city banks and regional banks, on a short-term basis by means of a uri-gensaki transaction. These transactions are termed "reverse" gensaki from the point of view of the securities firm since it is buying the gensaki rather than selling gensaki.[10]

Securities firms aggressively utilize jiko-gensaki transactions for several reasons. First, the firm readily holds inventories of target securities that can easily be used for collateral in a gensaki transaction. Even though the securities firms have other short-term funding vehicles (such as bank borrowing, call money, and foreign exchange loans), the readiness of the jiko-gensaki market in terms of timing and procedure makes it attractive to the securities firms.

Second, gensaki is considered a main commodity in the open market of Japan. Investors find gensaki attractive even as other commodities are developed such as CDs, CP, large time deposits, foreign currency deposits, and banker's acceptances. Government-related corporations and agencies using gensaki are limited as to what securities they can invest in, which increases the demand for gensaki.

Finally, jiko-gensaki satisfies the demand for gensaki that is not covered by itaku-gensaki. That is, not every gensaki transaction could have a buyer and a seller agreeing on all the terms of the transaction. Sometimes unique terms arise, and securities firms will have to own the position. Just like itaku-gensaki, transaction standards exist for jiko-gensaki in order to promote sound business practices by the securities companies and to protect investors (see Exhibit 7 for restrictions).

Gensaki Transactions After the MOF Report in 1976

Rules for the gensaki market were clarified in March 1976, when the chief of the Securities Bureau of the MOF issued the report recognizing gensaki. The rules were developed in order to standardize transactions and increase efficiencies in the market. The rules related to the establishment of contracts, target securities, prices, qualifications of investors, terms, and denominations.

Contracts. Any gensaki transaction must have a contract between buyer and seller. The contract specifies the kind of target security,

EXHIBIT 7: JIKO-GENSAKI BALANCE RESTRICTIONS

The four largest securities companies must satisfy conditions A and B below. All other securities companies are allowed to exceed A if they satisfy B.

A

$$\frac{\text{Total Liabilities} + \text{Jiko–Gensaki Balance}}{\text{Net Assets}} < 8$$

Net assets and liabilities taken at previous year end.

B

$$\frac{\text{General Sales of Bonds during Month} \times .5}{\begin{array}{c}\text{General} \\ \text{Bond} \\ \text{Balance}\end{array} + \begin{array}{c}\text{Jiko–Gensaki} \\ \text{Balance}\end{array} - \begin{array}{c}\text{Net Finished} \\ \text{Transaction} \\ \text{Balance}\end{array}} > 1$$

$$\text{General sales amount} = \begin{array}{c}\text{Total} \\ \text{Sales} \\ \text{Amount}\end{array} - \begin{array}{c}\text{Gensaki} \\ \text{Sales} \\ \text{Amount}\end{array}$$

$$\begin{array}{c}\text{Net finished} \\ \text{transaction balance}\end{array} = \begin{array}{c}\text{Sales Made} \\ \text{Prior to} \\ \text{Settlement Date}\end{array} - \begin{array}{c}\text{Purchases Made} \\ \text{Prior to} \\ \text{Settlement Date}\end{array}$$

Each number is the average of two months.

---

the unit price, terms, interest rate, and duties of each party to the agreement. A copy of a *Basic Agreement Concerning Gensaki Transactions* is shown in Exhibit 8.

Target securities. Most domestic bonds (such as government bonds, local government bonds, corporate bonds, bank debentures, and special bonds) are eligible target securities for gensaki transactions. Foreign bonds with similar characteristics to domestic bonds are also

EXHIBIT 8: BASIC AGREEMENT CONCERNING "GENSAKI" TRANSACTIONS

THIS BASIC AGREEMENT CONCERNING "GENSAKI TRANSACTIONS" (hereinafter the "Basic Agreement") has been made and entered into this _____ day of _____, 19__ between _____ with its principal office at _____ (hereinafter the "Buyer") and _____, having its main office at _____ (hereinafter the "Seller") in connection with the "Gensaki" transactions to be entered by and between the Buyer and the Seller.

WHEREAS, each individual agreement for a "Gensaki" transaction shall be concluded in accordance with and subject to the terms and conditions of the Basic Agreement.

NOW THEREFORE, it is hereby agreed by and between the Buyer and the Seller as follows:

1. In this Basic Agreement and in each individual Agreement for a "Gensaki" transaction, the following terms shall have the respective meanings set forth in the following paragraphs:
   (1) "Gensaki Transaction" shall mean, with respect to a given description and quality of bonds, a trading of such bonds (hereinafter, the "Bonds") between the two parties hereto on a promise that the Seller will buy the Bonds back from the Buyer on an agreed settlement date at agreed prices.
   (2) "Starting Transaction" shall mean such transaction that the Seller sells the Bonds to the Buyer as stipulated in the individual Agreement for a Gensaki Transaction.
   (3) "Ending Transaction" shall mean such transaction that the Seller repurchases the Bonds from the Buyer as stipulated in the individual Agreement for a Gensaki Transaction.
   (4) "Settlement Date for the Starting Transaction" shall mean the date stipulated as the date of settlement of the Starting Transaction in the individual Agreement for a Gensaki Transaction.
   (5) "Settlement Date for the Ending Transaction" shall mean the date stipulated as the date of settlement of the Ending Transaction in the individual Agreement for a Gensaki Transaction.
   (6) "Amount Payable for the Starting Transaction" shall mean the cash amount which is stipulated as the amount to be paid by the Buyer for a Starting Transaction in the individual Agreement for a Gensaki Transaction.
   (7) "Amount Payable for the Ending Transaction" shall mean the cash amount which is stipulated as the amount to be paid by the Seller

(exhibit continues)

EXHIBIT 8: BASIC AGREEMENT CONCERNING "GENSAKI" TRANSACTIONS (continued)

(repurchaser) of the Bonds for an Ending Transaction in the individual Agreement for a Gensaki Transaction.

2. An Individual Agreement for each Gensaki Transaction shall be offered, negotiated and concluded by and between the parties hereto by telephone, telegraph or any other means of communication.

3. Upon conclusion of an Individual Agreement for a Gensaki Transaction, the Seller shall send to the Buyer a confirmation by telex indicating description of bonds to be used for the transaction, their prices, settlement dates, the Amount Payable and other necessary items. In return, the Buyer shall give instructions to the Seller for the settlement of the transaction.

The Seller's confirmation by telex shall be deemed to be an Individual Agreement for the Gensaki Transaction duly made and entered into between the Seller and the Buyer.

4. The settlement of the transaction shall be made between the trading account for the Buyer opened with the Seller and the Seller itself. Bonds bought by the Buyer shall be kept under Seller's safe custody.

5. In the event that one of the parties hereto becomes insolvent or an application for bankruptcy, corporate reorganization or similar relief has been filed by or against that party, the other party hereto may demand the immediate performance of all individual agreements for the Gensaki Transactions then in effect between the two parties hereto.

6. In the event that one of the parties hereto (hereinafter the "Defaulting Party") shall fail to perform the settlement for the Ending Transactions or the settlement, or fail to make the immediate performance of all individual Agreements in accordance with the provisions of Section 5 above, the other party (hereinafter the "Non-defaulting Party") may elect to cancel any or all individual agreement for the Gensaki Transactions then existing between the two parties hereto. The Defaulting Party shall immediately compensate the Non-defaulting Party any loss caused by the difference between the total sum including all of the Amount Payable for the Ending Transactions and for the Gensaki Transactions cancelled by the Non-defaulting Party in accordance with the above provisions and the amount calculated or disposed on the actual market prices of the Bonds stipulated in the cancelled Individual Agreements at the time of the cancellation.

If the Defaulting Party shall fail to make immediate payment for compensation, the Defaulting Party shall pay interest on the unpaid amount until actual payment shall be made at the rate of __% per annum above the Japanese official discount rate prevailing at that time on the unpaid amount.

**EXHIBIT 8:   BASIC AGREEMENT CONCERNING "GENSAKI"
TRANSACTIONS (continued)**

7. This Basic Agreement and each individual Agreement for the Gensaki Transaction shall be governed by and construed in accordance with the laws of Japan.
8. A Japanese court shall have jurisdiction in any and all disputes arising under this Basic Agreement and each individual Agreement for the Gensaki Transaction.
9. No modification of this Basic Agreement shall be in effect unless the Buyer and Seller agree to it in writing. The Buyer or the Seller may terminate this Basic Agreement by giving 30 days prior written notice. Any modification or termination, however, shall not affect the rights and obligations of both parties in connection with any individual Agreement for the Gensaki Transaction entered into prior to such modification or termination.

SIGNED BY_____   SIGNED BY_____
        for and on behalf of   for and on behalf of

Source: Daiwa Securites Co. Ltd.

are also included as possible target securities. In a broad sense, other money market instruments are also target securities. For example, domestic and foreign CDs, domestic and foreign CP, yen-denominated BA, and T-bills are all permitted to be sold by the gensaki method.

Newly issued government bonds that have trading restrictions for 40 days after issuance are not allowed to be sold under a gensaki transaction during this period.[11] In addition, stocks, convertible bonds, warrant bonds, investment trusts, and securities in loan trusts are also excluded as target securities for gensaki transactions. Registered bonds must be registered in the name of the gensaki seller since the bonds must be owned by the seller and maintained by the seller in a typical uri-gensaki transaction.

Contracted price. Gensaki is an "open market" investment in that the transaction price is determined freely by the supply and demand for gensaki. As such, the buyers and sellers negotiate the transaction price of a gensaki contract. However, in order to avoid wild swings in gensaki rates during periods of tight money supply, the MOF determined that gensaki prices should reflect the underlying price of the target security. The gensaki price theoretically should trade within a specific range of the security price. However, in practice there are many cases in which the book value of a security is far apart from the gensaki price.

Qualification of investors. Participants in the gensaki market are limited to corporations whose stocks are listed as well as similar companies that are not listed but are "trustworthy economically and socially."[12] Individuals are not allowed to participate in the market as either investors or fund-raisers. It is strictly an institutional market.

Term. A characteristic of itaku-gensaki is that the term of the seller must match the term of the buyer. In general, a gensaki contract can have a maturity of up to one year. Most of the transactions are for terms of between one and three months. It is important to note that gensaki contracts cannot be cancelled during the term of the agreement. As such, there is limited liquidity within the specified term of each contract. A firm could set up a reverse transaction with another party to, in effect, unwind the position, but the initial contract itself cannot be reversed.

Denomination. Gensaki is generally traded in amounts over 100 million yen in units of 10 million yen. Both the number of transactions and the dollar volume of transactions of contracts over 500 million yen have increased since 1984 (see Exhibit 9). For example, in 1984, approximately 22% of the kai-gensaki contracts and 86% of the dollar volume were in contracts of over 500 million yen. In 1987, these figures increased to 37% and 92%, respectively.[13]

Transactions became modernized and standardized as a result of the MOF report in 1976. During the earlier periods, when there were few open market short-term investments, the efficiency of the gensaki market was relatively low compared to the repurchase agreement markets in other countries, particularly in the U.S. Following the quick expansion of the CD market after it was introduced in 1979, interest rates between markets became linked, and the efficiency and commodity nature of the gensaki market increased. The volume of transactions naturally decreased between 1980 and 1984 as the open market developed and diversified. However, since 1984, gensaki volume has increased due to the increase in target securities, many of which are tax exempt.[14]

Major sellers, such as financial institutions, varied their fund-raising efforts by using CDs, large amount time deposits, foreign-denominated currency deposits, and the Euro markets. Life insurance companies decreased their use of gensaki during the low interest rate period in the early 1980s when other fund-raising vehicles were developed in the short-term market. However, uri-gensaki retains an important role during the settlement of accounts (mainly March and September) when banks demand greater deposit levels and companies respond by raising money in the gensaki market to increase deposits.

The bond inventories of securities companies have increased following the development and expansion of the bond market. The number of market participants has increased due to the allowance of financial institutions in the distribution of bonds. However, the increase in inventory has not led to an increase in gensaki transactions. The main reason for this is that securities companies now have alter-

EXHIBIT 9:   KAI-GENSAKI DEALINGS OF MAJOR SECURITIES COMPANIES

(1) Number Of Transactions

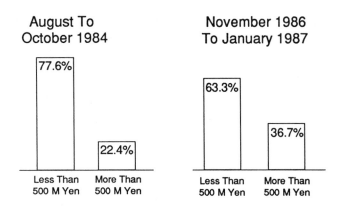

2) Amount Of Money

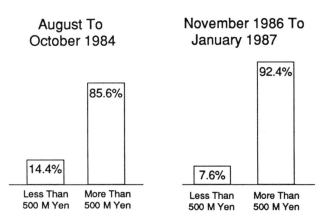

native fund-raising means. In addition, the firms do not carry as wide a range of bonds because of the increase in market participants. Securities companies are also holding more quality bonds in their portfolio for investment purposes and these bonds are still included in inventory.

MARKET PARTICIPANTS

Corporations have historically been the largest buyers of gensaki. Their liquidity positions have had a substantial impact on the level of gensaki rates. Like corporations, government and public authorities cannot participate in the call or bill markets (the inter-bank markets) so they are also active buyers in the gensaki market. Financial institutions, especially regional banks, agricultural financial institutions, and credit associations are mainly buyers. However, these institutions now seek to arbitrage rates by selling gensaki and investing in other short-term investments.

Securities companies have been the largest sellers of gensaki in order to carry out their bond-dealing businesses.[15] Their bond inventories fluctuate widely due to the fast-changing environment in Japan, and these inventory shifts have a significant influence on gensaki rates. For example, when inventories increase, the supply of gensaki also increases, which puts upward pressure on gensaki rates. City banks and life insurance companies have also been sellers of gensaki, mainly using itaku-gensaki. They sell gensaki both to raise short-term funds and to manage their bond portfolios.

We will now take a closer look at some of the major market participants in order to better understand their roles in the formation of the market. The major participants include securities companies, city banks, business corporations, governmental and public authorities, investment trusts, and finally, foreigners (see Exhibit 10).

Securities Companies

Securities companies, as stated earlier, hold large inventories of bonds in order to carry out their dealer function.[16] They raise funds by using these inventories as collateral in primarily jiko-gensaki transactions (transactions in which the securities companies use their

EXHIBIT 10: GENSAKI BALANCES OF MARKET PARTICIPANTS

(units 100M yen)

S = Sold (Uri)
B = Bought (Kai)

		1981	1982	1983	1984	1985	1986	1987
City Banks	S	6,028	4,201	2,467	1,299	303	1,885	2,249
	B	195	13	319	158	914	190	587
Regional	S	600	1,124	480	311	315	82	38
Banks	B	1,105	1,523	1,346	992	806	706	374
Long-Term	S	50	0	0	0	0	23	30
Credit Banks	B	254	188	7	0	52	14	0
Trust Banks	S	847	961	700	358	268	93	86
	B	478	600	614	1,479	4,333	12,005	13,540
Agriculture	S	2,677	966	3,164	1,051	299	1,982	727
& Forestry Banks	B	513	431	1,856	1,030	2,446	1,005	859
Mutual	S	357	989	313	396	114	183	92
Banks	B	705	279	373	223	93	1,131	936
Credit	S	399	1,202	841	286	10	177	117
Associations	B	2,014	869	1,542	243	349	481	1,108
Other	S	1,161	1,013	1,236	1,143	584	9,479	10,251
Financial	B	788	1,247	1,190	571	1,576	3,953	3,789
Institutions								
Insurance	S	1,710	2,373	5,194	3,099	7,043	5,934	8,955
Companies	B	2	72	377	426	251	92	900
Investment	S	0	0	14	0	0	0	
Trusts	B	0	1	12	13	14	2,397	2,782
Mutual Benefit	S	265	10	15	0	0	0	17
Associations	B	1,428	1,548	1,454	1,841	1,260	1,091	517
Business	S	2,344	2,401	1,717	1,079	1,000	1,613	2,498
Corporation	B	25,026	22,043	21,343	15,106	16,156	16,105	8,990
Other	S	33	66	35	58	171	48	2
Corporation	B	1,382	1,386	1,517	1,773	2,267	2,173	1,312
Foreigners	S	40	10	5	0	0	21	26
	B	8,117	5,505	3,249	2,198	4,045	4,058	5,203
Others	S	136	193	196	64	750	1,107	662
	B	2,803	7,330	7,679	9,529	11,633	19,197	19,579
Bond	S	28,163	27,626	26,510	26,474	35,562	48,532	32,473
Dealers	B	0	0	0	36	224	6,571	8,747
Total Balance		44,810	43,035	42,878	35,618	46,419	71,169	69,223

Source: Japan Securities Dealers Association.

own bonds and are the main parties to the transactions). As secondary market transactions increase, the amount of jiko-gensaki transactions should also increase in order to finance inventory between settlement dates of purchases and sales by securities companies. After the large increase in government bond sales after 1976, as well as the expansion of the secondary trading market for bonds, the share of uri-gensaki transactions by securities companies increased from 45% to 75%.

The expansion of the short-term money markets in Japan now gives the securities firms other choices for short-term funding for bond inventories. However, gensaki is still the best way to expand market participation and to increase investment funds. To cope with the needs of their clients, securities companies now hold target securities for gensaki that are not subject to the securities transfer tax (to be discussed later).

City Banks

City banks are one of the largest borrowers in the call money and bill discount markets. They are also one of the largest sellers, behind securities companies and insurance companies, in the gensaki market. The Bank of Japan had originally restricted the uri-gensaki balances of city banks. These restrictions were loosened beginning in 1978 as the government began to issue large amounts of government bonds. In October 1978, the balance restriction was increased from 5 billion yen to 20 billion yen. The restrictions were then increased to 50 billion yen in April 1979, then to 70 billion yen and finally to 100 billion yen before the restrictions were substantially abolished in April 1980.[17] City banks were allowed to deal freely in kai-gensaki in April 1981.

Following the liberalization of uri-gensaki, the balance of city banks has increased dramatically; their share of the total market has been between 14% and 18% of the total uri-gensaki balance since 1980.[18] However, because of the diversification of fund-raising vehicles such as CDs, large amount time deposits, and the call and bill discount markets, the weight of uri-gensaki is decreasing.

Business Corporations

Corporations hold a relatively high share of kai-gensaki, currently around 15% of the total balance. However, between 1976 and 1984, corporations held a much higher share of the kai-gensaki market—between 60% and 70%.[19] The decline in the balance can be attributed mainly to the diversification of the short-term market.

Corporations are still major participants, using the gensaki market as an efficient investment vehicle for idle funds. When the Japanese economy slows down in terms of GNP growth, corporations gain idle funds as investment in plant and equipment slows and inventory levels are reduced. Corporations then begin to place importance on the return on short-term funds under "zai-tech"; as a result, investment funds continue to flow into gensaki. The short-term nature of gensaki is also important as companies desire to maintain liquidity for unexpected needs for funds. Therefore, companies tend to invest in short-term investments with maturities corresponding to dividend payments dates, tax payments, bonus payments, etc.

Every year in June and December, when tax, bonus, and dividend payments concentrate, and again in March and September, when corporations cooperatively deposit funds in banks for the banks' settlement of accounts, the supply and demand in the gensaki market becomes thin compared to other months.[20] This seasonal demand for funds has an impact on the gensaki rates as well.

Of course, the diversification of the short-term markets has given corporations a wider range of investment opportunities. The CD market was created in 1979, the new Foreign Exchange Law was executed in 1980, open market sales of T-bills by the Bank of Japan began in 1981, and foreign CD and CP was introduced in 1984. Above all, large amount time deposits were allowed in 1985, causing large amounts of funds to flow away from gensaki. The corporations' share of gensaki has decreased each year since 1984.

Government and Public-Related Corporations

The Japanese government and related agencies hold the biggest balance of kai-gensaki (see Exhibit 10). The governmental agencies, (such as the Post Office Life Insurance Bureau, the Postal Savings

Bureau, and the Trust Fund Bureau) as well as the public corporations (such as the Japan Highway Corporation and the Japan Tobacco and Salt Corporation) have a combined market share of about 25% of the outstanding kai-gensaki.[21]

These agencies increasingly invest idle funds in the gensaki market rather than bank deposits because of the recent movement to improve the return on short-term funds. The curtailment of public finance payments under the "revolution of administration" means that governmental financial institutions and local public bodies have increased amounts of idle funds to invest in kai-gensaki.

In fact, kai-gensaki operations by the Trust Fund Bureau have been performed since 1980, not only to increase the efficient investment of funds, but also to adjust the short-term interest rates and support the government bond market. The Trust Fund Bureau and other agencies and public corporations generally buy gensaki from many securities companies and banks by means of competitive bidding.

Investment Trusts and Trust Banks

Following government-related corporations and agencies, trust banks are the next largest buyer of gensaki. Investment trusts hold a smaller share but their share is growing rapidly because of the recent "zai-tech" boom. Money trusts and investment trusts are mainly engaged in the general sale of stocks and bonds. However, they use the gensaki market as a short-term investment for the cash position of their portfolios, which varies depending on the condition of the stock and bond markets. These entities used to invest in the call and bill discount markets, but have increasingly moved to gensaki, CP, and CDs in order to improve returns on short-term investments.

Foreign Participation in Gensaki

Kai-gensaki by foreigners has increased steadily since 1979, when the Foreign Exchange and Foreign Trade Control Law was modified to allow overseas investors access to the gensaki market. These investors include central banks, governmental organizations, banks, and corporate investors. In December 1980, the Foreign Exchange and Foreign Trade Control Law was further amended to allow securities firms the opportunity to trade foreign currencies in connection with securities transactions. Securities firms thus were able to offer gensaki transactions in foreign currencies utilizing foreign exchange swap markets. Since this revision, foreign investors have become important participants in the gensaki market, holding about a 9% market share of kai-gensaki balances since 1981.[22]

Foreign volume of gensaki purchases has fluctuated widely, mainly due to changes in interest differentials between Euro-yen and gensaki rates. As mentioned earlier, Japanese gensaki rates increase seasonally, particularly in March, September, and December. For example, banks settle their accounts at the end of June and September. It is customary for corporations to oblige banks at these times by increasing bank deposits. Corporations increase deposits by moving out of gensaki, which causes rates to rise temporarily. These seasonal fluctuations in gensaki rates also cause the spread between Euro-yen rates and gensaki to widen. The increase in interest differentials causes foreign investors to enter the market and purchase gensaki.

In general, if the interest rate on gensaki is higher than interest rates on similar foreign investments plus swap costs, then foreign investors will purchase gensaki until the point where gensaki rates are again in line with foreign rates. These arbitrage transactions by nonresidents cause the gensaki market to be responsive to the overseas rates plus the swap costs reflected in the foreign exchange.

PROBLEMS OF THE BOND GENSAKI MARKET

The bond gensaki market is growing much slower than other short-term open-market vehicles. Of course, one of the reasons is the diversification and proliferation of competitive investments. However, the bond gensaki market itself has some significant problems.

High Cost of Fund Raising

A bond gensaki transaction is, substantially, a financial transaction between a borrower of funds and an investor of funds. However, the MOF defines bond gensaki as a method of bond sales so that a securities transaction tax is imposed on the seller of the bonds (the borrower of funds). Currently, the tax rate is 3/10,000 of the transfer price for both government and straight bonds. For securites companies that sell bonds, the tax rate is 1/10,000 of the transfer price. Banks and other financial institutions that deal in gensaki are treated as securities companies in terms of the transaction tax (Securities Transaction Law, Article 65-2-1).[23] There is no transaction tax for Treasury bills (discount short-term government bills).

The securities transaction tax is imposed on the bond when it is sold, so that bond gensaki transactions are taxed at the initial sale of the bond and also again at the time of repurchase. Therefore, each jiko-gensaki transaction is taxed at the rate of 4 sen (1 sen = 1/100 yen) per 100 yen in face value. For itaku-gensaki, the tax is 8 sen per 100 yen in face value. (See Exhibit 11 for a tax illustration.)[24]

The seller in a bond gensaki transaction generally bears the tax of the buyer in that the gensaki rate is quoted as the net rate after consideration of the transaction tax. For example, a bond gensaki rate quoted at 4% to the buyer (investor) means that the cost to the seller (borrower) is 4% plus the securities transaction tax (the tax on the initial sale plus the tax at repurchase).

The transaction tax has two negative effects on bond gensaki. The first is that the shorter the term of the gensaki contract, the larger the percentage increase in the gensaki rate. For example, a jiko-gensaki transaction for 5 days will have a 2.92% increase in the gensaki rate attributable to the transaction tax. A jiko-gensaki transaction with a term of 90 days will have only a .162% increase in the gensaki rate (see Exhibit 12).[25] This cost-up effect of shorter maturities is a major problem, particularly because of the strong demand for shorter-term maturities.

The second major problem is that the transaction tax causes bond-gensaki to carry significantly higher costs than other short-term investments such as the call and bill discount markets and the CD market. For example, assume that a company wanted to raise 1 billion yen for one month. The call and bill discount markets would carry an added cost of 200 yen from a revenue stamp tax. A CD gensaki transaction would cost 600 yen in notary charges (administrative fees). An itaku-gensaki transaction would carry a much larger cost of 800,000 yen due to the transaction tax (see Exhibit 13).[26] Securities companies are currently demanding that the securities transac-

EXHIBIT 11: SECURITIES TRANSACTION TAX

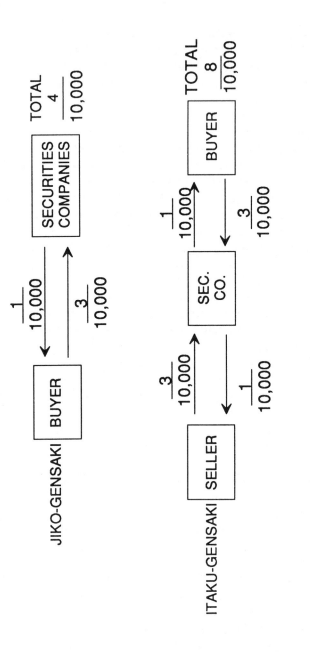

EXHIBIT 12: INTEREST RATE INCREASE (COST-UP) DUE TO SECURITIES TRANSACTION TAX

(%)

	Days					
	5	10	20	30	60	90
Jiko-Gensaki	2.92	1.46	0.73	0.49	0.24	0.16
Itaku-Gensaki	5.84	2.92	1.46	0.97	0.49	0.32

tion tax be abolished, or at least reduced, so that bond gensaki transactions can remain competitive with other investments.

Shortening the Settlement Period for Bonds

Another problem under the current system of gensaki is that the settlement period for bonds was shortened in August 1987. Prior to that time, settlement occurred three times per month—on the 10th, 20th, and the end of the month. After August 1987, three additional days were added per month—the 5th, 15th, and 25th. That is, the period between one settlement date and the next was shortened from 10 days to 5 days.

Bond gensaki transactions are used by securities companies and financial institutions to finance inventory between settlement dates. By shortening the period between settlements, the terms of the

EXHIBIT 13: TRANSACTION COSTS OF MAJOR SHORT-TERM MARKETS

Case: Raise 1 billion yen for 1 month

Market	Call	Bill Discount	CD Gensaki	Bond Itaku-Gensaki
Cost	200 Yen	200 Yen	600 Yen	800,000 Yen
Type	Revenue Stamp	Revenue Stamp	Notary Charges	Securities Transaction Tax

gensaki transactions were also shortened to match financing needs. The shortened gensaki term tends to increase the number of rollovers for longer-term financings, which increases volume and increases the securities transfer tax. The shortened period also has the cost-up effect described above, in that shorter maturities have higher percentage increases in gensaki rates than do longer maturities due to the transfer tax.

The shortened settlement period also makes it more cumbersome to transfer the bonds used for gensaki transactions because of the volume increase. The settlement period is expected to become shorter and shorter in the future as the bond market develops. Therefore, the gensaki market will become less competitive with other short-term investments unless changes are made in the tax system and the delivery system under gensaki contracts.

DETERMINANTS OF THE GENSAKI RATE

The gensaki market is quite different from the call and bill discount markets where rates are restricted by the Bank of Japan. These markets are known as the interbank markets and are generally limited to financial institutions. The gensaki market was the first "open market" short-term investment with rates determined freely by supply and demand of funds. Rates are determined by buyers and sellers of gensaki contracts and are influenced by five major elements.

Supply and Demand

The supply and demand characteristics in the market will affect gensaki rates. For example, when securities companies hold a large inventory of bonds, they will try to finance the inventories through gensaki contracts. The increase in supply causes the rates to rise as the securities companies try to attract investors. On the other hand, when inventories are low, rates tend to fall as demand exceeds supply.

Financial Condition

Economic conditions strongly influence gensaki rates. Tight monetary conditions cause the demand for funds (supply of gensaki) to increase, which tends to drive rates up. The most striking example was during the oil shock and tight monetary period between 1973 and 1975. Gensaki rates increased dramatically to close to 20% as institutions rushed into the gensaki market to raise short-term funds. During periods of easy money, the demand for funds is low and rates tend to fall.

The level and trend of the call and bills discount rates will also have an impact on gensaki rates. The call market rates are restricted by the Bank of Japan and more or less serve as the official policy rate of the government. Financial institutions will use the differential between these markets to earn arbitrage profits and, at the same time, to cause rates to move closer together. As the gensaki market matures, it is becoming difficult to see whether the gensaki rates are influencing the official rates or vice versa.

The financial conditions overseas will also influence gensaki rates. As noted previously, if gensaki rates are higher than the cost to borrow abroad plus swap costs, then rates will be arbitraged and pushed back in line with foreign participants. The revision of the Foreign Exchange and Foreign Trade Control Laws in 1980 has significantly increased the influence of foreign markets on gensaki rates.

Competitive Investments

The diversification of the open markets through the proliferation of new short-term vehicles has altered the supply and demand characteristics for gensaki. Investments such as CDs and large amount time deposits have taken a larger share of the total open market over the past few years. Many of the new investments have tax advantages over gensaki that have increased the movement toward the other investments.

Seasonal Effects

Money becomes scarce at certain times of the year due to the settlement of accounts for corporations and financial institutions (see Exhibit 14). March, September, and December are particularly tight months in which gensaki rates tend to increase. In other months, like April, October, and January, the abundance of funds increases after

EXHIBIT 14a: TYPICAL MONTHLY PATTERN FOR SUPPLY AND DEMAND FOR FUNDS

Bank of Japan Note Issue

Month	+ Withdrawal – Increased Note Issuance	Major Influential Factors for		+ Net payment – Net receipt
		Increase	Withdrawal	
January	Large +		Flowback of December bonuses and year-end spendings on a large scale	Large –
February	Small –	Outlays for upcoming school registration fees / Funds procurement before closing of fiscal year		Small –
March	Small –	Funds for settling bills at fiscal year-end, tuition fees and leisure		Large +
April	Small –	Fund demand for tuition fees, annuities and leisure	Reflux of term-end settlement funds	Large +
May	Fairly large +		Flowback of the money spent by the public during spring vacation	Small +
June	Large –	Fund demand for summer bonuses and for mid-year gift giving		Small –

EXHIBIT 14a (continued): TYPICAL MONTHLY PATTERN FOR SUPPLY AND DEMAND FOR FUNDS

Bank of Japan Note Issue

Month	+ Withdrawal – Increased Note Issuance	Major Influential Factors for Increase	Major Influential Factors for Withdrawal	+ Net payment – Net receipt
July	0	Funds demand for leisure and "bon" season related travel	Flowback of the cash paid out in summer bonuses or for mid-year gifts during the month of June	Small –
August	Small +		Reflux of bonus funds and "bon" season spendings	Large –
September	0			Small +
October	Small –	Consumption up after payments for new crops of rice		Small +
November	Small –	Funds for the purchase of rice and for leisure		Large +
December	The largest in the year –	Payments of year-end bonuses Increases in cash requirements for year-end gift giving, preparations for new year and payment of year-end bills		Large +

(exhibit continues)

EXHIBIT 14b: TYPICAL MONTHLY PATTERN FOR SUPPLY AND DEMAND FOR FUNDS

Treasury Funds

Month	Major Factors for Receipts	Major Factors for Disbursements	Credit Facility of the Bank of Japan	The Money Market
January	Receipt of withholding taxes on bonuses and year-end adjustment of income taxes Increases in postal savings		Contraction	Relaxes
February	Repayments on long-term loans made by the Trust Fund Bureau to local public bodies	Special grants-in-aid	Increases	Tightens
March	Corporate income tax for the term ending September Declared income tax	Payments for public works projects General payments and increased payments by the National Railways and Telegraphic Corporation	Breaks even	Tightens
April		Adjustment payments of appropriations authorized for the preceding fiscal year Trust Fund Bureau and Postal Insurance loans Grants-in-aid Annuities	Sharp contraction	Relaxes
May	Premiums on workers' compensation insurance	Trust Fund Bureau and Postal Insurance loans	Contraction	Relaxes

Month	Receipts	Major Factors for Disbursements	Credit Facility of the Bank of Japan	The Money Market
June	Corporate income taxes for the term ending in March Postal savings out of bonuses	Grants-in-aid Summer bonuses to public employees	Increases sharply	Tightens
July	Withholding taxes on summer bonuses and increases in postal savings	Payments made by the government for the purchase of rice and tobacco	Increases	Tightens
August	Withholding taxes on bonuses paid by private firms Declared income taxes for the first quarter Repayments on Trust Fund Bureau loans (long-term)		Increases sharply	Tightens
September	Income taxes (deferred payments) for the term ending in March Repayments of Trust Fund Bureau loans (long-term) Payment of workers' compensation insurance premiums	Grants-in-aid Payments for early harvested rice	Contraction	Relaxes
October		Funds for the purchase of rice and tobacco	Contraction	Relaxes

(exhibit continues)

EXHIBIT 14b (continued): TYPICAL MONTHLY PATTERN FOR SUPPLY AND DEMAND FOR FUNDS

Treasury Funds

Month	Major Factors for		Credit Facility of the Bank of Japan	The Money Market
	Receipts	Disbursements		
November		Funds for the purchase of rice and tobacco (which reaches a peak) Grants-in-aid	Sharp contraction	Relaxes sharply
December	Corporate income taxes (those previously deferred for the term ending in September) Declared income tax Repayment of principal and interest on long-term loans made by Trust Fund Bureau	Payments for public works projects General payments by the National Railways and Telegraph Corporation	Increases sharply	Tightens sharply

Source: Daiwa Securities Co. Ltd.

cooperative deposits are released from banks, causing gensaki rates to fall.[27]

Interest Rate Arbitrage

Transactions that focus on the difference between gensaki rates and other rates, such as systematic deposit rates, the Euro-yen rates and other open market rates, will cause these rates to move together. Arbitrage activities are very important to the efficiency of the market. As the Japanese market continues to liberalize, arbitrage will play more of a role in influencing all rates, including gensaki.

APPLICATIONS OF GENSAKI

Kai-Gensaki

A kai-gensaki transaction involves the purchase of gensaki (lending funds). Kai-gensaki transactions are used for several different reasons by various participants in the market.

One use of kai-gensaki is to capture the seasonal changes in the gensaki rates. An institution could purchase gensaki in March, September, and December when rates increase due to the scarcity of funds. Foreigners are particularly aware of this type of investment pattern.

Kai-gensaki is also used for interest rate arbitrage transactions. If rates are lower in other markets such as the CD and CP markets, then companies will borrow in the other markets and lend funds in the gensaki market in order to earn arbitrage profits between the two markets. Foreign investors will also invest funds in kai-gensaki as part of their arbitrage efforts between overseas short-term rates and Japanese short-term rates.

A third use is to purchase kai-gensaki as a strategy to pursue high current income. This is done by entering into kai-gensaki transactions where the underlying collateral are high coupon bonds.

A fourth use of kai-gensaki is to purchase it as a super short-term (within a week) investment. Securities companies hold certain types of bonds that are not subject to the transaction tax, such as Treasury bills. These securities are attractive collateral for short-term gensaki transactions at competitive rates. Rates usually match the rate that an investor could get in the restricted call market.

Business corporations use kai-gensaki in order to boost reserves for uncollectible accounts receivable at the end of the year to produce tax advantages. Kai-gensaki is allowed to be counted in the reserves for uncollectible accounts if the term of the gensaki agreement spans two tax years. As a result, corporations will invest in kai-gensaki near year end to increase the loss reserve and produce tax write-offs.

Banks in Japan must establish a reserve against possible price fluctuations of their government bond portfolios. Profits at year-end will be affected by the increase or decrease in the balance of government bonds held. Banks can adjust their balances through the use of gensaki transactions with government bonds as the underlying collateral.[28] Kai-gensaki is used to increase the balance of government bonds.

Uri-Gensaki

Uri-gensaki is used when an institution wants to raise funds by selling gensaki (borrowing funds). As with kai-gensaki, there are a variety of motives for using uri-gensaki.

Companies can lower the cost of borrowing funds by using uri-gensaki with starting dates on settlement dates such as the 10th, 20th, and end of the month. On these dates, there are generally more buyers because the securities houses clear their inventory and are not performing jiko-gensaki operations. Therefore, the cost of borrowing tends to be lower as the demand for collateral exceeds supply. Similarly, uri-gensaki transactions, in order to achieve a lower cost, can be set for longer maturities, say 2 or 3 months, than typical jiko-gensaki transactions by securities firms.

In an opposite manner from kai-gensaki, banks can use uri-gensaki of government bonds in order to avoid the increase in reserve for price fluctuations of government bonds.

It is also possible to lower the book value of a target bond by means of uri-gensaki. To lower the book value, a company must use a bond that will have a repurchase price that is lower than the initial price of the gensaki contract. In Japan, this is known as "tanka-sage," which means "lowering below the unit price," or "boka-sage," which means "below the book value."[29] There are two conditions that must be met in order to produce this result. First, the target security must be an interest-bearing bond. Second, the coupon of the bond divided by the selling price plus accrued interest must be greater than the gensaki rate. That is, when the accrued interest during the gensaki term is greater than the equivalent interest on the gensaki, then the repurchase price is reduced to compensate for the difference. Therefore, the lower the gensaki rate and the higher the coupon interest, the greater the reduction in book value of the target security. The sellers can raise funds and at the same time lower the book value of their bond holdings. However, the sellers also forfeit the accrued interest on the bonds that they would have received if they held the bonds outright.

Uri-gensaki is often sold to nonprofit organizations such as local public authorities that do not have to pay the transaction tax. These sales lower the cost of funds since no transfer tax is due on the repurchase of the bonds.

Companies also use gensaki transactions near year-end to reduce their portfolios of low coupon bonds and less liquid bonds. By doing so, the companies improve the constitution of their portfolios for financial reporting purposes at year-end.

INTEREST RATE ARBITRAGE

Gensaki versus Other Open-Market Investments

The proliferation of open-market securities in the short-term money market since 1979 has improved the efficiency and coordination of short-term rates through arbitrage transactions. Investors can now choose from a variety of open-market securities including domestic and foreign CP and CD, large amount time deposits, foreign currency-denominated deposits, CD gensaki, and bond gensaki. The flow of funds will be attracted to the higher rates: for example, if the CD rate increased, the CD gensaki rate would also tend to increase and idle funds would flow to CD gensaki. The demand for bond gensaki would decrease, which would then cause rates to increase toward the CD gensaki rates. The open market forces the liberal interest rate vehicles to sharply influence one another.

Gensaki versus Call and Bill Discount Rates

Generally speaking, financial institutions take part in the call and bill discount markets as a means of raising funds or investing funds on a short-term basis. The bill discount rate is normally higher than the call rate because of its longer maturities. If gensaki rates are above the call and bill discount rates, then financial institutions will raise funds in the call market and invest the funds in kai-gensaki in order to earn the interest rate spread. On the contrary, if gensaki rates (including the transaction tax) drift below the cost of raising funds in the call and bill discount markets, financial institutions will raise funds through uri-gensaki and invest the proceeds in the call market. These arbitrage activities of financial institutions help correlate the movements of the open market with the movements of the more restricted interbank markets. It is becoming less clear as to whether the call and bill discount rates are influencing the open-market rates or whether the open-market rates are forcing the BOJ to set interbank rates in line with the open market.

Gensaki versus Foreign Interest Rates

As discussed earlier, since the amendment of the Foreign Exchange and Foreign Trade Control Laws in 1980, foreigners have increased their activity in the gensaki market. Overseas investors will arbitrage the spread between gensaki rates and Euro-yen rates plus swap costs. For example, as bond gensaki rates increase above Euro-yen plus swap costs, foreigners will increase kai-gensaki operations in order to earn the spread between rates. Nonresident purchases of gensaki tend to increase in March, September, and December when seasonal factors force gensaki rates to rise. Foreign investors are becoming increasingly important participants in the Japanese open markets, forcing Japanese rates to respond to foreign market rates.

RATE OF RETURN CALCULATIONS FOR GENSAKI

In general, there are two types of collateral used for bond gensaki transactions. The first are interest-bearing bonds, and the second are discount bonds. The return calculations for gensaki transactions are different depending on which type of collateral underlies the transaction. In addition, with interest-bearing securities, the return calculations will vary depending on whether an interest payment occurs during the gensaki term. Also, with interest-bearing bonds, any accrued interest incurred prior to the transaction date is paid to the seller of the gensaki contract by the buyer of the contract. Regardless of the type of collateral, gensaki transactions are calculated on a single-day basis (i.e., March 1 to March 3 = 2 days) using simple interest. The gensaki rate is usually calculated on an annual basis using 365 days. In the case of kai-gensaki, the rate represents the net interest earned. However, in the case of uri-gensaki, it is necessary to calculate the total cost of funds including the transaction tax which is charged to the original seller.

Return (Cost) Calculations For Kai-Gensaki (Uri-Gensaki)

The following examples show the basic calculations for both kai-gensaki and uri-gensaki transactions. The examples are classified by three broad categories. The first is the calculation for gensaki transactions involving discount bonds including examples of both kai and uri-gensaki transactions. The second illustration is for interest-bearing bonds that do not incur an interest payment during the term of the gensaki. Again examples are included for both kai and uri-gensaki. Finally, illustrations of interest-bearing bonds that incur interest payments during the gensaki term are given for the two types of gensaki.

Calculating rates of return (cost of funds) for kai-gensaki (uri-gensaki) varies somewhat depending on the nature of the collateral and the timing of the contract. The two major types of gensaki transactions that affect return (cost) calculations are those that use discount bonds as collateral and those that use interest-bearing bonds as collateral. In addition, interest-bearing bonds may or may not have coupon payments during the gensaki term which will also affect return (cost) calculations. Examples are shown below for kai-gensaki and uri-gensaki transactions using both discount and interest-bearing bonds. We will focus on interest-bearing bonds where there is no coupon payment during the term of the gensaki, since this is far more prevalent than interest-bearing bonds with coupon payments during the gensaki term.

First, we need to present two basic identities:

1. Basic Equation of Kai-Gensaki

$$\frac{\text{purchase}}{\text{payment}} \times \left(1 + \frac{\text{kai–gensaki}}{\text{rate}} \times \frac{\text{No. of}}{\text{gensaki days}} \right) = \frac{\text{sales}}{\text{payment}} - \frac{\text{securities}}{\text{transaction tax}}$$

2. Basic Equation of Uri-Gensaki

$$\frac{\text{repurchase}}{\text{payment}} = \frac{\text{sales}}{\text{payment}} \times \left(1 + \frac{\text{uri–gensaki}^*}{\text{rate}} \times \frac{\text{No. of}}{\text{gensaki days}} \right)$$

*Use gross rate =
$$\frac{\text{kai–gensaki}}{\text{rate}} + \frac{.0002^{\#} + .0003^{\#\#}}{\text{No. of gensaki days}} \times 365$$

#Securities company transaction tax
##Buyer's transaction tax.

The first two examples below are of kai-gensaki return calculations showing both the discount bond method and the interest-bearing bond method. The last two examples are of uri-gensaki cost of capital calculations, again demonstrating the discount bond method and the interest-bearing bond method.

EXAMPLE I: Kai-Gensaki Discount Bond Method

- — invest in kai-gensaki from Sept. 30 to Oct. 31 (31 days)
- — face value of discount bond = 100M yen
- — gensaki rate = 4.6%
- — unit purchase price = 105 yen

1. Calculation of sell-back price

Sell-back price =

$$\frac{105 \times \left(1 + .046 \times \dfrac{31}{365}\right)}{\left(1 - \dfrac{3}{10,000^*}\right)} = 105.442M$$

*Transfer tax

2. Calculation of purchase payment

Face value × unit price =

$$100M \times \frac{105}{100} = 105,000,000 \text{ yen}$$

3. Calculation of sell-back proceeds

Face value × sell–back price =

$$100M \times \frac{105.442}{100} = 105,442,000 \text{ yen}$$

Transaction tax =

$$100M \times \frac{105.442}{100} \times \frac{3}{10,000} = (31,632)$$

Total sell-back proceeds = 105,410,368 yen

4. Verification of gensaki rate

Gensaki rate =

$$\frac{105,410,368 - 105,000,000}{105,000,000} \times \frac{365}{31} \times 100 = 4.6\%$$

EXAMPLE II: Kai-Gensaki Interest-Bearing Bond Method

— invest in kai-gensaki from Sept. 30 to Oct. 31 (31 days)
— face value of bond = 100M yen
— coupon = 6% paid on June 20 and Dec. 20
— gensaki rate = 4.6%
— unit purchase price = 104 yen

1. Calculation of sell-back unit price

$$\frac{\left(104 + 6.0 \times \frac{102}{365}\right)^{*} \times \left(1 + .046 \times \frac{31}{365}\right) - \left(6.0 \times \frac{133}{365}\right)^{**}}{\left(1 - \frac{3}{10,000}\right)^{***}} = 103.935$$

*Accrued interest - start
**Accrued interest - end
***Transfer tax

2. Calculation of purchase payment

Face value × unit purchase price =

$$100M \times \frac{104}{100} = 104,000,000 \text{ yen}$$

Accrued interest =

$$100M \times \frac{6}{100} \times \frac{102}{365} = 1,676,712$$

Total payment = <u>105,676,712</u> yen

3. Calculation of sell-back proceeds

Face value × sell–back unit price =

$$100M \times \frac{103.935}{100} = 103{,}935{,}000 \text{ yen}$$

Accrued interest =

$$100M \times \frac{6}{100} \times \frac{133}{365} = 2{,}186{,}301$$

Transaction tax =

$$100M \times \frac{103.935}{100} \times \frac{3}{10{,}000} = (31{,}180)$$

Total sell-back proceeds = <u>106,090,121</u> yen

4. Verification of gensaki rate

Gensaki rate =

$$\frac{106{,}090{,}121 - 105{,}676{,}712}{105{,}676{,}712} = 4.6\%$$

EXAMPLE III: Uri-Gensaki Discount Bond Method

— raise funds using uri-gensaki from Sept. 30 to Oct. 31 (31 days)
— face value of discount bond = 100M yen
— gensaki rate = 5.0% (gross rate)
— unit sales price = 98 yen

1. Calculation of unit repurchase price

$$98 \times \left(1 + .05 \times \frac{31}{365}\right) = 98.417$$

2. Calculation of sales proceeds

Face value × unit sales price =

$$100M \times \frac{98}{100} = 98,000,000 \text{ yen}$$

Transaction tax =

$$100M \times \frac{98}{100} \times \frac{3}{10,000} = (29,400)$$

Total sales proceeds = 97,970,600 yen

3. Calculation of repurchase payment

Face value × unit repurchase price =

$$100M \times \frac{98.417}{100} = 98,417,000 \text{ yen}$$

4. Verification of gensaki rate

Gensaki rate =

$$\frac{98,417,000 - 98,000,000}{98,000,000} \times \frac{365}{31} \times 100 = 5.0\%$$

5. Net cost of funds after transaction tax

Net cost =

$$\frac{98,417,000 - 97,970,600}{97,970,600} \times \frac{365}{31} \times 100 = 5.364\%$$

EXAMPLE IV: Uri-Gensaki Interest-Bearing Bond Method

— raise funds using uri-gensaki from Sept. 30 to Nov. 30
— face value of bond = 100M yen
— coupon = 7.5% paid on March 20 and Sept. 20
— gensaki rate = 5.0% (gross rate)
— unit sales price = 110 yen

1. Calculation of unit repurchase price

$$\left(110 + 7.5 \times \frac{10}{365}\right) \times \left(1 + .05 \times \frac{61}{365}\right) - \left(7.5 \times \frac{71}{365}\right) = 109.668$$

2. Calculation of sales proceeds

Face value × unit sales price =

$$100M \times \frac{110}{100} = 110,000,000$$

Accrued interest =

$$100M \times \frac{7.5}{100} \times \frac{10}{365} = 205,479$$

Transaction tax =

$$100M \times \frac{110}{100} \times \frac{3}{10,000} = (33,000)$$

Total sales proceeds = <u>110,172,479</u> yen

3. Calculation of repurchase payment

Face value × unit repurchase price =

$$100M \times \frac{109.668}{100} = 109,668,000 \text{ yen}$$

Accrued interest =

$$100M \times \frac{7.5}{100} \times \frac{71}{365} = 1,458,904$$

Total repurchase payment = 111,126,904 yen

4. Verification of gensaki rate

Gensaki rate =

$$\frac{111,126,904 - 110,205,479}{110,205,479*} \times \frac{365}{61} \times 100 = 5.0\%$$

*Pre-tax sales proceeds

5. Net cost of funds after transaction tax

Net cost =

$$\frac{111,126,904 - 110,172,479}{110,172,479} \times \frac{365}{61} \times 100 = 5.183\%$$

SUMMARY

The Japanese gensaki market has been a major factor in the liberalization of Japanese interest rates. Gensaki was the first "open market" investment with rates determined freely by the supply and demand for funds. The development of the open markets in Japan has been dramatic since 1976, when Gensaki was first officially recognized by the Ministry of Finance (MOF). Due to the expansion of the open markets since 1980, gensaki now represents a smaller market share. However, the importance of gensaki as the instrument that stimulated the liberalization of Japanese interest rates should not be diminished just because its market share has declined.

This chapter focused mainly on gensaki, from its historical development to current market trends. Of course, other short-term markets are significant. However, to fully understand the open markets, one must have an understanding of gensaki. The development of other short-term open markets was caused by the success of the gensaki market.

ENDNOTES

[1] Japan Securities Research Institute, *Securities Market in Japan 1988*, Tokyo, December 1987, p. 93.

[2] Ibid., p. 96.

[3] Nihon Keizai Shimbunsha [Nihon Keizai Shimbun, Inc.], *Tanki Kinyu Shijou* [in Japanese, titled translated as *Short-Term Financial Market*], Tokyo, 1987, p. 96.

[4] Ibid., p. 97.

[5] Ibid., p. 132.

[6] Ibid., p. 133.

[7] Japan Securities Research Institute, op. cit., p. 93.

[8] T. Morita and M. Hara (eds.), *Tokyo Money Market* [in Japanese, titled translated as the same], Tokyo: Yuhikakusensho, 3rd edition, 1988, p. 128.

[9] *Introduction to Japanese Bonds*, Daiwa Securities Co., Ltd., 1987, p. 65.

[10] Ibid.

[11] Nihon Keizai Shimbunsha, op. cit., p. 109.

[12] Ibid.

[13] Ibid., p. 110.

[14] Ibid., p. 111.

[15] Morita and Hara, op. cit., p. 67.

[16] Ibid., p. 138.

[17] Ibid., p. 139.

[18] Ibid.

[19] Ibid., p. 140.

[20] *Introduction to Japanese Bonds*, op. cit., p. 67.

[21] Morita and Hara, op. cit., p. 142.

[22] *Introduction to Japanese Bonds*, op. cit., p. 67.

[23] Morita and Hara, op. cit., p. 134.

[24] Ibid.

[25] Ibid., p. 135.

[26] Ibid.

[27] *Introduction to Japanese Bonds*, op. cit., p. 69.

[28] Morita and Hara, op. cit., p. 153.

[29] Ibid.

CHAPTER 7

Japanese Government-Related Organization Bond Market

Yiu C. Chan
New York, N.Y.

Shigeo Sasahara
Tokyo, Japan

In fiscal year 1987, nine government-related organizations issued a total of ¥2.2 trillion (US$16 billion) worth of bonds through public placement that carried explicit guarantees on interest and principal from the Japanese government. In the same year, ¥36 trillion of government-guaranteed bonds (GGBs) were traded. GGBs are the second largest public bond sector, ranking after the Japanese government bonds (JGBs) in both the primary and secondary markets. While the issuance and trading in the secondary market of government-guaranteed bonds resemble closely those of the JGBs, they nonetheless provide some unique features that deserve attention.

GGBs also can be issued through private placements. This chapter, however, will only briefly discuss GGBs issued through this method because most privately placed GGBs are not traded in the secondary markets and hence are of little interest to investors. Unless otherwise specified, all discussion and information on GGBs refer to those that are publicly offered.

Many small Japanese domestic investors and foreign financial institutions are unfamiliar with government-guaranteed bonds. During the process of writing this chapter, we found that even the Japanese securities firms do not have organized information on this relatively small segment of the public bond market. The lack of information and the dominance of the GGB market by major Japanese institutions have hindered the growth of the secondary market.

The origin of the GGB can be traced back to the early 1950s when they were first introduced and became a very significant source of public finance for the postwar Japanese economy. The appeal of the GGBs, however, decreased when the Japanese government started to issue government bonds in the mid-1960s. As part of a broad economic liberalization move by the Japanese government starting in the early 1980s, several of the government-related organizations were privatized; this reduced the number of organizations eligible to issue government-guaranteed bonds. In fact, issuance of GGBs has dropped from a peak of ¥2.8 trillion in fiscal year 1986.

Given the likelihood of further privatization and the reduced appeal of the GGBs, questions seem to arise around the future of the GGBs within the public bonds sector. Thus, the chapter has two objectives: (1) to provide as complete as possible a description of the current state and practice of the GGB primary and secondary markets, and (2) to give some indication on the future of the GGBs.

ROLE OF GOVERNMENT-RELATED ORGANIZATION BONDS

Government-related organization bonds are bonds issued by public corporations and special-purpose companies established under special laws. These government-related organizations are involved in various public activities, ranging from infrastructure construction to promotion of small businesses. Funding of these activities comes primarily from two sources: loans from the government and governmental organizations, and the sale of bonds.

These organizations issue two kinds of bonds: government-guaranteed bonds and non-government-guaranteed bonds. Principal and interest on government-guaranteed bonds are guaranteed by the Japanese government. The amount to be issued with government guarantees is determined each year by the Fiscal Investment and Loan Program which is administered by the Ministry of Finance and has to be approved by the Diet. Essentially, the Ministry of Finance determines how much government-guaranteed bonds each of the government-related organizations can issue in each year. Very often, the annual approved issue volumes of government-guaranteed bonds by these organizations meet only part of their annual budgets and they still need other financing means, e.g., loans and non-government-guaranteed bonds. The mix of the several financing sources varies for each organization.

All bonds issued by government-related organizations are secured by a "general mortgage" as required by law. The general mortgage entitles the bondholders to a second priority claim on all assets of the issuing organizations in case of insolvency. (Debt holders with "preferential right" have the first priority claim.[1])

Government-Guaranteed Bonds

Immediately after World War II, the Japanese government was prohibited from guaranteeing financial obligations of other institutions. However, as the need for public finance expanded rapidly with the postwar economy, and the Japanese government was chronically in financial difficulties, the ban on government guarantees was lifted. Issuance of government-guaranteed bonds by government-related organizations was an essential means for public financing as the Japanese government did not issue any government bonds until 1966.

Issuance of the government-guaranteed bonds began in 1953 as an important source of financing the revitalization of the postwar Japanese economy. Railway and telephone businesses, which used to issue public bonds, were reorganized into public corporations, the Japanese National Railways (JNR) and the Nippon Telegraph and Telephone Public Corporation (NTT). These were the first issuers of the government-guaranteed bonds.[2]

The government-guaranteed bonds provided a unique role in financing the postwar Japan, to the mid-1960s. Since the mid-1960s when the government started to issue government bonds, the reliance on government-guaranteed bonds for public financing decreased. Since the late 1970s, as part of a fiscal policy to liberalize the Japanese economy, several of the prominent government-related organizations have been privatized. From the government's point of view, the government-guaranteed bonds serve as an alternative to

JGBs for raising government debt. Yet given the privatization drive, it becomes questionable whether GGBs can continue to have a unique role within the government's portfolio of financing tools. From the investors' point of view, these government-guaranteed bonds are not so different from the JGBs or the local government bonds (LGBs) and carry very similar terms and creditworthiness.[3]

GGBs are issued through public offerings and private placements. We will focus on publicly offered GGBs, of which the issuance methods and trading patterns will be discussed later in this chapter. Privately-placed GGBs will be addressed briefly here.

Most of the privately placed GGBs are not allowed to be transferred to another entity by the original investors and hence cannot be traded on the secondary markets. These bonds, therefore, are not obtainable by many investors and have only a minor role in the secondary markets.

Private-placement GGBs provide more variety of coupon rate and maturity structures, e.g., super long-term bonds (15 years) and floating rate bonds. They are acquired mainly by the Norinchukin Bank, the Zenshinren Bank, trust banks and sometimes local governments.[4] Exhibit 1 provides two examples of private-placement GGBs.

Non-Government-Guaranteed Bonds

The other kind of bonds which government-related organizations issue are non-government-guaranteed bonds. As mentioned previously, the issuing organizations do not have much influence on the annual appropriation of government-guaranteed bond issues, and non-guaranteed bonds represent one alternative when there is insufficient funding. The non-government-guaranteed bonds do not carry explicit guarantees from the government, and, therefore, in principle are riskier than guaranteed bonds. In practice, however, the difference in risk is not significant for two reasons. First, the Japanese government will not easily allow these government-related organizations to get into financial distress. Second, if these organizations are threatened by bankruptcy, the government will likely honor these bonds. There has not been any incidence in which these non-government-guaranteed bonds have been in default.

The riskiness of the non-government-guaranteed bonds, however, can increase if the issuing organizations become privatized. Un-

EXHIBIT 1: TWO EXAMPLES OF PRIVATE-PLACEMENT GGBS

Issuer:	Japan Highway Public Corp.	Japanese National Railways
Issue date:	3/27/85	12/26/85
Maturity:	15 years	15 years
Issue size:	¥50 billion	¥40 billion
Coupon:	Floating*	Floating**
Issue price:	100	100
First coupon:	7.31%	6.76%
Coupon date:	28th of Feb/Aug	19th of Feb/Aug
Yield:	7.31%	6.76%
Subscriber:	Norinchukin	Norinchukin (¥25 bil.) Zenshinren (¥15 bil.)
Transfer:	No	No

*After one year of issue, coupon rate will be set each year 0.2% above the average yield of the public-placement GGBs which were issued during the previous year.

**After one year of issue, coupon rate will be set each year at the average yield of the public-placement GGBs.

Source: Kaichi Shimura, ed., *Gendai Nihon no Koushasai Shijou (Bond Market of Modern Japan)*.

like government-guaranteed bonds,which continue to be guaranteed even if the issuing organizations are privatized, the non-government-guaranteed bonds do not have explicit guarantees. When these organizations are privatized and become totally independent of the government, the implicit guarantees will likely be less significant.

Of the government-related organizations, the Nippon Telegraph and Telephone Public Corporation and the Japanese National Railways (both of which are now private)[5] were the largest issuers of non-government-guaranteed bonds. Many of these bonds are still being traded actively in the secondary market.

The non-government-guaranteed bonds can be placed privately or publicly. NTT's privately placed bonds used to be subscribed under a mandatory system, which required the subscribers of NTT's service to purchase the bonds. This system was abolished in 1984. NTT issued both coupon bonds and discount bonds. The balance will be outstanding until March 1993 for coupon bonds and August 1992 for discount bonds.

The Japanese National Railways (JNR) issued non-guaranteed bonds because of insufficient funding from government-guaranteed bonds. JNR was able to attract local governments to subscribe to its bonds through private placements as the proceeds generated allowed the expansion of the railway systems to the more remote prefectures, and the construction created business and job opportunities for the local economies.[6]

An example of publicly placed non-guaranteed bonds is the Special NTT Bond. It was first issued in 1972 and had been issued for a total of 94 times until March 1985.[7] This type of bond is still actively traded in the secondary markets: as of March 1988, the outstanding volume was ¥776 billion.

THE PRIMARY MARKET

Issuers

Government-related organizations are responsible for a variety of infrastructures and economic activities: the highway and transportation systems, water resources, energy, housing and urban development, and providing financing for certain segments of the economy. Since 1985, with the privatization of several public corporations, e.g., NTT, the number of corporations eligible to issue government-guaranteed bonds has decreased. As seen in Exhibit 2, there were 23 organizations eligible to issue as of December 1988. The issuers' role in the government-guaranteed bonds issuance is extremely limited. They do not contribute much influence over the amount and terms of the issues. The variations in creditworthiness and issuance terms among the issuers are negligible.

Size of the Market

Government-guaranteed bonds are the second largest type of public sector bonds both in terms of new issue volume and outstanding

EXHIBIT 2: GOVERNMENT-GUARANTEED BOND ISSUERS

East Japan Railway Company
Electric Power Development Company, Ltd.
Finance Corporation of Local Public Enterprises
Hanshin Expressway Public Corporation
Hokkaido-Tohoku Development Corporation
Honshu-Shikoku Bridge Authority
Housing and Urban Development Corporation
Japan Highway Public Corporation
Japan National Oil Corporation
Japan Railway Construction Public Corporation
Japan Regional Development Corporation
JNR Settlement Corporation
Kansai International Airport Company, Ltd.
Maritime Credit Corporation
Metropolitan Expressway Public Corporation
Organization for Promoting Urban Development
Overseas Economic Cooperation Fund
Shinkansen Holding Corporation
Small Business Corporation
Small Business Finance Corporation
Tohoku District Development Company
Trans Tokyo Bay Highway
Water Resources Development Corporation

Source: Daiwa Securities Co., Ltd., *Saiken no Joushiki (Practical Knowledge of Bonds)*.

volume. From an annual issue volume of ¥400 billion in the mid-1970s, volume grew to ¥2.8 trillion in fiscal year 1983. Since then it has remained flat, and in 1987, it dropped to ¥2.2 trillion (see Exhibit 3). While the outstanding amount has remained at around 10% of all public sector bonds, new issues of government-guaranteed bonds have actually declined in relative terms compared to the other public sector bonds, Japanese government bonds and local government bonds (see Exhibit 4). From 12.6% in 1983, the new issue volume as a percent of all public sector bonds declined to 7.3% in 1987. The trend of declining new issues is primarily due to the privatization of several public corporations, including the Nippon Telegraph and

EXHIBIT 3:   NEW ISSUE VOLUME OF GOVERNMENT-GUARANTEED BONDS

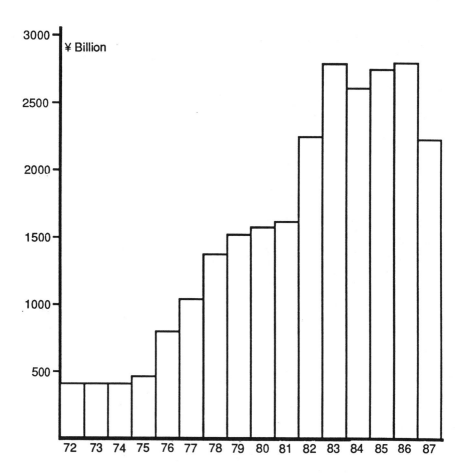

Source: The Bond Underwriters Association of Japan, *Koushasai Nenkan*, 1988.

EXHIBIT 4: PUBLIC SECTOR BONDS

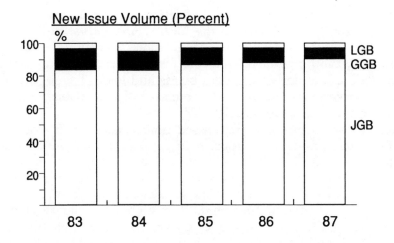

New Issue Volume (Percent)

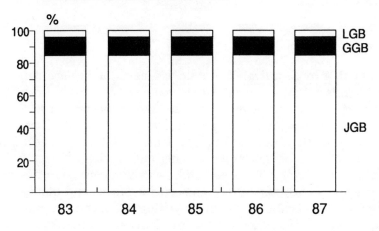

Outstanding Volume (Percent)

Telephone. Issue volume of government-guaranteed bonds per government-related organizations, however, has increased because the number of government-guaranteed bond issuers has decreased in the last few years.

There are several factors that will affect new issue volume of government-guaranteed bonds in the future. First, privatization has reduced the number of eligible organizations. Second, the Trust Fund Bureau, the largest lender to the Fiscal Investment and Loan Program through underwriting both bonds and loans, has to underwrite more government bonds and, therefore, allocate a smaller proportion of funds to the program.

Issuance of government-guaranteed bonds made up 5% of the Fiscal Investment and Loan Program in fiscal year 1975 but constituted about 9% in 1987. Thus the reduction of support from the Trust Fund Bureau to the program had the most impact on government-guaranteed bonds issuers. With smaller lending from the Bureau, these issuers have to raise funds through bond issuance. Third, the rapid increase in new issuance of government-guaranteed bonds in the late 1970s, which are now 10 years in maturity, has resulted in a large amount of refinancing needs in the late 1980s.[8] Thus, given these several countervailing factors, it is not clear whether the issuance volume of government-guaranteed bonds will increase or decrease in the future.

Issuance Procedures

Underwriting by Syndicates. Public issuance of government-guaranteed bonds follows two different channels. A portion of each underwriting goes through the syndicate while the rest goes through the "Policy Cooperative Subscription System." Underwriting syndicates are typically composed of city banks, long-term credit banks, local banks, trust banks, mutual loans and savings banks, Shinkin banks,[9] the Norinchukin Bank[10] and securities companies. Basically there are no restrictions on foreign securities firms and banks to participate in syndicates for underwriting government-guaranteed bonds. The real difficulties for foreign firms are in breaking into the inner circle of the entrenched underwriting syndicates. The number of syndicate members for each issue varies but is usually between 33 to 39. Only the syndicate for Finance Corporation of Local Public Enterprises consists of 50 members.[11]

The issuing organizations are the official entities to conclude the contracts for the underwriting and public offerings of the bonds with the syndicate, and for bond subscription with the trustees. The new issues, however, have to be authorized by the Ministry of Finance under the Fiscal Investment and Loan Program. The Ministry of Finance negotiates with the syndicate on the terms of the issue without the involvement of the issuing organizations. The Ministry of Finance used to dominate the negotiations with the syndicates and may impose terms on the syndicates that result in underwriting losses. For example, prior to 1985, the yield spread between primary issues of government and government-guaranteed bonds was fixed. Only since 1985 was the spread allowed to reflect secondary market conditions. Syndicate members had to accept the terms imposed by the Ministry of Finance and sometimes even underwrite losses because being part of the syndicate was essential for full participation in the government-guaranteed bond market (see Exhibit 5).

Policy Cooperative Subscription System. The other public issuance method is through non-syndicate underwriting. Almost 90% of non-syndicate underwritings of guaranteed bonds are under the "policy cooperative subscription system." The system is designed to attract certain institutional investors with surplus funds, such as pension funds and insurance companies, which are implicitly obliged to subscribe the issues. Banks do not play a role in this subscription system; only the securities firms handle the underwriting for the policy cooperative subscription system.

Using the system ensures that at least part of the public issuance will be subscribed to, thereby raising the likelihood that the entire issue will be sold. However, the system understandably cannot be overplayed. It should be used as a complementary means of channeling funds to the issuing organizations. For example, during periods of unfavorable market conditions, the system is more likely to be sought after. Thus, the Ministry of Finance not only determines the needs and terms of the bond issue but also exercises its influence to ensure a successful offering.

Syndicate underwritings continue to be the main public offering channel for guaranteed bonds but placement under the policy coop-

EXHIBIT 5: PROCEDURES FOR THE ISSUANCE OF GOVERNMENT-GUARANTEED BONDS

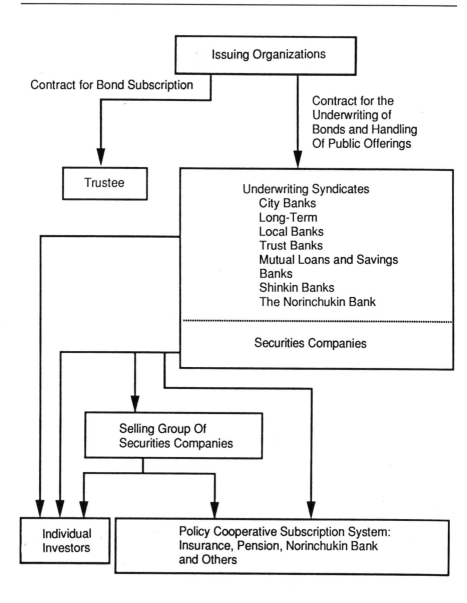

Source: The Bond Underwriters Association of Japan, *Koushasai Nenkan,* 1988.

erative subscription system has grown substantially in recent years (see Exhibit 6). Of all underwritings, syndicates took up 75% in 1982 (referred to fiscal year hereafter) but have since dropped to 61% in 1987. Underwriting through the policy cooperative subscription system climbed from 20% of all underwriting in 1982 to 35% in 1987. City banks, long-term credit banks and local banks are the major syndicate members who together account for almost 36% of new issue volume in 1987. The major participant in the policy cooperative subscription system, pension funds, alone account for 24% of the total issue volume.

For each issue, a trustee is assigned. The Industrial Bank of Japan is appointed as the trustee for all GGBs. There are several issues in which the Long-Term Credit Bank and the Hokkaido Takushoku Bank are assigned as additional trustees.[12]

The Trust Fund Bureau, which manages surplus funds for the government, plays a pivotal role in financing the government-related organizations and compensates for inadequacy of syndicate underwriting. During difficult market conditions, it increases its subscription of private-placement non-government-guaranteed bonds. This reduces the reliance on GGB issuance to provide financing for government-related organizations. The Bureau can also lend directly to those organizations instead of investing in their bonds. Most non-government-guaranteed bonds held by the Bureau are kept permanently, but it may release some excess transferrable bonds when market conditions improve. The role of the Bureau, however, has been reduced in recent years because of its increasing commitment to JGB underwriting. Thus, while the Ministry of Finance may mandate the terms of the syndicates, which at times may be unfavorable terms, the Trust Fund Bureau serves as a counter mechanism to reduce the negative impact on the syndicates.

Investors

The majority of investors in the government-guaranteed bond primary market are domestic private institutions. The major private institutional investors are city banks, long-term credit banks, trust banks, insurance companies, the Norinchukin Bank, Shinkin banks, and mutual loans and savings banks. Many of these are also major participants in the underwriting syndicates (see Exhibit 7). Public in-

**EXHIBIT 6:   UNDERWRITING CHANNELS OF GGBs BY RELATIVE VOLUME,
1982-1987**

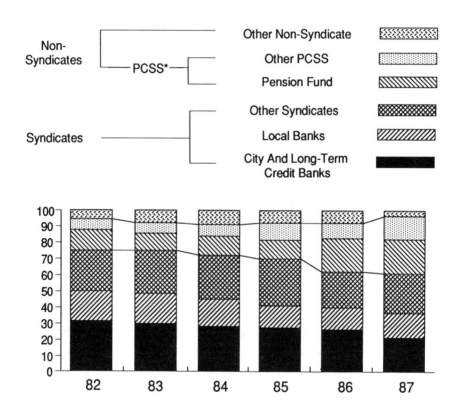

EXHIBIT 7: INVESTORS IN PRIMARY ISSUES OF GOVERNMENT-GUARANTEED BONDS: 1982 VS. 1987

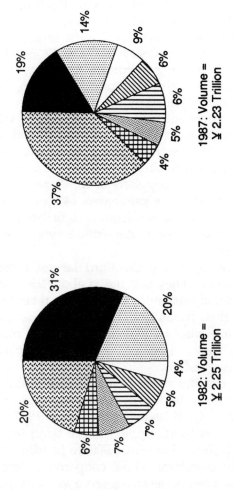

1982: Volume =
¥ 2.25 Trillion

1987: Volume =
¥ 2.23 Trillion

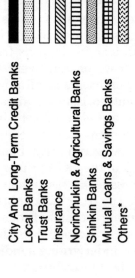

City And Long-Term Credit Banks

Local Banks

Trust Banks

Insurance

Norinchukin & Agricultural Banks

Shinkin Banks

Mutual Loans & Savings Banks

Others*

stitutional investors, such as the Trust Fund Bureau and Post Office Life Insurance, invest in bonds issued by government-related organizations which carry no government guarantees.

City banks (comprising 13 banks) and long-term credit banks (the Industrial Bank of Japan, the Long-Term Credit Bank of Japan and the Nippon Credit Bank) are the most important purchaser in the primary market of government-guaranteed bonds. In fiscal year 1987, this group acquired 19% of the primary issues of GGBs, down from 31% in 1982. In the underwriting syndicate for government-guaranteed bonds, these banks are also the major members, often taking the largest portion for their own account.

The second largest purchasers in the primary market of GGBs are local banks, 63 in total. Local banks are relatively small and their business is based mostly in their respective regions. These small local banks take in deposits from people in their areas, and because of a lack of major borrowers, they are net suppliers of funds and important purchasers of all public bonds: they purchased 14% of the new guaranteed issues in fiscal year 1987, down from 20% in 1982. Local banks are also actively involved in the underwriting syndicates of government-guaranteed bonds.

The seven trust banks in Japan are the third largest investor group in the GGB primary market. They purchased about 9% of new GGB issues in fiscal year 1987, significantly higher than their 4% in 1982. The trust banks obtain their funds from customer deposits and corporate pension funds. They also issue loan trusts and money trusts for additional funding. They are one of the most active players in the underwriting syndicates of GGBs.

The Norinchukin Bank and the other financial institutions for agricultural and forestry make up the fourth largest investor group for GGB, purchasing 6% of new GGB issues in fiscal year 1987. This group has been consistently a net fund supplier to the bond market. Farmers run cooperatives, which total almost 6,000, to handle credit, insurance and purchasing for members. These cooperatives are organized under 82 federations. The cooperatives serve as the deposit-taking and lending institutions at the local level for farmers, and they also deposit their extra funds at the federations, which in turn deposit funds at the Norinchukin Bank. The Norinchukin Bank is actively involved in the underwriting syndicates as well as the policy cooperative subscription system of the GGBs.

The fifth largest investor group in the GGB primary market is comprised of insurance companies. There are 25 life insurance companies and 23 non-life-insurance companies in Japan. Life insurance companies are the larger of the two in the GGB market. Most life insurance companies are mutual ones and profits are distributed to policyholders as dividends. These companies seek high yield investments, and the relatively higher yield offered on GGBs compared to JGBs makes the former more appealing to this group of investors. Insurance companies are not involved in the underwriting syndicates, but they are the second largest group in the policy cooperative subscription system.

Mutual loans and savings banks are small financial institutions targeting the small business enterprises. As lending opportunities decreased in recent years, they became more active in bond investing. They are both investors and underwriting syndicate members.

Shinkin banks are the other investor group for GGBs. Shinkin banks are credit associations and their real operations are very similar to banks. These credit associations have a national federation as their central organization with which they place their surplus funds. Shinkin banks are also active syndicate underwriters for GGBs.

Individual investors are almost negligible in the GGB primary market.

Two governmental organizations invest in bonds that carry no government guarantees and are issued by the government-related organizations: the Trust Fund Bureau, which manages government funds (e.g., post office savings and national welfare insurance) and invests in many public bonds, and the Post Office Life Insurance Bureau, which sells life insurance to individuals through post offices. As of October 1984, they collectively held almost ¥11 trillion of non-government-guaranteed bonds.[13]

The Trust Fund Bureau uses its funds to lend to the government, government-related organizations and local governments. Its investing activities increase during times when the bond market is depressed, therefore providing a stabilizing alternative for raising new funds for government-related organizations. As of October 1984, it held about ¥4.1 trillion non-guaranteed bonds issued by these organizations.

The Post Office Life Insurance Bureau collects premiums on life insurance and annuities through over 20,000 post offices. Most of the premium proceeds are transferred to a special account with the Ministry of Post and Telecommunications, which also manages the fund. As of October 1984, this account held over ¥6.8 trillion of non-guaranteed bonds issued by government related organizations.

Terms of an Issue

As stated earlier, the terms of a government-guaranteed issue are negotiated between the Ministry of Finance and the underwriting syndicate's members. The issuing organization itself is not involved. The terms set forth, therefore, do not depend on which issuing organizations are involved and are the same for all government-related organizations. Until recently, the terms of GGBs were identical to those of local government bonds. Since the volume of GGBs is relatively small compared to JGBs, there have been few variations in the issuing terms and methods.

All GGBs are coupon bonds with semiannual payments. All government-guaranteed bonds issued since 1982 had a maturity of 10 years. (Prior to that, they all had a maturity of 7 years.) Most of these bonds are issued at a slight discount to par value.

GGBs are issued almost every month. There are some months that, due to unsuccessful negotiations between the syndicate and the Ministry of Finance, no bonds are issued. Based on data from 1984–1988, with the exception of July 1986, in any month during which government-guaranteed bonds were issued, local government bonds were also offered. The appendix to this chapter provides a comparison of terms for public sector bonds. The maturity, coupon, issue price and yield of all government-guaranteed and local government bonds are also the same. Prior to July 1981, guaranteed-bond issuers were able to command more favorable terms than their local government counterparts. In the future, the terms of the two different bonds, however, will be different as a result of the new Bank for International Settlements (BIS) capital regulations. Under those new regulations for bank capital requirements, the risk weight of guaranteed bonds is zero and that of local governments is 10%, meaning banks will now be more reluctant to hold LGBs.[14]

Prior to 1985, yields of GGBs in the primary market were closely linked to those of JGBs. The Ministry of Finance set the yields of GGBs within the band of yields of the highest graded corporate bonds, the upper limit, and the yields of JGBs. It was a general rule that the yield on GGB primary issues be changed the same number of basis points as the yield on JGBs. Very often, they were about five basis points below the yield on LGBs. However, the yield spread between GGBs and LGBs has disappeared since late 1982 when the yield spread between corporate bonds and JGBs narrowed. Thus, given the restrictions on setting yield spread, the syndicates would occasionally find the terms to be too unprofitable, resulting in some failures to conclude the issuance.

Since 1985, yield spreads in the primary market between GGBs and JGBs have been allowed to gradually reflect secondary market conditions. During most of the period 1984 to 1988, the yield spread between GGBs and JGBs was positive, ranging from less than 10 to almost 80 basis points, except in the last few months of 1988 (see Exhibit 8).

As indicated in Exhibit 8, deregulation of the yield spread between GGBs and JGBs was carried out in several phases over almost a two-year period. The yield spread had been controlled at around 1 to 2 basis points until the first quarter of 1985. The yield spread was then allowed to increase to 10 basis points, which continued for six months. Then it was adjusted upward to 20 basis points, remaining fixed until April 1986 when the yield spread on primary issues of GGBs was completely allowed to reflect secondary market conditions. Thus, since April 1986, the yield spreads of GGB issues have been much more volatile than before.

While the credit risks of GGBs presumably are very similar to those of JGBs, there are inherent risks of regulatory changes, like the new BIS capital regulation, that can potentially decrease the attractiveness of the bonds for certain segments of investors. Guaranteed bonds issued before April 1987 are subject to the early redemption system (discussed later), and therefore, are less attractive to investors because of their call risk. JGBs, on the other hand, while callable in principle, have never been called. The positive spread between GGBs and JGBs, therefore, reflects both the higher credit risk and call risk associated with GGBs, as well as the lower marketability of GGBs.

The negative yield spread in the last few months of 1988 reflected what was happening in the secondary market, where the spread also turned negative. Later in this chapter when the secondary market is discussed, the reason for the negative spread will be

**EXHIBIT 8: YIELD SPREAD OF GOVERNMENT-GUARANTEED BONDS
OVER GOVERNMENT BONDS IN THE PRIMARY MARKET**

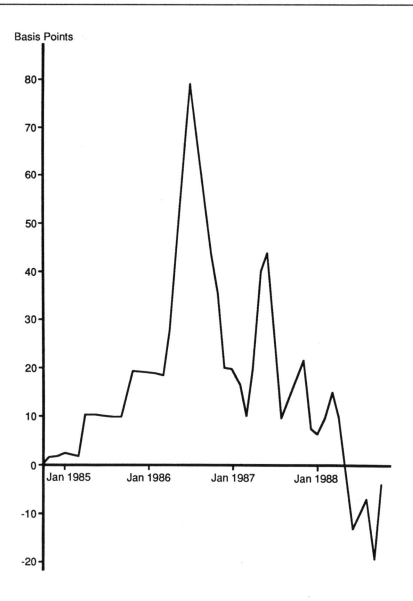

Source: The Bond Underwriters Association of Japan, *Koushasai Nenkan*, 1988.

explained. The more interesting development is the evidence that the Ministry of Finance is increasingly willing to accommodate the market movement during negotiations with the syndicates. As discussed previously, the Ministry of Finance can essentially dictate the terms of the issue with the syndicates. The changing attitude of the Ministry of Finance parallels the development of a more deregulated capital market in Japan.

Average issue size of GGBs has been increased to make them more marketable. Issue amount per organization each year is basically set at over ¥30 billion.

Details of issuing terms and market practices are described below.

Coupon Payment Date. All coupons are paid semiannually in arrears. If the coupon date is a nonbusiness day, the coupon will be paid on the preceding business day. Coupon payment dates vary among the issuing organizations but each organization tends to have a fixed coupon payment date for its issues.

First Coupon. The first coupon will be paid on an accrued interest basis. The following formulae are used depending on whether the first coupon date is more than half a year from the issue date:

(1) over half a year between issue and first coupon date:

First coupon = Face value × Coupon rate × 0.5 × [(A/B) + 1]

where

A = the number of days between the issue date and the day half a year before the first coupon date, and

B = the number of days of the half year before the first coupon date.

For example, suppose the issue date is April 1st 1991 and the first coupon date is October 30th 1991. A is then equal to the number of days between April 1st and April 30th, i.e., 29 days. B is the number of days between April 30th and October 30th, i.e., 183 days.

(2) less than half a year between first coupon and issue date:

First coupon = Face value × Coupon rate × 0.5 × (C/B)

where
C   =   the number of days between the issue date and the first coupon date.

For example, suppose the first coupon date is October 30th 1991 and the issue date is October 1st 1991. C is then equal to the number of days between October 1st and October 30th, i.e., 29 days. B is the number of days between April 30th and October 30th, i.e., 183 days.

Last Coupon. The last coupon will be paid on an accrued interest basis. The following formulae are used depending on whether the next to last coupon date is more than half a year from the maturity date.

(1) over half a year between next to last coupon and maturity date:

Last coupon = Face value × Coupon rate × 0.5 × [(D/E) + 1]

where
D   =   the number of days between the maturity date and the day half a year after the next to last coupon date, and
E   =   the number of days of the half year before the last coupon date.

For example, suppose the maturity date is October 30th 1991 and the next to last coupon date is April 1 1991. D is then equal to the number of days between October 1st and October 30th, i.e., 29 days. E is the number of days between April 30th and October 30th, i.e., 183 days.

(2) less than half a year between next to last coupon and maturity date:
Last coupon = Face value × Coupon rate × 0.5 × (F/E)

where
F   =   the number of days between the maturity date and the next to last coupon date.

For example, suppose the next to last coupon date is October 1st 1991 and the maturity date is October 30 1991. F is then equal to the number of days between October 1st and October 30th, i.e., 29 days. E is the number of days between April 30th and October 30th, i.e., 183 days.[15]

Ex-dividend. GGBs go ex-dividend 21 days before the coupon date. Normally, if the coupon date is not a business day, coupon interest will be paid on the preceding business day.[16] Bonds will not be traded for a settlement date that is up to 21 days before the coupon date. Instead, trades will be conducted for settlement on the coupon date (or the preceding business day if the coupon date is a holiday).

Early Redemption System. Previously, all GGBs were subject to the early redemption system. That is, GGBs could be redeemed before the maturity date. The system required that 3% of the initial issue amount be redeemed every half year after a nonredeemable period of three years. Periodic redemption is made by drawing of bonds by lot. While in principle all JGBs are callable, in practice they are not, which essentially eliminates any call risk for JGB investors. Thus, at one time all GGBs had higher call risks than the JGBs. In order to reduce the call risks for GGB investors, the government introduced the following redemption rule: only GGBs issued before April 1987 continue to be subject to the early redemption system; for issues since April 1987, no early redemption is allowed.[17]

Denominations. There are various denominations. The minimum denomination is ¥100,000.

Form. About 95% of the GGBs are in registered form and the rest in bearer form.[18] The register is kept by the trustees. For foreign investors who want to trade these bonds, the bonds must be kept in a custodian account with a Japanese clearing bank. The custodian account safekeeps the securities, collects interest and redemption proceeds, and files reports and tax documents. An investor's broker does not have to be a custodian bank, though. If desired, an investor in a new issue may apply, at subscription, for bearer instead of registered bonds.

Issuing Schedule. The issuance of GGBs follows a regular schedule. Around the end of the month before the issuing month, the size and terms of the issue are confirmed at a meeting between the Ministry of Finance and the underwriting syndicates. Since the financing needs of the government-related organizations are predetermined annually in the Fiscal Investment and Loan Program, most negotiations focus on the coupon rate and price. Subscriptions usually start on the day when terms are confirmed. The deadline for subscription and the payment date are around the 20th and 25th day, respectively, of the following month.[19]

Commission of Underwriters. Underwriting fees for syndicates are fixed at ¥1.15 per ¥100 face value. It consists of three components: underwriting responsibility fee (¥0.15), principal agent fee (¥0.05) and subscription transaction fee (¥0.95). Fees for the selling group are fixed at ¥0.95 per ¥100 face value, of which ¥0.40 is the subscription fee.[20] The selling group handles the selling for the policy cooperative subscription system and private investors.

SECONDARY MARKET

Trading Conventions

Pricing and Quotations of GGBs. Among dealers, GGBs are quoted in terms of simple yield.[21] GGBs, as other Japanese public sector bonds, are mostly traded in the over-the-counter markets, of which Tokyo is the largest. Since prices are determined by private negotiations between brokers and investors in the OTC market, public information on the actual market movement is limited.

The Japan Securities Dealers' Association has published two quotation lists for straight bonds, the *Representative Bond Quotation List* and the *Standard Bond Quotation List,* since January 1977. As of February 1989, the *Representative Bond Quotation List,* published daily, includes two GGBs. Fifteen securities companies designated by the Association (for public issues, an additional five banks) provide the Association with the bid-ask prices for each of these bonds on amounts of ¥100 million or so for trading, which starts at 10 A.M. each day. The Association announces the highs, lows and averages (simple average excluding the highest and lowest prices) using quotations from securities firms and banks at 1:30 P.M. every business day.

Another list that investors can obtain is the *OTC Market Quotation List* that appears in the newspaper and can be retrieved through on-line database. Data are furnished by the financial institutions participating in the market. Published daily, this list covers yields of issues which are especially representative among those on the *Representative Bond Quotation List*. Twenty-nine securities firms and all the banking institutions authorized by the Ministry of Finance to deal in government bonds, government-guaranteed bonds, and local government bonds provide bid-ask yields for each of these bonds trading on amounts of ¥100 million or so at 10 A.M. Quotation also includes the name of the quoting institution.[22]

Settlement. Since almost all GGBs are in registered form, only the settlement of registered bonds will be discussed. The mechanics are as follows:

(1) Purchase: Submit a form for registration transfer. Receive a receipt slip (certificate of custody) against payment on the settlement day. Receive certificate of registration, when it is ready, in exchange for the receipt slip.

(2) Sale: Submit certificate of registration and form of agreement and receive a receipt slip. Receive payment in exchange for the receipt slip on the settlement day. [23]

Settlement dates, although not mandatory, are usually on the 5th, 10th, 15th, 20th, 25th and the last day of the month (or next business day if a holiday, the preceding business day if the last day is a holiday). The settlement date picked should be within 10 days after the trade is conducted.[24] The six settlement dates allow some of the trade to be settled in either one or the other settlement date within the 10 day period. For example, a bond traded on the 8th can be settled on the 10th or 15th of the same month.

Settlement prices are calculated based on whether the transaction occurred on an exchange or in the OTC market. For an exchange transaction, the invoice price is as follows:

Buy:
Invoice price = Agreed-upon price + Accrued interest + Commission

Agreed-upon price = Agreed-upon unit price × (Face value/100)

Commission = Brokerage commission rate × (Face value/100)

Sell:
Invoice price = Agreed-upon price + Accrued interest +
Commission − Transfer tax
Transfer tax = Agreed-upon price × 0.03%

For an OTC transaction, the invoice price is:

Buy:
Invoice price = Agreed-upon price + Accrued interest

Sell:
Invoice price = Agreed-upon price + Accrued interest − Transfer tax[25]

Trading Number. GGBs are identified by the issuing organizations, trading numbers, and often Japanese alphabets. For example JNR # represents a bond by the Japanese National Railways.

Market-making System. The marketing-making system for GGBs was introduced in September 1986. Market-makers include domestic and foreign securities firms and banks authorized to deal in GGBs.[26] Each market-maker chooses a number of GGBs and provides bid-ask quotations every day.

Trading Patterns

Only a limited number of bond issues are listed on the stock exchanges of Tokyo, Osaka and Nagoya. As of June 30, 1988, there is only one government-guaranteed bond listed on each of the stock exchanges. Like other Japanese bonds, with the exception of convertible bonds, government-guaranteed bonds are mostly traded in the over-the-counter market rather than in the stock exchanges (see Exhibit 9). Over 99% of GGBs are traded in the OTC markets.

Trading of GGBs on the stock exchanges has several disadvantages relative to the OTC markets. First, the most obvious one is the liquidity. Second GGBs traded on stock exchanges have to be in bearer form. Third, the settlement date is inflexible. Fourth, the commission is set at a relatively higher level. Exhibits 10 and 11 show the trading rules and commission rates on the Tokyo Stock Exchange. Despite all these disadvantages, the stock exchanges do provide a

**EXHIBIT 9: ANNUAL TRADING VOLUME OF
GOVERNMENT-GUARANTEED BONDS, 1978-1987**

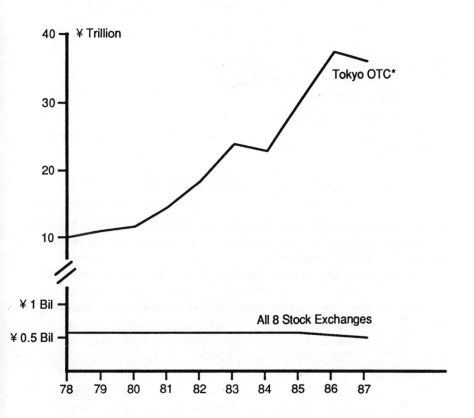

* Including Both Buy and Sell Volume.

Source: The Bond Underwriters Association of Japan, *Koushasai Nenkan*, 1988.

EXHIBIT 10: TRADING RULES FOR GOVERNMENT-GUARANTEED BONDS ON THE TOKYO STOCK EXCHANGE

Trading session	From 9:30 A.M.
Trading unit	In multiples of ¥1 million
Bid and ask	In units of 5 sen (1 sen is a hundredth of 1 yen)
Normal settlement date	On the 4th day from the date of transaction (inclusive)
Accrued interest	Subject to taxation
Mandatory trading on a stock exchange	Not applicable
Type of bonds	Bearer
Restriction on settlement price	Within 1 yen of the last price of the preceding day

Source: Daiwa Securities Co., Ltd., *Saiken no Joushiki.*

significant role for the trading of GGBs by giving prices to the representative issue, which acts as an indicator of market movement for trading in the OTC market.

Behavior of the major players affects the trading volume and patterns in the secondary markets. As the largest investors in the primary market, city banks were also the largest net sellers in the secondary market. This, however, has changed since 1983 when city banks were allowed to sell to the public through their retail networks JGBs, GGBs, and LGBs. In addition, to facilitate their fight for the right to deal in the secondary markets, the city banks became more supportive of public bond prices by curbing their selling activities in the markets. Local banks increased their selling activities in the secondary market as underwriting volume increased. For reasons similar to the city banks, local banks have also curbed their selling and became net buyers in the secondary market. The other major investors in the primary market (trust banks, insurance companies, mutual loans and savings banks and the Norinchukin Bank) are, on average, net buyers in the secondary market.

Development of the secondary market for GGBs has been handicapped by several factors. There is a lack of variety in the offerings,

**EXHIBIT 11: BROKERAGE COMMISSION RATES FOR GOVERNMENT-
GUARANTEED BONDS (TOKYO STOCK EXCHANGE)**

(per face value of ¥100)

Face value	Commission rate
¥5 mil. or less	60 sen
Over ¥5 mil. and up to ¥10 mil.	50 sen
Over ¥10 mil. and up to ¥50 mil.	40 sen
Over ¥50 mil. and up to ¥100 mil.	30 sen
Over ¥100 mil. and up to ¥1 bil.	15 sen
Over ¥1 bil.	10 sen

Source: Daiwa Securities Co., Ltd., *Saiken no Joushiki.*

as basically only one type of bond is available, the 10-year coupon bond. In addition, the relatively large holdings by banks and other institutions have hindered individual participation. Compared to JGBs and major private companies, issuers of GGBs are less well-known and the issuing sizes are much smaller.[27]

Trading Volume in the Secondary Markets. GGBs are the second most actively traded public bonds in the OTC markets. Annual turn-over is over ¥36 trillion.[28] Their trading volume as a share of all public bonds, however, has decreased in the last five years as trading of JGBs sky-rocketed. Trading of GGBs grew steadily at 15% per year from 1978 to 1987 (see Exhibit 12). For the same period, trading of government bonds increased at an annual rate of 61%. The increases in trading rates of both JGBs and GGBs were the most rapid in the second half of the period.

Although the outstanding volumes of both JGBs and GGBs increased by about 50% in the last five years, the turnover rate of JGBs has increased by more than tenfold and surpassed that of GGBs (see Exhibit 13). While on average, outstanding GGBs maintained a steady turnover rate of 4-6 times each year, JGBs, on average, turned over about 33 times in fiscal year 1987, up from 3 times in 1983.

An important development in the Japanese capital market in 1984 was that banks were permitted to start dealing in government and other government-related organization bonds. Prior to that, only

**EXHIBIT 12: TRADING VOLUME: GOVERNMENT, GOVERNMENT-GUARAN-
TEED AND LOCAL-GOVERNMENT BONDS, 1978 VS. 1987**

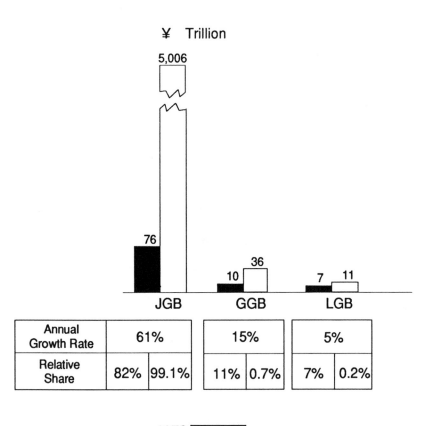

¥ Trillion

	JGB		GGB		LGB	
Annual Growth Rate	61%		15%		5%	
Relative Share	82%	99.1%	11%	0.7%	7%	0.2%

1978 ■■■■
1987 ▭

EXHIBIT 13: TURNOVER RATE OF PUBLIC BONDS*

	JGBs	GGBs	LGBs
1983	2.9	4.6	0.73
1984	5.9	4.0	0.54
1985	18.3	4.9	0.55
1986	23.5	5.9	0.65
1987	32.9	5.3	0.56

*Trading volume divided by outstanding volume.

securities firms were allowed to deal in those securities. Since then the trading volume of both JGBs and GGBs has increased much more rapidly than in previous years. The increase of JGB trading was even more phenomenal, for the reasons explained in Chapter 5.

GGBs do have an advantage over JGBs. For accounting purpose, Japanese companies investing in securities not listed on the stock exchanges have to choose the acquisition cost method. If the securities they hold are listed on the stock exchanges, they can choose to report by either the acquisition cost method or the lower of cost (or market value) method. In order to provide financial reporting on a comparable basis. Companies usually avoid changing from one reporting method to another for listed securities. Thus, for those companies that choose the second reporting method, if the market value of the securities they hold is lower than the acquisition cost, it must be reflected in the annual financial statements. For this reporting purpose, market value is based on the price of the securities as they are listed on the stock exchanges. The advantage of GGBs over JGBs is that only one GGB is listed on the stock exchanges, and therefore only that GGB has a market value for reporting purposes. Thus, for companies choosing the lower of cost or market value method, even if the value of their GGB holdings falls below the acquisition cost, they do not have to report the loss on any GGBs which are not listed on the stock exchanges. Most JGBs, on the other hand, are listed on the stock exchanges, and therefore they do have a reportable market value. Hence, many companies may choose to shift from JGBs to GGBs toward the end of a fiscal year in order to reduce "the noise" in their financial statements. This increase in demand for GGBs reduces their yields temporarily.

Beginning from the second quarter of the calendar year of 1988, Japanese bond prices fell significantly and many public sector bonds traded below their book values. JGBs reacted even more strongly than the other public sector bonds. The overshooting of JGBs' price decline was the major cause for the negative spread between the GGBs and the JGBs discussed earlier in this chapter.

Exhibit 14 provides a monthly breakdown of trading volume of GGBs. The volume trend demonstrates a strong seasonal pattern. Volume is heaviest around the end of the fiscal year for Japanese companies, i.e., end of March. It falls sharply in May and will not recover until the end of the calendar year.

Changes in GGB yields. The principal factors affecting the yields of GGBs in the secondary market are the performance of JGBs and the regulatory climate. Yields of JGBs affect the yields of GGBs in two ways. The nature of the risks of GGBs are very similar to those of JGBs. Thus, the economic factors that move the price of the JGBs also affect the GGBs in similar ways. Another way that the performance of JGBs affects the yields of GGBs is the accounting rule on bond

EXHIBIT 14: TRADING VOLUME IN THE SECONDARY MARKETS

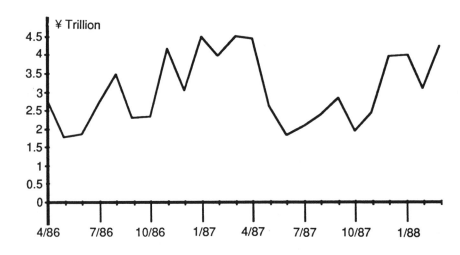

Source: The Bond Underwriters Association of Japan, *Koushasai Nenkan*, 1987 and 1988.

holding discussed earlier. Regulatory changes potentially can alter the risk of GGBs as the BIS capital regulations did on the LGBs.

Yield Spread. The yield spread between GGBs and JGBs depends on the relative supply and demand of the bond issues involved. The yield spreads between any GGBs and a specific JGB issue are essentially the same. That is, who the GGB issuer is does not affect the spread. The yield spread between a certain GGB and two different JGBs, however, can be very different. Exhibit 15 illustrates this phenomenon. The yield spread between a GGB and the benchmark JGB, is consistently higher than that between the GGB and a non-benchmark JGB of similar maturity. The benchmark JGB is usually very heavily traded and the yield is usually much lower than non-benchmark JGBs. As previously discussed, the yield spread between GGBs and non-benchmark JGBs turned negative in the second quarter of 1988. The yield spread between GGBs and the benchmark JGB, meanwhile, continued to be significantly positive.

Bid-ask Spread. The bid-ask spreads of quoted yields on GGBs are usually 5 basis points for trades of ¥100 million or so. The spreads are comparable to those for non-benchmark government bonds, reflecting their thinner volume.

REGULATIONS AND TAXES

Restrictions on Price Quotation in the OTC Market

Prices of GGBs traded in the OTC market are negotiated between brokers and investors. Since most of these bonds are not included in the daily price quotation lists, investors are subject to risks of mispricing and malpractice by brokers. To reduce the mispricing and protect small investors, certain restrictions on pricing have been established. These are listed in Exhibit 16.

Restrictions on Bond Investments by Nonresidents

Buying of GGBs by nonresident investors has been fully liberalized since the end of 1980 when the Amended Law Concerning Foreign Exchange and Foreign Trade Control went into effect. Under this

**EXHIBIT 15: YIELD SPREAD BETWEEN GGB AND JGB IN
SECONDARY MARKETS**

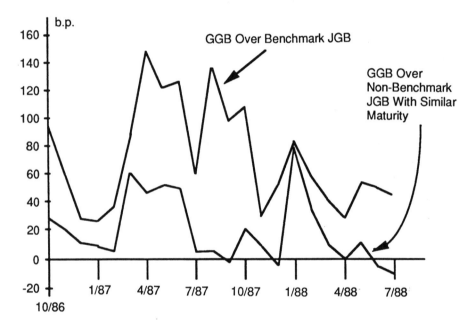

Sources: 1) Nomura Research Institute, *Koushasai Youran;* 2) Research and Statistics
Bureau, Bank of Japan, *Toukei Binran.*

law, when a nonresident investor purchases Japanese securities, he (or his agent) must file a notifying form with the Ministry of Finance. This requirement can be waived if the investor uses one of Japan's designated securities houses. No restrictions are imposed on selling of the bonds nor on remittance of the interest or proceeds abroad.[29]

Taxes on Investing in GGBs

Similar to investing in JGBs, coupon payments are subject to a 20% withholding tax. The degree of tax burden borne by foreign investors is a function of the withholding tax on interest income under bilateral tax treaties between Japan and the investor's country. For U.S. and U.K. investors, the rate is 10%. No withholding tax is imposed on central banks and supranational banks.[30]

Selling GGBs is subject to a transfer tax of 0.03% of the selling price calculated to the nearest yen. The tax rate for dealers is 0.01%.

Short Selling of GGBs

Short sale on settlement basis, that is, sell short and borrow for delivery, is prohibited. Only short sale on dealing basis, that is, selling short and buying back before settlement is permitted. There are limits on the volume of short sales of bonds depending on the kind of institution.[31]

Ratings of GGBs

There are no official or private agency credit ratings for GGBs. Creditworthiness of these bonds is consistently just below that of government bonds and similar to that of local government bonds.

CONCLUSION

In this chapter, we have focused on market practices of, and participants in, the publicly issued government-guaranteed bonds primary and secondary markets. In terms of opportunities in the primary market, while deregulation has allowed foreign participation, the real barrier lies in breaking into the inner circle of the Japanese institutional underwriters. The profitability of syndicate underwriting,

EXHIBIT 16: RESTRICTIONS ON PRICE IN OTC MARKET

Issues Listed on Stock Exchange

Up to ¥ million to brokerage	Standard price ± amount equal commission
More than ¥1 million and up to ¥10 million	Standard price ± 1% of standard price
More than ¥10 million	Standard price ± 2% of standard price

Note: Standard price is the last transaction price on the stock exchange.

Issues on Standard Bond Quotation List

Up to ¥5 million	Standard quote ± 60 sen
More than ¥5 million and up to ¥10 million	Standard quote ± 1% of standard quote

Other Issues

Other issues are also expected to follow the above guidelines

Source: Daiwa Securities Co., Ltd., *Practical Knowledge of Bonds.*

however, may not be appealing to foreign banks and securities firms. The closely linked relationship between the Ministry of Finance and the financial institutions, and the dominance of the former, necessarily requires new participants to "pay their dues" in order to establish themselves in this network. The real profitability lies more in the long term, as the established relationship between the two can give rise to other opportunities. The movement toward an auction system in JGB underwriting may spill over to the GGB market. If this happens, foreign firms will find it easier to participate in the primary market.

GGBs, most of the time, provide higher yields than JGBs with essentially identical risks. The setback is in lower liquidity. The new restriction on the early redemption system reduces the call risk of GGBs.

The role of GGBs in public financing of the Japanese economy has declined. This, together with the privatization trend, has reduced the issue volume of bonds with government guarantees. On the other hand, the Japanese government is interested in reducing its budget deficits, and issuing GGBs can be an ideal alternative for deficit reduction. Thus, it remains unclear if the issue volume will pick up significantly in the near future.

ENDNOTES

[1] The Bond Underwriters Association of Japan, *Wagakuni no Koushasai Shijou* [in Japanese, title translated as *Japanese Bond Market*], 1988, pp. 8-11.

[2] Daiwa Securities Co, Ltd., *Saiken no Joushiki* [in Japanese, title translated as *Practical Knowledge of Bonds*], 1988, pp. 10-11.

[3] JGBs and LGBs are discussed in Chapters 5 and 8, respectively.

[4] These financial institutions are discussed in Chapter 3.

[5] The Japanese government continues to have a significant shareholding of NTT although plans are under way for further reduction of the government holdings by public stock issuance.

[6] Nihon Keizai Shimbun, *Koushasai Ryutsu Shijou* [in Japanese, title translated as *Secondary Bond Market*], 1987, p. 30.

[7] Daiwa Securities Co., Ltd. *Saiken no Joushiki*, p. 18.

[8] Kaichi Shimura, ed., *Gendai Nihon no Koushasai Shijou* [in Japanese, title translated as *Bond Market of Modern Japan*], (Tokyo: Tokyo Daigaku Shuppankai, 2nd edition, 1987), p. 47.

[9] Shinkin banks are credit associations. See Chapter 3.

[10] Norinchukin Bank coordinates and invests for agricultural federations and cooperatives. See Chapter 3.

[11] Nomura Research Institute, *Koushasai Youran* [in Japanese, title translated as *Bond Handbook*, 1988, pp. 240-241.

[12] Ibid., pp. 240-241.

[13] Daiwa Securities Co., Ltd. *Introduction to Japanese Bonds*, fourth edition, 1985, pp. 38-41.

[14] For a discussion of these regulations and their implications see: David J. Askin, Llewellyn Miller and N. R. Vijayaraghavan, "The

Bank Capital Guidelines: Implications for Bank Asset Portfolios and Financial Markets," in Frank J. Fabozzi (ed.), *Managing Institutional Assets* (New York, NY: Harper & Row, 1990).

[15] Daiwa Securities Co., Ltd., *Saiken no Joushiki*, p. 143.

[16] Ibid., p. 384.

[17] The Bond Underwriters Association of Japan, *Koushasai Nenkan 1988* [in Japanese, title translated as *Bond Almanac*], 1988, p. 57.

[18] Daiwa Securities Co., Ltd., *Introduction to Japanese Bonds*, p. 81.

[19] Daiwa Securities Co., Ltd., *Saiken no Joushiki*, p. 60.

[20] The Bond Underwriters Association of Japan, *Koushasai Nenkan 1988*, p. 289.

[21] See Chapter 4 for an explanation of simple yield.

[22] Daiwa Securities Co., Ltd., *Saiken no Joushiki*, pp. 115-117.

[23] Ibid., pp. 126-127.

[24] The Bond Underwriters Association of Japan, *Koushasai Nenkan 1988*, p. 80.

[25] Daiwa Securities Co., Ltd. *Saiken no Joushiki*, pp. 129-130.

[26] The Bond Underwriters Association of Japan, *Koushasai Nenkan 1987*, pp. 8-9.

[27] Shimura, *Bond Market of Modern Japan*, p. 83.

[28] This includes trading volume for the Tokyo OTC market and all stock exchanges.

[29] Daiwa Securities Co., Ltd., *Introduction to Japanese Bonds*, p. 85.

[30] Credit Suisse First Boston *The Yen Bond Markets* (Chicago, Ill.: Probus Publishing Company, 1988), p. 57.

[31] The following are short selling limits of bonds imposed on institutions: 30% of net asset for domestic securities firms, 30% net asset value of foreign securities companies' branches, 20% of net worth for banks authorized to deal in JGBs, GGBs and LGBs, and 10% of those banks authorized less than a year. For more information, see The Bond Underwriters Association of Japan, *Koushasai Nenkan 1988*, p. 25.

Appendix A
TERMS OF PUBLIC BOND ISSUES 1984-1988

	Local Government Bonds				Government-guaranteed Bonds				Long-term Government Bonds			
	Issue Price	Coupon Rate (%)	Maturity	Yield (%)	Issue Price	Coupon Rate (%)	Maturity	Yield (%)	Issue Price	Coupon Rate (%)	Maturity	Yield (%)
Nov-84	99.00	6.900	10	7.070	99.00	6.900	10	7.070	98.50	6.800	10	7.055
Dec-84	99.50	6.900	10	6.984	99.50	6.900	10	6.984	99.00	6.800	10	6.969
Jan-85	99.50	6.600	10	6.683	99.50	6.600	10	6.683	99.00	6.500	10	6.660
Mar-85	98.75	6.900	10	7.113	98.75	6.900	10	7.113	98.25	6.800	10	7.099
Apr-85	99.25	6.900	10	7.027	99.25	6.900	10	7.027	99.25	6.800	10	6.926
Jun-85	98.75	6.600	10	6.810	98.75	6.600	10	6.810	98.75	6.500	10	6.708
Jul-85	99.25	6.600	10	6.725	99.25	6.600	10	6.725	99.25	6.500	10	6.624
Aug-85	98.75	6.300	10	6.506	98.75	6.300	10	6.506	98.75	6.200	10	6.405
Oct-85	99.25	6.100	10	6.221	99.25	6.100	10	6.221	99.25	6.000	10	6.120
Nov-85									98.75	6.500	10	6.708
Dec-85	99.00	6.600	10	6.767	99.00	6.600	10	6.767	99.50	6.500	10	6.582
Jan-86	98.50	6.200	10	6.446	98.50	6.200	10	6.446	99.00	6.100	10	6.262
Feb-86	99.50	6.100	10	6.180	99.50	6.100	10	6.180	100.00	6.000	10	6.000
Mar-86	99.00	5.800	10	5.959	99.00	5.800	10	5.959	99.50	5.700	10	5.778
Apr-86	99.50	5.300	10	5.376	99.50	5.300	10	5.376	100.00	5.100	10	5.100
May-86	99.50	5.500	10	5.577	99.50	5.500	10	5.577				
Jun-86	99.50	5.800	10	5.879	99.50	5.800	10	5.879				
Jul-86					98.00	5.800	10	6.122	98.50	5.100	10	5.329
Aug-86	98.50	5.800	10	6.040	98.50	5.800	10	6.040	97.00	5.100	10	5.567
Oct-86	98.25	5.700	10	5.979	97.50	5.600	10	6.000	99.50	5.700	20	5.753
Nov-86	98.00	5.600	10	5.918	98.00	5.600	10	5.918	99.00	5.400	10	5.555
Dec-86	99.00	5.500	10	5.656	99.00	5.500	10	5.656	99.00	5.300	10	5.454

(table continues)

	Local Government Bonds				Government-guaranteed Bonds				Long-term Government Bonds			
	Issue Price	Coupon Rate (%)	Maturity	Yield (%)	Issue Price	Coupon Rate (%)	Maturity	Yield (%)	Issue Price	Coupon Rate (%)	Maturity	Yield (%)
Jan-87	99.50	5.500	10	5.577	99.50	5.500	10	5.577	99.50	5.300	10	5.376
Feb-87	0.99	5.200	10	5.314	0.99	5.200	10	5.314	99.00	5.700	20	5.808
									99.00	5.000	10	5.151
Mar-87	99.50	5.100	10	5.175	99.50	5.100	10	5.175	99.50	5.000	10	5.075
Apr-87	99.75	4.900	10	4.937	99.75	4.900	10	4.937	99.75	4.700	10	4.736
May-87	99.00	4.400	10	4.545	99.00	4.400	10	4.545	99.50	4.000	10	4.141
									99.75	4.800	20	4.824
Jun-87	99.25	4.300	10	4.408	99.25	4.300	10	4.408	99.50	3.900	10	3.969
Jul-87									97.50	4.300	10	4.666
Aug-87	99.00	5.000	10	5.151	99.00	5.000	10	5.151	97.00	4.600	10	5.051
Sep-87									98.50	4.900	10	5.126
									96.93	5.600	20	5.934
Nov-87	98.75	5.100	10	5.291	98.75	5.100	10	5.291	99.50	5.000	10	5.075
Dec-87	99.50	5.000	10	5.075	99.50	5.000	10	5.075	100.00	5.000	10	5.000
Jan-88	99.25	5.000	10	5.113	99.25	5.000	10	5.113	99.00	4.900	10	5.050
Feb-88	99.50	4.900	10	4.974	99.50	4.900	10	4.974	99.50	4.800	10	4.874
Mar-88	99.00	4.800	10	4.949	99.00	4.800	10	4.949	100.00	4.800	10	4.800
									100.03	5.300	20	5.296
Apr-88	99.00	4.700	10	4.848	99.00	4.700	10	4.848	99.00	4.600	10	4.747
May-88									100.00	4.600	10	4.600
									99.05	4.900	20	4.993
Jun-88	99.50	4.900	10	4.974	99.50	4.900	10	4.974	98.00	4.800	10	5.102
Jul-88	100.00	5.000	10	5.000	100.00	5.000	10	5.000	100.00	5.000	10	5.000
Aug-88	99.50	5.000	10	5.075	99.50	5.000	10	5.075	99.00	5.000	10	5.151
									98.68	5.300	20	5.437
Sep-88	98.75	5.000	10	5.189	98.75	5.000	10	5.189	97.50	5.000	10	5.384
Oct-88	99.00	5.000	10	5.151	99.00	5.000	10	5.151	98.75	5.000	10	5.189

CHAPTER 8

Japanese Local Government Bonds

David Lee
Associate
Global Risk Management
Chase Manhattan Bank N.A.

Kenji Sakagami
Manager
Bank of Tokyo

Local government bonds (LGBs) are debt instruments issued by the various cities, prefectures, towns and villages of Japan. In 1986, these municipalities issued a total of ¥2.7 trillion of LGBs.[1] This figure included both public subscription and private placement LGBs issued. Local governments in 1986 were the fourth largest issuers of publicly-issued bonds in Japan (behind government, government-guaranteed and corporate bonds).[2] In the same year, over ¥27.6 trillion worth of LGBs were traded in the secondary markets (both exchange and OTC trading). LGBs ranked fifth in turnover in the secondary markets behind government bonds, short-term government bills, convertible bonds, and government-guaranteed bonds.[3]

Despite the importance of LGBs as indicated by the statistics mentioned above, little organized data is available about them, even from securities houses in Japan. Recently, government bonds have

261

dominated the spotlight in both the primary issuance and secondary trading markets in Japan. No doubt this development has adversely impacted the popularity and growth of LGBs in the primary and secondary markets.

The bulk of LGBs were issued by Japanese local governments after World War II to facilitate public finance and reconstruction efforts of the post-war Japanese economy. Since then, LGBs have been primarily issued to finance construction, education, agriculture, disaster preparation and sewage projects initiated by local governments. In the recent past, LGB financing has provided for around 33% of the financing needs of local governments, with the rest of the financing coming from direct loans from the government's Trust Fund and Post Office Life Insurance Bureaus, and also from *sho-shos borrowings*.[4] Sho-shos are certificates of borrowings issued by local governments to financial institutions for borrowing funds. These certificates are negotiated privately between local governments and lenders and are like simple bank loans. Currently there is no secondary market trading for these instruments; therefore, this chapter will concentrate on the LGB markets and not on other funding sources available to Japanese local governments.

In this chapter, we will provide information on the past and current trends and practices of the LGB primary and secondary markets, and discuss the problems and future developments of the LGB markets.

PRIMARY ISSUANCE MARKET

Who are the Issuers?

Public Subscription LGBs. The criteria for public issuance are the reputation of the local government body in the marketplace, and the outstanding amount of private placement bonds that the local government body has issued in the past. Also these entities are expected to issue public subscription LGBs regularly in the future.

In 1972, there were only eight metropolitan prefectures, municipalities, and cities that issued public subscription LGBs. They were Tokyo, Metropolitan Osaka Prefecture, Hyogo, Yokohama, Nagoya, Kyoto, City of Osaka, and Kobe. In 1973, ten additional cities and prefectures were added to the list. They were Hokkaido, Kanagawa, Shizuoka, Aichi, Hiroshima Prefecture, Fukuoka Prefecture, Sapporo, Kawasaki, Kitakyushu and the City of Fukuoka. In 1975, four additional prefectures, Miyago, Saitama, Chiba and Kyoto, started to issue public subscription LGBs. In 1982, Hiroshima became the last city to join the ranks of the local governments issuing these bonds.[5] Therefore, there are currently 23 municipalities, prefectures and cities issuing public subscription LGBs.

Exhibit 1 provides a detailed breakdown of the issuers of public subscription LGBs from 1982 to 1986. This exhibit also shows the annual issuance and outstanding amounts of public subscription LGBs for each issuer during this time period. In 1986, ¥868.7 billion worth of public subscription LGBs were issued. Tokyo was the largest issuer, accounting for approximately 40% of all public subscription LGBs issued that year. The city of Osaka was second, accounting for 8.5% of the total issuance that year. Yokohama and Nagoya came in third and fourth, accounting for 6.1% of total issuance and 5.5% of total issuance that year, respectively.[6] As can be seen from the above statistics and from Exhibit 1, the issuance of public subscription LGBs was dominated by large cities or prefectures.

The Ministry of Home Affairs and the Ministry of Finance have jurisdiction over the issuance terms of these bonds. The issuance terms are identical among the 23 participating cities and prefectures. Later in this chapter, the issuance terms and market practices will be discussed in more depth.

Private Placements LGBs. There are no central government regulations restricting any local governmental bodies from issuing private placement bonds. Therefore, even small villages in Japan can issue private placement LGBs. The size of issuance in the private placement market is usually much smaller than public subscription LGBs, and there are relatively few bondholders involved.

Exhibit 2 provides a detailed breakdown of investors in private placement LGBs in 1986. That year, ¥1,852 billion worth of private placement LGBs were issued and placed with various financial institutions and private investors.[7] The total amount of private placement LGBs issued in 1986 was more than twice the amount of public subscription LGBs (¥868.7 billion) issued that year.[8] In 1986, local governments also issued ¥502.4 billion of certificates of borrowings.[9]

EXHIBIT 1: ANNUAL BREAKDOWN OF PUBLIC SUBSCRIPTION LGBs BY ISSUERS

(Yen billions)

	1982		1983		1984		1985		1986	
	Issuing	Outstanding	Issuing	Outstanding	Issuing	Outstanding	Issuing	Outstanding	Issuing	Outstanding
Tokyo Muni.	240.9	1,769.0	276.0	1,927.6	335.6	2,132.9	321.4	2,287.6	346.9	2,423.1
Osaka Met.	24.7	225	42.8	253.1	42.8	279.7	41.3	301.1	45	321.8
Hyogo Pre.	14.7	123.1	21.2	138	23	155.1	21.5	165.9	25.2	177.9
Yokohama	45.7	310.2	50.7	341	52.8	371.7	53	395.5	53	413.7
Nagoya	29.3	305.1	50.1	329.2	45	346.9	42	357.1	48.4	367.6
Kyoto City	23.1	165.7	23.9	181.2	24.2	195.5	23.6	206.4	27.1	216.4
Osaka City	48.7	452.7	73.2	487.1	71.5	517.8	70.3	540	73.9	562.4
Kobe	23.9	166.6	27.9	184.4	31	203.8	29.1	218.5	28.7	230.4
Hokkaido	15	116.6	19.6	130.5	21.6	145.4	24.5	159.6	29.4	175.3
Kanagawa	22	186.2	35.2	212.9	30.6	233	25.8	240.8	28.4	249.5
Shizuoka Pre.	7	50.7	9	56.6	9.7	63.4	9.6	69.1	10.2	74.6
Aichi Pre.	9	69.1	11	77	12.5	85.7	12.5	93.2	13	99.1
Hiroshima Pre.	4	43.5	6	47.1	6.5	50.8	6.5	51.4	7.5	52.7
Fukuoka Pre.	6	40.7	7.6	46.3	8.6	52.5	9.2	58.4	9.2	64.1
Sapporo	12	112.3	20	125.3	17.7	135.2	20.7	142.4	23.2	151.4
Kawasaki	12	108.5	12.3	116	11.2	121.4	10.3	124.5	11.5	124.2
Kitakyushu	10	58.9	10.6	116.7	11.2	74.1	10.2	80	9.7	84.6
Fukuoka City	16	107.5	15.9	119.1	14.6	128.5	15.7	136.8	17.5	144.3
Miyagi Pre.	5	39.9	7	45.6	8	51.9	8	56.9	8.6	62.1
Saitama Pre.	10	97.1	19	112.2	16	123.3	19	131.9	19.8	140
Chiba Pre.	15	134.3	24	153.7	20	157.8	22.6	177.9	21.8	187.8
Kyoto Metr.	4	140.1	6	44.5	6	48.5	6.6	52.2	6.7	54.7
Hiroshima City	3	30	3	6	3	9	4	13	4	16.8
Total	601.0	4,725.7	771.8	5,201.0	823.0	5,683.4	807.3	6,060.0	868.7	6,394.5

Source: *Local Government Bonds*, the Ministry of Finance, June 1988.

EXHIBIT 2:   1986 BREAKDOWN OF INVESTORS IN PRIVATE PLACEMENT LOCAL GOVERNMENTS' DEBT

(Yen millions)

	Bond	Sho-sho (certificate)	Total
City Banks	764,186	99,407	863,593
Local Banks	773,309	191,938	965,247
Long-term Credit Banks	39,846	220	40,066
Trust Banks	54,162	3,331	57,498
Mutual Banks	49,375	16,914	66,289
Credit Union	27,333	32,218	59,551
Agricultural Banks	33,488	81,581	115,069
Accidental & Life Insurance Cos.	25,737	4,691	30,428
Mutual Funds	84,526	68,637	153,163
Others	150	3,430	3,580
Total	1,852,117	502,367	2,354,484

Source: *Annual Data of Local Government Bonds,* Japan Public Bond Underwriters' Association, 1987.

Therefore, the breakdown of private placement debt financing for local governments in 1986 was 78.6% private placement bonds and 21.4% private placement sho-shos. Unlike public subscription LGBs, the issuance terms and conditions (i.e., price, yield) of private placement LGBs vary from issuer to issuer. More on the issuance terms of private placement LGBs will be discussed later in this chapter.

Methods of Underwriting

Private Placement LGBs. The underwriting or issuance methods used by local governments for private placement bonds differ from public subscription LGBs primarily with respect to the issuance amount. If the issuance amount is small, then the local government tends to place the whole issue with a few local financial institutions with which it has a close relationship. However, if the issuance is large, then normally an underwriting syndicate consisting of many financial institutions will be formed, and the issue will be distributed among this syndicate. Most of the privately placed local government bonds are issued in registered form.

Public Subscription LGBs. In issuing public subscription LGBs, an underwriting syndicate consisting of banks/securities houses will be employed by the local government. One or several members of the syndicate will normally be appointed as principal agents responsible for managing the issue. Traditionally, the big four securities houses (Nomura, Daiwa, Nikko, and Yamaichi) will take turns in becoming principal agents. Each member in the syndicate will be allocated a fraction of the issue and they may sell the newly issued bonds directly to public investors. If they cannot sell all of their allotments, they are obligated to purchase the unsold bonds.

Every accounting year, when the Minister of Finance and the Minister of Home Affairs get together for the determination of the national budget and investment schedule, they also discuss the amount of public subscription LGBs that should be issued in the coming 12 months. Therefore, every month, using this discussion as a guideline, each local government can formulate its needs and determine what its issue amount will be in that month. Also, each local government decides the details such as coupon rate, maturity, and the underwriting syndicate for each issue after considering its budget. After such details are drafted, the selected syndication group will discuss with the Minister of Finance and the Minister of Home Affairs the final details of the bond issuance and solicit their approval. If the proposal is accepted, the final details will be disclosed to the public on the same day or one to two days later. The public investor can subscribe once the details of the issue are disclosed. The common subscription and settlement dates are on the 20th and 25th of each month, respectively.[10] More on the issuance terms and mechanics will be described in the next section.

Primary Market Issuance Terms and Market Practices

Public Subscription LGBs. Exhibit 3 details the terms of all public subscription LGBs issuances from April 1984 to April 1988. Note that the issuance terms were identical for all issuers of public subscrip-

EXHIBIT 3: SHIFTS IN THE ISSUANCE TERMS OF PUBLIC SUBSCRIPTION LGBs

	4/84	8/84	9/84	10/84	11/84	12/84	1/85	3/85	4/85	5/85	6/85	7/85	8/85
Coupon Rate (%)	7.1	7.4	7.2	7.2	6.9	6.9	6.6	6.9	6.9	6.9	6.6	6.6	6.3
Issuing Price	98.50	98.25	98.00	98.50	99.00	99.50	99.50	98.75	99.75	99.25	98.75	99.25	98.75
Years to Maturity	10	10	10	10	10	10	10	10	10	10	10	10	10
Avg. Maturity (Years)	8.635	8.635	8.635	8.635	8.635	8.635	8.635	8.635	8.635	8.635	8.635	8.635	8.635
Subscriber's Yield (%)	7.36	7.709	7.551	7.461	7.07	6.984	6.683	7.113	7.027	6.942	6.81	6.725	6.506
Issuer's Yield (%)	7.759	8.12	7.965	7.864	7.454	7.357	7.05	7.504	7.406	7.309	7.194	7.097	6.884

	10/85	12/85	1/86	2/86	3/86	4/86	5/86	6/86	8/86	9/86	10/86	11/86	12/86
Coupon Rate (%)	6.1	6.6	6.2	6.1	5.8	5.3	5.5	5.8	5.8	5.6	5.7	5.6	5.5
Issuing Price	99.25	99.00	98.50	99.50	99.00	99.50	99.50	99.50	98.50	98.50	98.25	98.00	99.00
Years to Maturity	10	10	10	10	10	10	10	10	10	10	10	10	10
Avg. Maturity (Years)	8.635	8.635	8.635	8.635	8.635	8.635	8.635	8.635	8.635	8.635	8.635	8.635	8.635
Subscriber's Yield (%)	6.221	6.767	6.446	6.18	5.959	5.376	5.577	5.879	6.04	5.832	5.979	5.918	5.656
Issuer's Yield (%)	6.583	7.145	6.828	6.537	6.321	5.69	5.895	6.192	6.375	6.168	6.318	6.26	5.975

	1/87	2/87	3/87	4/87	5/87	6/87	8/87	11/87	12/87	1/88	2/88	3/88	4/88
Coupon Rate (%)	5.5	5.2	5.1	4.9	4.4	4.3	5	5.1	5	5	4.9	4.8	4.7
Issuing Price	99.50	99.25	99.50	99.75	99.00	99.25	99.00	98.75	99.50	99.25	99.50	99.00	99.00
Years to Maturity	10	10	10	10	10	10	10	10	10	10	10	10	10
Avg. Maturity (Years)	8.635	8.635	8.635	8.635	8.635	8.635	8.635	8.635	8.635	8.635	8.635	8.635	8.635
Subscriber's Yield (%)	5.577	5.314	5.175	4.937	4.545	4.408	5.151	5.291	5.075	5.113	4.974	4.949	4.848
Issuer's Yield (%)	5.885	5.622	5.476	5.223	4.838	4.694	5.455	5.603	5.369	5.412	5.267	5.25	5.147

Note: Issuing price is per ¥100.

Source: *Local Government Bonds,* the Ministry of Finance, June 1988.

tion LGBs because of government regulations. During the period 1984 to 1988, the average issue size was around ¥3 billion and issuance coupon rates fluctuated between 4.3% and 7.4%. Issuance prices were mostly between 98% and 99.75% of face value. Therefore, most public subscription LGBs issued during this period were issued at discounts. During this period, all LGBs issued were 10-year semiannual pay coupon bonds with an average maturity of around 8.635 years.[11]

Almost all public subscription LGBs were issued with a compulsory periodic retirement schedule. This schedule requires the issuer to redeem a certain portion of the bonds semiannually after a set number of years from issuance. For example, in the current 10-year public subscription LGB issues, 3% of the initial issue amount is retired semiannually by the issuer after a grace period of three years.

Additional issuing terms and market practices are described below.[12]

Denominations. Public subscription LGBs are normally issued with ¥10,000, ¥100,000 or ¥1,000,000 denominations. In certain special circumstances, ¥500,000 denomination LGBs can be issued.

Form. Most of the public subscription LGBs are issued in registered form. The purchaser of a registered bond may apply for issuance of the bond in bearer form by submitting the registration certificate and the necessary form to the registrar.

Coupon Payment. All coupons are paid semiannually in arrears. If the coupon date is a non-business day, the coupon will be paid on the next available business day.

First Coupon. The initial coupon payment will be made on an accrued interest basis.

Issuance Yield Calculation. The conventional yield quoted in the primary market is the simple yield as explained in Chapter 4.

Fees for Underwriters. Underwriting fees for syndicates are fixed at 1.25% of the issuance amount. This fee can be broken down into: underwriting responsibility fee (0.15%), principal agent fee (0.05%) and subscription transaction fee (1.05%). Underwriting fees for selling agents and custodians are broken down as follows: sales consignment fee (0.13% of issuance amount), initial registration fee (0.07% of issuance amount), principal repayment fee (0.20% of principal payment), interest payment fee (0.3% of interest payment), and miscellaneous fee (0.05% of issuance amount).

In principle, the underwriting and selling commission rates should be negotiated and jointly determined by the underwriting syndicate and the local government issuer. Currently, the commission rates are set by the Ministry of Home Affairs and the Ministry of Finance and these rates are identical for all issuers and underwriters of public subscription LGBs. Periodically, these government ministries will revise the rates according to changes in financial market conditions. However, the two ministries consult with the Industrial Bank of Japan before doing so.

The problem with this fixed commission structure is that since commissions represent compensation for the underwriter's expenses and risks, then the commission rate should be quite different for an issuer such as Tokyo compared to an issuer such as Hiroshima. Therefore, this fixed commission rate structure penalizes larger cities and prefectures with higher credit standings like Tokyo and Osaka.

Private Placement LGBs. Unlike public subscription LGBs, there are no government guidelines dictating the terms and conditions for the issuance of private placement LGBs. Therefore, a wide divergence of issuance coupon rates among the various issuers can be observed. For example, in 1985, for large cities in Japan, Aichi issued private placement LGBs at a 5.337% coupon rate while Tokyo issued private placement LGBs at a 6.78% coupon rate. This represented a difference of nearly 140 basis points on issuance coupon rates. For small cities, towns and villages, the divergence of issuance coupon rates was even larger. In 1985, for example, Nagano issued bonds with a 3% coupon while Sendai issued bonds with a 7.181% coupon, representing a spread of over 410 basis points.[13] The divergences in the issue coupon rates were primarily due to the differences in each local government's credit rating and financial strength. Therefore, in the private placement markets, credit analysis is becoming more important. More on credit evaluation conventions will be discussed later.

There is currently little public information available on the issuance terms and conditions of private placement LGBs. This is be-

There is currently little public information available on the issu-ance terms and conditions of private placement LGBs. This is be-cause the terms and conditions of each private placement issue are privately negotiated between the issuer and the investors and are not subject to government regulations. Therefore, the wide divergence of terms (i.e., issuance coupon rates) across issuers will also apply to other aspects of issuance. For example, unlike public subscription LGBs, which currently have a fixed maturity of 10 years, the matu-rity of private placement LGBs can vary from 7 to 15 years. Also the coupon and principal repayment schedule can vary a great deal from issuer to issuer. In the past, the average issue size of private place-ment LGBs was around ¥100 million. This figure is small compared to the average issue size of public subscription LGBs (¥3 billion).[14]

Trends and Statistics of the Primary Issuance Market for LGBs

Previously, we have described the issuers, the underwriting meth-ods, and the issuance terms and practices for both public subscrip-tion and private placement LGBs. In this section, we will describe the trends and volume of public subscription and private placement LGBs in the primary issuance market.

Public Subscription LGBs. A year-by-year breakdown of the issu-ance volume of public subscription bonds in Japan is provided in Exhibit 4. In 1986, JGBs accounted for 71.5% of the total public bonds issued in Japan. This was followed by government guaranteed bonds, corporate bonds, and LGBs. Their shares of the issuance vol-ume that year were 17.4%, 6.1% and 5%, respectively.[15] As can be seen, in the primary issuance market, the total volume of public sub-scription LGBs issuance was small compared to JGBs and the other issuers. The relatively small volume of public subscription LGB issu-ances was not much different between 1971 and 1986 (4% of all pub-lic bond issuance in 1971 to 5% in 1986).[16] The interesting things to note in Exhibit 4 are the relative growth in issuances of JGBs and the relative decline of corporate bond issuances. In 1971, corporate bond issuances accounted for 33.3% of the total public subscription bond issuances that year.[17] In 1986, this figure declined to 6.1%. No doubt, the relatively small volume of public subscription LGB issuances and the relative decline of the share of corporate bonds can be attributed

**EXHIBIT 4: NEW ISSUE VOLUME OF PUBLIC SUBSCRIPTION BONDS,
1971-1986**

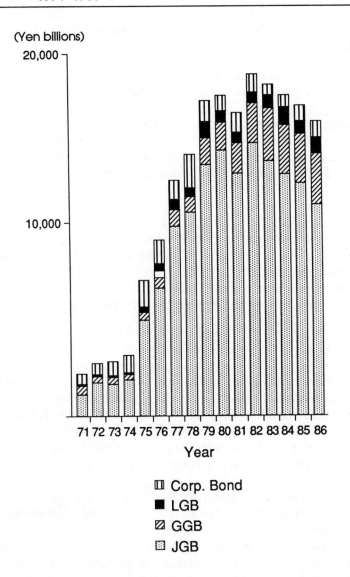

(Yen billions)

20,000

10,000

71 72 73 74 75 76 77 78 79 80 81 82 83 84 85 86
Year

▥ Corp. Bond
■ LGB
▨ GGB
▦ JGB

Source: *Discussion of LGBs,* by Shozo Takayose, July 1988.

to the growth in popularity of JGBs. The important point is that it was not the absolute issuance volume which had declined for public subscription LGBs (which actually went up from ¥601 billion in 1982 to ¥868.7 billion in 1986), but the relative issuance volume of LGBs compared to JGBs that had remained stagnant.[18]

Private Placement LGBs. Year-to-year issuance volume for private placement LGBs are not widely available to the public. According to a 1987 survey in the Local Government Annual Census, the share of private placements with respect to total local governments' borrowings has been declining steadily.[19] Exhibit 5 summarizes some of the important statistics from that survey. In 1976, private placements represented 49.2% of all local governments' funding sources. In 1986, private placements represented only 25.1% of their funding sources.[20] Surprisingly, public subscription LGB issuances did not increase significantly during this period either. It appeared that local governments have reverted back to more reliance on the Japanese government for funds. This recent trend might be the result of JGBs' domination of the bond markets in Japan. Also, the relatively thin liquidities of both public and private placement LGBs in the secondary markets may have caused the decline in their issuance volumes.

Investors of LGBs in the Primary Market

Private Placement Investors. Banks are normally the largest investors in private placement LGBs. These banks include city banks, local banks, long-term credit banks, trust banks, and mutual banks. In 1986, local banks and city banks were the two largest investors of private placement LGBs issued that year, purchasing 41.8% and 41.3% of the issuances, respectively.[21] Other investors in private placement LGBs include credit unions, agricultural cooperatives, insurance companies, and mutual funds. Their investments normally account for less than 20% of the private placement LGB issues in a particular year.[22]

In terms of the importance of private placement LGBs as investments for banks, local banks invested proportionally a larger percentage of their funds in these instruments than in any other banks. For example, in 1987, local banks invested 12.3% of their total invest-

EXHIBIT 5: FUNDING SOURCE RATIOS OF LOCAL GOVERNMENTS

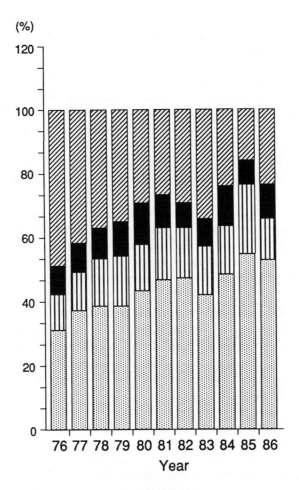

(%)

Year

☒ Private Placement
■ Public Subsor. Bond
▥ Gov't Related Banks
▨ Gov't Funds

Source: *Annual Data of LGBs,* Japan Public Bond Underwriters' Association, 1987.

ment in marketable securities in private placement LGBs. In contrast, city banks in 1987 invested only 5.3% of their total investment in marketable securities in private placement LGBs. Currently, all banks' investments in private placement LGBs are about 3 to 5 times their investments in public subscription LGBs.[23]

This current large ownership of private placement LGBs by banks (especially local banks) poses several problems. First, as the funding needs of local governments and LGB issuances have escalated drastically in recent years, banks may have already been saturated with the flood of private placement LGBs issued. As the liquidity of private placement LGBs is quite low in the secondary markets, banks might find it difficult to sell their LGBs. In the recent past, some local banks were forced to sell their private placement LGBs at a capital loss because of thin secondary markets. Therefore, in the future we should see banks increasing their holdings in public subscriptions rather than in private placement LGBs. Second, as banks normally invest in private placement LGBs for the longer term, they tend to trade these LGBs as a last resort (i.e., when they are desperate for funds). This situation indirectly created the thin liquidity in the secondary markets. Third, as mentioned before, private placement LGBs are not permitted as collateral against borrowing from the Bank of Japan. In the past, banks have largely ignored this disadvantage because of their strong relationships with the local governments. However, this might change in the future with banks shying away from private placement and investing more in public subscription LGBs.

Public Subscription LGB Investors. Exhibit 6 provides a historical breakdown of investors in public subscription LGBs. Similar to private placement LGBs, the principal investors in public subscription LGBs are banks. In 1986, bank investments accounted for over 40% of the public subscription LGBs issued that year.[24] City and long-term credit banks normally are the largest investors within the banking group. This is because city banks and long term credit banks have traditionally enjoyed a good banking relationship with larger cities and municipalities. As public subscription LGBs are currently issued by 23 large cities and prefectures in Japan, these banks would normally be the most active investors. However, this will change if the federal government grants smaller cities and prefectures the right

EXHIBIT 6: INVESTORS IN PUBLIC SUBSCRIPTION LGBs IN THE PRIMARY MARKET

(Yen Billion)

Year	City Banks Amt.	%	Local Banks Amt.	%	Trust Banks Amt.	%	Insurance Co. Amt.	%	Agric'l Banks Amt.	%
1982	268.2	44.6	32.8	5.5	21.5	3.6	3.2	0.5	25.0	4.2
1983	292.5	37.9	33.9	4.4	26.7	3.5	5.5	0.7	34.9	4.5
1984	333.6	40.5	34.7	4.2	24.9	3.0	7.2	0.9	33.6	4.1
1985	344.4	42.7	37.0	4.2	26.1	3.2	3.7	0.5	17.0	1.8
1986	337.5	38.8	41.6	4.8	26.4	3.0	6.4	0.7	45.9	5.3

Year	Credit Union Amt.	%	Mutual Banks Amt.	%	Individual Amt.	%	Others* Amt.	%	Total Amt.	%
1982	23.6	3.9	8.5	1.4	32.0	5.3	186.2	31.0	601.0	100
1983	43.3	5.6	15.5	2.0	44.8	5.8	274.6	35.6	771.8	100
1984	40.3	4.9	12.5	1.5	36.1	4.4	300.1	36.5	823.0	100
1985	17.0	2.1	10.6	1.3	31.0	3.8	322.7	40.0	807.3	100
1986	23.2	2.7	17.3	2.0	18.9	2.2	351.6	40.5	868.7	100

*Includes government mutual fund, religious groups, schools and enterprising companies.

Source: *Local Government Bonds*, the Ministry of Finance, June 1988.

to issue public subscription LGBs. As smaller cities have stronger ties with local banks, these banks might increase their investments in public subscription LGBs.

From 1975 to 1986, other investor groups such as government mutual funds, religious groups, schools, and companies have all increased their investments in public subscription LGBs. Their investments in these bonds increased from 10.1% of all public subscription LGBs issued in 1975 to over 40% in 1986.[25] The reasons for this increase are that these investor groups are usually long-term, stable investors and do not require a high degree of liquidity (as in JGBs) on their investments. Therefore they were naturally attracted to the relatively higher coupon rates offered by public subscription LGBs.

One final group of investors in public subscription LGBs is individual investors. In 1986, individuals purchased 2.2% of all the public subscription LGBs issued that year. In the same year, individuals purchased 10.1% of the JGBs issued.[26] It is apparent that individuals have not invested heavily in LGBs.

Simple Yield Spreads between LGBs and the Benchmark JGB in the Primary Market

As mentioned previously, the primary yields of public subscription LGBs are determined by the Ministry of Home Affairs and not by the market. Therefore, in order for public subscription LGBs to compete with government bonds and other debt instruments offered in Japan, the primary yield to subscribers at issuance must be competitive for LGBs. In Exhibit 7, a historical breakdown of average issuance yield spreads between LGBs and the benchmark JGB is shown. All the yield figures presented in Exhibit 7 and the rest of this section are in terms of simple yield.

Spreads were mainly the result of the difference in credit quality and liquidity between LGBs and the benchmark. Another reason for the spread is that the government tries to price JGBs in line with market trends, and LGBs were most often priced artificially low and out of line with the market. Of course, the Japanese government, with its higher credit standing and liquidity, almost always enjoyed lower issuance yields. However, in July 1987, the simple yield of the benchmark JGB exceeded that of the LGBs in the primary market. Prior to July 1987, the yields of benchmark JGBs in the primary market were on a downward trend. This bull market was caused by the appreciation of the yen against the U.S dollar, which gave rise to unrealistic expectations of cuts in short-term yen rates. The price rise in the benchmark JGB was further fueled by a large increase in speculative activity. In the summer of 1987, to discourage the excessive speculations on the benchmark, the Bank of Japan installed measures such as requiring securities houses to adopt more frequent settlement dates on their benchmark trades. These measures, along with the fear of inflation due to a rise in oil prices, caused a sharp rise in the simple yield of the benchmark in the primary market and a bear market for the benchmark. In a market rally or decline, the price of

**EXHIBIT 7:   YIELD SPREAD IN THE PRIMARY MARKET BETWEEN
JGB AND LGB, 1975-1987**

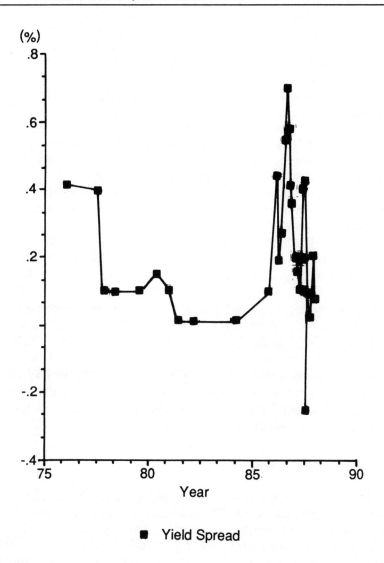

■ Yield Spread

Source: *Discussion of LGBs,* by Shozo Takayose, July 1988.

the benchmark usually moves first because of the speculative interests surrounding it. Therefore, in August 1987, when the simple yield of the benchmark JGB rose in the primary market, the yields of the JGB-side issues and LGBs followed, albeit more slowly. This created a negative spread between the benchmark JGB and LGBs, where the yield of the benchmark JGB was actually higher than that of LGBs in the primary market.[27]

During the last 15 years, there were fluctuations in the simple yield spreads between LGBs and the benchmark JGB in the primary market. In 1975, the average simple yields to subscriber were 8.637% and 8.227% for LGBs and the benchmark JGBs, respectively. This represented an average yield spread of 41 basis points.[28] In the late 1970s and early 1980s, the government issued huge amounts of JGBs and drove the average yield of JGBs up in the primary market. During this period, the average simple yield spread between LGBs and JGBs declined to around 10 basis points.[29] In 1983 and 1984, the average yield spread fell to an all time low of 1 basis point, as JGBs issuances continued to saturate the market. As JGB issuances have slowed down a little recently, spreads widened to 10 to 50 basis points.[30]

When analyzing the yield spreads between the benchmark and LGBs in the primary market, there are several points that should be realized. First, the primary yields on the benchmark are usually biased downward because of the excessive investor speculation. Second, the primary yields on LGBs are fixed by the Ministry of Home Affairs, and they are also biased downward. Therefore, the fluctuations in yield spreads between the benchmark and LGBs in the primary market are the result of these factors.

Non-Yen Local Government Bonds

Part of local governments' issuances of public subscription bonds are non-yen denominated LGBs. These bonds are issued overseas and are denominated in foreign currencies. Currently, all non-yen local government debts are financed through bond issuance and not other debt instruments. Permission from the Ministry of Finance and the Ministry of Home Affairs is needed before local governments can issue non-yen bonds. Unlike yen-denominated LGBs, currently all non-yen LGBs are issued with the guarantee of the Japanese government.

The first foreign currency LGB was issued in 1899. The city of Kobe issued 25,000 British-pound-denominated private placed bonds that year. In 1902, Yokohama and Osaka were the first two cities in Japan to issue public subscription non-yen bonds. The issue size amounted to 92,000 and 316,000 British pounds, respectively.

Before World War II, 17 non-yen LGBs were issued. Only two of these issues were guaranteed by the government. After World War II, as the need for reconstruction intensified, and domestic financing proved inadequate, more non-yen LGBs were issued. All non-yen LGBs issued after World War II were guaranteed by the government. The total amount of government guarantees provided for non-yen local government bonds is determined each year during the central government's budgetary process. There are currently no withholding taxes on non-yen LGBs.

Exhibit 8 provides a detailed breakdown by issuers of all non-yen LGBs issued after World War II and up to January 1988. Currently there are only four cities in Japan that issue non-yen LGBs: Tokyo, Osaka, Kobe and Yokohama. After World War II, 18 deutschemark-denominated issues were floated in the West German market, 13 Swiss-franc-denominated issues were floated in the Swiss market, six issues were Eurodollar issues, and five issues were floated in the U.S market. After World War II, Kobe led all issuers with 16 issues, followed by Tokyo with 13 issues, Yokohama with six issues and Osaka with five issues.[31] Most of these issues were used to finance public projects such as subway construction, sewage system construction and recreational land development.

If a local government decided to use a non-Japanese financial institution to underwrite its bond issuance, which might also include the handling or remittance of interest and principal of the bonds, it would first have to obtain permission from the Ministry of Home Affairs. Of course, the non-yen LGB issuers and underwriters must also follow the rules, procedures and regulations of the country where the bonds are issued.

There are several advantages for local governments to issue non-yen bonds. First, by taking advantage of the interest rate differentials between Japan and overseas, and timing the issue appropriately, the local government may be able to issue the bonds at more advanta-

EXHIBIT 8: BREAKDOWN OF NON-YEN LGBs BY ISSUERS AND ISSUING AMOUNT

Issuing Date	Issuer	Issuing Amt. Millions	Equiv. ¥ Amt. ¥ Million	Coupon %	Issuing Price ¥	Maturity Year	Subscri. Yield %	Issuing Place
2/12/62	Osaka Met.	DM100	900	6.500	96.500	15	6.970	W. Germany
3/20/63	Osaka Met.	DM100	900	6.500	98.500	15	6.700	W. Germany
1/7/64	Osaka Met.	DM100	900	6.500	99.750	15	6.532	W. Germany
4/15/64	Tokyo	ES22.5	810	5.750	96.500	15	6.200	Euromarket
2/8/65	Osaka Met.	DM100	900	6.250	99.000	15	6.380	W. Germany
6/15/65	Tokyo	US20	720	6.000	95.250	15	6.631	U.S.A.
6/12/68	Kobe	DM100	900	7.000	99.500	15	7.067	W. Germany
8/26/68	Yokohama	DM100	900	6.750	99.000	15	6.885	W. Germany
5/22/69	Kobe	DM100	900	6.750	98.500	15	6.954	W. Germany
9/26/69	Yokohama	DM100	980	7.000	96.500	15	7.495	W. Germany
2/11/71	Kobe	DM100	980	7.750	100.000	15	7.750	W. Germany
8/16/71	Yokohama	DM100	900	8.000	100.000	15	8.000	W. Germany
5/17/72	Kobe	DM100	960	6.750	99.500	15	6.817	W. Germany
5/30/75	Kobe	DM50	620	8.250	100.000	5	8.250	W. Germany
6/2/77	Kobe	DM100	1,150	7.500	99.000	7	7.720	W. Germany
6/15/77	Kobe	DM100	1,160	6.500	99.000	10	6.666	W. Germany
7/12/78	Kobe	DM100	980	5.750	100.250	8	5.704	W. Germany
9/20/79	Kobe	DM150	1,850	7.125	100.250	10	7.082	W. Germany
6/26/80	Kobe	DM100	1,230	8.000	100.000	10	8.000	W. Germany
7/22/81	Kobe	SF100	1,100	7.000	100.500	10	6.915	Switzerland
5/25/82	Kobe	SF100	1,200	6.125	100.250	10	6.085	Switzerland
11/23/82	Tokyo	SF100	1,250	5.375	100.000	10	5.375	Switzerland
5/19/83	Kobe	DM120	1,200	7.000	99.500	10	7.085	W. Germany
8/11/83	Tokyo	SF100	1,200	5.750	100.000	10	5.750	Switzerland

Issuing Date	Issuer	Issuing Amt. Millions	Equiv. ¥ Amt. ¥ Million	Coupon %	Issuing Price ¥	Maturity Year	Subscri. Yield %	Issuing Place
7/25/84	Tokyo	E$50	1,200	12.875	100.000	10	12.875	Euromarket
11/5/84	Kobe	SF100	1,000	5.750	100.000	10	5.750	Switzerland
12/17/84	Tokyo	SF80	800	5.250	99.500	10	5.316	Switzerland
9/19/85	Tokyo	SF100	1,030	5.375	100.000	8	5.375	Switzerland
11/20/85	Yokohama	SF100	1,030	5.375	97.750	10	5.408	Switzerland
12/16/85	Tokyo	E$100	2,370	10.125	101.000	10	9.926	Euromarket
9/19/86	Tokyo	SF100	970	5.125	99.750	20	5.125	Switzerland
11/7/86	Tokyo	E$200	2,090	8.250	101.500	10	8.030	Euromarket
12/10/86	Yokohama	SF100	970	4.750	100.000	10	4.750	Switzerland
2/16/87	Kobe	SF100	970	4.500	100.250	10	4.470	Switzerland
3/18/87	Tokyo	US100	2,090	7.500	99.515	10	7.570	U.S.A.
9/17/87	Kobe	SF100	1,100	4.750	99.500	10	4.810	Switzerland
10/20/87	Tokyo	US150	1,440	10.375	100.000	10	10.375	U.S.A.
11/10/87	Osaka Met.	E$120	1,480	5.000	100.250	7	10.117	Euromarket
12/10/87	Yokohama	SF100	1,050	5.000	100.250	10	4.968	Switzerland
1/7/88	Tokyo	E$200	1,320	9.500	101.500	5	9.110	Euromarket

Source: *Local Government Bonds*, the Ministry of Finance, June 1988.

geous terms (i.e., lower coupon rates and issuance costs). Second, the local governments of Japan can tap a larger overseas investor base for its financings and diversify its sources of funding. Third, in most countries, the regulations for bond issuance are not as restrictive as in Japan. Therefore, local government issuers have more flexibility in choosing the terms and conditions of issuance.

The drawbacks of local governments issuing non-yen bonds are foreign exchange risks, higher information costs, and unexpected foreign developments. The yen costs of coupon and principal payments depend highly on fluctuations in the foreign exchange markets. Recently, with the introduction of currency hedging instruments such as swaps, foreign exchange risks can be minimized somewhat. Also, the costs to learn the regulations and language for foreign issuance could result in high information costs. Finally, changing foreign market conditions and regulations could mean the cancellation of an issuance at any time. This would present substantial risks to the Japanese local government issuer.

SECONDARY MARKET FOR LGBs

Trading Conventions

Quotations of LGBs in the Secondary Markets. Trading in the over-the-counter market is based on private negotiations between brokers and investors; therefore, it is difficult for the public to know about actual market movements. In order to maintain a fair market, the Securities Dealers of Japan have published two quotation lists: the *Representative Bond Quotation List* and the *Standard Bond Quotation List*. Both of these lists are based on bond prices reported by major securities houses and are reported daily. Some representative LGB issues are listed in these quotation lists. Also, some banks in Japan have started to offer real time, on-line systems for institutional investors to monitor the median prices of LGBs issued by major cities or prefectures such as the Tokyo metropolitan government, Yokohama, Nagoya, Osaka, Kyoto, and Kobe.[32] This system will eventually expand to cover smaller local issues.

Pricing of LGBs in the Secondary Markets. Like almost all yen-denominated bonds trading in the secondary markets, LGBs are quoted and priced by dealers in terms of simple yields. When LGBs are traded between interest payment dates, the accrued interest is paid by the buyer to the seller.

Bid-ask Spread. The average bid-ask spread of LGBs is currently between 10 and 15 basis points. For the benchmark JGBs it is one basis point. For the more active side-issues of the JGB, the spreads are between two to five basis points, and for the less active issues, five to ten basis points. The large bid-ask spread for LGBs in the secondary market is a relection of its thin liquidity.

Transfer Taxes. If a nonresident foreign investor sells LGBs to a Japanese resident, a flat-rate transfer tax of 0.045% of the principal amount involved will be levied on the foreign investor. There is no transfer tax when a nonresident investor sells LGBs to another nonresident investor. The transfer tax for securities companies is currently 0.015%.

Trading Activity of LGBs

Earlier we described the trends and statistics of the primary issuance market of public subscription and private placement LGBs. Here, we will describe the trading trends of LGBs in the secondary markets (both exchange and OTC).

Exchange Trading. There are currently three stock exchanges in Japan in which public subscription LGBs are listed and traded—the Tokyo, Osaka, and Nagoya stock exchanges. At present, only one issue of public subscription LGBs is listed and traded in each of the three exchanges. In 1986, the turnover of LGBs on these exchanges was ¥855 million. This represented much less than 0.01% of the public subscription LGBs traded in the OTC markets. In the same year, the turnover of exchange-listed LGBs was less than 0.01% of all the public bonds traded on these three exchanges.[33] Exhibit 9 provides a detailed breakdown of these trends. As can be seen from the exhibit and the above data, most of the secondary market trading of LGBs is not on the exchanges. Over the period 1976 to 1986, the turnover of LGBs on the exchanges was stagnant.

EXHIBIT 9: TRENDS OF PUBLIC SUBSCRIPTION LGbs TRADING ON THE MAJOR STOCK EXCHANGES (TOKYO, OSAKA AND NAGOYA)

(Yen million)

	Public Subscription LGBs	Public Bond Total	Percentage
1976	855	1,137,257	0.00075
1977	855	2,213,665	0.00039
1978	855	4,811,075	0.00018
1979	858	3,488,473	0.00025
1980	855	4,447,950	0.00019
1981	855	7,384,488	0.00012
1982	858	8,619,656	0.00010
1983	861	22,948,368	0.00004
1984	852	39,998,259	0.00002
1985	855	78,744,047	0.00001
1986	831	78,744,047	0.00001

Source: *Local Government Bonds,* the Ministry of Finance, June 1988.

OTC Trading. Tokyo based institutional brokers and dealers are the most active traders of debt instruments in Japan. Therefore, the OTC activities in Tokyo, which we shall refer to as the Tokyo OTC market, provide a good indication of the overall trend of OTC trading in Japan. In Exhibit 10, an annual breakdown of the Tokyo OTC trading volume of private placement and public subscription LGBs is provided. In 1975, ¥917.4 billion worth of public subscription LGBs were traded in the Tokyo OTC market. In 1986, this volume had increased to ¥11.6 trillion. This represented an increase of 1172% in OTC trading volume for public subscription LGBs in 11 years.[34] However, as can be seen in Exhibit 10, most of this growth in secondary trading of public subscription LGBs came between 1975 and 1978. From 1979 to 1986, the growth was modest. The growth in popularity of JGBs not only overshadowed the relative volume of public subscription LGBs issuances, but also their trading volume in the secondary market.

The growth in the Tokyo OTC trading for private placement LGBs between institutional brokers and dealers in the Tokyo area

EXHIBIT 10: ANNUAL TRADING VOLUME (OTC MARKET IN TOKYO) FOR PUBLIC AND PRIVATE PLACEMENT LGBs

(Yen billion)

	Public Subscription LGBs	Private Placement LGBs	LGBs Total	Public Bonds Total	Percentage
1975	917.4	12,313.5	13,230.9	55,698.6	23.8
1976	2,529.0	17,112.1	19,641.1	71,399.6	27.5
1977	5,107.4	25,379.2	30,486.6	133,676.4	22.8
1978	7,338.6	24,018.6	31,357.2	196,646.3	15.9
1979	7,170.7	25,569.2	32,739.9	222,731.5	14.7
1980	6,874.0	22,990.7	29,864.7	281,011.4	10.6
1981	6,849.7	16,219.2	23,068.9	297,527.5	7.8
1982	8,480.4	19,872.7	28,353.1	332,888.9	8.5
1983	9,195.3	21,555.3	30,750.6	416,191.0	7.4
1984	7,838.1	17,098.3	24,936.4	798,024.9	3.1
1985	9,063.6	14,170.5	23,934.1	2,514,653.1	1.0
1986	11,670.5	16,032.8	27,703.3	3,490,263.7	0.8

Source: *Discussion of LGBs*, by Shozo Takayose, July 1988.

has been much slower than for public subscription LGBs. In 1975, ¥12.3 trillion worth of private placement LGBs were traded in the Tokyo OTC market. In 1986, this volume increased to only ¥16 trillion. This represented an increase of only 30% in Tokyo OTC trading volume for private placement LGBs over 11 years.[35] As can be seen from Exhibit 10, the major growth period for private placement LGB trading was between 1975 and 1977. From 1978 to 1986, trading volume of private placement LGBs in the Tokyo OTC market actually declined.

The lower growth in OTC trading for private placement LGBs was the result of several factors. First, unlike public subscription LGBs, private placement LGBs were sometimes issued by smaller cities and prefectures. These local governments normally are not well-known by investors outside of their locality. Therefore, most interest in trading these private placement LGBs would only come from local investors. Second, as the primary issuance terms and conditions of private placement bonds were specifically tailored for the local government issuers and specific investors at the time of issuance, secondary market investors might find these terms to lack the standardization of more popular public bonds such as JGBs and even public subscription LGBs. Third, the average issue size of ¥100 million for private placement LGB is usually too small to trade effectively in the secondary market. The average transaction lot-size in the secondary market is between ¥500 million and ¥1 billion. Therefore, many private placement LGBs have to be traded as "broken lots," which has adversely impacted their liquidity in the secondary market. Finally, as mentioned earlier, private placement LGBs are not acceptable as collateral for borrowing from the Bank of Japan. Many institutional investors in secondary markets stayed away from investing in private placement LGBs for this reason.

In conclusion, one should realize that LGBs, in general, are not actively traded in the secondary market compared to JGBs and other debt instruments. To illustrate our point, in 1975, LGBs (both private placements and public subscription) accounted for 23.8% of the trading volume of debt instruments in the Tokyo OTC market. However, in 1986, this figure declined to 0.8%.[36]

Yield Spreads Between Primary Issuance and Secondary Markets

Here we will examine the yield spreads between the primary and secondary markets. Once again, all yields used in this analysis are simple yields.

The issuance terms and conditions of public subscription LGBs are determined largely by the Ministry of Home Affairs and not by any sort of market mechanism. Therefore the yields to subscribers could change drastically after a new issue is trading in the secondary market. Historical yield spreads between yields to subscribers of public subscription LGBs in the primary and yields in the secondary markets are plotted in Exhibits 11a and 11b. In the late 1970s and early 1980s, the yields to subscribers in the primary market were usually lower than in the secondary market, resulting in a positive yield spread between the primary issuance and secondary markets. This was the result of the regulated issuance system used by the Ministry of Affairs to keep issuance yields low. In a few selected months in the late 1970s and early 1980s, the yield spread between

**EXHIBIT 11(a): LGB YIELD SPREAD BETWEEN PRIMARY AND
SECONDARY MARKET, 1977–1984**

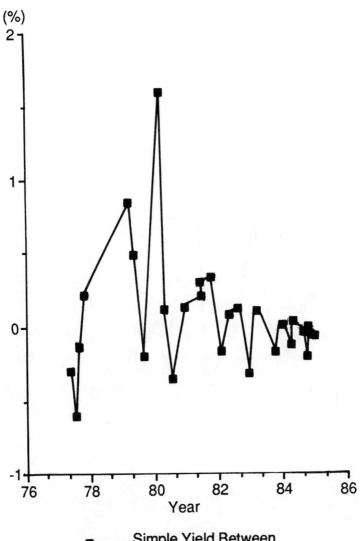

Simple Yield Between
Prim. & Sec.

Source: *Manual for Public and Corporate Bonds,* Nomura Research Inst., 1988.

EXHIBIT 11(b): LGB YIELD SPREAD BETWEEN PRIMARY AND SECONDARY MARKET, 1985–1987

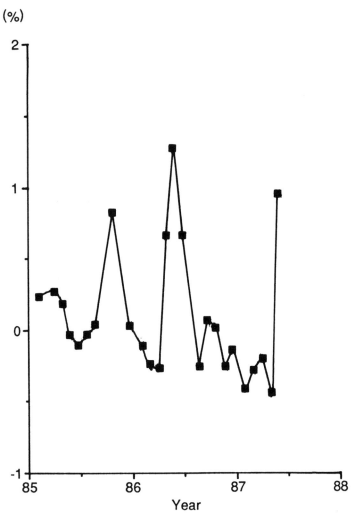

(%)

Year

■   Simple Yield Between
Prim. & Sec.

Source: *Manual for Public and Corporate Bonds,* Nomura Research Inst., 1988.

the primary and secondary markets were as follows: 84.3 basis points in March 1978, 47.9 basis points in May 1979, and 160.1 basis points in March 1980.[37]

From 1983 to 1987, the wide positive yield spreads that previously existed for public subscription LGBs between the primary and secondary markets almost disappeared. In selected months during this period, the positive spread declined to 7.6 basis points in September 1986, and 3.5 basis points in October 1986.[38] Surprisingly in the last two months of 1986 and the first four months of 1987, there were even small negative spreads (i.e., primary market yields higher than secondary market yields). This trend of smaller positive spreads, and even negative spreads, was partly due to the Ministry of Home Affairs' increased awareness of the market trend in pricing public subscription LGBs.

REGULATIONS AND TAXES FOR INVESTORS

Regulations for Nonresident Investors

Since December 1980, when the Amended Law Concerning Foreign Exchange and Foreign Trade Controls went into effect, purchases of Japanese bonds and debentures by nonresident investors have been permitted.[39] This law requires that a notice be filed with the Ministry of Finance by a nonresident investor (or his agent) prior to his buying of any Japanese securities. However, if the foreign investor made his purchase through one of Japan's designated securities companies, he is not required to file a notice. There are currently no restrictions on selling LGBs by foreign investors. Any interest or redemption proceeds can be freely remitted out of Japan back to the investor's country.

Withholding Taxes on Coupon Payments

According to the Japanese Income Tax Law, LGB coupon payments made to nonresident investors are subject to a 20% withholding tax.[40] Japan has tax treaties with numerous countries to avoid the double levying of taxes. Most of these treaties stipulate the maximum tax rate applicable in Japan on interest coupon payments made to foreign nonresident investors. In special cases, if the foreign investor submits a special form to the Japanese tax authorities through his custodian in Japan, he may have the tax rate reduced. Depending on his country of citizenship, an investor may claim a foreign tax credit in his country of residence for the withholding tax he paid in Japan.

CREDIT EVALUATION TECHNIQUES FOR LGBs

Previously, we discussed the lack of trading activity for public and private LGBs in the secondary markets. One reason for this is the lower credit quality of LGBs as compared to either JGBs or government-guaranteed bonds. Despite the higher credit risks of Japanese local governments as compared to the federal government, until now, no local governments have defaulted on any of their bond obligations. In addition, public subscription LGBs are currently issued by 23 of the largest cities and prefectures in Japan, and their bond repayment abilities are backed by their enormous local tax revenues. Therefore, the overall quality of LGBs, especially that of public subscription bonds, is very sound.

Currently, under the restricted guidelines determined by the Ministry of Home Affairs and Ministry of Finance, every local government has been issuing public subscription LGBs under the same conditions and terms. However, as deregulation of the Japanese financial markets continues, individual credit evaluation will become increasingly important for LGBs to trade successfully in the secondary markets.

Currently for LGBs, there are no standardized bond ratings used like Moody's or Standard & Poor's municipal bond ratings in the United States. However, there are many conventional yardsticks that are used by Japanese investors in gauging the creditworthiness of each LGB issue.

One widely used measure is the ratio of bond expenses. This ratio is calculated by dividing the bond coupon and principal repayments of the issue by the budget of the local government. Nikkei (Japanese Economic Journal Company) developed the *debt service coverage ratio* (DESC),[41] which is similar to the ratio of bond expenses and has supplied this ratio to most financial institutions and individual investors in Japan. The key assumption underlying this ratio is that principal and coupon payments on LGBs should only be financed by local tax revenues. However, local government revenues are comprised of not only local taxes, but also local grant taxes and other revenues. Also, this ratio assumes that other local government expenses, such as salary and welfare, should have priority over bond payment expenses. Therefore, the DESC ratio is a somewhat conservative estimate of the repayment ability of the local government borrower.

In using the DESC, the larger the ratio, the higher the creditworthiness of the borrower. Conventionally speaking, a rule of thumb of 3.5 times is desirable, and the acceptable minimum is usually around 2.0 times. Local governments can achieve high DESC ratios in several ways. First, the larger the local tax revenues not earmarked for other purposes, the larger is the DESC ratio. Second, the smaller the current expenses (e.g., salary expenses) of the local government, the larger the DESC ratio. Finally, the smaller the amount of bonds already outstanding (therefore the smaller amount of principal and coupon payments), the higher is the local government's DESC ratio.

In the future, as more financial information is compiled and revealed by the local governments of Japan, the credit evaluation techniques will no doubt increase in accuracy. Still, even though this type of credit evaluation is imperfect, it helps private placement and OTC investors in identifying the value of local government bonds.

CURRENT PROBLEMS IN THE LGB MARKET

We mentioned earlier that all public subscription LGBs were issued with the same terms and conditions irrespective of the issuer's credit quality and market conditions. Also, the issuance terms of LGBs and government guaranteed bonds have been identical since 1981, despite their difference in credit quality.

This rigid licensing/permission system enacted by the government created tensions and problems for underwriters, issuers and investors. For example, in March 1989, no public subscription LGBs were issued in Japan due to the disagreement between the Ministry of Home Affairs, the local government issuers, and an underwriting syndicate consisting of banks and securities firms.[42] Their disagreement centered around the issuance terms of the new 10-year public subscription LGB. The underwriting syndicate asked the Ministry of Home Affairs to differentiate the issuance terms of LGBs from those of government guaranteed bonds so as to reflect a wide gap of yields between the two in the secondary market. Government guaranteed bonds were traded at 0.40 to 0.60 yen higher in the secondary market than those of LGBs, thereby creating huge losses for firms underwriting public subscription LGBs. The suggestion by the syndicate group to the Ministry of Home Affairs of raising the issuance yield of LGBs above government guaranteed bonds was rejected by the government. Because of this snag in the negotiations between the participants, 12 local governments that had planned to issue LGBs had to procure funds through other means.

Another recent development that created problems for LGBs was the enactment of the Bank for International Settlement's (BIS) capital adequacy ratio in 1988.[43] This ratio required banks to assign different risk weightings for LGBs versus government guaranteed bonds in their investment portfolios. This resulted in banks buying more government guaranteed bonds (i.e., lower risk weighting) and driving their yields below those of LGBs in the secondary market, adversely affecting the relative attractiveness of LGBs. Because of this, LGB underwriting syndicates claimed that different issuance terms should be applied to LGBs and government guaranteed bonds.

No doubt all these tensions and frictions between the participants will affect LGB issuances. The monthly negotiation process between the participants for LGB issuance was severely mired since the summer of 1988. Since February 1989, fewer public subscription LGBs came to the market, and for those that were issued, the issuance size was smaller. Only large cities like Tokyo and Yokohama, with their high credit status, issued public subscription LGBs.[44]

FUTURE DEVELOPMENTS IN THE LGB MARKET

As the deregulation environment continues in Japan, it will just be a matter of time before public subscription LGBs are allowed to be priced separately for each issuing entity and independently from government guaranteed bonds. There are other developments in the LGB market which can be expected to continue in the future.

Pooling of Smaller Tranches of Private Placement LGB Issues

On June 19, 1986, the Ministry of Home Affair's section chief for LGB sent the following message to all local governments: "In recent years, as the public bond market expands, investors strongly prefer high liquidity bonds. Therefore, in order to issue and sell more LGBs, it is necessary to increase the liquidity of LGBs now."[45] The message was clear that the government was concerned with the lack of liquidity of LGBs in the secondary market and wanted to improve this situation. The first recommendation was to increase the issuing amount of each private placement LGB issue. In the past, the average issue size of around ¥100 million for private placement LGBs was simply too small for these bonds to trade actively in the secondary market. Therefore the future development in this market would be that more and more local governments and their underwriting syndicates would pool together smaller tranches of private placement LGBs issues that have the same issuance dates and conditions (price, due date, deferment, repayment schedule), and issue one mega tranche. This effectively would increase the issue size of private placement LGBs and increase their liquidity in the secondary market.

Securitization of Sho-shos (Certificate of Borrowings)

As previously mentioned, local governments can issue either bonds or certificates of borrowings in their private placement debt offerings. Certificates of borrowings are more like simple bank loans made by the creditor banks to the local government. In the past, these certificates have had no secondary market trading capabilites and their terms were strictly negotiated between the issuing local government and the institutional lender. However, this may change somewhat in the future.

On March 10, 1989, the Financial System Research Committee, an advisory panel to the finance minister of Japan, suggested measures for certificate lenders to sell pools of these certificates of borrowings or loans to investors.[46] Under the recommended system, a certificate representing various sho-shos (loans) made by the creditor bank to local governments can be sold to investors. The investor, however, will not be allowed to transfer the certificate to a third party without approval of the debtor (creditor bank). The creditor bank will not have to guarantee the repayment of the loans or repurchase the certificates. The investor can entrust the bank with its loan management, including the collection of interest and principal repayments. The minimum value of the certificate will be ¥100 million. The bank's name will not have to appear on the certificate.

It is premature to say what the future volume of this instrument will be or how it will affect the LGB market. However, the trend of securitization of sho-shos will no doubt benefit local governments. More banks will be willing to invest in private placement debt of local governments as there would be a larger secondary market for them to sell these instruments. Also, more investors (besides banks) can participate in financing local governments.

CONCLUSION

In this chapter, we have focused on the market practices, trends, current problems and the future development of LGBs in both the primary and secondary markets. In this concluding section, we will summarize the investment merits of LGBs (especially for non-Japanese investors).

Currently, yields of yen LGBs are higher than those of JGBs in both the primary and secondary markets. Also, yields of LGBs are higher than those of government guaranteed bonds in the secondary markets. LGBs' higher yields should attract foreign investors interested in investing in yen-dominated bonds. The credit quality of these LGBs is very sound, since only the larger cities or prefectures with excellent credit standing in Japan are allowed to issue public subscription LGBs. Until now, no Japanese local government has defaulted on its public subscription or private placement LGBs.

Non-yen LGBs should provide an alternative for foreign investors interested in Japanese LGBs, but are unwilling to assume foreign exchange risk. Another attractive feature of non-yen LGBs is that the Japanese government usually guarantees the interest and principal payments of these bonds. In contrast, yen-denominated LGBs currently do not enjoy this advantage.

Despite the above-mentioned attractiveness of both yen and non-yen LGBs, there are several facts that foreign investors should be aware of when they buy LGBs. The liquidity of LGBs is substantially less than that of JGBs, resulting in wider bid-ask spreads for LGBs. Foreign investors should realize this and be ready to pay higher transaction costs for these bonds.

ENDNOTES

[1] The Ministry of Home Affairs, *Census of Local Government Debt* [in Japanese, title translated], 1987.

[2] The Ministry of Finance/Local Government Bond Committee, *Local Government Bonds* [in Japanese, title translated], June 1988, p. 175.

[3] Nomura Research Institute, *Manual of Public and Corporate Bonds* [in Japanese, title translated], 1984–1987.

[4] Japan Public Bonds Underwriters Association, *Annual Data of Local Government Bonds* [in Japanese, title translated], 1987, p. 10.

[5] *Local Government Bonds*, p. 173.

[6] Ibid, p. 180.

[7] *Annual Data of Local Government Bonds*, p. 234.

[8] *Local Government Bonds*, p. 180.

[9] *Census of Local Government Debt*

[10] Daiwa Securities Company Ltd., *Introduction to Japanese Bonds* [in Japanese, title translated], October 1988, p. 58.

[11] *Local Government Bonds*, pp. 187-191.

[12] *Introduction to Japanese Bonds*, pp. 55-58.

[13] Shozo Takayose, *Discussion of Local Government Bonds* [in Japanese, title translated], July 1988, p. 120.

[14] Hirotoshi Sugihara, *How to Manage Local Government Bonds*, October 1988, pp. 66-67.

[15] *Discussion of Local Government Bonds*, p. 175.

[16] Ibid.

[17] Ibid.

[18] Ibid.

[19] *Annual Data of Local Government Bonds,* p. 10.

[20] Ibid.

[21] *Annual Data of Local Government Bonds,* p. 234.

[22] Ibid.

[23] *Local Government Bonds,* pp. 176–177.

[24] Ibid.

[25] Ibid.

[26] Ibid.

[27] Credit Suisse/First Boston, *The Yen Bond Markets,* Probus Publishing, 1988, p. 64.

[28] *Discussion of Local Government Bonds,* p. 96.

[29] Ibid.

[30] Ibid.

[31] *Local Government Bonds,* p. 211.

[32] "Banks to Offer Municipal Bond Price Information," *Nikkei Financial Daily,* January 13, 1989.

[33] *Local Government Bonds,* p. 181.

[34] Ibid.

[35] Ibid.

[36] Ibid.

[37] *Manual of Public and Corporate Bonds.*

[38] Ibid.

[39] *Introduction to Japanese Bonds,* p. 295.

[40] Ibid, p. 296.

[41] *Discussion of Local Government Bonds,* p. 115.

[42] "March Municipal Bond Issuances Suspended," *The Japan Economic Journal*, April 1, 1989.

[43] "Background of the Tokyo Market," *The Tokyo Financial Letter*, February 27, 1989.

[44] "Negotiations On Local Bond Terms Stalmated," *Nihon Keizai Shimbun*, March 23, 1989.

[45] *Discussion of Local Government Bonds*, p. 115.

[46] "Background of the Tokyo Market," *The Tokyo Financial Letter*, March 20, 1989.

CHAPTER 9

The Bank Debenture Market

Satoshi Doi
System Analyst
The Bank of Tokyo, Ltd.

INTRODUCTION

Bank debentures are bonds issued by banks as their primary means of raising funds. As of 1989, under Japanese laws, only six Japanese banks are allowed to issue debentures. Those banks include the Industrial Bank of Japan (IBJ), the Long-Term Credit Bank of Japan (LTCB), the Nippon Credit Bank (NCB), the Norinchukin Bank (the Central Cooperative Bank for Agriculture and Forestry), the Shoko Chukin Bank (the Central Cooperative Bank for Commerce and Industry), and the Bank of Tokyo (BOT). Although all six banks are in the commercial banking business, some of them concentrate on certain specific services. As their primary businesses, the first three banks finance long-term industrial projects, the next two banks provide funds for small farms and businesses, and the Bank of Tokyo finances foreign trade and exchange operations. Unlike other commercial banks in Japan, the domestic branch networks of these six banks are not sufficiently widespread to attract deposits from the general public. Each of these banks, therefore, is allowed to issue two types of bank debentures, namely, one-year discount debentures and five-year coupon debentures. (The BOT's coupon debentures have a maturity of three years.)

Bank debentures are issued each month and subject to guide-lines of the Ministry of Finance (MOF), and the Bank of Japan. Since the issuance of bank debentures is a primary means of raising funds for these banks, they are granted preferential treatment to ensure that debentures are issued smoothly. First, when issuing bonds, ordinary corporations cannot start subscription until the application for issuance is granted and validated by the Ministry of Finance. The issuers of bank debentures, in contrast, have only to report to the MOF the amount and terms of the issue whenever they want to issue debentures. It is as if only bank debentures were eligible in the U.S. for "shelf registration." Second, while most corporate bonds are required to be issued on a secured basis, bank debentures are not. The reason is that the issuers of bank debentures are considered to have little credit risk because they are under strict supervision of the Ministry of Finance and obliged to preserve their assets to ensure the refunding of debentures. For instance, when lending longer than six months, the issuing banks must require collateral of a certain value to ensure the safety and collectability of the loan. In practice, bank debentures have higher credits than any other corporate bond, and are used as collateral when banks borrow from the Bank of Japan or in the call money market.

The new issue volume of bank debentures in FY 1987 was ¥32.9 trillion, the largest of any class of Japanese debt, exceeding even that of Japanese government bonds. (See Exhibit 1.) The outstanding balance of bank debentures at the end of March 1987 was about ¥51.7 trillion (¥33.6 trillion in coupon debentures and ¥18.1 trillion in discount debentures), which was about 17.5% of the total outstanding balance of Japanese bonds. (See Exhibit 2.) As shown in Exhibit 3b, about 70% of new issues of coupon debentures were purchased by "individuals and others," including private corporations and nonresidents, while 30% was bought by financial institutions. Nearly 100% of discount debentures are purchased by "individual investors and others." (See Exhibit 3a.)

EXHIBIT 1:   NEW ISSUE VOLUME OF BONDS IN FY 1987

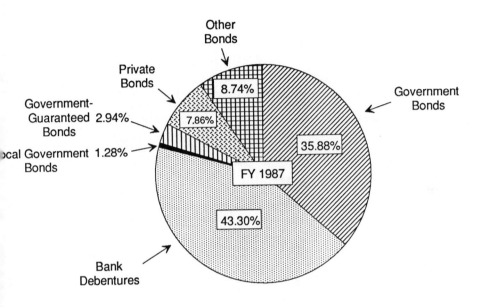

		(¥ billion)	
Category	*FY 1987*	*FY 1986*	*FY 1985*
Bank Debentures	32,908.6	28,645.9	26,300.4
Government Bonds	27,268.6	25,897.4	22,998.0
Local Government Bonds	976.2	868.6	807.3
Government-guaranteed Bonds	2,231.1	2,799.9	2,747.9
Private Bonds	5,970.0	4,552.0	2,584.0
Other Bonds	6,640.4	6,055.3	6,332.4
Total	75,994.9	68,819.1	61,770.0

Source: Nomura Research Institute.

EXHIBIT 2:   OUTSTANDING BALANCE OF BONDS IN FY 1987

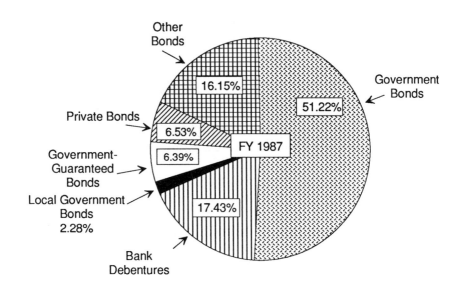

		(¥ billion)	
Category	*FY 1987*	*FY 1986*	*FY 1985*
Bank Debentures	51,659.9	47,179.9	43,515.0
Government Bonds	151,809.4	145,126.8	133,431.5
Local Government Bonds	6,751.7	6,394.5	6,060.0
Government-guaranteed Bonds	18,946.5	18,099.9	16,443.1
Private Bonds	19,353.5	16,634.3	13,826.9
Other Bonds	47,870.6	14,656.6	48,207.8
Total	296,391.6	281,092.0	261,484.3

Source: Nomura Research Institute.

EXHIBIT 3a: INVESTORS IN DISCOUNT DEBENTURES

(million yen)

FY	Total Amount Issued	City Banks Long-term	%	Local Banks	%	Trust Banks	%	Insurance Companies	%	Agricultural Financial Institutions	%	Shinkin Banks	%	Mutual Banks	%	Individuals & Others	%	Total	Trust Fund Bureau	Post Office Life Insurance Bureau
1972	2,902,598		0.0		0.0		0.0	55	0.0	472	0.0	21	0.0		0.0	2,646,157	100.0	2,646,705	237,420	18,474
1973	3,569,878	30	0.0		0.0		0.0	68	0.0	649	0.0	2	0.0	110	0.0	2,996,017	100.0	2,996,876	549,060	23,943
1974	4,089,156	30	0.0		0.0		0.0	182	0.0	969	0.0	1,500	0.0		0.0	3,345,054	99.9	3,347,735	713,953	27,468
1975	5,160,228		0.0		0.0		0.0	146	0.0	1,799	0.0	3	0.0		0.0	4,294,863	100.0	4,296,811	841,165	22,252
1976	6,002,160		0.0		0.0		0.0	212	0.0	2,099	0.0	3	0.0		0.0	5,322,783	100.0	5,325,097	653,200	23,863
1977	6,884,781		0.0		0.0	39	0.0	174	0.0	1,845	0.0	3	0.0	413	0.0	6,340,902	100.0	6,343,376	516,191	25,216
1978	7,490,292		0.0		0.0		0.0	215	0.0	2,568	0.0	7	0.0		0.0	6,976,920	100.0	6,979,710	485,939	24,643
1979	8,260,858		0.0		0.0		0.0	208	0.0	2,544	0.0	7	0.0	509	0.0	7,564,188	100.0	7,567,456	693,401	
1980	8,874,594		0.0		0.0		0.0	264	0.0	3,082	0.0	1	0.0		0.0	8,138,650	100.0	8,141,997	732,597	
1981	9,234,735		0.0		0.0		0.0	282	0.0	3,217	0.0		0.0		0.0	8,762,222	100.0	8,765,721	469,014	
1982	10,430,369		0.0		0.0	1	0.0	292	0.0	2,977	0.0		0.0		0.0	9,591,028	100.0	9,594,297	836,072	
1983	12,110,401		0.0		0.0		0.0	306	0.0	2,874	0.0		0.0		0.0	11,239,905	100.0	11,243,086	867,315	
1984	14,276,280		0.0		0.0		0.0	300	0.0	3,011	0.0		0.0		0.0	13,177,292	100.0	13,180,603	1,095,677	
1985	18,879,449		0.0		0.0		0.0	269	0.0	2,999	0.0		0.0		0.0	17,685,168	100.0	17,688,436	1,190,996	
1986	20,493,694		0.0		0.0		0.0	257	0.0	3,047	0.0	410	0.0		0.0	19,313,079	100.0	19,316,793	1,176,902	
1987	24,091,233		0.0		0.0		0.0	229	0.0	3,176	0.0	330	0.0		0.0	22,916,913	100.0	22,920,648	1,170,585	

Source: The Bond Underwriters Association of Japan.

EXHIBIT 3b: INVESTORS IN COUPON DEBENTURES

(billion yen)

FY	Total Amount Issued	City Banks & Long-term Credit Banks	%	Local Banks	%	Trust Banks	%	Insurance Companies	%	Agricultural Financial Institutions	%	Shinkin Banks	%	Mutual Banks	%	Individuals & Others	%	Total	Trust Fund Bureau	Post Office Life Insurance Bureau
1972	2,124	388	19.9	180	9.2	5	0.3	96	4.9	9	0.5	175	9.0	181	9.3	915	46.9	1,949	144	33
1973	2,077	394	20.3	212	10.9	5	0.3	102	5.2	4	0.2	133	6.8	212	10.9	881	45.3	1,943	104	31
1974	2,427	417	18.3	216	9.5	7	0.3	107	4.7	5	0.2	144	6.3	213	9.4	1,165	51.2	2,274	141	13
1975	2,919	458	16.4	261	9.4	10	0.4	118	4.2	18	0.6	200	7.2	239	8.6	1,485	53.2	2,789	116	16
1976	3,435	498	14.9	326	9.8	13	0.4	135	4.1	12	0.4	178	5.3	280	8.4	1,889	56.7	3,331	85	19
1977	3,608	463	13.2	348	10.0	14	0.4	166	4.7	11	0.3	249	7.1	311	8.9	1,935	55.3	3,497	94	16
1978	3,904	462	13.2	391	11.1	12	0.3	188	5.3	6	0.2	250	7.1	335	9.5	1,871	53.2	3,515	373	15
1979	3,464	411	12.6	391	12.0	13	0.4	185	5.7	4	0.1	168	5.2	311	9.6	1,773	54.5	3,256	208	
1980	4,689	531	11.5	454	9.8	26	0.6	236	5.1	9	0.2	262	5.7	341	7.4	2,755	59.7	4,614	74	
1981	5,539	519	9.5	518	9.5	24	0.4	264	4.8	10	0.2	291	5.3	352	6.4	3,484	63.8	5,462	78	
1982	5,968	476	8.1	525	8.9	26	0.4	288	4.9	8	0.1	294	5.0	359	6.1	3,918	66.5	5,894	75	
1983	6,390	481	7.6	572	9.1	31	0.5	317	5.0	8	0.1	329	5.2	406	6.4	4,171	66.0	6,315	75	
1984	5,334	414	7.9	569	10.9	31	0.6	331	6.3	8	0.2	259	4.9	365	7.0	3,262	62.3	5,239	95	
1985	7,421	547	7.5	670	9.2	38	0.5	396	5.4	25	0.3	324	4.4	432	5.9	4,887	66.8	7,319	102	
1986	8,152	537	6.7	770	9.6	43	0.5	448	5.6	33	0.4	370	4.6	434	5.4	5,397	67.2	8,032	91	
1987	8,817	486	5.6	802	9.3	43	0.5	483	5.6	51	0.6	412	4.8	479	5.6	5,863	68.0	8,619	198	

Source: The Bond Underwriters Association of Japan.

DEVELOPMENT AND ROLE OF BANK DEBENTURES

The History of Bank Debentures

Japanese bank debentures were first issued in 1896, when huge amounts of funds were needed to encourage agriculture and other industries. To finance these needs, the Kangyo Bank of Japan and the Noukou Bank were founded based on the Chartered Bank Laws in 1896, and were permitted to issue coupon debentures for fund raising. The Industrial Bank of Japan, founded in 1902, started issuing discount debentures in the midst of serious stagnation in 1922 to provide emergency financing to small firms.

After World War II, the Chartered Bank Laws were abolished, and replaced in 1950 by the Law Concerning Issuance of Debentures by Banks. This law allowed any bank to issue debentures for fund-raising, however, only four banks—the Kangyo Bank of Japan, the Noukou Bank, the Industrial Bank of Japan, and the Bank of Tokyo—did issue them. In 1952 this law was replaced by the Long-Term Credit Bank Law, which aimed at separating long-term financing from short-term financing. This law prohibited commercial banks that were bound by the Ordinary Bank Law from issuing debentures. Therefore, the Industrial Bank of Japan, Long-Term Credit Bank of Japan, the Norinchukin Bank, and the Shoko Chukin Bank were the only issuing banks in 1952. In 1957, the Real Estate Bank of Japan (the predecessor of the Nippon Credit Bank) was established as the third long-term credit bank, and started issuing debentures. The government revised the Foreign Exchange Bank Law in 1962 to allow the BOT, which has a limited network in Japan, to support its operating funds with debentures.

Role of Bank Debentures

The role of coupon debentures is different from that of discount debentures. Coupon debentures were created to meet long-term financing needs. Japanese commercial banks, in general, raise funds through deposits such as time and savings deposits. Time deposits are deposits for which the term of the deposit is fixed and which, in principle, cannot be withdrawn during this period.[1] The term is usually one year or less. Since those funds are mostly short-term, they are usually loaned out on a short-term basis to maturity to match the banks' assets and liabilities. In the postwar recovery period, some banks specializing in long-term loans were needed to provide sufficient and stable funds to growing industries. For that purpose the Norinchukin Bank, the Shoko Chukin Bank and the three long-term credit banks were founded, and they were allowed to issue bank debentures as their primary source of raising long-term funds. Those banks, in fact, played an extremely important role in long-term financing throughout the high growth period of the 1950s and 1960s.

Purchased by commercial banks and other financial institutions, coupon debentures work as the vehicle to transform short-term funds collected by those institutions into long-term funds. In other words, financial institutions which are supposed to take charge of short-term financing also participate in long-term financing indirectly by purchasing coupon debentures.

Nearly 100% of discount debentures, in contrast, have been consistently held by individual investors as a handy instrument for short-term investment because of a lower tax rate applicable to these securities and relatively higher yield. (This tax rate will be discussed later.) When interest rates are high, discount debentures are an important source of funds for the issuing banks. Issuing banks temporarily reduce their total fund-raising costs by concentrating their issuance activities on discount debentures rather than coupon debentures, because the cost of discount debentures is usually lower than that of coupon debentures reflecting their shorter maturity and tax advantage.

Long-Term Prime Rate System and Coupon Debentures

The long-term prime rate system maintains order in the long-term loan market in Japan. That is, the long-term prime rate, which is based on the coupon rate of debentures, has been accepted among various financial institutions as the base rate for long-term loans. There are, however, some indications which suggest that the system has already lost its effectiveness.[2] This section highlights the relationship between coupon debentures and the long-term prime rate system, and addresses the role of coupon debentures from a different point of view.

Japanese banks may determine their lending rate individually, either for short-term or long-term loans. They use the same base rate for lending, however, maintaining large profit margins by excluding competition among them. For instance, the long-term (longer than one year) lending rate is determined based on the long-term prime rate which is a certain number of basis points higher than the coupon debenture rate. Long-term credit banks as well as trust banks, insurance companies, and government financial institutions (such as the Japan Development Bank) use this long-term prime rate as their basic long-term loan rate. City banks and local banks often adopt the long-term prime rate as the base rate for their long-term lending. The coupon rate on debentures, therefore, has had a great impact on long-term lending rates through the long-term prime rate.

The long-term prime rate system began in 1961, and had provided a sort of "standard" rate for the long-term loan market. In those days, the difference between the long-term prime rate and the coupon rate on the coupon debentures, which was called the "basic profit margin," was 1.4%. This profit margin generated large profits for issuing banks. As lending opportunities gradually shrank in the late 1970s owing to a general move from indirect to direct financing (i.e., issuance of bonds or equity), the profit margin declined to 0.9%. Recently financial institutions have been lending at a rate below the long-term prime rate because of the intense competition between them. The long-term prime rate system, therefore, has lost its significance as a standard lending rate in the long-term credit market. The rapid expansion of the Euroyen lending market, due to the deregulation and internationalization of Japanese financial markets, has also accelerated this trend.

Changes in the Environment Affecting Debentures. Exhibit 4 shows the trend of the outstanding balance of bank debentures since 1955. Outstanding volume has increased smoothly, on the whole, and there are two notable trends in the annual growth rate and proportion of coupon and discount debentures. First, the annual growth rate of the outstanding balance of bank debentures has slowed down over the last 35 years. It dropped from 24.3% during the period 1956–1960 to 16% during the period 1966–1970. It recovered to 20.2% in the early 1970s, but again dropped to about 10% in the 1980s. Second, the growth rate of discount debentures exceeded that of cou-

**EXHIBIT 4:   OUTSTANDING BALANCE AND ITS ANNUAL
GROWTH RATE OF BANK DEBENTURES (1955–1985)**

| | Outstanding balance (billion yen) | | | | |
Year	Coupon debentures	%	Discount debentures	%	Total
FY 1955	308.3	82.4	65.8	17.6	374.1
FY 1960	761.5	68.5	349.8	31.5	1,111.3
FY 1965	2,228.7	73.8	791.3	26.2	3,020.0
FY 1970	4,460.0	70.3	1,881.7	29.7	6,341.7
FY 1975	11,128.7	˙69.9	4,791.0	30.1	15,919.7
FY 1980	17,671.4	67.5	8,485.8	32.4	26,157.2
FY 1985	28,385.9	65.2	15,129.1	34.8	43,515.0

| | Annual growth rate | | |
	%	%	%
1956–60	19.8	39.7	24.3
1961–61	24.0	17.7	22.1
1966–70	14.9	18.9	16.0
1971–75	20.1	20.6	20.2
1976–80	9.7	12.1	10.4
1981–85	9.9	12.3	10.7

Source: The Bond Underwriters Association of Japan.

pon debentures in 1965, and has remained higher since. Accordingly, the proportion of discount debentures to total bank debentures rose from 17.6% in FY 1960 to 35.0% in FY 1985.

The Decade of Rapid Change in Composition of Investors in Bank Debentures (1966–1975). During the period of 1956–1965 the largest holders of coupon debentures were commercial banks, who purchased about 70% of the total outstanding amount. (See Exhibit 5.) Of these, city banks held 44.1% of coupon debentures at the end of FY 1965. Coupon debentures were very attractive to those banks because of their high marketability and liquidity. Coupon debentures, like Japanese government bonds and selected local government bonds, may be used as collateral when banks borrow funds from the Bank of Japan. In addition, in 1963, the Bank of Japan added coupon

EXHIBIT 5: HOLDERS OF COUPON DEBENTURES ISSUED BY THREE LONG-TERM CREDIT BANKS (OUTSTANDING BASIS)

	(Billion yen)		
	FY 1965	FY 1975	FY 1985
Commercial banks	1,304.6	4,478.4	7,953.7
	(71.4%)	(49.7%)	(39.5%)
City banks	804.9	1,469.1	1,656.3
	(44.1%)	(16.3%)	(8.2%)
Other banks	499.7	3,009.3	6,297.4
	(27.3%)	(33.4%)	(31.3%)
Insurance companies & agricultural financial institutions	47.9	1,059.6	2,690.8
	(2.6%)	(11.8%)	(13.4%)
Individuals & others	393.9	3,298.6	8,418.1
	(21.6%)	(36.6%)	(41.8%)
The Fund Trust Bureau & The Post Office Life Insurance Bureau	80.6%	178.9	1,085.7
	(4.4%)	(2.0%)	(5.4%)
	1,827.0	9,015.6	20,148.3
Total			
	(100.0%)	(100.0%)	(100.0%)

Source: Research by the Ministry of Finance "Other banks" include local banks, trust banks, sogo banks, and Shinkin banks.

debentures to its intervention account through which the BOJ sold or bought bonds to carry out monetary policy. Those banks which held coupon debentures could, therefore, raise funds whenever they wanted to by either selling debentures to the BOJ or borrowing from the BOJ while using the debentures as collateral.

The situation changed, however, in 1966 when the long-term government bond was issued for the first time after World War II. In that year, the BOJ removed coupon debentures from its intervention account, and the merits derived by banks from holding debentures almost disappeared. For city banks especially to purchase the debentures continuously became very difficult because of the expansion of lending opportunities and the increasing burden on them to underwrite large amounts of government bonds. Accordingly, the share of coupon debentures held by commercial banks dropped from 71.4% at the end of FY 1965 to less than 50% at the end of FY 1975. (See Exhibit 5.) The share of the amount held by city banks dropped sharply, from 44.1% to 16.3% over this period. Issuing banks thus had to broaden the investment appeal of debentures so that other institutional and individual investors would invest in them.

The growth rate of discount debentures, on the other hand, was stable in this decade, and was always higher than that of coupon debentures. One of the reasons is that issuing banks stressed selling discount debentures through their own networks to diversify sales channels and promote overall transactions. In 1965, most discount debentures were distributed by securities firms, but the proportion of the debentures sold by issuing banks increased gradually during this period. (See Exhibit 6.) There were two major changes which had an important effect on investment attitudes toward discount debentures.

First, the "separate tax withheld at source" was introduced to discount debentures in 1967. Prior to that year, the discount on discount debentures had been classified not as interest income but as "other income," and subject to a consolidated income tax. That is, a tax rate on the discount was determined based on the total income earned by the entity in that year. In 1967, however, a 5% separate tax on the discount levied at issuance was introduced, while a withholding tax rate on the income from interest and dividends rose from 15% to 20%.[3] That gave a tax advantage to discount debentures relative to other financial instruments such as coupon bonds and time deposits.

EXHIBIT 6: DISTRIBUTION CHANNELS OF DISCOUNT DEBENTURES ISSUED BY THREE LONG-TERM CREDIT BANKS

	(Billion yen)		
Distribution Channels	FY 1965	FY 1975	FY 1985
Securities Firms	482.5	1,759.0	4,313.5
	(84.4%)	(63.4%)	(45.5%)
Issuing Banks	89.1	1,016.5	5,176.9
	(15.6%)	(36.6%)	(54.5%)
Total	571.5	2,775.5	9,490.4
	(100.0%)	(100.0%)	(100.0%)

Source: Research by the Ministry of Finance.

Second, discount debentures also offered a yield advantage. The discount rate on discount debentures, which had been closely linked to the call rate until the 1950s, started to be set at a certain number of basis points above the interest rate on one-year time deposits in 1967. Sales of discount debentures expanded rapidly due to the lower tax rate and relatively higher yield during the period from 1966 to 1975.

The Decade of Continuous Issuance of a Huge Amount of Government Bonds (1976–1985). The rapid increase in new issuance of government bonds after 1975 had various impacts on the coupon debenture market, as well as other Japanese bond markets.

City banks, who were major holders of coupon debentures, became less enthusiastic about subscribing to coupon debentures due to the heavy burden of underwriting government bonds. However, other commercial banks, institutional investors, corporations, and individual investors found them more appealing as an investment vehicle as they sought to diversify their portfolios. For example, the share of "individuals and others" in the primary market of coupon debentures rose from 56.7% in FY 1976 to 66.8% in 1985. (See Exhibit 3b.) Local banks and Sogo banks (mutual loan and savings banks) became the second largest purchasers of coupon debentures, purchasing 15.1% of new issues in 1985.

Another important effect was that the coupon rate of debentures began to reflect the real demand-supply situation in the market. Prior to this period, there was a hierarchy of interest rates, reflecting the credit of each bond issuer. Yields of Japanese government bonds were always the lowest, followed by those of government-guaranteed bonds and local government bonds, while yields of corporate bonds were the highest. Although the bank debentures are shorter term and, in an upward sloping yield curve environment, should offer a lower yield, the coupon rate on five-year coupon debentures had always been set slightly above that of 10-year government bonds for the purpose of preserving competitiveness with government bonds. This hierarchy of yields collapsed, however, as the amount of government bonds increased. The collapse took place in three phases. (See Exhibit 7.)

First, the government had to raise the yield of 10-year government bonds to encourage successful underwriting of the bonds. The coupon rate of debentures was also raised, but not as much as that of

EXHIBIT 7: ISSUE TERMS OF 5-YEAR COUPON DEBENTURES AND 10-YEAR GOVERNMENT BOND

		5-year Coupon Debentures Coupon/Yield	10-year Government Bond		
			Coupon	Price	Yield
	1975–8	8.8	8.0	98.25	8.320
	11		8.0	98.75	8.227
	12	8.3			
	1977–5	7.5	7.4	99.50	7.487
	7	7.7	7.2	99.50	7.286
	8	7.0	6.9	99.50	6.984
	10	6.7	6.6	99.50	6.683
	1978–4	6.2	6.1	99.50	6.180
	1979–3		6.5	99.50	6.582
	4		7.2	99.50	7.286
	5	6.8			
Phase 1	8				
	9		7.7	99.50	7.788
	1980–3	7.9	8.0	99.50	8.090
	4	8.6	8.7	99.00	8.888
	7		8.5	99.75	8.546
	12	7.9	8.0	98.75	8.227
	1981–5	7.6	7.6	98.50	7.868
	6			98.00	7.959
	9		8.0	98.00	8.367
	11	8.0			
	1982–1	7.7	7.7	98.25	8.015
	4	7.5	7.5	98.25	7.811
	8		8.0	98.50	8.274
	9	8.0			
	12		7.7	98.50	7.969
	1983–1	7.7	7.5	98.50	7.766
	2	7.5			
Phase 2	3		7.5	98.00	7.857
	9		7.5	97.25	7.994
	10		7.5	97.75	7.902
	11	7.3	7.3	97.75	7.698
	1		7.3	98.50	7.563
	3		7.3	99.00	7.474
Phase 3	1984–4	7.4	7.0	98.00	7.346

EXHIBIT 7:   (continued)

Issue Date	5-year Coupon Debentures Coupon/Yield	10-year Government Bond Coupon	10-year Government Bond Price	10-year Government Bond Yield
8		7.3	97.75	7.698
9		7.1	97.50	7.538
10		7.1	98.00	7.448
11	6.5	6.8	98.50	7.055
12		6.8	99.00	6.969
1985–1	6.7	6.5	99.00	6.666
2	6.5			
3		6.8	98.25	7.099
4	6.8	6.8	99.25	6.926
5		6.8	99.75	6.842
6	6.6	6.5	98.75	6.708
7		6.5	99.25	6.624
8	6.3	6.2	98.75	6.406
10	6.1	6.0	99.25	6.120
11		6.5	98.75	6.708
12	6.6	6.5	99.50	6.582
1986–1	6.3	6.1	99.00	6.262
2	6.0	6.0	100.00	6.000
3	5.5	5.7	99.50	5.778
4		5.1	100.00	5.100
5		5.1	100.00	5.100
6		5.1	100.00	5.100
7		5.1	98.50	5.329
9		5.1	99.00	5.252
		5.1	97.00	5.567
11		5.4	99.00	5.555
12		5.3	99.00	5.454
1987–1		5.3	99.50	5.376
2	4.9	5.0	99.00	5.151
3	4.6	5.0	99.50	5.075
4	4.3	4.7	99.75	4.736
5	4.0	4.0	99.00	4.141
6		3.9	99.50	3.969
7		4.3	97.50	4.666
8	4.3	4.6	97.00	5.051
9		4.9	98.50	5.126
10	4.8			
11		5.0	99.50	5.075
12		5.0	100.00	5.000
1988–1	4.6	4.9	99.00	5.050
2		4.8	99.50	4.874
3		4.8	100.00	4.800

Note: 5-year coupon debentures were always issued at par.
Source: The Bond Underwriters Association of Japan.

10-year government bonds. Therefore, the yield on new issues of government bonds often exceeded that of coupon debentures by 30-40 basis points during the period from March 1979 to May 1981.

Second, from May 1981 to August 1984, the coupon rate of debentures was identical to that of 10-year government bonds during most of this period. Government bonds became the core of the secondary market for medium-term and long-term bonds, with their share of trading volume increasing from 63.4% in 1981 to 84.1% in 1984. As a result, the coupon rate of 10-year government bonds significantly influenced the yields of other bonds. Bank debentures offered the same coupon rate as 10-year government bonds though they were different in maturities and credit risk. However, 10-year government bonds were issued below par to increase the yields to compensate for their longer maturity. The yields of 10-year government bonds were, on average, 30-40 basis points higher than those of 5-year coupon debentures during this period, as well as in the previous period.

Third, since August 1984, the coupon rates on bank debentures are no longer regulated by the government, but are now market determined. Specifically, the issue terms of government bonds and coupon debentures were, for the first time, determined independently taking into account the actual market situation at the time of issuance. The expansion of the bond secondary market, which was due to the advent of bank dealing in 1984, has encouraged this change. The coupon rate of debentures was revised as often as seven times in FY 1985, while the coupon rate and issue price of government bonds were adjusted every month except September in the same fiscal year.

The growth rate of discount debentures slowed down during this decade. There are several reasons for this.

First, the tax rate on discount debentures was increased from 5% to 16% in the tax reform of 1978, and through further tax reform of 1987, it was raised by another 2% to 18% as of April 1988. The tax advantage of holding discount debentures (18% versus a 20% withholding tax for interest income), therefore, became very small, which resulted in a decline in the annual growth rate of discount debentures after 1975 as shown in Exhibit 4.

Another important reason for this decline was that several financial instruments emerged in that decade which competed for funds with discount debentures. The first was government bonds. The Japanese government introduced new types of bonds to broaden their investor base. The government began issuing 5-year discount bonds in 1977, but its impact on bank debentures was limited because the issued amount was relatively small. But the medium-term government coupon bonds, such as the three-year bond introduced in 1978, the 2-year bond in 1979, and the 4-year bond in 1980, competed directly with bank debentures, providing individual investors with handy instruments for medium-term investment. The second competitor was "the medium-term government bond trust fund," developed by securities firms in 1980.[4] Because of their high yield and liquidity, these trust funds became a strong rival for discount debentures. These new financial instruments have disrupted the stable sale of discount debentures.

To overcome these unfavorable situations, issuing banks increased marketing efforts through their salespeople. As a result, the share of discount debentures sold by issuing banks themselves increased further, from 36.6% in FY 1975 to more than 50% in FY 1985. (See Exhibit 6.) Although it dropped from 19.73% in the previous decade, the annual growth rate of discount debentures in terms of outstanding balance was, on average, 12.2% during this decade, paralleled by the increase in savings by households at the same rate.

PRIMARY MARKET

Issuing Banks

As stated earlier, the six banks eligible to issue bank debentures are the Industrial Bank of Japan, the Long-Term Credit Bank of Japan, the Nippon Credit Bank, the Norinchukin Bank, Shoko Chukin Bank, and the Bank of Tokyo. The laws that permitted these banks to issue debentures also regulate the amount, terms, and procedures of issue. Following is a profile of each issuing bank.

The Industrial Bank of Japan. The IBJ was organized under a special law in the prewar period, and converted to an ordinary bank in 1950. It was reconverted to a long-term credit bank in December 1952 to supply industrial funds. The IBJ, like the two other long-term credit banks, concentrates its operations on making long-term loans. That is, it is supposed to provide credit for plants and equipment and long-term working capital, but cannot supply short-term working capital funds over the limits of the deposits. The IBJ put more resources into the securities business than before, including underwriting of public and corporate bonds, and is expanding into international loans and investment operations. About 54% of the IBJ's funds came from the issuance of debentures in FY 1988.[5]

The Long-Term Credit Bank of Japan. The LTCB, established in 1952, is the second largest long-term credit bank. Recently it has emphasized development of loans to new fields in wholesale, retail and service industries, shifting from its former emphasis on mainline lending in heavy and chemical industries. It has expanded into international businesses, and has increased loans to local firms in North America. The LTCB raised 67% of its funds through the issuance of debentures in FY 1988.

The Nippon Credit Bank. The NCB was established in 1957 as the third long-term credit bank. The NCB has developed on the basis of long-term loans to medium and small sized businesses and mortgage credits, primarily housing loans and loans to the distribution industry. The NCB, like the IBJ and the LTCB, is expanding into international loans and investment operations. NCB raised 67% of its funds by issuing debentures in FY 1988.

The three banks described above were established under the Long-term Credit Bank Law which permits them to issue debentures up to a limit of 30 times the amount of their capital and reserves.

The Norinchukin Bank. The Norinchukin Bank was established as a special corporation with limited liability based on the Norin-chuo-kinko Law in 1923, and converted to a private corporation in 1986. It is the central financial institution for cooperatives serving the agricultural, forestry, and fishery industries. The financing for these industries is carried out through organizations of cooperatives based on a spirit of mutual support and with government protection and aid.

The Shoko Chukin Bank. The Shoko Chukin Bank is a special corporation organized under the Shokokumiai-chuo-kinko Law of 1936. Its purpose is to facilitate the financing of cooperative societies of small businesses and also of organizations of small business operators. Originally it was chartered for a 50-year period, however, in a revision of the law in 1985 it was converted into a permanent organization. In FY 1988, about 75% of its total funding was obtained from the issuance of debentures.

The above two special banks are allowed to issue debentures up to a limit of 30 times the amount of their paid-in capital and reserves.

The Bank of Tokyo. The Bank of Tokyo, successor to the Yokohama Specie Bank, was established in 1946 and designated Japan's sole specialized foreign exchange bank in 1954. With an extensive worldwide network, the BOT earns 70% of its gross profit from international operations. The amount it has lent to debtor countries is the largest among Japanese banks. In FY 1988, the BOT raised 26% of its funds by issuing debentures. The Foreign Exchange Bank Law permits the BOT to issue debentures up to a limit of 10 times the amount of its capital and reserves.

Size of the Market

The new issue volume of bank debentures exceeded ¥30 trillion in FY 1987 and was the largest of all types of Japanese bonds. From an annual issue volume of ¥802.8 billion in FY 1962, it has grown at an average annual rate of 16% to ¥32.9 trillion in FY 1987. (See Exhibit 8.) In FY 1987, new issues of coupon debentures rose 8.2% to ¥8.8 trillion because loan demand for plant and equipment increased due to the economic recovery. At the same time, investors were attracted to coupon debentures because of the surplus of money they had and the relatively high coupon rate compared to other instruments. The new issue amount of discount debentures rose 17.6% to ¥24.1 trillion in FY 1987 since individual investors rushed to buy them in the face of the abolition of the "Maru-yu" system[6] or tax exemption of small savings, scheduled in April 1988. As a result, the total outstanding balance of coupon and discount debentures amounted to ¥51.66 trillion in FY 1987, and was the largest of any category of bonds except that of Japanese government bonds.

EXHIBIT 8:   ISSUE AMOUNT OF BANK DEBENTURES

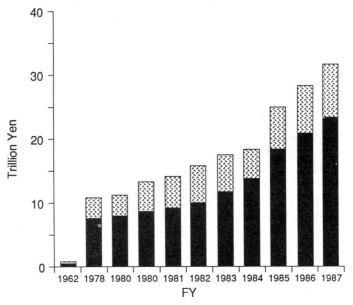

☒ Coupon

■ Discount

| | | (¥ billion) | |
| | | Coupon | Discount |
Year	Total	Debentures	Debentures
FY 1962	802.8	371.2	431.6
FY 1978	11,394.0	3,903.7	7,490.3
FY 1979	11,725.1	3,464.2	8,260.9
FY 1980	13,563.3	4,688.7	8,874.6
FY 1981	14,774.2	5,539.5	9,234.7
FY 1982	16,398.0	5,967.7	10,430.4
FY 1983	18,500.9	6,390.5	12,110.4
FY 1984	19,610.5	5,334.2	14,276.3
FY 1985	26,300.4	7,420.9	18,879.4
FY 1986	28,645.9	8,152.2	20,493.7
FY 1987	32,908.6	8,817.4	24,091.2

Source: The Bond Underwriters Association of Japan.

Issuance Procedures

Since there is no syndicate for bank debentures, issuance follows one of the following two procedures.

Direct Subscription. Like other corporate bonds, bank debentures can be issued through "direct subscription." That is, the issuing bank announces the issuing amount and other terms to the public, and prepares application forms for purchasing the debentures. Then, investors submit application forms, and the issuer allocates a certain amount to each investor.

Uridashi Issue. Bank debentures may be issued through "Uridashi" as well. Uridashi means selling debentures to the public during a certain period of time designated by the issuing banks. The issuing date of debentures is always the 27th of every month (or the preceding business day if the 27th is a holiday), but, under Uridashi, investors can buy them from the 28th of the previous month. Issuers do not have to prepare application forms, and investors are saved the trouble of subscribing. Investors obtain the certificates as soon as they pay the proceeds. Since debentures are the primary source of funding for issuing banks, issuance through Uridashi is permitted so that they can sell these securities to the general public in order to raise sufficient funds.

Roughly 30% of coupon debentures are sold to financial institutions through subscription, while 70% of coupon debentures and all discount debentures are sold through Uridashi.[7] Note that Uridashi includes the distribution of debentures by securities firms. That is, securities firms obtain debentures from issuing banks at a fixed price, and then sell them to investors at the same price. Securities firms, in turn, receive a fixed commission from issuing banks. In 1987, commissions for coupon debentures and discount debentures were ¥130 and ¥60 per ¥10,000 of face value, respectively.[8] The Big Four securities companies sell 5% of coupon debentures and about half of all discount debentures.[9]

While issues of bank debentures are under strict regulation, there are some preferential treatments concerning issuance.

Issuing Limits. For regular corporations, the ceiling for corporate issues, specified by the Commercial Code, is the total of a corporation's capital and reserves or the value of outstanding net assets on the latest balance sheet, whichever is lower. This restriction is relaxed for the six banks that are allowed to issue debentures. For example, the Long-term Credit Bank Law allows the long-term credit banks to issue up to 30 times the amount of capital plus reserves.

Gengaku Hakkou (Issuance with Reduced Amount). According to the Japanese Commercial Code, ordinary corporate bonds are considered unestablished when the amount subscribed to does not reach the total issuance amount reported to the MOF. Even in that case, however, debenture issuers can reduce the amount of the issue to the amount already subscribed. In other words, other firms have to give up financing a particular business when there is a subscription shortage, while debenture issuers can raise funds continuously.

Investors

As shown in Exhibit 3b, "individuals and others" are the largest purchasers in the primary market of coupon debentures. This category includes households, small businesses, large corporations, and nonresidents. The amount purchased by this investor category increased from ¥914.9 billion in FY 1972 to ¥5863.4 billion in FY 1987, and its share in the primary market also increased from about 50% in the early 1970s to 70% in FY 1987.

Local banks are one of the most important purchasers in the primary market. Japanese local banks are relatively small and their business is based mostly in their respective regions. They take in deposits from individuals in their areas, and because of a lack of major loan demand, they are net suppliers of funds in the bank debenture primary market. They consistently had about 10% of this market during the last 15 years.

In FY 1987, city banks and long-term credit banks were the third largest purchasers in the primary market, consistently holding about ¥480 billion worth of coupon debentures for the last 10 years. However, their share dropped from 13.2% in FY 1978 to 5.6% in FY 1987. As explained earlier, in recent years, city banks have been reducing the amount purchased because of the heavy burden of underwriting government bonds.

In FY 1987, both Sogo banks and insurance companies accounted for 5.6% of the market. The Sogo banks are small financial institutions that target small business enterprises in their regions. As lending opportunities decreased in recent years, they became more active in bond investing. Insurance companies seek high yield investment opportunities and have gradually increased their investments in bank debentures every year.

The sixth largest purchaser in the market are trust banks. These seven banks purchased 4.8% of the new issues in FY 1987, down from 9.0% in FY 1972. Trust banks obtain their funds through customer deposits and corporate pension funds. They also issue loan trusts for additional funding.

Governmental organizations also invest in coupon debentures. The Trust Fund Bureau of the MOF, which manages government funds (e.g., postal savings deposits, the Welfare Pensions, and the National Pensions), invests in various bonds. It invested ¥1,368.4 billion in bank debentures in FY 1987. At one time the Post Office Life Insurance Bureau, which sells life insurance to individuals, invested in debentures. However, it stopped subscribing to debentures in 1979.

Terms of an Issue

Bank debentures are issued on the 27th of every month (or the preceding business day if the 27th is a holiday), but investors can purchase debentures from the 28th of the previous month at either issuing banks or securities firms. The issue terms of bank debentures are decided by individual issuers, but subject to guidelines of the Ministry of Finance and the Bank of Japan.

Coupon Debentures. Coupon debentures are 5-year coupon bonds with semiannual payments. (The BOT's coupon debentures are 3-year bonds.) Recent coupon debentures have been issued at par value. Following are details of issuing terms and the market practices.

1. *Coupon rate and yield.* Although issuing banks are allowed to determine the coupon rate individually, their practice is to offer debentures with the same coupon rate. The coupon rate often remains constant for several months unless other interest rates change greatly. As can be seen in Exhibit 9, the coupon rate on 3-year coupon debentures was set 30 basis points lower than that of 5-year coupon debentures during January 1974 through February 1980. The difference, however, decreased to 20 basis points in March 1980 and has remained at this level since.

2. *Price.* Five-year coupon debentures have always been issued at par since 1959. Three-year coupon debentures were sometimes issued below par during the period from 1962 to 1983, but have been issued at par since November 1983.

3. *Early redemption system.* While provisions do exist for optional early redemption of coupon debentures after a one-year period, they have never been applied because of the perceived adverse effect they would have on the market.

4. *Coupon payment.* All coupons are paid semiannually, usually on the 27th of the corresponding month (or the preceding business day if the 27th is a holiday). Interest accrued before the issue date is calculated at the coupon rate on a 365 day basis and subtracted from the pay-in amount.

   For example, suppose an investor purchases an April issue of a coupon debenture with a 4.6% coupon rate (sales period is from March 28 through April 27) on April 20 for a face value of one million yen. An investor obtains ¥882 (=1,000,000 × .046 × 7/365) as interest for seven days, and he/she pays ¥999,118 to get ¥1,000,000 of the coupon debenture. On October 27th and April 27th, 23,000 yen (=1,000,000 × .46 × .5) of coupon will be paid at either issuing banks or any securities firms. If the coupon date is a nonbusiness day, the coupon will be paid on the preceding business day.

5. *Denomination.* Coupon debentures are available in the following six denominations: ¥10,000, ¥100,000, ¥1,000,000, ¥5,000,000, ¥10,000,000, and ¥50,000,000.

EXHIBIT 9:   TERMS OF ISSUE (1978–1987)

Year	Coupon	Price	Yield	Coupon	Price	Yield	Price	Yield
	5-year Debenture	*Coupon Debenture*		*3-year Debenture*			*Discount Debenture*	

Year	Coupon	Price	Yield	Coupon	Price	Yield	Price	Yield
1978 Apr	6.2	100.00	6.200	5.9	99.95	5.919	95.19	5.141
1979 May	6.8	100.00	6.800	6.5		6.519	94.44	5.887
Aug	7.3	100.00	7.300	7.0	99.80	7.080	93.78	6.632
1980 Mar	7.9	100.00	7.900	7.7	99.85	7.761	92.91	7.631
Apr	8.6	100.00	8.600	8.4	99.80	8.483	92.27	8.377
Dec	7.9	100.00	7.900	7.7	99.85	7.761	92.91	7.631
1981 May	7.6	100.00	7.600	7.4	99.95	7.420	93.56	6.883
Nov	8.0	100.00	8.000	7.8	99.95	7.861		
1982 Jan	7.7	100.00	7.700	7.5	99.95	7.561		
Feb		100.00					94.00	6.382
Apr	7.5	100.00	7.500	7.3	99.95	7.361		
Sep	8.0	100.00	8.000	7.8	99.95	7.861		
1983 Jan	7.7	100.00	7.700	7.5	99.95	7.561		
Feb	7.5	100.00	7.500	7.3	99.95	7.361		
Nov	7.3	100.00	7.300	7.1	100.00	7.100		
Dec		100.00					94.22	6.134
1984 Apr	7.0	100.00	7.000	6.8	100.00	6.800		
Nov	6.5	100.00	6.500	6.3	100.00	6.300		
1985 Jan	6.7	100.00	6.700	6.5	100.00	6.500	94.40	5.932
Feb	6.5	100.00	6.500	6.3	100.00	6.300		
Apr	6.8	100.00	6.800	6.6	100.00	6.600		
Jun	6.6	100.00	6.600	6.4	100.00	6.400		
Aug	6.3	100.00	6.300	6.1	100.00	6.100	94.56	5.752
Oct	6.1	100.00	6.100	5.9	100.00	5.900		
Dec	6.6	100.00	6.600	6.4	100.00	6.400		
1986 Jan	6.3	100.00	6.300	6.1	100.00	6.100		
Feb	6.0	100.00	6.000	5.8	100.00	5.800		
Mar	5.5	100.00	5.500	5.3	100.00	5.300	95.01	5.252
Apr		100.00			100.00		95.79	4.395
1987 Feb	4.9	100.00	4.900	4.7	100.00	4.700		
Mar	4.6	100.00	4.600	4.4	100.00	4.400		
Apr	4.3	100.00	4.300	4.1	100.00	4.100	96.47	3.659
May	4.0	100.00	4.000	3.8	100.00	3.800		

Source: The Bond Underwriters Association of Japan.

6. *Form.* Investors may hold bank debentures either in bearer form or in registered form. An investor in a new issue may apply at subscription for registered instead of bearer form.

Discount Debentures. Discount debentures are one-year discount bonds. Discount debentures are, of course, issued below par value. Interest accrued before the issuance date is calculated at the same discount rate on a 366 day basis and subtracted from the pay-in amount. The yield calculation of discount bonds is explained in Chapter 4.

Discount debentures are available in the following eight denominations: ¥10,000, ¥50,000, ¥100,000, ¥500,000, ¥1,000,000, ¥5,000,000, ¥10,000,000, and ¥50,000,000.

The form of issuance for discount debentures is the same as for coupon bonds.

SECONDARY MARKET

As shown in Exhibit 10, trading volume of bank debentures in the secondary market was between ¥28.8 trillion and ¥55.2 trillion during the ten year period from 1978 to 1987. Until 1977, the trading volume of bank debentures had been the largest in the secondary bond market. The total turnover in the OTC market was ¥46.5 trillion in FY 1977, making up about 34.8% of the trading volume in the Tokyo OTC market. (See Exhibit 11.) However, the share of bank debentures in the secondary bond market has been decreasing since then, as the amount of new issues of government bonds has increased.

This trend has been obvious since 1984, when the city banks that had been the largest participants in the secondary bond market were permitted to start dealing in public bonds.[10] Accordingly, the trading volume of government bonds has increased much more rapidly than in previous years, while that of bank debentures has gradually shrunk. In 1987, the trading volume was still as large as ¥39 trillion, including Tokyo OTC and all stock exchanges, but it accounted for only .7% of total trading volume in the market. Bank debentures seem to have become less active and less important in the bond secondary market.

**EXHIBIT 10: TRADING VOLUME VS. OUTSTANDING BALANCE
OF BANK DEBENTURES**

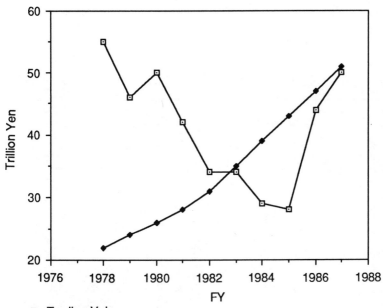

-□- Trading Vol
-◆- Outstanding Vol

(¥ billion)

Year	Trading Volume	Outstanding Volume	Turnover Rate
FY 1978	55,236.6	22,856.3	2.42
FY 1979	46,338.3	24,072.1	1.93
FY 1980	50,191.2	26,157.1	1.92
FY 1981	42,355.6	28,624.8	1.48
FY 1982	34,538.4	31,503.6	1.10
FY 1983	34,543.3	35,669.5	0.97
FY 1984	29,842.1	39,481.8	0.76
FY 1985	28,761.0	43,515.0	0.66
FY 1986	44,161.2	47,197.9	0.94
FY 1987	50,418.0	51,660.0	0.98

Source: The Bond Underwriters Association of Japan.

EXHIBIT 11: TRADING VOLUME OF BANK DEBENTURES IN THE BOND SECONDARY MARKET

Year	8 Stock Exchanges		Tokyo OTC Market				Total Trading Volume
	Coupon Debentures	Total Trading	Coupon Debentures	%	Discount Debentures	%	
FY 1977	3.990	2,213.7	43,158.1	32.3	3,345.9	2.5	133,676.4
FY 1978	3.990	4,811.1	51,222.6	26.0	4,010.0	2.0	196,646.3
FY 1979	4.004	3,488.5	40,235.0	18.1	6,099.3	2.7	222,731.5
FY 1980	3.991	4,447.9	43,437.0	15.5	6,750.2	2.4	281,011.4
FY 1981	3.990	7,384.5	36,779.5	12.4	5,572.1	1.9	297,527.5
FY 1982	4.004	8,619.7	29,168.0	88.8	5,366.4	1.6	332,888.9
FY 1983	4.018	22,948.4	29,632.5	7.1	4,906.8	1.2	416,191.0
FY 1984	3.976	39,998.3	24,502.1	3.1	5,336.0	0.7	798,024.9
FY 1985	3.990	78,744.0	22,838.2	0.9	5,918.8	0.2	2,514,653.1
FY 1986	3.878	123,589.4	36,193.9	1.0	7,963.4	0.2	3,490,263.7
FY 1987	3.850	110,815.1	38,628.3	0.8	11,785.8	0.2	5,094,292.3

Source: The Bond Underwriters Association of Japan.

Trading Conventions

Bank debentures are quoted in terms of simple yield among dealers, and are traded both on the eight stock exchanges and in the over-the-counter market. Most bank debentures—all discount debentures and more than 99% of coupon debentures—are traded in the OTC market.

Since prices in the OTC market are determined by private negotiations between dealers and investors, public information on the actual market movement is limited. The Japan Securities Dealers' Association has published two quotation lists for straight bonds, *the Representative Bond Quotation List* and the *Bond Quotation List*, since January 1977. Yields are quoted in terms of simple yield, as explained in Chapter 4.

The settlement procedures of bank debentures are the same as those of other bonds. While they are not mandatory, settlement dates are usually on the 5th, 10th, 15th, 20th, 25th, and the last day of the month (or next business day if a holiday, the preceding business day if the last day is a holiday). Settlement prices are calculated as for stock exchange and OTC trades.

Bank debentures are identified by the issuing banks and trading numbers. For instance, "Tougin Rikinsai 322" indicates the April issue of coupon debenture issued by the Bank of Tokyo (Tougin = the Bank of Tokyo, Rikinsai = coupon debentures).

The bid-ask spreads of quoted yields on bank debentures are determined based on the actual market situation at the time of transactions. They are usually 4 to 5 basis points.

There is no special market making system for bank debentures. Market makers are Japanese securities firms. Dealers and investors trading debentures refer to the price indicated by securities firms on the stock exchanges.

Trading Patterns

Only a limited number of debenture issues are listed on the stock exchanges of Tokyo, Osaka, and Nagoya. As of April 30, 1989, there were five coupon debentures listed on the Tokyo and Osaka Stock Exchanges, and four on the Nagoya Stock Exchange. As shown in

Exhibit 11, most bank debentures are traded in the over-the-counter market rather than on the stock exchange.

Trading bonds on the stock exchanges has several disadvantages relative to the over-the-counter market. The first, most obviously, is liquidity. Second, bank debentures traded at the exchanges have to be in bearer form. Third, the settlement date at the exchanges is inflexible. Despite the disadvantages, the stock exchanges do provide a significant role for the trading of bank debentures by pricing the representative issue, which acts as an indicator of market movement for trading in the over-the-counter market.

The behavior of the major players affects the trading volume and patterns in the secondary markets. There is no data available on which category of investors sells or buys exactly how much of debentures in the secondary market, but overall trading patterns of each category of investors in the bond secondary market can still be addressed.

As the important investors in the primary market, city banks were the largest net-seller in the secondary market before 1984. (See Exhibit 12.) This changed, however, when city banks were allowed, in 1984, to sell directly to the public, through their retail networks, newly issued public bonds. City banks became supportive of government bonds by curtailing their selling activities in order to gain further admission to deal bonds in the secondary market. Local banks, being a net seller before FY 1986, gradually decreased their selling activities for reasons similar to those of the city banks. The other major investors in the primary market, such as the trust banks, insurance companies, Sogo banks and the Norinchukin Bank, have been, on average, net buyers in the secondary bond market.

REGULATIONS AND TAXES

Restrictions on debenture investments by nonresidents, as well as restriction on short selling, are the same as for other bonds described in this book. Similar to investing in government bonds, coupon payments on coupon debentures are subject to a 20% withholding tax. The degree of tax burden borne by foreign investors is a function of the withholding tax on interest income under bilateral tax treaties

EXHIBIT 12a: TRADING VOLUMES OF BONDS BY INVESTOR GROUP

(billion yen)

	Commercial banks		Local banks		Long-term credit banks		Trust banks		Agricultural financial institutions	
	sell	buy	sell	buy	sell	buy	sell	buy	sell	buy
FY 1982	10,151.5	5,841.9	7,630.4	5,283.9	2,436.4	1,698.7	6,668.0	9,113.8	5,943.2	7,402.7
	[-4,309.6]		[-2,346.5]		[-737.7]		[2,445.8]		[1459.5]	
FY 1983	13,428.9	10,826.3	8,448.8	6,785.3	4,540.6	4,307.2	11,592.1	13,223.2	8,405.2	9,197.3
	[-2,602.6]		[-1,663.5]		[-233.4]		[1,631.1]		[792.1]	
FY 1984	17,861.9	16,584.0	11,617.5	10,774.2	6,214.1	6,282.2	23,159.1	25,381.2	10,685.5	11,801.5
	[-1,277.9]		[-843.3]		[68.1]		[2,222.1]		[1,116.0]	
FY 1985	16,265.3	16,428.1	15,274.3	15,017.5	7,251.0	6,795.2	48,110.4	49,889.8	22,263.2	23,614.7
	[162.8]		[-256.8]		[-455.8]		[1,779.4]		[1,351.5]	
FY 1986	28,778.5	31,514.6	10,089.8	10,686.3	12,333.4	11,889.1	64,704.4	64,569.5	14,820.0	15,076.8
	[2,736.1]		[596.5]		[-444.3]		[-134.9]		[256.8]	
FY 1987	44,764.5	49,703.0	9,683.3	11,686.2	21,145.9	20,444.1	95,203.0	96,859.3	15,404.5	14,676.2
	[4,938.5]		[2,002.9]		[-701.8]		[1,656.3]		[-728.3]	

Note: "Agricultural financial institutions" include the Norinchukin Bank and agricultural cooperative societies.

Source: The Bond Underwriters Association of Japan.

EXHIBIT 12b: TRADING VOLUMES OF BONDS BY INVESTOR GROUP

(billion yen)

	Sogo banks			Shinkin banks			Other banks			Insurance companies			Investment trusts		
	sell	buy	[net]	sell	buy	[net]	sell	buy	[net]	sell	buy	[net]	sell	buy	[net]
FY 1982	2,676.7	2,090.6	[-586.1]	3,249.2	3,652.0	[402.8]	4,606.3	2,495.3	[-2,111.0]	2,407.3	2,469.0	[61.7]	2,919.4	5,649.8	[2,730.4]
FY 1983	2,308.0	1,580.3	[-727.7]	4,367.5	3,658.7	[-708.8]	4,503.2	3,163.1	[-1,340.1]	2,397.4	2,191.5	[-205.9]	3,989.5	8,454.4	[4,464.9]
FY 1984	3,008.2	2,691.8	[-316.4]	9,637.7	9,411.3	[-226.4]	17,253.6	9,183.6	[-8,070.0]	2,807.4	2,553.0	[-254.4]	6,998.7	10,040.3	[3,041.6]
FY 1985	5,863.6	5,456.8	[-406.8]	9,936.6	9,451.5	[-485.1]	22,427.5	13,075.1	[-9,352.4]	7,668.6	7,756.8	[88.2]	6,883.7	8,194.9	[1,311.2]
FY 1986	5,664.7	5,998.0	[333.3]	6,052.9	5,867.0	[-185.9]	6,838.7	9,552.1	[2,713.4]	8,459.4	10,496.6	[2,037.2]	7,860.0	13,213.9	[5,353.9]
FY 1987	6,987.0	8,237.5	[1,250.5]	6,986.7	7,211.8	[225.1]	7,813.2	11,831.9	[4,018.7]	16,830.4	16,936.5	[106.1]	13,934.1	18,415.5	[4,481.4]

Source: The Bond Underwriters Association of Japan.

EXHIBIT 12c: TRADING VOLUMES OF BONDS BY INVESTOR GROUP

(billion yen)

	Governmental organizations		Individual and Others		Bond dealers		TOTAL	
	sell	buy	sell	buy	sell	buy	sell	buy
FY 1982	1,372.5	1,873.9	22,203.6	24,194.1	24,077.0	23,834.4	96,341.9	95,600.1
	[501.4]		[1,990.5]		[-243.0]		[-741.8]	
FY 1983	1,456.7	1,826.8	34,317.1	33,704.1	42,742.5	41,638.0	142,497.5	140,556.2
	[370.1]		[-613.0]		[-1,104.5]		[-1,941.3]	
FY 1984	1,808.0	2,263.1	81,124.1	82,104.7	133,386.2	131,562.3	325,562.0	320,633.2
	[455.1]		[980.6]		[-1,823.9]		[-4,928.8]	
FY 1985	2,306.6	3,027.5	100,224.9	99,323.6	742,540.0	737,887.8	1,007,015.7	995,919.3
	[720.9]		[-901.3]		[-4,652.2]		[-11,096.4]	
FY 1986	1,859.2	2,305.6	85,016.5	76,818.5	832,365.0	822,094.7	1,084,842.5	1,080,082.7
	[446.4]		[-8,198.0]		[-10,270.3]		[-4,759.3]	
FY 1987	2,058.5	2,452.5	80,412.5	72,497.1	1,008,750.0	994,334.9	1,329,973.6	1,325,286.5
	[394.0]		[-7,915.4]		[-14,415.1]		[-4,687.1]	

Source: The Bond Underwriters Association of Japan.

between Japan and the investor's country. Since April 1988, an 18% tax is levied on the discount at issue for discount debentures.

THE FUTURE OF THE BANK DEBENTURE MARKET

Bank debentures were introduced to the Japanese financial market so that certain banks could raise long-term low-cost funds and then funnel those funds to the basic and primary industries, small-sized enterprises, and international trade industries. To carry out this mission successfully, bank debentures were granted several advantages (such as yield and tax advantages) to attract funds. Bank debentures, through issuing banks' lending activities, played an extremely important role in promoting production, especially during the postwar period. However, they are destined to lose significance when this mission becomes obsolete, the advantages given to debentures would be withdrawn, and the favorable environment would disappear.

There are two general trends that will affect the future of the bank debenture market. First, the most essential industries for the Japanese economy until the late 1960s were the heavy industries, such as shipbuilding, automotive, iron and other metal, and chemical industries. Since those industries required a huge amount of long-term funds to build plants and purchase equipment, they depended to a large extent upon the loans from long-term credit banks. However, the service and other "soft" industries like banking, information and communication, and fast food have become important in the economy since the 1970s. For instance, those industries accounted for 57.0% of GNP[11] and 58.1% of all workers in 1988.[12] Since, unlike the heavy industries, those industries do not need a vast amount of long-term funds in general, the debenture issuing banks may have a difficult time finding good lending opportunities. As shown in Exhibit 13, long-term credit banks, therefore, have gradually shifted their lending operations from long-term to short-term loans. In that sense, the mission given to the issuers of bank debentures is becoming ambiguous.

Second, Japanese interest rates have been strictly regulated by the Ministry of Finance and the Bank of Japan after World War II. The interest rates offered by financial institutions must fall within a certain range determined by the Temporary Interest Adjustment

EXHIBIT 13: CHANGES IN THE RATIOS OF LONG-TERM VS. SHORT-TERM LOANS

	Term	FY 1955	FY 1965	FY 1975	FY 1984	FY 1985
City banks	long-term	5.2	10.1	29.7	36.2	35.2
	short-term	94.8	89.9	70.3	63.8	64.8
Long-term	long-term	87.3	91.7	92.5	73.3	72.8
credit banks	short-term	12.7	8.3	7.5	26.7	27.2

Note: "long-term"—loans for longer than one year.

Source: The Bank of Japan.

Law. Under the regulation, the rigid interest-rate systems, such as the hierarchy of the interests in the bond market, and the long-term prime rate system which was discussed earlier, have maintained order in the Japanese financial markets for a long time.

However, the deregulation of interest rates began proceeding in May 1984, when the MOF agreed with the U.S. Treasury Department on the gradual liberalization of the Japanese financial market. Regulations applying to Negotiable Certificate of Deposit (NCD) interest rates have been the first step toward total interest rate deregulation. Commercial banks introduced money market certificates in March 1985 whose interest rates were linked to the NCD rate. Interest rates on time deposits with ¥1 billion or more were also deregulated in October 1985, and the deregulation has rapidly proceeded to small denomination deposits since. Money Market Certificates are now available from 10 million yen at city banks, and "Large Denomination Time Deposits" are available from ¥20 million. In addition, trust banks introduced in 1988 a new type of trust fund called "Super Hit" which is available from ¥3 million. City banks introduced "Super MMCs" in June 1989 which are also from ¥3 million. With the advent of these competitors, sales of discount debentures went into a slight slump in 1989. To maintain the competitiveness of discount debentures, the bank debenture issuing banks introduced a new type of discount debenture in June 1989 whose yields fluctuate between the rate on two-year Super MMCs and the rate on the one-year Super

Hit.[13] Since discount debentures are available from ¥10,000, interest rate deregulation will have reached denominations as small as ten thousand yen. The introduction of a new type of discount debenture is expected to maintain their investment attractiveness, while the fund-raising costs will go up, placing a heavy burden on the issuing banks.

Coupon debentures are also facing potential competition from city banks who are eager to introduce a three-year time deposit. Historically, the Japanese government has separated long-term financing from short-term so that banks in each area could manage the maturity match of their assets and liabilities. However, city banks expanded long-term lending activities as a result of the decrease in total lending opportunities. (See Exhibit 13.) They are trying to obtain permission from the Ministry of Finance to introduce three-year time deposits to support their long-term lending activities. (As of April 1989, they had time deposits with a maximum maturity of two years.) If the three-year time deposits are permitted, they will compete directly with three-year coupon debentures and, to a lesser extent, with five-year debentures.

Deregulation might bring efficiency to the Japanese capital market on the whole. However, from the issuing banks' point of view, it has also brought intense competition and, thus, an increase in fund-raising costs. Bank debentures are still important for the issuing banks as a primary source of funds today. However, considering that the two general trends discussed above are not reversible, it can be expected that the expansion of the bank debenture market is likely to level off in the near future.

ENDNOTES

[1] Time deposits were available with a maturity of 3 months, 6 months, 1 year, and 2 years as of April 1989.

[2] See Yoshio Suzuki ed., *The Japanese Financial System* (Oxford University Press. New York, 1987), pp. 146–147 and Nihon Keizai

Shimbun Inc., *Kaoushasai Hakkou Shijou [Bond Primary Market]* (Nihon Keizai Shimbun Inc., Tokyo, 1987), pp. 212–214.

[3] See Nomura Research Institute, *Koushasai Youran [Bond Handbook]*, 1988 edition, (Nomura Research Institute, Tokyo, 1988) for more information about the history of tax rates on interest income.

[4] Security firms became less enthusiastic about selling bank debentures, because they had their own short- and medium-term vehicles.

[5] Toyo Keizai Shimposha, Japan Company Report, 1989 Spring edition (Toyo Keizai Shimposha, Tokyo, 1988).

[6] "Maru-yu" system was introduced in 1968. Under this system, the interest payments on a certain account are tax-free as long as the original principal deposited in the account is below ¥3 million.

[7] Nihon Keizai Shimbun Inc., *Koushasai Hakkou Shijou [Bond Primary Market]* (Nihon Keizai Shimbun Inc., Tokyo, 1987).

[8] Daiwa Securities Co. Ltd., *Saiken No Joushiki [Practical Knowledge of Bonds]* (Daiwa Securities Co. Ltd. Tokyo, 1987).

[9] Aron Viner, *Inside Japanese Financial Markets* (Homewood, IL: Dow Jones-Irwin, 1988).

[10] Prior to 1984, only securities firms were allowed to deal in those bonds.

[11] The Japanese Government, *White Paper on Japanese Economy*, 1987 edition.

[12] The Bank of Japan, *Economics Statistics Annual, 1987 edition* (The Bank of Japan, Tokyo, 1987).

[13] Nihon Keizai Shimbun Inc., *Nihon Keizai Shimbun*, April 5, 1989.

CHAPTER 10

Commercial Paper Market

Jeffrey L. Dickson
Associate Investment Manager
Prudential Capital Corporation

Hiroaki Fuchida
Vice President
The Mitsubishi Bank, Ltd.

Yutaka Nishizawa
Senior Vice President
The Mitsubishi Bank, Ltd.

HISTORICAL BACKGROUND

Commercial paper (CP) is an unsecured promissory note through which corporations raise short-term funds directly in the money market as a means of circumventing borrowing from banks. Due to the ease and speed of issuance, the outstanding balance of commercial paper in the U.S. has grown to a level comparable to that of U.S. Treasury bills. The volume on European markets has risen dramatically as well.

The worldwide trend among businesses to shift financing activities from bank borrowing to debt financing directly in the capital and money markets is one of the main reasons for the liberalization of the CP market in Japan. Another reason for the development of

the CP market in Japan is the growing complaint by foreign investors of the lack of money market instruments with a maturity of less
than one year. Furthermore, Japanese overseas subsidiaries have
been issuing CP in foreign markets for some time now.

As a further step to promote internationalization of the Yen, the
Ministry of Finance (MOF) approved the issuance of domestic CP by
Japanese entities as well as issuance of Euroyen CP by non-Japanese
entities in November 1987. The MOF also approved the issuance of
domestic yen CP by non-Japanese entities in January 1988—so-called
"Samurai CP." Since the ban on issuance was lifted, the oustanding
balance of the CP market has increased rapidly to 9,300 billion yen
as of December 1988 (see Exhibit 1). Also, the number of issuers increased dramatically to 100 by December 1988.

**EXHIBIT 1: CHANGES IN DOMESTIC COMMERCIAL PAPER
MARKET BALANCE IN JAPAN (ESTIMATE)**

		(10 billion yen)
1987	November	108
	December	165
1988	January	235
	February	220
	March	275
	April	394
	May	438
	June	508
	July	560
	August	630
	September	596
	October	772
	November	825
	December	930
1989	January	870

Source: The Mitsubishi Bank.

LEGAL CHARACTERISTICS OF COMMERCIAL PAPER

Under the current legal framework in Japan, CP could be classified as either (1) a promissory note, (2) a corporate bond, or (3) some new classification. In order to develop the market quickly, the CP market had to be created under the current legal system, which meant that a new classification was not feasible.

If CP was classified as a corporate bond, then the current law posed several problems for the development of the CP market. First, under Commercial Law, new bond issues must be approved via a board meeting (Commercial Law 296).[1] This would put serious limitations on the readiness-to-issue factor, which is critical in the CP market. There is also a limitation on the amount of corporate bonds that may be issued (Commercial Law 297) and most corporations would have little capacity to issue CP based on this restriction. Also under Commercial Law 301 companies must submit an application to issue a security with the MOF.

Another problem, if CP was considered to have the legal characteristic of a bond, is that financial institutions would not be able to deal the paper under Securities and Exchange Law 65. Also, under Securities Laws 4 and 8, companies have to wait 30 days after application before the bond can be issued.[2] This provision would be prohibitive in issuing a short-term instrument like CP.

CP viewed as a promissory note has the problem that CP is sold randomly to numerous investors, whereas a promissory note is issued between parties of a business transaction under the draft law. However, as long as the elements of the draft are the same as a promissory note, the law could be used formally, even though it does not fit the expected transactions.

As for the problem with the Commercial Law regarding prior approval of the board before issuance of CP, it was determined under Commercial Law 260-2 that approval was necessary. However, the amount could be set in advance such as "within X million yen" and the company would be free to issue within this limit without subsequent board approval.[3]

Some people argue that CP is a kind of accommodation bill (draft) only because it is not backed by a real business transaction. However, CP is backed up by the creditworthiness of the company.

The term of CP was limited from 2 weeks to 9 months in order to emphasize the short-term nature of the instrument and, more importantly, to distinguish the paper from corporate bonds. As such, CP was finally manifested under the laws regarding promissory notes.

ISSUERS OF COMMERCIAL PAPER

In general, CP is issued and backed by the company's good faith and credibility, so it is limited to large creditworthy companies. In the U.S., companies are selected according to their rating which is given by independent commercial rating companies such as Moody's, Standard & Poor's, Fitch and Duff & Phelps (see Exhibits 2 and 3). However, in England and France, where ratings companies are not well developed, standards are set to determine eligibility to issue CP.[4] Like these countries, Japan also established standards of eligibility in November 1987. In December 1988, the MOF issued new rules that altered the standards and required newly issuing companies to obtain a rating for their commercial paper from the rating companies in order to issue new paper. Companies that issued paper under the old rules can continue to issue CP without acquiring a CP rating. However, these companies must still meet the eligibility standards set forth in November 1987.

EXHIBIT 2: RELATIVE RATING COMPARISONS AMONG THE RATINGS AGENCIES IN THE U.S.

Standard & Poor's	Moody's	Fitch	Duff & Phelps
A – 1+			Duff 1+
A – 1	Prime – 1	F – 2	Duff 1
			Duff 1–
A – 2	Prime – 2	F – 2	Duff 2
A – 3	Prime – 3	F – 3	Duff 3

**EXHIBIT 3:   SHORT-TERM AND LONG-TERM RATING
COMPARISONS BETWEEN S&P AND MOODY**

| Standard & Poor's | | Moody's | |
Short-term Rating	Long-term Ratings	Short-term Rating	Long-term Rating
A – 1+	AAA	P – 1	Aaa
	AA+		Aa1
	AA		Aa2
	AA–		Aa3
A – 1	A+		A1
	A		A2
	A–		A3
A – 2	BBB+	P – 2	Baa1
	BBB		Aaa2
	BBB–		Baa3

Eligibility Standards

One standard states that companies that can issue straight bonds without collateral and companies that can issue straight bonds with collateral and whose stocks are listed on the stock exchange are allowed to issue CP. Under this standard, there are eleven companies permitted to issue CP, including nine electric power companies (Hokkaido, Tohoku, Tokyo, Chubu, Hokuriku, Kansai, Chugoku, Shikoku, and Kyushu), as well as NTT (Nippon Telegraph and Telephone) and KDD (Kokusai Denshin Denwa).[5]

Another standard sets minimum net worth levels and ratio requirements that must be met (see Exhibit 4). The net worth levels are divided into three categories: (1) ¥55 billion or more, (2) ¥110 billion or more, and (3) ¥300 billion or more.[6] At each of these levels, companies must meet various ratio requirements in order to be eligible to issue CP. It is important to note that financial institutions (banks,

EXHIBIT 4: ELIGIBILITY TO ISSUE YEN CP IN JAPAN

I)   Either (1) or (2) stated below are the eligibility standards.

(1)

A. Net asset	300 billion yen or more	110 billion yen or more	55 billion yen or more
B. Shareholders' equity over total assets	30% or more	40% or more	50% or more
C. Working income over total assets*	8% or more	10% or more	12% or more
D. Net assets over paid-in capital	3 times or more	4 times or more	5 times or more
E. Interest coverage ratio**	3 times or more	4 times or more	5 times or more
F. Dividend	Dividend paid in the last fiscal year		
Conditions	Compulsory: A Optional: 4 items out of B-F should be satisfied		Compulsory: A&B Optional: 3 items out of C-F should be satisfied

$$* \quad \frac{\text{Operating Income + Interest Received + Dividend Received}}{\text{Total Assets}}$$

$$** \quad \frac{\text{Operating income + Interest Received + Dividend Received}}{\text{Interest Paid}}$$

(2)

2.   Companies who have rating
   1)   AA rating or better
   2)   A rating with net assets of 55 billion yen or more.

II)   Eligibility to issue without backup line
   1.   AAA rating or,
   2.   AA rating with net assets of 300 billion yen or more or net assets and acid assets* : 200 billion yen or more respectively and, current ratio: 100% or more and acid-test ratio (quick ratio): 80% or more.

*Acid Assets – Liquid Assets – Inventory

Source: Tomoko Amaya, *CP in the Run*, 1988.

securities companies, and finance companies) are *not* allowed to issue CP.

Finally, the ratings standard allows corporations with a rating of AA, or corporations with a net worth of more than ¥55 billion and a rating of A, to issue CP.

The new CP rating rules allow companies that have the best CP ratings (such as A1 or an A2 rating), but also have a net worth of more than ¥55 billion, to issue CP. The companies must obtain ratings from at least two rating agencies. Also, if the company's stock is not listed on the Tokyo Stock Exchange, the company can issue CP if it meets the disclosure requirements under the Securities and Exchange Laws for three consecutive years.

As of December 1988, it was estimated that 400 companies were eligible to issue CP in addition to the nine electric power companies.

Backup Credit Line

Most CP is paid off by rolling the paper, that is, the issuer sells new paper in order to satisfy maturing paper. This situation creates the risk that issuers will be unable to pay off maturing paper. As a result, investors usually require issuers to back their outstanding paper with bank lines of credit.

In Japan, in general, it is necessary to have a backup facility or a guarantee of a financial institution in order to issue CP. However, companies that satisfy certain conditions, as well as companies that can issue straight bonds with collateral and that are listed on a stock exchange, are not required to have a backup or a guarantee.

No backup facility is required for those companies that can issue straight bonds without collateral if they meet the following standards:

1. Companies with a AAA rating.

2. Companies with a AA rating and net worth of ¥300 billion.

3. Companies with a net worth and acid assets (current assets minus inventory) more than ¥200 billion and current and acid ratios of more than 100% and 180%, respectively.

As of November 1987, approximately 40 companies satisfied these standards, and another eleven companies can issue straight bonds with collateral. Therefore, about 51 companies were allowed to issue CP without a backup facility.[7]

As of December 1988, rating agencies can determine the level of the backup needed by issuers that have a CP rating. In general, the backup should be no less than 50% of the issue. However, the rating agencies may require issuers to obtain higher backup. In the future, the determination of backup facility standards will be left solely to the rating agencies.

COMMERCIAL PAPER INVESTORS

The CP market is limited primarily to institutional investors, including corporations that have sufficient funds and information. By making the minimum face value ¥100 million and excluding foreign currency denominations, general investors are excluded from the market. CP is considered an investment vehicle that is only suitable for professional investors. It has simple but limited disclosure, so general investors would lack sufficient protection even if they were allowed to invest in the paper.

In the U.S., investment companies as a group comprise one of the largest investors in CP in Japan. Japanese Securities Law limits the acceptable investment alternatives of investment company funds to securities, so that they cannot invest in short-term financial instruments like CP as the primary asset of a fund. Therefore, investment trusts are strictly limited as to the amount of CP they can purchase. In practice, each investment company policy specifies the amount they can invest in CP, within a limit of 20% of the total net asset value of the fund.[8]

Investors in CP are not given protection under the disclosure rules of the Securities and Exchange Laws. The main reasons for this are that investment in CP is limited to institutional investors and issuance of CP can only be made by companies listed on the Tokyo Stock Exchange. The sophistication of the players and the fact that CP is such a short-term instrument make it unnecessary to enforce strict disclosure rules.

Prior to the sale of CP, the issuing company must provide a brief report to the dealers and investors of the paper. The report must include a description of the issuer with a balance sheet and income statement, information regarding the backup facility, the rating of the CP (if available), and other information for the investors. The report is only necessary for primary issuance and does not have to be provided for secondary transactions. However, original dealers keep copies of the report available for investors during the term of the CP. Reports are revised after each settlement of accounts.

DEALERS

CP must be issued through an intermediary, i.e., a financial institution or securities company. As of November 1987, 99 companies, including foreign securities companies, were permitted to deal CP.[9] In the secondary market, short-term credit brokers (Tanshi) also can trade CP.

Financial Institutions

Legally, a financial institution's inherent business is "discounting the drafts" (Banking Law 10-1-2). Formally, the dealing of CP is considered the discounting of a promissory note. However, the character of the genuine business of "discounting the drafts" is quite different from that of dealing CP. Therefore, the dealing of CP is considered as an additional business and, after revisions of the rules of bank law, was included in money credit (including certificates of deposits (CDs) or other certificates defined by the Ministry of Finance Act).

Financial institutions that deal CP include banks, mutual banks, credit unions, the Shokochukin Bank (Shokokumiai-chuo Kinko), and the Norinchukin Agricultural Bank (Norin-chuo Kinko). All institutions must report to the MOF before they begin to deal an issue of CP.

Securities Companies

A securities company cannot do business other than securities business except as permitted by the MOF (Securities and Exchange Law 43). The dealing of CP was not considered part of the securities business because of the legal character of the paper. Therefore, dealing

CP was permitted as a side business, or "agency business." Admission into a side business is judged on a company-by-company basis based on business performance.[10]

Foreign securities companies and banks that have a license in Japan are treated the same way as Japanese dealers. As of November 1987, 49 foreign banks and eight foreign securities companies were allowed as dealers of CP as well as the short-term money brokers in the secondary market.

ISSUANCE OF COMMERCIAL PAPER

In order to promote an orderly market, CP must be issued through dealers. In Japan, unlike the U.S., direct issue placement is not permitted. The two indirect methods of issuance are the Kaitori (purchase) method and the Assen (conciliation) method. Under the Kaitori method, dealers purchase the entire issue of CP from the issuing company and then sell the issue to investors. The dealers, in effect, assume the risks of issuance. Under the Assen method, dealers use a "best-efforts" method to try and sell the issue as the agent for the issuing company. The dealers have no responsibility to purchase any unsold CP. The issuing company assumes the placement risk. In Japan, the Kaitori method is more popular than the Assen method.

The issuing company must negotiate a contract with a dealer and also choose an issuing agent. In addition, the company must approve the issue of CP via a board meeting, unless it was done in advance. A brief report must also be written by either the issuing company or the dealer and submitted to MOF. The dealer then assists the company in determining the amount of the issue, the term, and the issuing conditions.

After the terms and conditions are established, the actual issuing procedure follows. If the Kaitori method is used and if there is an issuing agent, then the issuing agent delivers notes on behalf of the issuing company to the dealers. The dealers then transfer funds into a special account for the issuing company. If there is a backup line of credit, then both the issuing company and the dealers will notify the backup line bank. Dealers then sell the issue to investors and either deliver the CP notes or retain the CP notes and deliver a certificate to the investors.

TAXATION OF COMMERCIAL PAPER

From a legal context, CP is considered a promissory note rather than a security. As such, no securities transaction tax or transfer tax is imposed on CP. However, CP does incur a revenue stamps tax according to the schedule outlined in Exhibit 5.

The revenue stamps impose a significant cost on the issuance of CP. For example, suppose a firm wanted to raise ¥10 billion by issuing CP (¥500 million × 20 pieces) for a term of one year (three-month notes × four times). The revenue stamps tax would be ¥8 million (¥100,000 × 20 × 4). As of November 1987, a banker's acceptance in Japan is only subjected to a ¥200 stamp and many feel that CP should be treated the same. If the change is adopted, the tax as calculated under the previous example would drop to ¥0.016 million (¥200 × 20 × 4).[11]

DOMESTIC COMMERCIAL PAPER BY NON-JAPANESE ENTITIES—"SAMURAI CP"

Non-Japanese corporations whose shares are listed on the Tokyo Stock Exchange and who meet certain standards, are eligible to issue domestic CP, popularly referred to as "Samurai CP." It has the legal

EXHIBIT 5:   STAMP DUTY TARIFF (EXCERPT)

Issued Amount	Stamp Duty	Percentage
100 million yen	20 thousand yen	2 b.p. on ¥100 M
over 100 million yen	40 thousand yen	2 b.p. on ¥200 M
over 200 million yen	60 thousand yen	2 b.p. on ¥300 M
over 300 million yen	100 thousand yen	2 b.p. on ¥500 M
over 500 million yen	150 thousand yen	1.5 b.p. on ¥1 B
over 1 billion yen	200 thousand yen	1 b.p. on ¥2 B

Source: Tomoko Amaya, *CP in the Run*, 1988.

character of a promissory note in Japan. The maturity must be between two weeks and nine months in order to remain similar to
other liberal interest rate instruments such as CDs.

Denominations must be ¥100 million or more and all issuers are
required to have a backup facility unless they clear certain eligibility
or rating requirements. Samurai CP is not subject to the Securities
Transaction Tax or Withholding Tax but is subject to a Stamp Duty
to be paid in accordance with the tariff (see Exhibit 5).

Samurai CP is issued through dealers, including financial institutions and securities houses in Japan. Settlement is made through a
special settlement account following the procedure required for the
issuance of promissory notes.

EUROYEN COMMERCIAL PAPER

Any entity whose bond rating is single-A or better, or whose CP
rating is A1, P1, or F1, is eligible to issue Euroyen CP. The qualifying
rating agencies include Moody's Investor Service, Standard & Poor's,
Fitch Investors Services, Duff and Phelps, Nippon Investors Service
Inc., Japan Credit Agency, Limited, and The Japan Bond Research
Institute.

Euroyen CP must be issued with maturities of less than one
year. It is sold at a discount with the rate determined by money market rates as well as the credit of the issuer of the CP. The paper is
normally issued in denominations of ¥100 million, although this is
not a requirement. Euroyen CP is not subject to the Securities Transaction Tax, the Withholding Tax, or the Stamp Duty.

Euroyen CP must be issued through a bank or security company. Dealers include both Japanese and non-Japanese financial institutions. Euroyen CP may not be sold in Japan within two weeks of
the issuance date. In addition, Euroyen CP traded in Japan should
have a remaining maturity of less than 180 days and should have a
denomination of ¥100 million, or more. Any issuer (except financial
institutions and securities companies) can bring CP funds into Japan
after being admitted by the MOF under the Foreign Exchange and
Foreign Trade Control Law. However, certain amounts can be approved in advance and shelved to avoid continuous MOF application and approval.

THE RAPID GROWTH OF THE DOMESTIC CP MARKET

The CP market has grown to over a ¥9000 billion market since its liberalization in November 1987. The number of issuing companies is over 100 and the range of companies includes trading companies and distribution and service industries. The market was expected to grow much more slowly to the level of ¥2000 billion over this time period. The larger than anticipated growth indicates that there was a strong demand for liberalized short-term securities in Japan. The reasons for the rapid growth of the domestic CP market are analyzed below.

From the Viewpoint of the Suppliers of Funds

One of the main reasons for the rapid growth is the fact that financial institutions, including investment trusts, shifted their investment funds from the interbank markets to CP where the rates were relatively higher. Investment trusts are the largest holders, followed by financial institutions, "Tokkin" (specified money trust), and local and mutual banks.

Moreover, in the distribution market, gensaki transactions of CP are actively done allowing buyers to select the term that they desire. CP is also an attractive target security for gensaki[12] because of its relative liquidity and ease of issuance compared to CD gensaki or bond gensaki.

From the Viewpoint of the Issuers of Commercial Paper

The CP market allows issuers to raise short-term funds at market rates. The market also provides a way to diversify methods of raising funds; this is important in Japan where previously, most companies were forced to borrow strictly from financial institutions. In addition, issuers have tried to arbitrage the market by issuing CP and investing the funds in large amount time deposits. In a sense, the current CP market can be regarded as a "Zai-tech" fund market.[13] However, this does not take away from the fact that CP is a real market that serves the fund-raising needs of institutions.

PROBLEMS IN THE COMMERCIAL PAPER MARKET AND REVISION OF THE RULES IN DECEMBER 1988

One year after the creation of the CP market, the MOF issued new rules in order to correct structural inefficiencies in the market. One problem in the market related to eligibility standards. The rules relating to the eligibility of issuing bonds were also applied to issuing CP. Considering the fact that CP is a short-term, fund-raising vehicle with frequent roll-overs, it is not appropriate to apply rules corresponding to a long-term fund-raising vehicle. Factors important for short-term fund-raising include daily working capital, liquidity, lines of credit, and the use of funds.

Backup facility in the form of a line of credit is important in order to eliminate the market risk due to economic and financial circumstances. In the U.S., even if a company is superior in terms of assets and liquidity, it generally will carry backup facility for its CP issues. When Penn Central Railroad went bankrupt in June 1970, its outstanding CP balance in the U.S. was $82 million. The market erupted into temporary chaos and many companies could not continue to borrow smoothly in the CP market. However, firms were able to repay their outstanding issues by making use of these backup lines of credit. In Japan, under the previous rules, certain companies could issue CP without any backup facility by meeting certain standards. Under these rules, an unexpected financial crisis similar to Penn Central could cause problems in the ability to retire outstanding CP issues.

Disclosure requirements presented another problem in the CP market. Under the original rules, companies had only to issue a brief report as well as financial statements in order to issue CP. The report included the CP issuing balance, limitation on issuing amount, and a description of the company's financial condition; the working capital movements of the company were hardly disclosed. Under these circumstances, neither the dealers who accepted CP nor the investors could accurately judge whether the issue amount was necessary or if the CP redemption was certain. Therefore, it was believed that new rules would be necessary to improve investor protection.

The purpose of the revisions presented by the MOF was to address these problems and to insure that the future growth of the market was orderly and efficient. One of the main revisions was to introduce a more comprehensive CP rating system similar to the one in the U.S. As mentioned previously, it was necessary to change the eligiblity standards of the CP market in order to reflect its short-term nature. By introducing CP ratings, the rating institutions can continuously analyze the issuing companies, i.e., their financial conditions, working capital and CP balances, and use of funds. This is a progressive step in market stabilization and investor protection. The introduction of CP ratings has increased the number of companies eligible to issue CP to over 450, and will dramatically affect the growth of the market over the coming years.

Another revision presented by the MOF related to the establishment of backup facility for CP. To a certain degree, the rating agencies became responsible for setting the appropriate lines of credit for companies issuing CP. Rating agencies can continuously analyze the market and companies to determine the amount of backup needed to minimize liquidity risk. The rating agencies, over time, will add consistency to the market, which will improve investor confidence. In a sense, the rating system and rating agencies are the keys to the future growth and development of the market.

Disclosure requirements were also tightened under the MOF revisions. It now is compulsory to disclose the limitation of issuance, the issuing balance, and the ratio of the backup facility to CP (if backup is necessary). This revision will also increase investor confidence in the market and allow companies to raise short-term funds efficiently.

The issuing periods of CP were also revised, from between 1 and 6 months to between 2 weeks and 9 months. (Most of the issuance of CP in the U.S. is less than 30 days.) Corporations wanted the ability to remain flexible in their fund raising and demanded a shorter term on CP. The change to two weeks will increase CP balance, as more companies will issue shorter maturities.

These revisions will undoubtedly improve the stability, efficiency, and growth of the CP market in the future. However, there are still some problems which must be addressed: the main and current issue is the Revenue Stamp Tax. The system of revenue stamps is like progressive taxation—the larger the amount, the larger the tax. This system results in an increasing cost, which is not consistent with the goals of the MOF. While the term has been reduced to two weeks, to make this change meaningful, the Stamp Tax should be revised.

Another important factor for the CP market and for the Japanese financial markets in general, is the further internationalization of the yen. Foreign investors will continue to play an important role in the short-term market as long as the yen continues to internationalize. Foreign investment will cause efficiency of the markets to improve through arbitrage activities. For example, in the U.S., there is a good balance between instruments of financial institutions and capital market instruments such as Treasury bills, commercial paper, etc. Internationalization of the yen depends on revision of the tax system in Japan and the development of more open market financial investments such as Treasury bills and CP.

ENDNOTES

[1] T. Amaya, *Ugokidashita CP* [translated as *CP in the Run*], Zeimukenkyukai Shuppankyoku, 1988, p. 100.

[2] Ibid., p. 101.

[3] Ibid., p. 101.

[4] Sumitomo Trust Bank, *Kinyu No Kiso-Text* [Translated as *Basic Text for Finance*], Nihon Noritsu Kyokai, March 1989.

[5] *CP in the Run*, p. 110.

[6] *Basic Text for Finance.*

[7] *CP in the Run*, p. 113.

[8] Ibid., p. 114.

[9] *Nihon-Ginkou No Kenkyu* [Translated as *Study on Bank of Japan*], Nihon Keizai Shimbun Sha, March 17, 1989.

[10] *CP in the Run*, p. 120.

[11] Ibid., p. 147.

[12] The gensaki market is described in Chapter 6.

[13] Amaya, *CP in the Run*, p. 97.

CHAPTER 11

The Japanese
Corporate Bond Market

Edward William Karp
Corporate Finance
Eli Lilly and Company

Akira Koike
General Manager
Mitsui & Co. (U.S.A.), Inc.

The Japanese corporate bond market consists of yen-denominated bonds that are issued in the Japanese domestic market by major Japanese corporations. The corporate bond market today is facing some major changes as a result of the lessening of restrictive controls and customs by the government and financial institutions, the development of new instruments such as convertible bonds, warrants, commercial paper, and the openness of the Eurobond market. In this chapter, we review the Japanese corporate bond market.

HISTORICAL BACKGROUND

The history of the Japanese corporate bond market can be divided into four distinctive periods: pre-World War II, post-World War II through 1970, 1970 through 1980, and 1980 to the present. These periods indicate major shifts in how the JCBM has developed, showing

353

how Japanese corporations are gradually moving from financing long-term debt via traditional bank loans to using highly sophisticated instruments issued in the international capital markets.

In 1870, the first Japanese bond was issued. It was a government bond that was issued in England and denominated in pounds. The purpose of the issue was to finance the construction of the railway system of Japan.[1] It was issued in England because a bond market was already in existence and the British pound was the recognized financial currency standard around the world. Two years later, in 1872, the first domestically traded Japanese government bond was issued.[2] This bond, however, was not a "modern" version of a bond, mainly because it was nontransferable. The bond was issued for the purpose of subsidizing the liabilities accrued from the previous government's administration.

The first Japanese corporate bonds were issued in Japan in 1890 by the Osaka Railway Company.[3] These bonds were fully guaranteed by the Japanese government in order to earn the confidence of investors. Even though corporate bonds were developed and traded in Japan in the late 19th century, their popularity was fairly moderate during this period through World War II for several reasons. First, the low interest rate on the bonds stipulated by the government made them unattractive to investors. Second, due to the strong relationship between banks and companies, corporations found bank loans more appealing as a form of financing. As mentioned earlier, most corporate debt was raised via bank loans. This was mainly because Japanese banks were protected by the full faith and credit of the Japanese government and the banks worked very closely to help build corporations. Bonds, instead, would be issued through a security house, bypassing the banks, thereby putting a strain on the relationship between banks and corporations. Finally, investors found bonds unattractive since many that were outstanding before World War II were significantly reduced in value after the reconstruction that took place after the war.

The relationship in Japan between the government, banks, and corporations is much closer than the relationship between their counterparts within the United States or Great Britain. Almost all economic policies and regulations are closely debated and worked on by the three entities to formulate a fairly unified policy. Seldom does one of the groups act independently of the others.[4]

Post-World War II through the early 1970s was a time of reconstruction and immense expansion by the private sector. The rebuilding of Japan took place as the government supplied funds to the private sector by purchasing corporate bonds. The main function of the government was not a "regulatory" but a "developmental" role.[5] Although funds were relatively scarce, the demand soared and corporations were willing to pay a higher interest rate for capital compared to the prime rate.

At the same time it was loaning capital, the government of Japan itself was rapidly expanding and spending. This rapid growth caught up with the government: several exogenous, non-Japanese factors started to play havoc with the Japanese economy. The first shock was the oil crisis of the early 1970s. Japan was particularly vulnerable because of its enormous dependence on foreign oil imports. Japanese corporations slimmed down their working capital requirements as a result of the oil crisis, which decreased the tax revenue for the government. This decrease in tax revenue, along with a steady increase of government expenditures, led to government deficits.

As a result of the readjustments resulting from the oil crisis, investment in the government was an attractive investment option for corporations. The Japanese government turned to the rebuilt private sector to help fund its financial problems. During the 1970s, in effect, the private sector became the principal supplier of funds to the government by investing in government bonds. Thus, after World War II, the government was the supplier of the corporations' financial demands, but in the 1970s, the govern-ment's financial needs grew exponentially while the corporate needs were also growing, but not nearly at the same rate.

From the mid-1970s until very recently, the supply of funds has not been the major concern for well-performing firms. In fact, it has been relatively plentiful. Unfortunately, even though the supply was adequate, the cost of capital had remained high in the 1970s. This was because banks were still the primary lenders and alternative sources of capital were not attractive due to many issuing restrictions.

The future for Japan is definitely one of continual reform. In the 1980s, the pressures of global competition and the development of new instruments and capital markets are forcing a movement for greater deregulation of the corporate bond market. The changes in financial institutions that are occurring in the United States and the proposals for change in 1992 in Europe have added fuel to the Japanese outcry for domestic reform.

Bank Relationships

Let us take a closer look at the relationship between Japanese banks and corporations. For around 300 years, the main economic power was not in the hands of the different governments, but in the hands of several very influential merchant families (such as, Zaibatsu families like Mitsui, Kohnoike, etc.). As these families developed into large conglomerates, one of their core businesses was banking. Today, this strong interrelationship between corporations and banks remains, with each company having a main bank that they work closely together with to finance projects. This "closeness" exists in different ways. In some cases, bank officials are on the board of the company and work with the corporation's president and treasurer to monitor the strategy and growth of the firm, unlike the U.S. system where banks and companies work independently of one another.

Banks in Japan are also very influential because they are the main creditors of the corporations.[6] Exhibit 1 compares the debt ratios of Japan, the United States, the United Kingdom and the Federal Republic of Germany from 1979 to 1985. As seen in this exhibit, debt financing is important to the economic structure of all countries but particularly important in Japan. Today, on average, Japanese firms have about a 80% debt ratio.

This interrelationship or "allegiance" between banks and corporations is particularly evident when a time of crisis exists for a corporation. The banks use their clout and power to help ensure the stability and survival of their corporate client. In addition, if a major corporation should go bankrupt, it would not only be a disaster for the firm, but also the reputation of the bank would be called into question.

Even though not a single Japanese bank has gone bankrupt since World War II, the number of corporate bankruptcies per year has been fairly constant. The vast majority of these cases have been smaller firms with capitalizations of less than ten million yen.[7] Ex-

**EXHIBIT:1   INTERNATIONAL COMPARISON OF CAPITAL AND
LIABILITIES FROM 1979 TO 1985 (IN PERCENTAGE)**

	Japan		United States	
Year	Equity Capital	Liability	Equity Capital	Liability
1979	15.4	84.6	64.8	35.2
1980	16.2	83.8	65.4	34.6
1981	16.6	83.4	65.4	34.6
1982	16.6	83.4	65.0	35.0
1983	17.1	82.9	64.5	35.5
1984	17.3	82.7	61.8	38.2
1985	18.5	81.5	59.5	40.5

	United Kingdom		F. R. Germany	
Year	Equity Capital	Liability	Equity Capital	Liability
1979	46.5	53.5	34.7	65.3
1980	46.6	53.4	34.3	65.7
1981	45.6	54.5	33.8	66.2
1982	45.0	55.0	34.6	65.4
1983	46.0	54.0	35.3	64.7
1984	46.3	53.7	36.2	63.8
1985	—	—	36.9	63.1

Source: Robert J. Ballon and Iwao Tomita, *The Financial Behavior of Japanese Corporations* (Tokyo: Kodansha International, Ltd., 1988), p. 86. Reprinted by permission. All rights reserved.

hibit 2 compares total insolvency cases over a nine-year period for five countries. One of the clear examples of this inter-relationship was the recent pooling of resources and the eventual bailout by the Japanese banks of Toyo Kogyo, or Mazda, the once ailing car company.[8]

This interrelationship has also caused some important liability management concerns due to the banks' lending practices. American banks place a greater proportion of their funds in security investments while Japanese banks invest more in loans. Although the ratios have been changing during the last thirty years, in 1980 the banks' asset ratio of loans to security investments in the U.S. was double that of Japanese banks'.[9]

EXHIBIT 2: INTERNATIONAL COMPARISON OF INSOLVENCY CASES (1978–1986)

Year	Japan	United States	United Kingdom
1978	15,875	6,619	8,988
1979	16,030	7,564	8,037
1980	17,884	11,742	10,928
1981	17,610	16,794	13,747
1982	17,122	24,908	17,767
1983	19,155	31,334	20,438
1984	20,841	52,078	21,950
1985	18,812	57,067	21,674
1986	17,476	—	21,557

Year	F. R. Germany	France
1978	5,952	—
1979	5,484	15,863
1980	6,312	17,375
1981	8,496	20,895
1982	11,915	20,462
1983	11,845	22,708
1984	12,018	25,018
1985	13,625	26,425
1986	13,500	27,802

Source: Robert J. Ballon and Iwao Tomita, *The Financial Behavior of Japanese Corporations* (Tokyo: Kodansha International, Ltd., 1988), p. 71. Reprinted by permission. All rights reserved.

These allegiances have caused concern and some strained relationships in the 1970s among the banks and corporations. As the Japanese corporations were tightening their belts in the 1970s, they were also beginning to be concerned about: (1) the cost of capital, (2) the restrictive market conditions of issuing corporate bonds, and (3) the high interest rates paid on the loans from their "company" bank. As a result, corporations began to look to foreign capital markets to reduce their financial costs. Because of the tight government regulations, as well as these long standing bank-corporation ties, it was not easy for corporations to go to foreign capital markets in the 1970s. Also, banks at that time were being exposed to international competition. Japanese banks were now competing in non-Japanese homelands, where the pressures and regulations were quite different than in Japan.

During the 1980s, Japan became a major player in the world financial markets. In particular, the 1980s ushered in a lessening of government restrictions as well as an attitude of "openness" towards the domestic financial markets. A major effort has been instigated to "open up" the Japanese corporate bond market. This has been primarily through government deregulation of banks as well as deregulation of foreign exchange controls. This caused a dramatic decrease in the volume of corporation funding by the banks. By 1984, bank lending dropped from over 80% of total funding in the early 1970s to 59.4%.[10]

Following are some of the major changes that have occurred as a result of deregulation: (1) banks are not as "protected" by the Japanese government, (2) foreign security trading houses are now allowed to compete in Japan, and (3) new instruments such as the commercial paper market have been established.

As time goes on, more of an effort will be made to deregulate the domestic markets in order to be more competitive on the world markets. As one of the world financial leaders, Japan is now faced with world responsibilities and tremendous exogenous pressures.

MARKET CHARACTERISTICS

Unlike in the United States, a formal corporate bond rating system was introduced in Japan only in 1977. From 1959 to 1977, the rating system in Japan was informal and mainly focused on the size of the corporation as opposed to any other requirements. Issuers of corporate bonds have been the corporations which meet the requirements discussed in the next section.

The large security houses, as underwriters, along with the Ministry of Finance and the banks (commissioned banks) are very influential in their internal policing of the rules and regulations for issuance of corporate bonds. The large security houses, referred to as "the big four," are Nomura, Daiwa, Nikko, and Yamaichi, followed by nine "semi-large" security houses (Nippon Kangyo Kakumaru, New Japan, Kokusai, Sanyo, Wako, Cosmo, Okasan, Universal, and Yamatane). While there is a significant difference in size between the

big four and these nine other security houses, the latter are influential too.[11]

The "big four" security houses have very close "links," or working relationships, with several of the smaller security houses. The
large houses act not only as leaders in the industry but work on a
cooperative basis with the smaller houses in sharing and parceling
out new business and ventures.

The Market Size of the Corporate Bond Market - Primary Market

The public issuance volume of the Japanese corporate bond domestic
market was about 915 billion yen ($7 billion at 130 yen/$) for the
fiscal year April 1987 to March 1988.[12] The main issuers of the 915
billion yen corporate bond market, by volume, were: nine electric
power companies, 75%; NTT, 22%; and governmental companies,
2.4%. During this period, there were only 27 issuances. Only one of
the issuances, totalling 5 billion yen (0.5% of the total volume), was
issued by a totally private company.

The breakdown of the investors in this primary corporate bond
market was as follows: city banks and long-term credit banks, 6.3%;
local banks, 1.1%; trust banks, 1.1%; insurance companies, 0.4%; central bank for agriculture and forestry, 2.3%; central bank for commercial and industrial associations, 4.0%; mutual banks, 1.1%; and
individuals, 14.6%. About 69% is acquired mainly by business corporations, government municipalities, and security houses.

During the same time period, corporate bond private issuance
volume was about one-quarter or 248 billion yen ($1.9 billion at 130
yen/$). In this private issuance market, nearly 75% is issued by the
nine electric companies and 22% by NTT, which recently went from
a public to a private telecommunication firm. Only 3% of the private
bond issuance is done by the major corporations.

Funds for financing growth can come from three sources: internal funding, stock sale and debt. During the prewar years, one-third
came from internal funding. Two-thirds came from external sources
of stock sales and debt, stock sales representing only one-third of the
total.[13] As a result of the major restructuring of the Japanese stock
market in the postwar years, funds obtained from the sale of stock
fell below 10% of the total corporate supply of funds.

Government bonds are by far the largest type of bond issue in Japan. Until recently, corporate bonds have not been very popular because the bond market is not a free market. The issues are tightly controlled by the Japanese government and the large security houses. For example, the coupon rates on corporate bonds are fixed and linked to those on long-term government bonds. Also, straight bond issues are regulated by the Kisai-kai (Bond Flotation Committee) which is a committee composed mainly of city banks.[14]

Another key reason why corporate bonds have not been very popular is because of the collateral requirement of the Japanese Commercial Law. Secured bonds became the norm in the 1930s after so many unsecured bonds defaulted in the 1920s.[15] The defaults also led to major financial reforms. The collateral requirement has made it difficult for smaller asset-rich firms to issue straight corporate bonds. They have turned to other types of bonds. As an example of the impact of the collateral requirement on the bond volume over time, consider that the domestic issuance of straight bonds peaked at 1.4 trillion yen in 1975 and decreased to 589.5 billion yen in 1985.[16] Since most Japanese corporations did not meet the strict requirements, they primarily issued convertible bonds.

The Size of the Secondary Market

The secondary market includes all of the transactions and trading of corporate bonds that occur after the bonds are issued by the corporation. It includes all of the trading between security houses, institutional investors, governmental agencies, corporations, and individual investors. They are traded on the three major Japanese security exchanges (Tokyo, Osaka, and Nagaya) and on the over-the-counter market.

The growth of the secondary market increased fiftyfold from 1976 to 1986; the most significant increase was in convertible bonds. The first convertible bond was made legal and issued in 1966 by the Nippon Express Company. As a result, the issuance of convertible bonds has risen significantly: since 1974, domestic issuance of convertible bonds rose by 771%.[17] In 1985, the volume was more than 1.9 trillion yen. Domestic issuance of convertible bonds has surpassed that of overseas issuance in both amount issued and number of issues. Even though the recent developments in deregulation and the recent attempts to develop a freer market have made corporate bonds more attractive than before, a great deal more deregulation is needed to significantly stimulate the Japanese corporate bond market.

Secondary market volume in fiscal year 1987, which includes the trading on the three major Japanese security exchanges and on the over-the-counter market, was 5,316 trillion yen ($41 trillion at 130 yen/$).[18] Of this total, only 7 trillion yen represented trading of nonconvertible corporate bonds.

Corporate Bond Quotes

Corporate bonds are usually quoted on a price basis. For example, a bond quote of 97.[40-70] means that the bid price is 97.40 yen per 100 yen, and 97.70 yen per 100 yen is the offering price. There are no corporate bond indexes, mainly because the market volume is so small.

The difference between the bid price and the offer price (bid-ask spread) is dependent upon market conditions at that time including each security house's inventory position. The volume of trading of each bond is also taken into consideration. Usually a government bond bid-ask spread is much smaller because it is much more liquid than the corporate bond. For example, the price quote on April 19, 1989 for the Tohoku Electric Power Company's bond (no. 341) was 97.[80] − 98.[10] yen (a 0.30 yen bid-ask spread), while the government benchmark bond traded on the same day had a 0.06 yen bid-ask spread.[19]

The Yield Spreads for the Primary and Secondary Corporate Bond Markets

It somewhat difficult to obtain the standardized corporate bond yield spreads due to the changing government bond benchmark. Exhibits 3 and 4 compare the corporate bond yield movements and spreads with those of the government bond benchmark from 1978 to 1987 for the primary market and from 1980 to 1987 for the secondary market.

EXHIBIT 3: LONG-TERM CORPOPRATE BOND YIELD MOVEMENT AND COMPARISON WITH GOVERNMENT BONDS (PRIMARY MARKET)

Year	Long-Term Corporate Bond Yield AA Rated	Long-Term Government Bond Yield	Yield Spread
1978	6.436%	6.180%	0.256%
1979	8.022	7.788	0.234
1980	8.842	8.546	0.296
1981	8.409	8.367	0.042
1982	8.324	8.274	0.050
1983	7.944	7.994	(0.050)
1984	7.497	7.538	(0.041)
1985	6.914	6.624	0.290
1986	6.035	5.100	0.935
1987	4.532	3.969	0.563

Source: Nomura Research institute, *Koushasai Youran 1988 (The 1988 Bond Handbook)*, pp. 176 and 188.

EXHIBIT 4: LONG-TERM CORPORATE BOND YIELD MOVEMENT AND COMPARISON WITH GOVERNMENT BONDS (SECONDARY MARKET)

Year	Long-Term Corporate Bond Yield (Electric Power Co.)	Long-Term Government Bond Yield	Yield Spread
1980	8.481%	8.250%	0.231%
1981	8.200	8.580	(0.380)
1982	8.568	8.521	0.065
1983	7.974	8.055	(0.081)
1984	7.939	7.475	0.464
1985	6.839	6.460	0.379
1986	6.813	4.770	2.043
1987	5.197	3.850	1.347

Source: Nomura Research institute, *Koushasai Youran 1988 (The 1988 Bond Handbook)*, p. 278.

The reason why the yields spreads fluctuate, and are even at times negative, is that the factors that affect the government bond yields may or may not have the same effect on the corporate bond yields. Some of these influential factors are political influences, issuance volume, and the restrictive market conditions.

FACTORS AFFECTING THE JCBM

In order to fully understand the Japanese corporate bond market, one must understand some of the underlying forces which have had and will continue to have a significant impact on this market. In particular, the major factors include: policies of the Ministry of Finance and the Bank of Japan, and the structure of the Japanese stock market. These forces affect the way corporations determine their fundraising sources as well as the basis for the government's future deregulation policies concerning corporate bonds.

The Role of the Ministry of Finance

The Ministry of Finance (MOF) is similar to the U.S. Treasury Department, the Office of Management and Budget, and the Securities and Exchange Commission combined. It is also one of the most important governmental organizations in Japan in terms of prestige and policy-making. The Ministry of Finance is composed of career officers from the elite Japanese universities.

The Ministry of Finance is also involved with the regulation of the financial sector and tax administration. The MOF drafts most of the legislation that comes before the Diet regarding intermediary financing, and uses its power to influence economic activity through administrative guidance. An important fact that should be noted is that the Ministry of Finance has never let a banking institution go bankrupt since World War II.

The Ministry of Finance became the major force in establishing the pro-growth financial policy and investment race that occurred after World War II. Based on two "temporary" laws enacted in 1949 and 1950, and remaining in effect throughout the rapid growth decades, the MOF made loan capital available to the largest private banks, which in turn were guided to make loans available to the largest and most innovative firms. What made the guidance effective was the fact that the MOF was empowered to control the full range of the rate structure, enabling the ministry to set a below-equilibrium rate for loans made to large firms. The MOF influenced and helped in establishing the corporate bond ratings as well as the corporate bond issuing structure. Also over this time, the chronic excess demand for loans created by the administered below-market rate allowed the MOF to engage in effective credit rationing to the point of guiding the largest banks to make loans to specific industries or even to specific firms engaged in the investment race.[20] This corporation and government interaction is illustrated by the practice of having retiring career officials of the Ministry of Finance sit on the boards of financial institutions.

The Role of the Bank of Japan

The Bank of Japan is Japan's central bank. It is similar to the United States Federal Reserve Board. The main functions of the Bank of Japan are to: (1) set the discount rate, (2) control the money supply, (3) audit the financial institutions, and (4) act like a clearing house for the local banks. It also keeps a watchful eye on the state of the economy in terms of the interest rates, open market operations, and unemployment levels. The Bank of Japan acts like a barometer for establishing the corporate bond rate.

The Role of the Ministry of International Trade and Industry

During most of the rapid growth era (from 1945 to the early 1970s), the Ministry of International Trade and Industry (MITI) had the power to selectively allocate foreign exchange for the purchase of imports. The MITI's role was as a doorman to vital imports of Western technology: it influenced the timing, composition, and allocation of a flow of knowledge that was essential to the competitive success of each rapidly innovating Japanese firm.[21]

Just as the ability of the MOF to pressure Japanese financiers to divert funds into strategic industries was a result of structural and procedural features of the Japanese capital market, the power of the MITI to influence the investment and marketing decisions of private

companies was a result of the ministry's control over essential con-
duits linking the Japanese economy to sources of raw materials and
technology.[22]

The MOF and the MITI maintained a standing committee to
identify the industries to benefit from their guidance. A policy of
providing capital to selected large firms (and depriving consumers
and small firms of funds) was feasible because the Japanese capital
market was insulated from international money markets. The MOF's
policies of preferentially directing credit to large, efficient firms in
each industry intensified the tendency toward the domination of
each sector of the economy by a small number of large firms. In addition to enjoying the cost reductions of mass scale, these firms had
more secure and ready lines of credit than did smaller competitors.[23]
The MITI's role in the corporate bond market is indirect. It mainly
identifies and supports the firms which are to be helped when issuing corporate bonds and it promotes Japanese firms issuing bonds
abroad.

The Corporate Bond Market Relationship with other Domestic Financial Sources

There are several sources of capital for Japanese corporations. The
major ones include: bank loans, depreciation allowance, retained
earnings, issuance of stocks, issuance of warrant bonds, issuance of
convertible bonds and foreign capital.

It is of interest to note how the sources of capital have changed
in priority for the Japanese over the last 20 years. Exhibit 5 provides
a list of these capital sources as ranked by executives and illustrates
the decrease of importance placed on bank loans over this relatively
brief time period.[24]

There also have been some major shifts in the sources of funds
available to Japanese manufacturing companies. As a result of the
deregulation occurring in the past 15 years, long-term borrowing has
decreased by 50% during the last ten years, internal reserves percentages have stabilized, and the issuance of bonds and stocks has become somewhat more popular.[25]

EXHIBIT 5: JAPANESE EXECUTIVES RANKING THE DIFFERENT METHODS TO OBTAIN CAPITAL FOR JAPANESE CORPORATIONS DURING THE 1970s AND 1980s

	1970s	*1980s*
Bank loans	1	7
Depreciation allowance	2	2
Retained earnings	3	1
Issuance of stocks	4	3
Issuance of bonds	5	6
Issuance of convertible bonds	6	4
Foreign capital	7	5

Source: Robert J. Ballon and Iwao Tomita, *The Financial Behavior of Japanese Corporations* (Tokyo: Kodansha International, Ltd., 1988), p. 84. Reprinted by permission. All rights reserved.

The Corporate Bond Market Relationship with the United States and the Euromarkets

Faced with many domestic restrictions and the high costs associated with domestic issuing, many Japanese firms are obtaining debt financing in non-Japanese markets. The main non-Japanese market has been the Euromarket. The main advantages of issuing bonds in the Euromarket are:

1. Fewer restrictions than in Japan even though more disclosure information is required.

2. No rating system.

3. Lower issuing costs compared to the domestic market.

4. More currency options.

The volume of Japanese straight corporate bonds issued in foreign markets increased 18 times from 1977 to 1986 ($935 million in 1977 to $17 billion in 1986).[26] It should be pointed out that even though a formal rating system has not been popular in Japan until recently, many of the firms have obtained a rating from Moody's or Standard & Poor's. Although ratings entail the fees charged by these agencies as well as extra disclosure requirements, they have been sought by the Japanese firms primarily to be able to issue bonds in the United States as well as for the domestic and international prestige associated with being rated by one of these agencies.

In Japan, there are currently five bond rating companies. These are Mikuni & Co., the Japan Bond Research Institute, Nippon Investors Service Inc., Japan Credit Rating Agency, Moody's Japan K.K. (which is the Japanese subsidiary of Moody's Investors Service) and Standard & Poor's Corp. of the United States.

Issuing bonds in non-Japanese markets has only taken place in the last ten to fifteen years. The lead bank and corporation relationship has very strong historical ties and even today it is not a very easy tie to break.

THE KEY FEATURES OF THE ISSUANCE REQUIREMENTS OF JAPANESE CORPORATE BONDS

Classification of Corporate Bonds

Corporate bonds can be classified in several ways, these are discussed in the categories below.[27]

Type of Security:

1. Securitized with collateral assets.
2. Securitized with a guarantee by another party.
3. Securitized with a general mortgage.
   a. Special laws permit that bondholders are given the priority of being repaid prior to the general creditors.
   b. Electric power companies and NTT are independently classified
4. Nonsecuritized basis (noncollateral).

Types of Redemption:

1. A lump sum basis at maturity (e.g., bullet).
2. Terminal redemption (i.e., sinking fund).
   a. Previously this was compulsory and was applied to all bonds.
   b. Recently, the lump sum at maturity basis is allowed for certain issues.
3. Call provisions—Even though the call provision is legally allowed, it has never been exercised, except for cases involving convertible bonds and yen-denominated foreign bonds. On some callable bonds there is a period of time when the bond cannot be called. For example, the Tokyo Electric Power Company bond issued in June 1985 with a maturity of 12 years has a call option available after five years from the date of issuance. The redemption price of this bond is set as follows:
   a. 5-6 years after issuance, the redemption price (with premium) is 103 yen per 100 yen.
   b. 6-7 years after issuance, the redemption price is 102.50 yen per 100 yen. For each year after until due, the call redemption price (premium) decreases by 0.50 yen.
   c. During year 12, if the call is exercised, the redemption price is par.[28]

Maturity Term:

1. Straight bonds at 6, 7, 10, 12, and 15 years to maturity.
2. Convertible bonds at 6, 8, 9, 10, 12, and 15 years to maturity.

Interest Payment Terms:

1. With coupon (fixed interest rate).
2. Discounted (zero coupon).
3. Floating rate bonds—Even though floating rate bonds are legally possible, they are generally not issued due to the high cost of

issuance to the issuer. The issuer would prefer to obtain a bank loan rather than issue a domestic floating rate corporate bond.

Eligibility Requirements to Issue Public Corporate Bonds

Eligibility requirements for the issuance of public corporate bonds depend on whether the bonds are securitized or nonsecuritized. The requirements for each are discussed below.

Corporate Bonds which are Securitized. Following are the requirements for a firm to issue public corporate bonds which are securitized:[29]

1. The net worth of the company must be at least 3 billion yen.
2. Either of the following must be met from the ratio requirements set forth in Exhibit 6:

   a. The dividend requirement and three out of the other four ratios set forth in Exhibit 6 must be met.

   b. For firms that already have outstanding balances of public corporate bonds, then the following has to be met:

   b-1. if the dividend requirement has been met for the last three years, then only one of the remaining four ratios set forth in Exhibit 6 must be met.

   b-2. if the dividend requirement has been met for the last year, then two of the remaining four ratios set forth in Exhibit 6 must be met.

It should be noted that there are different issuing requirements for the general trading companies.

Corporate Bonds that are Nonsecuritized. There are different requirements for issuing nonsecuritized public corporate bonds. The following are the requirements for a firm to issue public corporate bonds which are not securitized:[30]

1. The net worth must by at least 55 billion yen.

EXHIBIT 6: MINIMUM ISSUANCE RATIOS BASED ON NET ASSETS (YEN) FOR SECURITIZED PUBLIC CORPORATE BONDS

		Net Assets (Yen)		
	Ratio	3–6 B	6–10 B	>10 B
1.	$\dfrac{\text{Shareholders' equity}}{\text{Paid in capital}}$	≥3.0	≥1.5	≥1.2
2.	$\dfrac{\text{Shareholders' equity}}{\text{Total Assets}}$	≥30%	≥12%	≥10%
3.	$\dfrac{\text{Operational Profit*}}{\text{Total Assets}}$	≥8%	≥6%	≥5%
4.	Interest coverage ratio	≥3.0	≥1.2	≥1.0
5.	Past dividend per share	≥5 yen for past 3 years	≥4 yen for past 3 years or 5 yen for last year	≥3 yen for past 3 years or 4 yen for last year

* Operational profit = Gross profit + Interest received + Dividend received + Deferred sales interest received

Source: Ministry of Finance, Securities Bureau, ed., *Dai-26-kai Ookurasho Shokenkyoku Nenpoo, Showa-63-nenban (26th Version of the Annual Bulletin for the Year Ending March 1988 of the Securities Bureau, Ministry of Finance)* (Tokyo: Kinyuu Zaiseii Jijoo Kenkyuukai, 1988), p. 64.

2. For firms with net worth between 55-110 billion yen, the second ratio in Exhibit 7 and three out of the remaining four ratios in the exhibit must be met. For firms over 110 billion yen, four out of the five ratios in Exhibit 7 must be met.

3. Generally, additional limitations are required on an individual basis (for example, a firm may be required to maintain a certain earnings ratio, certain profit levels, or dividend restrictions, etc.).

However, if a firm has a "AA" rating *or* their net worth is at least 55 billion yen and simultaneously has a "A" rating, then a firm can issue nonsecuritized public corporate bonds without meeting any of the above ratio requirements.

EXHIBIT 7: MINIMUM ISSUANCE RATIOS BASED ON NET ASSETS (YEN) FOR NONSECURITIZED PUBLIC CORPORATE BONDS

	Ratio	Net Assets (Yen) 3–6 B	6–10 B	>10 B
1.	Shareholders' equity / Paid in capital	≥5.0	≥4.0	≥3.0
2.	Shareholders' equity / Total Assets	≥50%	≥40%	≥30%
3.	Operational Profit* / Total Assets	≥12%	≥10%	≥8%
4.	Interest coverage ratio	≥5.0	≥4.0	≥3.0
5.	Past dividend per share	≥6 yen for past 5 years	≥6 yen for past 5 years	≥6 yen for past 5 years

* Operational profit = Gross profit + Interest received + Dividend received + Deferred sales interest received

Source: Ministry of Finance, Securities Bureau, ed., *Dai-26-kai Ookurasho Shokenkyoku Nenpoo, Showa-63-nenban (26th Version of the Annual Bulletin for the Year Ending March 1988 of the Securities Bureau, Ministry of Finance)* (Tokyo: Kinyuu Zaiseii Jijoo Kenkyuukai, 1988), p. 61.

As with the securitized bonds, certain general trading companies also have a different set of requirements for issuing nonsecuritized bonds.

Issuance Volume Limitations. When issuing either securi-tized or nonsecuritized public corporate bonds, there are certain limitations placed on the volume of bonds to be issued. Historically, the volume limitation was set by Japanese commercial law that stated that the total outstanding bond volume of a corporation could exceed neither its capital plus reserve amount nor its total net worth.[31] However, a temporary law was passed in 1977, which is still in effect today, stating that the volume limitation placed by the 1977 law could be doubled for all securitized bonds, convertible bonds, and bonds issued outside Japan.

Private Placement Issuing Requirements. Private corporate bond placement is usually initiated between the corporation and certain identified investors. The benefits of private placement are low transaction and administrative costs, and the speed and flexibility of the transaction.

Historically, this method was used by small corporations that were not eligible for public offering and the total placement amount could not exceed 2 billion yen in any one year. In fact, once a corporation issued public offered bonds, they were not allowed to return and issue private placement bonds. This was called the "no return rule."

As a result of the global trends within the bond securitization market and the lobbying of large corporations, the "no return rule" was abolished in 1987 with the following revisions.[32]

First, the private placement amount can not exceed a corporation's past aggregate public offering amount.

Second, the total private placement amount per year can not exceed 10 billion yen for corporations that do not qualify for public offering. As for the corporations who are eligible to issue public bonds, they can issue private placements up to 6 times in a year with a 10 billion yen limitation per placement (i.e., the total private placement amount is 60 billion in any one year).

Third, for private placement above 2 billion yen, a "go-between," or mediator (such as a bank, security company, or a life insurance company), is required to help facilitate the transaction. Mediators are limited to purchasing up to 10% of any transaction which they are involved in.

Fourth, in order to qualify as a private placement, the number of investors per issue can not exceed 50. The investors can not resell these bonds within a two-year period.

The private placement bond market doubled during the nine month period that the new 1987 regulation was enacted. It increased from 123 billion yen during the April 1986–March 1987 fiscal year to 248 billion yen during the April 1987–March 1988 fiscal year.[33]

Rating System for the Primary Corporate Bond Market

The rating of Japanese corporations began in 1959. Today, corporations can be rated by several different methods and there is still ample room for establishing guidelines that are accepted by all market participants. The rating of a firm has a direct effect upon its issuance costs.

The Bond Floatation Committee assigns ratings based on the ratios listed in Exhibit 8.[34] The assignment of a rating is as follows:

1. If a firm meets the minimum net worth requirement, then it has to meet only one of the other four requirements set forth in the

EXHIBIT 8: BOND FLOATATION COMMITTEE RATING SYSTEM
             RATIO REQUIREMENTS

	Ratings (units: yen)				
Ratio	AA	A	BB	B	
Net Worth Amount	≥110 B	≥55 B	≥10B	≥6B	≥3B
Shareholders' Equity Total Assets	≥15%	≥15%	≥15%	≥20%	≥30%
Shareholders' Equity Total Capital	≥1.5	≥1.5	≥1.5	≥2.0	≥3.0
Operational Profit* Total Assets	≥6%	≥6%	≥6%	≥7%	≥8%
Interest Coverage ratio	≥1.2	≥1.2	≥1.2	≥1.5	≥3.0

	Qualitative Standards	
Ratio	Standard No. 1	Standard No. 2
Shareholders' Equity Total Assets	≥25%	≥15%
Shareholders' Equity Total Capital	≥3.2	≥2.0
Operational Profit* Total Assets	≥10%	≥7%
Interest Coverage ratio	≥2.5	≥1.5

*Operational Profit = Gross profit + Interest received + Dividend Received + Deferred Sales Interest Received

Source: Nomura Research Institute, *Koushasai Youran 1988 (The 1988 Bond Handbook)*, p. 224.

top panel of Exhibit 8 to be rated. If it exceeds 120% of the minimum net worth requirement, then none of the four requirements needs to be met in order to be rated.

2. If a firm does not meet either one of the requirements as stated in (1), it will then be rated one rank below.

3. A firm will be rated one rank above its level if it meets the following requirements:

   a. Its net worth must be at least 60% of the rank above its minimum net worth requirement, and its dividends per year for the last 3 years must exceed 6 yen per year.

   b. A firm must satisfy all four ratio requirements in the bottom panel of Exhibit 8 for Standard No. 1 *or* three out of the four requirements of Standard No. 1 with the unsatisfied one meeting the corresponding number in Standard No. 2.

Issuance Costs

The costs associated with the issuance of corporate bonds are described below. The issuance yield to the issuer is determined by the following method:[35]

$$\text{Issuance Yield} = \frac{[\text{initial cost} + \text{period costs} + (\text{par value} - \text{issuance price}) + \text{principal redemption handling charge}]}{\{\text{total par value} - [\text{initial cost} + (\text{par value} - \text{issuance price})]\} \times \text{average maturity years}}$$

where:

Initial cost includes the fees associated with the underwriting, trustee banker, and the registration fee.

Period costs include coupon payment and the handling charges of such payments to the commissioned bank.

The following is a summary of issuance costs for the years 1985 through 1987:[36]

Corporate Bond Rating	Year	Coupon Rate	Issuing Price*	Issuance Yield
AA	1985-Oct	6.3%	99.25	6.833%
	1986-June	6.0%	99.75	6.393%
	1987-March	5.3%	99.50	5.709%
BB	1985-Oct	6.5%	99.50	7.419%
	1986-June	6.2%	100.0	6.944%
	1987-March	5.5%	99.75	6.270%

*Issuing price units are: yen/100 yen par value.

The following is a detailed breakdown of the major costs:[40]

Item	Costs (yen/per 100 yen)
Underwriting fee:	
7-15 yrs. maturity	1.6
6-7 yrs. maturity	1.5
4 yrs. maturity	1.3
commissioned bank fee:	
—nonsecuritized	0.2
—securitized	0.25
Initial registration fee:	0.1
Mortgage registration fee:	
—only for securitize	0.25 - 0.4
Handling charge for coupon payments:	0.6% of the coupon
Period costs by the commissioned bank:	
—nonsecuritized	0.05
—general mortgage	—
—securitized	0.2 - 0.25
Handling charge for the redemption of the principal:	0.4

SUMMARY

In this chapter we have focused on the Japanese corporate bond market. The unique features of the Japanese corporate bond market as compared to other markets around the world can be summarized as follows.

First, a formal rating system similar to Moody's was introduced in 1977 and it still needs further development. Actually, the original rating system was introduced in Japan in 1959, but the ratings were only based upon the size of the corporation. However, many large firms have been rated by non-Japanese rating agencies such as Moody's or Standard & Poor's in order to participate in joint ventures with United States firms as well as for good relationships and prestige.

Second, very strong and long historic corporate and bank relationships still exist. Even now, banks subsidize corporations in case of default.

Third, even though there is a weak formal rating system, there are very tight restrictions for issuance. These restrictions include volume limitations and collateral requirements.

Fourth, the disclosure system is not as open as it is in the United States. This has resulted in heavy reliance by investors on the government authorities for information.

Fifth, the tight restrictions have forced many corporations to issue straight corporate bonds outside Japan. Therefore, many investors find it difficult to invest in the domestic market because of the limited volume and options.

Sixth, hedging in the corporate bond market through futures or option transactions is still in the infancy state.

Seventh, even though callable corporate bonds are legally possible, they are not used in Japan except for convertible bonds.

Investors in this market sector are concerned with the following issues.

First, since hedging is limited, investors are more likely to invest in other instruments, like government or convertible bonds, because of the larger transaction volume in the market.

Second, since the corporate bond market trading volume is low compared to other markets like the stock market, investors are concerned with liquidity.

Third, at times, investors feel that not enough information is available because the disclosure and rating systems are not fully developed.

Future developments include the following:

1. Attempts to attract domestic corporate issuances by lowering the minimum issuance requirements.
2. Push for a more acceptable and standardized formal rating system.
3. Development of different hedging contracts (futures and options).

ENDNOTES

[1] Daiwa Security Company, *Saiken no Joushiki* (*Practical Knowledge of Bonds*) (Tokyo: Daiwa Security Co., 1986), p. 3.

[2] Ibid., p. 3.

[3] Ibid., p. 3.

[4] The Japanese business philosophy is one that is built on harmony. However, the Japanese also believe that competition is beneficial for society. The three entities work together to create a business atmosphere that is competitive but where no one emerges as the dominant player at the expense of others. In other words, competition is not to develop a clear cut winner. Instead, competition is a goal in itself. An example of this philosophy is: a firm beginning to dominate in their field without caring for its weaker competitors is not looked upon favorably. By working together and being interdependent with competitors and creditors, wealth can be achieved by all.

[5] Robert J. Ballon and Iwao Tomita, *The Financial Behavior of Japanese Corporations* (Tokyo: Kodansha International, 1988), p. 27.

[6] Ibid., p. 86.

[7] Ibid., p. 70.

[8] See: Robert B. Reich, "Bailout: A Comparative Study in Law and Industrial Structure," *International Competitiveness*, 21 (1986), p. 312-318.

[9] S. Yoshihara, *Ginkoo Torihiki no Chishiki (Information on How to Deal with Banks)* (Tokyo: Nihon Keizai Shinbunsha, 1977), p. 95.

[10] Ballon and Tomita, *The Financial Behavior of Japanese Corporations*, p. 91.

[11] Motohiro Ikeda, "Foreign Securities Firms," *The Japan Economic Journal*, (Summer 1988), p. 45.

[12] Nomura Research Institute, *Koushasai Youran 1988 (The 1988 Bond Handbook)* (Tokyo: Nomura Research Institute, 1988), p. 220 and 224.

[13] Ballon and Tomita, *The Financial Behavior of Japanese Corporations*, p. 84.

[14] Ibid., p. 96.

[15] Ibid., p. 99.

[16] Ibid., p. 99.

[17] Ibid., p. 101. Convertible bonds are discussed in more detail in Chapter 12.

[18] Nomura Research Institute, *Koushasai Youran 1988 (The 1988 Bond Handbook)*, p. 272.

[19] Per telephone interview with Mitsui & Co. USA on April 28, 1989.

[20] Kozo Yamamura, "Caveat Emptor: The Industrial Policy of Japan," *Strategic Policy and the New International Economics* (Cambridge: MIT Press, 1987), p. 172.

[21] Yamamura, "Caveat Emptor: The Industrial Policy of Japan," p. 173.

[22] Ibid., p. 174.

[23] Ibid., p. 172.

[24] Ballon and Tomita, *The Financial Behavior of Japanese Corporations*, p. 84.

[25] Ibid., p. 85.

[26] Nomura Research Institute, *Koushasai Youran 1988 (The 1988 Bond Handbook)*, p. 528.

[27] Nakajima, *Zusetsu, Nihon no Shooken Shijoo (Chart Method Explanation Series, The Japanese Security Market)*, p. 103.

[28] Daiwa Security Company, *Saiken no Joushiki (Practical Knowledge of Bonds)*, p. 100.

[29] Ministry of Finance, Securities Bureau, ed., *Dai-26-kai Ookurasho Shokenkyoku Nenpoo, Showa-63-nenban (26th Version of the Annual Bulletin for the Year Ending March 1988 of the Securities Bureau, Ministry of Finance)* (Tokyo: Kinyuu Zaisei Jijoo Kenkyuukai, 1988), p. 64.

[30] Ibid., p. 61.

[31] N. Sassa and H. Matsuzaki, *Ginshoo Sensoo (The War—Banks vs Security Houses)* (Tokyo: Zaikei Shoohoosha, 1987), p. 130.

[32] Ministry of Finance, Securitities Bureau, ed., *Dai-26-kai Ookurasho Shokenkyoku Nenpoo, Showa-63-nenban (26th version of the Annual Bulletin for the Year Ending March 1988 of the Securities Bureau, Ministry of Finance)* p. 66.

[33] Nomura Research Institute, *Koushasai Youran 1988 (The 1988 Bond Handbook)*, p. 224.

[34] Ibid., p. 451.

[35] Ibid., p. 790.

[36] Ibid., p. 194.

[37] Ibid., p. 790.

CHAPTER 12

Yen-Denominated Convertible Bonds

Yoshiki Kaneko
Associate
The Sanwa Bank Ltd.

Luca Battaglini
Senior Researcher
Research Department
Instituto Mobiliare Italiano

Convertible bonds have been the most important public security form of financing for Japanese companies in the 1980s. The trend is evident from Exhibit 1, which compares the funds raised by Japanese corporations in the domestic and in the overseas markets. In the domestic market, convertible bonds have been predominant since 1983, while warrant bonds have been the most popular Japanese security overseas after 1986. Convertible bonds and warrant bonds are the two most important types of equity-linked bonds. Warrant bonds are similar to convertible bonds, except that the debt and warrant portions of the unit can be traded separately as distinct securities. In this chapter, we review the yen-denominated convertible bond market in Japan. We begin with a description of the basic terms and investment characteristics of convertible bonds.

381

**EXHIBIT 1: DISTRIBUTION OF BOND AND STOCK ISSUES OF
JAPANESE COMPANIES IN THE DOMESTIC AND
OVERSEAS MARKETS**

Domestic Market
(¥ 100 Million)

	SB		CB		WB		Stocks	
FY 1980	(101)	9,935	(12)	965	(—)	—	(256)	11,601
FY 1981	(127)	12,690	(52)	5,260	(3)	200	(285)	17,932
FY 1982	(91)	10,475	(46)	4,175	(9)	470	(172)	10,154
FY 1983	(62)	6,830	(67)	8,610	(3)	170	(126)	8,494
FY 1984	(55)	7,200	(125)	16,115	(1)	30	(152)	8,146
FY 1985	(63)	9,435	(142)	15,855	(5)	550	(131)	6,513
FY 1986	(61)	9,800	(204)	34,680	(11)	1,040	(110)	6,315
FY 1987	(27)	9,150	(302)	50,550	(—)	—	(149)	20,839

Overseas Market

	SB		CB		WB		Stocks	
FY 1980	(34)	1,680	(73)	5,149	(—)	—	(13)	1,077
FY 1981	(8)	491	(132)	10,248	(5)	443	(24)	2,874
FY 1982	(96)	6,812	(75)	6,275	(9)	658	(11)	626
FY 1983	(62)	4,039	(152)	11,914	(33)	3,231	(6)	778
FY 1984	(96)	11,345	(153)	12,272	(61)	4,336	(10)	495
FY 1985	(155)	14,393	(87)	9,480	(91)	8.662	(2)	107
FY 1986	(175)	16,392	(49)	4,853	(202)	19,932	(1)	6
FY 1987	(86)	8,240	(91)	10,766	(223)	34,390	(2)	390

Notes
( ) = number of issues
SB, CB and WB stand for straight, convertible and warrant bonds,
respectively.
FY stands for fiscal year.

Source: *Koushasai Nenkan 1988 ed. (The Bond Yearbook of Fiscal Year 1988.)* The
Bond Underwriters Association of Japan.

Exhibit 2 demonstrates that, until 1983, convertible bonds were more popular overseas than in the domestic market. Prior to that time, issuing in the overseas markets had several advantages. For example, coupon rates on convertible bonds were lower, especially in the Swiss market. Also, convertibles were usually unsecured bonds (while in Japan the regulations were such that, for most companies, these bonds had to be secured), and the issuance procedure was simple.

In 1983, however, the relaxation of the restrictions on the issuance of convertible bonds made the domestic public securities markets generally easier for companies to access. The decrease in domestic interest rates was another positive factor, having the effect of lowering issuing costs for companies. Also, during this time both the stock and the bond markets were generally favorable for issuing convertible bonds.

EXHIBIT 2: CONVERTIBLE BOND ISSUES OF JAPANESE COMPANIES IN THE DOMESTIC AND OVERSEAS MARKETS

	Domestic Market		Overseas Market	
Fiscal Year	Number of Issues	Amount (¥ 100 million)	Number of Issues	Amount (¥ 100 million)
1974	56	2,835	5	203
1975	42	3,310	15	1,820
1976	14	555	22	1,538
1977	26	1,625	34	2,211
1978	27	2,770	81	4,281
1979	31	3,535	91	5,561
1980	12	965	73	5,149
1981	52	5,260	132	10,248
1982	46	4,175	75	6,275
1983	67	8,610	152	11,914
1984	125	16,115	153	12,272
1985	142	15,855	87	9,480
1986	204	34,680	49	4,853
1987	302	50,550	91	10,766

Source: *Koushasai Nenkan 1988 ed. (The Bond Yearbook of Fiscal Year 1988.)* The Bond Underwriters Association of Japan.

Exhibit 3 compares the trends in the domestic primary markets of convertible bonds and straight (that is, nonconvertible) bonds. The rapid rise of the amount of convertibles issued resulted mainly from the deregulation of the eligibility of companies that may issue convertible bonds. Some major companies were able to launch large issues (as much as ¥100 billion), but, more importantly, access to the market became easier for medium-sized companies.

EXHIBIT 3: STRAIGHT AND CONVERTIBLE BOND ISSUES OF JAPANESE COMPANIES IN THE DOMESTIC MARKET

	Straight Bonds			Convertible Bonds		
	Number of Issues	Amount (¥ 100 million)	Avg. Issue Amount	Number of Issues	Amount (¥ 100 million)	Avg. Issue Amount
1969	386	49,521	128	4	125	31
1970	426	6,083	14	22	1,145	52
1971	414	8,535	21	18	850	47
1972	167	6,553	39	65	2,880	44
1973	178	8,540	48	91	4,103	45
1974	187	9,867	53	56	2,835	51
1975	310	15,042	49	42	3,310	79
1976	171	11,664	68	14	555	40
1977	142	12,408	87	26	1,625	63
1978	153	13,133	86	27	2,770	103
1979	126	12,981	103	31	3,535	114
1980	101	9,935	98	12	965	80
1981	127	12,690	100	52	5,260	101
1982	91	10,475	115	46	4,175	91
1983	62	6,830	110	67	8,610	129
1984	55	7,200	131	125	16,115	129
1985	63	9,435	150	142	15,855	112
1986	61	9,800	161	204	34,680	170
1987	27	9,150	339	302	50,550	167

Source: *Koushasai Nenkan 1988 ed. (The Bond Yearbook of Fiscal Year 1988.)* The Bond Underwriters Association of Japan.

THE ISSUERS

Exhibit 4 shows the market share of straight bonds, convertible bonds, and warrant bonds in the primary market of Japanese corporate bonds. The share of convertibles has increased dramatically since 1983, reaching more than 80% of the total.

Exhibit 5 shows the distribution of convertible bonds according to the industry of the issuing company. The market share calculation in the exhibit is based on the total face value of outstanding convertible bonds issued by each industry at the end of fiscal years 1986 and 1987. The electronics industry is the major issuer of convertible bonds, followed by the financial sector, which more than doubled its share in fiscal year 1987. The increase is primarily due to the recent relaxation of regulations with respect to the issuance of convertible bonds by banks. As a result, Japanese banks also used convertible bond financing to increase their primary capital ratio to 8% in order to satisfy the capital requirements of the Bank for International Settlements.

EXHIBIT 4: DISTRIBUTION OF TOTAL BOND ISSUES OF JAPANESE COMPANIES IN THE DOMESTIC PRIMARY MARKET

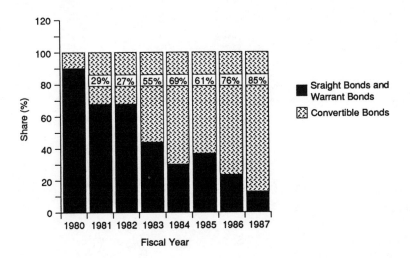

Source: *Koushasai Nenkan 1988 ed. (The Bond Yearbook of Fiscal Year 1988.)* The Bond Underwriters Association of Japan.

**EXHIBIT 5:   DISTRIBUTION BY ISSUING INDUSTRY OF OUTSTANDING
JAPANESE CONVERTIBLE BONDS**

	Fiscal Year 1987		Fiscal Year 1988	
	¥ Billion	%	¥ Billion	%
Electronics	1,751	23.78	1,904	18.84
Financial Services	381	5.18	1,201	11.89
Chemical	703	9.56	947	9.37
Commercial	445	6.04	865	8.56
Construction	448	6.09	745	7.36
Transportation Machinery	665	9.03	664	6.57
Ground Transportation	351	4.76	398	3.94
Real Estate	127	1.73	352	3.48
Food	244	3.31	339	3.35
Machinery	400	5.43	338	3.34
Textile	204	2.77	289	2.85
Electrical Utilities	226	3.06	269	2.66
Other Manufacturing	174	2.36	235	2.32
Glass	156	2.12	225	2.23
Precision Instruments	216	2.93	167	1.65
Other Metals	172	2.34	163	1.61
Media	98	1.33	146	1.44
Other Services	79	1.08	137	1.35
Oil & Coal	50	0.68	130	1.28
Paper & Pulp	111	1.51	111	1.10
Steel	160	2.17	106	1.05
Air Transportation	16	0.21	105	1.04
Other Metal Products	50	0.68	67	0.66
Gas	32	0.44	54	0.54
Warehousing	10	0.14	53	0.52
Shipping	74	1.01	44	0.44
Rubber	5	0.07	44	0.44
Fishery	10	0.13	6	0.06
Other Transportation	1	0.01	5	0.05
Mining	4	0.05	2	0.01
Total Face Value	7,363	100	10,111	100

Source: *Koushasai Nenkan 1988 ed. (The Bond Yearbook of Fiscal Year 1988.)* The
Bond Underwriters Association of Japan.

Incentives for Japanese Corporations

There are two main incentives for the use of convertible bonds by Japanese corporations, the first of which is the less stringent issuing standards required for this security compared to straight bonds. As deregulation on the eligibility of issuers of convertible bonds went progressively into effect, many major companies relied on convertibles as the principal fund-raising vehicle. Second, while convertibles help a company raise the funds necessary for the expansion of its business, at the same time they also improve its primary capital. This is not only true for banks, but also for Japanese manufacturing firms. Historically, Japanese companies tended to be heavily dependent on debt financing from banks, especially in the 1960s and 1970s, when they actively expanded their businesses. Because of this dependence, Japanese companies had, on average, a low primary capital ratio. Convertible bonds provided the best way for a company to increase its primary capital—if the company showed a good performance after issuance of the convertibles. In this case, as the stock price increases, the company can expect bondholders to convert into stock.

INVESTMENT FEATURES OF CONVERTIBLE BONDS

Convertible bonds are securities combining many of the features of straight bonds and warrants. Like straight bonds, convertible bondholders receive fixed coupon payments and principal at the maturity date, and have priority over the stock in the event of bankruptcy. At the same time, convertible bonds, like warrants, can be exchanged at the discretion of their owners into a specified number of shares of stock. Unlike warrants though, the exercise price for convertible bonds is, in effect, the value of the future coupon and principal payments which is foregone when the security is converted into the company's stock. Actually, a convertible bond is the equivalent of a package of a straight bond and a warrant with a variable exercise price. The exercise price is variable because it is equal to the value that the convertible would have as a straight bond. This value will typically change over time, according to changes in interest rates and in the credit risk of the issuer.

An important provision associated with nearly every convertible bond is that the issuing firm has the right to repurchase ("call") the outstanding securities at given times and at given conditions specified at the time of issuance. Call provisions can reduce the potential attractiveness of convertible bonds, since the firm may be able to force conversion into its common stock earlier than security holders would prefer.

Either a *conversion ratio* or a *conversion price* is stated in each convertible bond's indenture. The conversion ratio specifies the number of shares of the issuing firm that can be obtained by surrendering the convertible security. In some cases, the specifications in the indenture may provide for changes in the conversion ratio over time. The conversion ratio is defined as:

$$\text{Conversion Ratio} = \frac{\text{Face Value of the Security}}{\text{Conversion Price}}$$

Of course, if the conversion ratio is stated directly in the indenture, then the conversion price can be derived as the ratio of the face (or par) value of the security to the conversion ratio.

The *market conversion price* of a convertible bond represents the cost per share of the common stock if it is obtained through the purchase of the company's convertible bonds and their immediate conversion into stock. The market conversion price per common share is typically higher than the current market price of the stock if purchased directly in the stock market. Convertibles are then said to be selling at a premium. If the conversion premium were negative, arbitrage opportunities would be available in the market. An arbitrage trade could be constructed by shorting the stock, buying the convertible, and immediately exercising it into the issuer's stock. The shares obtained through conversion would be delivered to cover the short position on the stock. The whole transaction would guarantee a profit at no risk, since the price at which the stock was shorted was higher than the price at which the stock could be obtained through conversion of the bond. It is unlikely though that such opportunities exist, meaning that conversion premiums will be the norm.

Conversion premiums are explained by the investment characteristics of convertible bonds: i.e., they have upside potential but limited downside risk compared to that of a stock. Nevertheless, dividends paid on a company's stock may create a situation during the life of a convertible bond where the conversion premium could be close to zero. The convertible's price will then just be equal to the value of the stocks into which the security can be converted. In this circumstance, early conversion into stocks is normally the optimal strategy. Still, in most situations, convertible bonds are typically traded at a premium over their stock-equivalent value.

To illustrate the investment characteristics of a convertible bond, consider the following Japanese issue:

Yamaichi Securities 11th, issued on 08/31/88.[1]
Maturity: 03/31/95
Coupon rate: 1.2%
Conversion price: ¥2,020
Market quotes as of 04/21/89:[2]
  Convertible bond = 98
  Stock price = ¥1,780

Convertible bond market prices are quoted with respect to the unit face value of the security. A quote of 98 means that the Yamaichi 11th convertible is selling at 98% of its face value. In addition, Japanese convertible bonds are traded in multiples of at least ¥100,000. Therefore, to buy ¥100,000 of Yamaichi 11th convertibles, an investor would then have to pay: (98/100) × ¥100,000 = ¥98,000. Key values for the security are calculated below:

Conversion ratio =
¥100,000/¥2,020 per share = 49.505 shares

Conversion premium per share =
¥98,000/49.505 shares – ¥1,780 per share = ¥199.6 per share

Conversion premium ratio =
100 × (¥199.6 per share / ¥1,780 per share) = 11.21

The conversion premium ratio, or *disparate ratio*, shows the percentage increase in the stock price necessary to reach a parity between the stock and the market conversion price of the convertible. The disparate ratio is an indicator of the premium at which a convertible bond is selling in the market.

A convertible bond offers the downside protection of a straight bond, while allowing investors to share in the upside potential for the common stock of a growing firm. If the stock of the issuer rises in price, the convertible will usually also rise to reflect the increased value of the underlying common stock. On the other hand, if the stock price declines, a convertible bond can be expected to decline only to the point where the security yields a satisfactory return on its value as a straight bond. In this case, the value of the warrant component of the convertible bond will drop close to zero, and the convertible will be at its lower bound, being worth only its value as straight debt. It should be noted, however, that the lower bound value of a convertible bond can be changing. If the interest rate applicable on a company's straight debt rises or if interest rates in the economy rise, the straight bond value of the convertible will decrease. Therefore, the downside risk potential of convertible bonds is not fixed, as is the case with standard options.

As a final note, it is important to point out that takeover risk faced by investors in U.S. convertible bonds is practically nonexistent for convertible bonds issued by Japanese companies. As a matter of fact, the structure of ownership in Japan makes it very difficult for takeovers to occur. Convertible bonds will rarely, if at all, be exposed to events, like takeovers, that are difficult to predict.

PRIMARY MARKET

The history of convertible bonds in Japan goes back to the revision of the Commercial Law in 1938. With this revision, convertible bonds were legislated for the first time in the domestic market. The initial objective was to attract overseas investors and introduce capital into Japan from the U.S. and Western Europe. The first convertible bond issue under the new law was floated in 1949. Since then, it took several revisions of the Commercial Law to bring the current form of convertible bonds into the primary market. Among these changes, the most important ones were the conversion at market value and the introduction of issuances of unsecured convertible bonds.

The revison of the Commercial Law of 1938 did not set particular restrictions on the price at which investors could exchange convertible bonds into stocks of the issuing company. The conventional practice in the marketplace was that bondholders could convert their bonds on the basis of the face value of the stock. The face value of a stock is the nominal price showing on the stock certificate. The conversion price was then set equal to the stock's face value, regardless of the stock market value; this feature prevented issuers from exploiting the real value of their stocks. The reason for this convention was that, even in the stock market, new issues at market value were considered out of question. Therefore, convertible bonds had to adjust to the same logic.

Meanwhile, more companies were advocating that convertible bonds should have a conversion price related to the market value of the stock. The advocators of the change were pointing out that this feature would permit an improvement in a company's capitalization. In 1962, *Hitachi* was the first company to float a convertible bond issue with a conversion price based on the market price of the stock. The issue was denominated in U.S. dollars, and launched in the U.S. market. Two other convertible bond issues were launched in 1962, and nine more in 1963, in the overseas markets. These convertible bonds were attractive to investors partly because of the outstanding growth of the Japanese economy at the time.

These first successful convertible issues launched overseas were a major factor for the introduction of convertible bonds based on the stock market value in the Japanese domestic market. In 1966, *Nippon Tsuuun* was the first to experiment with this type of convertible in the domestic market, with a ¥10 billion issue. However, both the primary and secondary markets for convertible bonds became active only after 1969, when the first stock issue at market value was successfully introduced in Japan. In May 1970, convertible bonds were listed for the first time on the Tokyo Stock Exchange. Thereafter, relaxation of the regulations governing the issuance of convertible bonds, together with the restrictions applying to the issuance of straight debt, have contributed to the success of convertibles as a major financing vehicle for Japanese corporations. Almost all convertible bonds are now listed on at least one of the Japanese exchanges and trade very actively. Unlike straight bonds, only a small fraction is traded over-the-counter. The number of outstanding issues is more than 1,000, with a total face value in excess of ¥13 trillion.

Reasons for the Growth of the Market

The Performance of the Stock and Bond Markets. A natural factor associated with the performance of the convertible bond market is the behavior of the stock market. Foreign investors have become increasingly involved in the Japanese financial markets, but they have different investment standards from Japanese investors. Unlike Japanese investors, who pay special attention to dividends and premiums, foreign investors focus on the earnings per share of a company, and its growth opportunities.[3] The latter approach was quite successful in evaluating the performance of the Japanese stock market. At the same time, the success of stock issues at market value supported the new issues of convertible bonds.

Another major reason for the success of convertible bonds was related to the limited opportunities available in the straight bond market. Since tight regulations have traditionally been applied to the issuance of straight bonds, companies have looked for ways to diversify their sources of funds. Convertible bonds represented for many companies a relatively more accessible form of financing.

Progressive Deregulation on the Issuing Side. Convertible bonds can be issued in different forms. The basic ones are secured convertible bonds, unsecured convertible bonds with reserved assets, and unsecured convertible bonds without reserved assets.

When a company issues secured convertible bonds, specific assets are reserved as collateral for that particular issue. There is a one-to-one relationship between the debt and the assets pledged as collateral. This type of convertible is traditionally secured with assets like plants, mines, railways, or real estate. Unsecured convertible bonds with reserved assets give their holders protection in the case of bankruptcy of the issuing company. Some designated assets are reserved for the convertible debt at the time of issuance. The type of assets that can be reserved are limited in general to the company's most important ones, like transferable securities, main plants, and real estate properties. The legal and operational terms of this form of debt are different from those applying to secured convertible bonds. Finally, unsecured convertible bonds without reserved assets do not require collateral for the issue.

The conventional rule, until 1973, was that all convertible bonds, like straight bonds, were to be secured by plants, mines, or real estate. The objective was to protect investors in case of insolvency of the company. However, as the international financial environment evolved, this rule was relaxed. In January 1973, companies were allowed to issue unsecured convertible bonds with reserved assets. In March 1979, unsecured convertible bonds without reserved assets were also permitted.

Companies have to meet particular standards in order to issue convertible bonds. These standards are part of a larger set known as the *voluntary adjustment standards*, which also covers some special items such as dividend payments. The voluntary adjustment standards are set jointly by the securities companies, with the informal approval of the Ministry of Finance. Standards for companies had been alleviated primarily in 1983, as well as in 1987. Exhibits 6, 7, and 8 describe the core of the standards currently applicable to the three forms of convertible debt.

The major improvement concerning secured convertible bonds was the reduction from ¥6 billion to ¥3 billion in the minimum net assets required before issuance. In the case of unsecured convertible bonds with reserved assets, companies with net assets of at least ¥33 billion should meet conditions both for net assets and dividends, and any two of the other four conditions. Instead, companies with net assets of less than ¥33 billion should meet conditions both for net assets and primary capital ratio, and any three of the other four conditions. In addition, companies that have either received a rating of "A" or better, or have ¥20 billion or more of net assets and at least a "BBB" rating, are eligible for issuing unsecured convertible bonds with reserved assets, regardless of the above conditions. In the case of unsecured convertible bonds without reserved assets, companies with net assets of ¥110 billion or more are required to meet conditions both for net assets and dividends, and any two of the other four conditions. Instead, companies with net assets of less than ¥110 billion are required to meet conditions both for net assets and primary capital ratio, and any three of the other four conditions. Also, companies that have either received at least a rating of "A," or have net assets of ¥33 billion or more and at least a "BBB" rating, are allowed to issue unsecured convertible bonds without reserved assets regardless of the above conditions.

EXHIBIT 6:   STANDARDS FOR ISSUING SECURED CONVERTIBLE BONDS

	Minimum Eligibility Requirements Based on Net Assets (in ¥ billion)		
	10	6	3
Primary Capital Ratio (%)	10	12	15
Net Asset Ratio (1)(times)	1.2	1.5	2
Profit/Total Assets (2)(%)	5	6	7
Dividend per Share (¥)	5	5	5
Earnings per Share after Taxes (¥)	7	7	7

The three net asset categories are: (1) greater than or equal to ¥10 billion; (2) greater than or equal to ¥6 billion but less than ¥10 billion, and; (3) greater than or equal to ¥3 billion but less than ¥6 billion.

A company with ¥10 billion and more of net assets has to meet the three standards of net assets, dividend per share and earnings per share after taxes, and at least any one of the other three.

A company with less than ¥10 billion of net assets has to meet the three standards of net asseets, dividend per share and earnings per share after taxes, and at least any two of the other three.

Notes:

(1) Net Asset Ratio = Net Assets/Capital Stock

(2) Profit/Total Assets = Operating Profits/Total Assets

Source: *Koushasai Nenkan 1988 ed. (The Bond Yearbook of Fiscal Year 1988.)* The Bond Underwriters Association of Japan.

In addition to these financial standards, other rules apply, such as the obligation of the issuer to complete a form describing the intended use of the funds to be raised. Overall, the result of the institutional changes was that the number of companies which could issue both unsecured and secured convertible bonds increased. In February 1987, the number of companies eligible for issuing unsecured convertible bonds without reserved assets increased from about 180 to 330. Also, the number of companies which could issue secured convertible bonds increased from about 940 to 1,030.[4] Exhibit 9

EXHIBIT 7: STANDARDS FOR ISSUING UNSECURED CONVERTIBLE BONDS WITH RESERVED ASSETS

	Minimum Eligibility Requirements Based on Net Assets (in ¥ billion) of:			
	55	33	20	10
Primary Capital Ratio (%)	15	20	40	50
Net Asset Ratio (1)(times)	1.5	2	4	5
Profit/Total Assets (2)(times)	67	10	12	(%)
Int. Cov. Ratio (3)(times)	1.2	1.5	4	5
Dividends	(4)	(4)	(5)	(5)

The four net asset classes are (1) greater than or equal to ¥55 billion; (2) greater than or equal to ¥33 billion but less than ¥55 billion; (3) greater than or equal to ¥20 billion but less than ¥33 billion, and; (4) greater than or equal to ¥10 billion but less than ¥20 billion.

Notes:

(1) Net Asset Ratio = Net Assets/Capital Stock

(2) Profit/total Assets = Operating Profits/Total Assets

(3) Int. Cov. Ratio = Interest Coverage Ratio

$$= \frac{\text{Operating Profits + Interest and Dividend Revenues}}{\text{Interest Expenses}}$$

(4) A company must have been paying dividends for the last five consecutive years, and at least ¥6 per share for the last five consecutive years.

(5) A company must have been paying at least ¥6 per share for the last five consecutive years.

Source: *Koushasai Nenkan 1988 ed. (The Bond Yearbook of Fiscal Year 1988.)* The Bond Underwriters Association of Japan.

shows the trend resulting from this deregulation. In particular, it should be noted that in fiscal year 1987 more than 85% of the convertible bonds issued were unsecured bonds without reserved assets.

Other changes contributed to the increase in the number of companies eligible for issuing convertible bonds. In July 1987, companies having their stocks traded only over-the-counter were allowed for the first time to issue convertible bonds. Previously, only companies

EXHIBIT 8: STANDARDS FOR ISSUING UNSECURED CONVERTIBLE BONDS WITHOUT RESERVED ASSETS

	Minimum Eligibility Requirements Based on Net Assets (in ¥ billion) of:			
	110	55	33	20
Primary Capital Ratio (%)	15	30	40	50
Net Asset Ratio (1) (times)	1.5	3	4	5
Profit/Total Assets (2) (%)	6	8	10	12
Int. Cov. Ratio (3) (times)	1.2	3	4	5
Dividends	(4)	(4)	(5)	(5)

The four net asset classes are (1) greater than or equal to ¥110 billion; (2) greater than or equal to ¥55 billion but less than ¥110 billion; (3) greater than or equal to ¥33 billion but less than ¥55 billion, and; (4) greater than or equal to ¥20 billion but less than ¥33 billion.

Notes:

(1) Net Asset Ratio = Net Assets/Capital Stock

(2) Profit/Total Assets = Operating Profits/Total Assets

(3) Int. cov. ratio = Interest Coverage Ratio

$$= \frac{\text{Operating profits} + \text{Interest and Dividend Revenues}}{\text{Interest Expenses}}$$

(4) A company must have been paying dividends for the last five consecutive years, and at least ¥5 per share for the last three consecutive years.

(5) A company must have been paying at least ¥6 per share for the last five consecutive years.

Source: *Koushasai Nenkan 1988 ed. (The Bond Yearbook of Fiscal Year 1988.)* The Bond Underwriters Association of Japan.

whose stocks were listed on the exchanges could issue convertible bonds. In fiscal year 1987, nine convertible bond issues (a total amount of ¥39 billion) were launched. Banks were also allowed to issue convertibles in the domestic market, under the condition that the funds raised had to be used only for investments in infrastructures and equipment. Actually, the motivation behind this change was that banks needed to increase their primary capital and upgrade

EXHIBIT 9: DISTRIBUTION OF CONVERTIBLE BOND ISSUES BY TYPE OF CONVERTIBLE IN THE DOMESTIC MARKET

Fiscal Year	Unsecured CB Without Reserved Assets			Unsecured CB Without Reserved Assets			Secured CB		
	# of Issues	Amount*	Share (%)	# of Issues	Amount*	Share (%)	# of Issues	Amount*	Share (%)
1979	1	500	14.2	7	1,500	42.4	23	1,535	43.4
1980	0	0	0	1	400	41.5	11	565	58.5
1981	1	600	11.4	15	2,080	39.5	36	2,580	49.1
1982	1	450	10.8	12	1,820	43.6	33	1,905	45.6
1983	9	2,570	29.8	23	4,065	47.2	35	1,975	23
1984	36	9,210	57.2	27	3,150	19.5	62	3,755	23.3
1985	32	7,250	45.7	26	3,160	19.9	84	5,445	34.4
1986	95	23,415	67.5	19	3,010	8.7	90	8,255	23.8
1987	205	43,370	85.8	23	2,430	4.8	74	4,750	9.4

*¥100 million

Source: *Koushasai Nenkan 1988 ed. (The Bond Yearbook of Fiscal Year 1988.)* The Bond Underwriters Association of Japan.

their computer-based systems. In fiscal year 1987, 28 convertible bond issues (a total amount of ¥463 billion) were floated by banks; this accounted for 30% of the increase in the amount of convertibles issued by all market participants between fiscal years 1986 and 1987.

The Role of Ratings Companies. As the restrictions on the eligibility of issuing companies became progressively more relaxed, the role of ratings companies grew in importance. The Japan Bond Research Institute was established as an independent entity in April 1985. Later in the same month, two other Japanese ratings companies were established: the Japan Credit Research and the Nippon Investors Service. Currently, S&P, Moody's, and Fitch, are also recognized as official ratings companies. Japanese companies can receive one of nine different ratings, ranging from AAA to C.

The ratings companies have a direct impact on the convertible bond primary market. As mentioned previously, a company's rating is one of the standards relevant for determining its eligibility to issue unsecured convertible bonds. Also, ratings have recently become a standard for determining a company's eligibility to issue secured convertible bonds. Ratings also affect the coupon rate set on convertibles, and they influence the redemption features of the issue. These last two points are described in more detail later in this chapter.

Euromarket

The Eurobond market has been the principal beneficiary of Japanese financial liberalization. The vast majority of bonds in this market are in bearer form, and issues are generally unsecured obligations of the issuer. For Japanese companies, the Eurobond market is a clearly favorable alternative to issuing in the Japanese domestic market. The advantages of the Eurobond market are derived basically from two factors. First, the issuance procedures are much simpler; second, issues can be denominated in different currencies, permitting the issuer to exploit swap opportunities that reduce the cost of funds.

The performance of Eurobonds is sensitive to movements in exchange rates. Investors' confidence in the maintenance of relative stability in exchange rate relationships is very important in determining their preferences across the various currencies and products available. The Eurobond market plays a major role as a reliable source of long-term financing to companies, and represents an attractive outlet for international portfolio investments. Investors are especially receptive to offerings by highly-rated borrowers, and access to the market is rather limited for second tier companies.

Equity-linked bonds are one type of instrument available to investors in the Euromarket. Exhibit 10 shows that during the 1980s, Japanese companies increased their recourse to the overseas market relative to the domestic market. Within the overseas markets, the Euromarket played a major role. Exhibit 11 shows the distribution of Japanese issues in the overseas market between 1986 and 1987 by currency of denomination and by type of security offered. Several facts should be noted. Traditionally, Japanese companies have been raising a relatively large fraction of funds directly in the Swiss market. In 1984, Japanese corporations were allowed to hedge their liabilities with forward contracts for the entire life of a bond. As a consequence, companies increasingly diversified their issues into the Euromarket, with a larger number of offerings denominated in currencies other than the yen. Another factor in this period was the pre-

EXHIBIT 10: DISTRIBUTION OF TOTAL BOND ISSUES OF JAPANESE COMPANIES IN THE DOMESTIC AND THE OVERSEAS MARKETS

	Domestic Market		Overseas Market	
	Amount*	%	Amount*	%
1980	10,900	61	6,829	39
1981	18,150	62	11,182	38
1982	15,120	52	13,745	48
1983	15,610	45	19,184	55
1984	23,345	46	27,953	54
1985	25,840	44	32,535	56
1986	45,520	53	41,177	47
1987	59,700	53	53,396	47

*¥100 million

Source: *Koushasai Nenkan 1988 ed. (The Bond Yearbook of Fiscal Year 1988.)* The Bond Underwriters Association of Japan.

EXHIBIT 11: DISTRIBUTION OF TOTAL BOND ISSUES OF JAPANESE COMPANIES IN THE OVERSEAS MARKET (¥100 MILLION)

	Straight Bonds		Convertible Bonds		Warrant Bonds		Total	
	1986	1987	1986	1987	1986	1987	1986	1987
Euro Market	10,439	5,038	1,732	4,384	16,004	32,625	28,174	42,048
U.S. $	4,285	1,502	1,732	4,039	14,976	32,293	20,991	37,834
DM	497	311	0	346	745	75	1,242	732
¥	4,720	3,120	0	0	0	0	4,720	3,120
ECU	458	0	0	0	163	203	621	203
Others	480	105	0	0	121	54	601	159
Swiss Market	5,953	3,182	3,123	6,381	3,928	1,765	13,004	11,328
Total	16,392	8,240	4,853	10,766	19,932	34,390	41,176	53,396

Source: *Koushasai Nenkan 1988 ed. (The Bond Yearbook of Fiscal Year 1988.)* The Bond Underwriters Association of Japan.

dominance of equity-linked bonds (warrant bonds, in particular) as a share of the total amount issued. Equity-linked bonds rose from 60% of total offerings in 1986 to 84% in 1987. Within the convertible bond market, banks issued the equivalent of ¥650 billion in 1987, accounting for 60% of the total amount of convertibles issued. Another feature of Japanese offerings is that no yen-denominated equity-linked issue was made in the Euromarket since 1986. Actually, there have been only five Euroyen convertible issues so far, all made in 1985 by Japanese industrial companies, and only two Euroyen issues of warrant bonds, both made in 1986. Of course, for their issues in yen, Japanese industrial companies also have the choice of using the domestic convertible bond market.

It is interesting to extend to the year 1988 the analysis of Japanese issuers' activity in the overseas markets. Considering the distribution, by country, of bond offerings in the Eurobond market, Japanese residents were the largest fund-raisers. As much as 90% of all new issues of equity-linked bonds were made by Japanese companies. Also, the share of equity-linked bonds in the total of Japanese bond issues rose to 68%, from a level of 44% in 1986. The bulk of the new issues took place in the market for warrant bonds. These instruments provide investors with greater flexibility for equity play as well as overall asset management, to the extent that warrants can be stripped off and negotiated separately from the underlying bond. On the other hand, issues of convertible bonds had a modest increase, and were heavily concentrated in the Swiss market.

In 1988, Japanese convertible offerings totaled a U.S. dollar equivalent of $7.1 billion. The Swiss market absorbed most of the new issues, while the Eurodollar share slumped to $1.6 billion. In the market for warrant bonds, new offerings reached a U.S. dollar equivalent of $28.6 billion, virtually all from Japanese companies. In view of the strong performance of the Japanese stock market, equity warrants were very attractive to investors during most of 1988. Concurrently, because of currency swaps, Japanese corporations were in a position to raise funds with a maturity of around five years at cheaper terms than those available in the domestic market.

Issuing Procedures

A convertible bond issue involves an issuing company (issuer), underwriting securities companies (underwriters), trust companies (trustees), and the Japanese Ministry of Finance. The issuing procedures are described in Chapter 3.

Technical Features of Japanese Convertible Bonds

All of the terms of a convertible bond issue are stated in the plan that the issuer provides to subscribers after the notification to the Ministry of Finance is made. In the issuing plan, investors can find not only the terms of the issue, but also financial data and other information on the issuer's businesses.

Total Amount of the Issue. There are two different regulations concerning the total amount of an issue of convertible bonds, the Commercial Law, and the voluntary adjustment rules set by securities companies.

The Commercial Law fixes the limits on the amounts that can be issued. An issuing company is allowed to offer convertible bonds if it has earned profits, but the amount issued cannot be greater than the difference between its primary capital plus legal reserve and the total amount of all types of bonds outstanding. However, another law is now temporarily allowing the issuance of convertible bonds, as well as secured bonds and foreign currency-denominated bonds, to reach up to two times the amount of this difference. There is no specific mention in the Commercial Law as to the minimum amount of an issue. However, ¥2 billion can be considered the minimum, since the security exchange's standards require the minimum amount of the issue to be listed to be at least ¥2 billion.

Voluntary adjustment standards set by securities companies also include a provision regarding the total amount of a convertible bond issue. According to the standards, the increase in the number of shares made possible through conversion of the bonds into stocks should be less than 20% of the outstanding number of stocks at the time of the issue. This rule limits the decrease in the stock price that could result from large issues of convertibles.

Convertible Bond Certificates. There are three kinds of certificates available: ¥100,000, ¥500,000 and ¥1,000,000. Unlike straight bonds, only one kind of certificate is conventionally offered in each issue of convertible bonds. The historical trend shows that the certificate of ¥100,000 was most widely used in the late 1960s and early 1970s, while the ¥500,000 certificate has recently become the most popular. The ¥1 million certificate is also gaining more widespread use.

Issuing Price. The issuing price of a convertible bond is always set at par at ¥100, unlike straight bonds, which can be issued at a discount or at a premium. Nevertheless, the initial listing price at securities exchanges can differ from the par value of the convertible bond.

Coupon Rate. Currently, the coupon rate on a convertible bond issue is based on the "standard rate" and the issuer's rating. The standard rate is a figure set by a committee of securities companies, whose meetings are held twice a month. The performance of convertibles on the secondary market is the main variable taken into account in fixing the rate. Other factors considered in determining the standard rate are the behavior of the stock and bond markets, and the total amount of new convertible bonds scheduled for future issuance. Once the standard rate has been set, the coupon rate differential of the specific convertible bond issue with respect to the standard rate is determined. The differential depends on the issuer's rating. The lead underwriter can still change the coupon rate differential at its discretion though, after taking into account all the factors affecting the value of the convertibles issued.

Standard Coupon Rate. The standard coupon rate is primarily determined on the basis of: the one-month average of the simple yield of all convertible bond whose parity price is not less than 90 and not more than 100, the yield on convertible bonds issued in the last 12 months, and the nearest-one-week average of the previous two yields. In addition to these yields, other factors are also taken into account in determining the rate, such as: the C.B.Q. average,[5] the initial listing prices of other issues, the average disparate ratio of outstanding convertible bonds having a parity price of not less than 90 and not more than 100, the ratio of the outstanding balance of convertible bonds on the securities exchanges and the total initial amount of the issues, and the bond and stock markets' performances.

The standard coupon rate will be the coupon rate set for issues of convertible bonds having 10 years to maturity, a conversion premium of not less than 5% and not more than 6%, and a rating of BBB.

Coupon Rate Differential. The coupon rate differential depends on several factors, according to rules set by the securities companies. First, it is a function of the years to maturity of the convertible debt, with the current coupon rate differential:

Years to maturity	Coupon rate(S)
10, 12, 15	S
8, 9	S – 0.1%
6, 7	S – 0.2%
4	S – 0.3%

The differential varies according to the conversion premium and the required simple yield of the issue. It also depends on the issuer's rating, with the current weights as follows:

Rating	Coupon rate(S)
AAA	S − 0.3%
AA	S − 0.2%
A	S − 0.1%
BBB	S
BB	S + 0.1%
No ratings	S + 0.2%

Finally, the lead underwriter can use its judgement in adjusting the coupon rate differential, within the range of +0.4% and -0.6%.

Coupon Payment Dates. If an issuer closes its accounts once a year, coupons on the convertible bonds are paid at the end of the accounting year. However, if the issuer pays interim dividends, it will pay coupons on a semiannual basis. There is a specific treatment in the case of conversion. If a convertible bond is converted into stock between two coupon payment dates, no interest payment is made to the new stockholder on the next coupon payment day. On the next dividend date though, the new stockholder will receive the same amount of dividends paid to the old stockholders. Dividend and coupon payment dates are stated in the convertible bond issuing plan.

Maturity. All issues used to have an initial maturity of ten years. Currently, however, new issues of convertible bonds are also offered with a maturity of four, six, seven, eight, nine, twelve, or fifteen years. Issues with seven and four years to maturity were introduced in March 1988 and May 1987, respectively. Exhibit 12 shows the recent distribution of the volume of issues of convertible bonds based on the years to maturity.

Redemption Provisions. Convertible bonds are redeemed at par value at maturity, if bondholders do not choose to convert their bonds into stock. However, an issuer may retire part or all of the

EXHIBIT 12: DISTRIBUTION OF CONVERTIBLE BOND ISSUES BY MATURITY IN THE DOMESTIC MARKET

Maturity (Years)	FY 1985 Amount*	%	FY 1986 Amount*	%	FY 1987 Amount*	%
15	0	0	14,195	40.9	22,710	44.9
12	3,740	23.6	6,100	17.6	4,260	8.4
10	7,555	47.7	5,710	16.5	2,290	4.6
9	0	0	2,725	7.9	15,300	30.3
8	445	2.8	2,575	7.4	975	1.9
7	0	0	0	0	2,680	5.3
6	4,115	25.9	3,375	9.7	2,035	4
4	0	0	0	0	300	0.6
Total	15,855	100	34,680	100	50,550	100

*¥100 million

Source: *Koushasai Nenkan 1988 ed. (The Bond Yearbook of Fiscal Year 1988.)* The Bond Underwriters Association of Japan.

outstanding convertible bonds before the maturity date. As with straight bonds, there are several possible ways to retire an outstanding issue before maturity.

First, an issuer can retire its outstanding bonds at any time by purchasing them back on the market at the prevailing market price. Second, optional redemption features can be included in the terms of the issue. In this case, an issuer may call part or all of its convertible bonds at a premium to par, but only after a certain number of years have elapsed from the issuance date (grace period). The grace period is five years for convertible bonds with a maturity of ten years, and three years for the six-year convertibles. These terms are set by law. Redemption prices are scaled down over time. For example, a ten-year issue can have a call price of ¥104 for the sixth year (there is an initial five-year grace period), ¥103 for the seventh year, ¥102 for the eighth year, ¥101 for the ninth year, and ¥100 for the last year. It should be noted that partial redemption of the issue must be exercised by lot. In Japan, there have been only two cases in which the issuer called back the convertibles before maturity.[6]

The third way to retire an outstanding issue deals with compulsory periodic retirement. If this feature is specified in the terms of the issue, the issuer will redeem at par, in semiannual or annual installments, the outstanding amount of convertible bonds. The grace period applies to compulsory redemption in the same way as with optional redemption. Retirement of the issue is made either by drawing the bonds by lot (sinking fund method), or by purchasing them on the market. Currently, it requires the issuer to deposit, after the grace period, a certain amount of reserves in a trustee bank. The amount is between 15% to 20% of the issue in the case of a ten-year convertible, and around 30% of the issue in the case of a six-year convertible. Also, the amount of reserves deposited depends on the balance of the issue outstanding in the market, which varies over time due to the exercise of conversion into stocks. When convertible bonds are drawn by lot, their holders have four weeks to choose whether to convert their bonds into stock.

Finally, an issue can be retired by redemption at maturity, the so-called *blanket redemption*. This method was introduced in October 1983, and only applies to convertibles having between six and nine years to maturity at the time of issue. An exception to this rule is made if a company has at least an A rating or more than ¥55 billion of net assets. Under either of these circumstances, the company can issue convertible bonds with ten or more years to maturity and blanket redemption.

Registration. Investors can choose to register their convertible bonds with particular institutions. In this case, they will not hold a bond certificate, but a registration certificate. According to the Bond Registration Act, the institution designated must be a trustee company. A pledge trustee company will be chosen in the case of secured convertibles, and a subscription trustee company in the case of unsecured convertibles. Investors can sell their registration certificates, or change the form from registration to bond certificate. In the second case, a certain number of days are needed for the change to occur. Only bond certificates can be traded on the securities exchanges, except if the two parties in a trade have an open account on the exchange. In this case, registered certificates can be transferred automatically between the investors' accounts.

Conversion Price. As in the U.S. and in the Euromarket, the conversion price in Japan is the price at which the issuer will set that the bondholder will have to pay by exchanging the bond for the stock. At one time, the issuer would set the conversion price equal to the par value of the stock. For example, if the par value of the stock was ¥50, the conversion price was set at ¥50. Today, the issuer sets the conversion price based upon the current price of the stock. For example, if the market price of a stock with a par value of ¥50 is ¥200, the issuer will set a conversion price at a premium above ¥200. When the issue is launched, the conversion price is usually set from 5% to 6% above the closing price of the stock one business day before the issuer agrees on the contract terms with the underwriters.

The conversion price can be changed only if the company issues new stocks. Two methods can be used to adjust the conversion price: the market price method and the conversion price method. The market price method specifies the following formula for the adjusted conversion price:

New conversion price = Old conversion price ×

$$\frac{(\text{outstanding shares} + \text{new shares} \times \text{issuing price}/\text{market price})}{(\text{outstanding shares} + \text{new shares})}$$

The market price in the formula is the average of the stock price for 30 trading days, starting from 45 trading days before the date when this new conversion price is applied.

With the conversion price method the adjusted conversion price is given by:

New conversion price = Old conversion price ("old price") ×

$$\frac{(\text{outstanding shares} + \text{new shares} \times \text{issuing price}/\text{old price})}{(\text{outstanding shares} + \text{new shares})}$$

At the time the issuer sets the original conversion price, it also decides which of the two methods will (possibly) be used later. Currently, the market price method is the most popular. The provision for the adjustments in the conversion price is called the *anti-dilution clause.* The objective of this clause is to protect holders of convertible bonds against the potential negative effects of new stock issues on the value of their securities.

Treatment of the Capital Resulting from Conversion. In the event bonds are converted into stocks, half of the total amount converted is usually posted by the issuer as primary capital, and the remaining half as capital reserve. The issuer cannot post more than half of the total amount resulting from conversion to capital reserve.

Conversion Periods. Convertible bondholders can theoretically exercise their right to convert at any time after the issuance and up to the maturity of the issue. The conversion of a convertible bond into stock becomes effective on the day the request form reaches the stock transfers office. An issuer usually appoints a trust bank or a security company as its representative in the procedure. It takes about two weeks for an investor to receive the stock from the issuer.

SECONDARY MARKET

Trading has been very active in the Japanese secondary market for convertible bonds, from the time the first issues were listed on the Tokyo Stock Exchange in 1970. The market average price of convertibles has fluctuated from period to period, following the changes in the overall performance of the Japanese economy. Recent years have shown a surge in trading volume, as a consequence of the strong recovery of the economy from the recession of the early 1980s, and the appreciation of the yen against the dollar.

Market Indicators

Several indicators are used to assess the performance of the secondary market for convertible bonds in Japan. The most popular indicators in the financial community are: (1) simple average price, (2) trading volume, (3) market average disparate ratio, (4) average of the direct yield, and (5) the deal ratio. These five market indices are quoted daily in the newspapers. The initial price on the exchanges of a newly listed convertible bond issue[7] is also used as a market indicator.

Simple Average Price. The simple average price is just the straight average of the closing prices of all convertible bonds traded on the exchanges.

Trading Volume. The trading volume is measured in terms of the face value of the convertible bonds traded on the exchanges.

Market Average Disparate Ratio. The market average disparate ratio is the simple average of the disparate ratios of the issues traded on the exchanges. Generally, a value higher than 20% is a signal of the excessive performance of the convertible bond market.[8]

Average of the Direct Yield. The direct yield of a convertible bond is defined as:

$$\text{Direct yield} = \frac{\text{Coupon rate (\%)}}{\text{Convertible bond price}} \times 100$$

The average of the direct yield is the simple average of the direct yields of the convertible bonds traded on the exchanges. This index is used by investors in making asset allocation decisions.

The Deal Ratio. The deal ratio is the ratio of the number of convertible bond issues traded to the total number of issues listed on an exchange. The higher the ratio, the more active the market, and vice versa. Normally, the deal ratio ranges between 40% and 70%.

Initial Listing Price on the Exchange. The initial price of a newly listed convertible bond can also be an indicator of the performance of the secondary market. A bond is initially sold to investors at the par price of ¥100. One or two weeks later, the issue is listed and traded on the exchanges. The initial price of new convertibles reflects the conditions prevailing in the convertible bond market in general, but in a different way from what is conveyed by the statistics on ordinary trades of seasoned issues. In the history of the Japanese market, the record high of an initial listed price of a convertible bond issue is ¥215.10, set by the 9th convertible issue of Sumitomo Mining Co., initially listed on November 7, 1981.

Historical Trends

Exhibit 13 shows the historical trend of the simple average price and of the trading volume of convertible bonds. The market has fluctuated over time, but trading volume basically followed an increasing trend during the 1980's. Both in terms of volume and average price, the market performed better over the previous year in the years 1972, 1978 and 1981. Improvements in trading systems have contributed partly to the expansion. More important though were the performance of the stock market and the changes in the official discount rate set by the Bank of Japan.

Since convertible bonds are equity-linked bonds, their value is affected by the factors relevant to both the stock and bond markets. The discount rate, which reached a high of 7.5% in the first quarter of 1975, declined steadily since then, down to 3.5% in March 1978.

EXHIBIT 13: TRADING VOLUME AND SIMPLE AVERAGE PRICE OF CONVERTIBLE BONDS

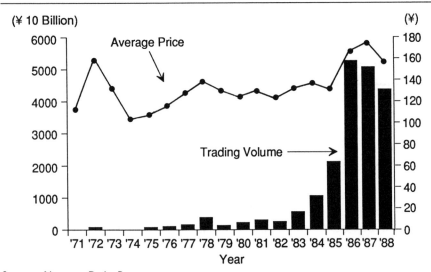

Source: Nomura Data Base.

As the rate declined, trading in convertible bonds became so active that the monthly average disparate ratio peaked to 21.55%[9] in September 1986. Subsequently, however, a new rising pattern in the discount rate adversely affected the convertible bond market's performance. In April 1979, the discount rate was at 4.25% and climbing; by March 1980, it was up to 9%. The poor performance of convertible bonds in the years 1979 and 1980 is indicated in Exhibit 13.

Exhibit 14 shows the strong effect of the stock market on the performance of convertibles. From the beginning of 1986, trading was very active in the stock market, and the Nikkei Heikin (the stock market index) reached its highest level of the year on August 20, at ¥18,936.42. Since then, it declined to the level of October 22, at ¥15,819.55. The convertible bond market followed the same trend. The simple average price kept increasing for most of the year, peaking in September at ¥194.07. Subsequently, however, the index slid to a low of ¥166.75 in November.

EXHIBIT 14: NIKKEI HEIKIN STOCK INDEX AND SIMPLE AVERAGE PRICE OF CONVERTIBLE BONDS IN 1986

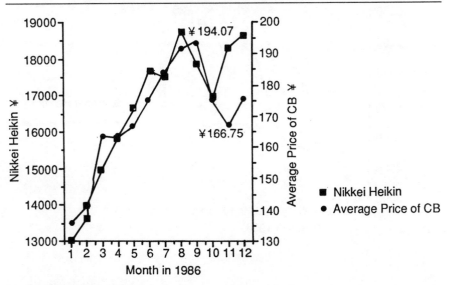

Source: Nikkei Data Base.

Exhibit 15 compares the performance of the stock and the convertible bond markets using the market average disparate ratio. The data support the results found for the year 1986. To a large extent, the stock market did influence the convertible bond market. The disparate ratio increased steadily from the beginning of the year, peaking to 24.14% in September. Since then, however, the index fell constantly, to a low for the year of 16.89% in November.

In contrast, in 1987 trading in the convertible bond market was affected to a large extent by factors other than the performance of the stock market. Until "Black Monday," trading was very intense in the Japanese stock market. However, unlike in 1986, the corresponding trading volume in the convertible bond market did not follow the same pattern. Exhibit 16 shows the trend of the average disparate ratio and of the turnover ratio[10] in the convertible bond market. The main factor explaining the downward trend was that as many as 279 convertibles issues were floated in fiscal year 1987. Therefore, the

EXHIBIT 15: NIKKEI HEIKIN STOCK INDEX AND AVERAGE DISPARATE RATIO OF CONVERTIBLE BONDS IN 1986

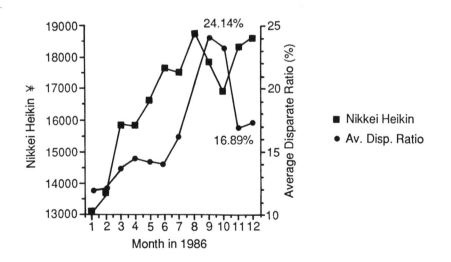

Source: Nikkei Data Base.

market for convertibles was saturated, and this resulted in lower trading volumes on the exchanges during the year. Exhibit 17 shows the performance of the convertible bond market in 1987. The secondary domestic market for convertibles was generally less active during the year, compared to the previous boom period.

Trading Mechanics

Trading in convertible bonds has undergone several changes aimed at expanding the secondary market. The improved features of trading systems on the securities exchanges, and the introduction of the transfer settlement system were the most important factors contributing to the growth of the convertible bond market.

Trading Features. In Japan, as well as in other major financial centers, securities are traded either on the securities exchanges or over-the-counter. In over-the-counter trading, securities companies play the role of dealer; they are the counterpart to investors who buy or sell stocks or bonds. On the other hand, these same securities compa-

EXHIBIT 16: TURNOVER AND AVERAGE DISPARATE RATIO OF CONVERTIBLE BONDS IN FISCAL YEAR 1987

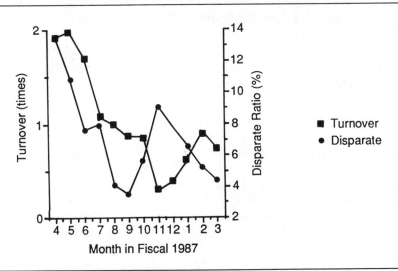

EXHIBIT 17: INITIAL LISTING PRICES ON THE EXCHANGES AND AVERAGE DISPARATE RATIO OF CONVERTIBLE BONDS

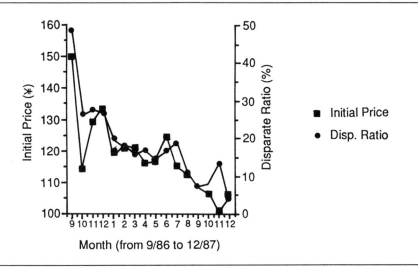

Month (from 9/86 to 12/87)

nies play the role of broker in the trading that is performed on the exchanges. That is, they find counterparts to close the deal.

Stocks are principally traded on the exchanges, through consignment sales and purchases of the securities. In contrast, most bond trading is performed over-the-counter. The low liquidity of bonds on organized exchanges, stemming from the limited number of issues listed, explains in part this feature of bond trading. Restrictions on the trading unit on the exchanges and on the trading of registered bonds are other contributing factors.

Since October 1987, almost all convertible bonds have to be traded on the securities exchanges in Japan. The exchanges have been, by far, the most important markets for convertible bonds, partly because the performance of convertibles is closely related to that of the stocks listed on the exchanges. At the present time, convertible bonds are listed and traded on eight securities exchanges in Japan. All convertible bonds are listed on the Tokyo Stock Exchange, and some are listed on more than one exchange. The trading practices regarding convertible bonds on the Tokyo Stock Exchange will be described next.

Requirements for Listing. Companies are allowed to list more than one issue of convertible bonds (as well as warrant bonds) on an exchange, but they can list only one issue of straight bonds. The requirements for listing are as follows:

1. The company's stock has to be listed on the exchange.
2. The total amount of the issue must be at least ¥2 billion.
3. There has to be sufficient trading activity in the convertibles by individual and general corporate investors (general corporate investors are corporations other than city banks, long-term credit banks, and insurance companies).
4. The issue should comply with the rules set by the security exchange.

Listing Commissions. Issuers initially pay a listing commission of 0.045% of the total principal amount of a new issue listed on the exchange. Depending on the total amount of principal, they also pay the following annual levy:

Principal amount unit from...	to...	Incremental unit	Commission per increment
	¥0.5 billion	¥0.1 billion	¥200,000
¥0.5 billion	¥0.6 billion	¥0.2 billion	¥20,000
¥6 billion	¥10 billion	¥0.5 billion	¥20,000
¥10 billion	¥50 billion	¥5 billion	¥20,000
¥50 billion	¥100 billion	¥10 billion	¥20,000
¥100 billion		¥20 billion	¥20,000

Trading Rules. The daily trading times are from 9 am to 11 am and from 1 pm to 3 pm. The trading days in a week are from Monday to Friday, with the exception of national holidays.

Convertible bonds minimum price change on the exchange is ¥0.1 yen. The face value of a convertible bond is ¥100 yen. For example, a typical bid could be ¥99.30, or ¥110.50. The trading unit is the same as the unit of the bond certificate, that is, ¥100,000, ¥500,000 or ¥1,000,000.

There is a limit on the daily change in price of a convertible bond. Unlike straight bonds, which have a restriction of ¥1 in the daily absolute price change,[11] convertible bonds are linked to the underlying stock price in the following way:

$$\text{Limit on the price change of convertible bonds} =$$

$$\frac{\text{Limit on the change of the stock price}}{\text{conversion price}} \times 100$$

The price limits on stocks are shown in Exhibit 18.

Trading on the exchange is settled with bond certificates. Therefore, registered convertible bonds should be unregistered in order to be traded on the exchanges. However, registered convertibles are tradable over-the-counter, although the market is not liquid. An important change was made with the introduction of the transfer settlement system, which went into effect on July 22, 1988, for all convertible bonds listed on the exchanges. Under this system, securities companies and their clients open their accounts at the Japan Se-

EXHIBIT 18: DAILY PRICE LIMITS ON THE TOKYO STOCK EXCHANGE

Opening Stock Price (P) in Yen	Price Change (±)
P < 100	30
100 ≤ P < 200	50
200 ≤ P < 500	80
500 ≤ P < 1,000	100
1,000 ≤ P < 1,500	200
1,500 ≤ P < 2,000	300
2,000 ≤ P < 3,000	400
3,000 ≤ P < 5,000	500
5,000 ≤ P < 10,000	1,000
10,000 ≤ P < 30,000	2,000
30,000 ≤ P < 50,000	3,000
50,000 ≤ P < 100,000	5,000
100,000 ≤ P	10,000

curities Settlement Co., and deposit their convertibles in these accounts in the form of bond certificates. From then on, investors can close their transactions just by account transfer. The new settlement system has facilitated trading on the exchanges in general, and helped corporate investors by making their transactions easier to accomplish. Trades are settled on the fourth business day following the transaction. Holidays are not included in the day count.

Investors have to pay a consignment commission to securities companies when placing their trades. This commission is determined by the securities exchanges, and depends on the amount traded, as follows:

Amount Traded from...	to..	Commission
¥0	¥1 million	1.00%
¥1 million	¥5 million	0.90%
¥5 million	¥10 million	0.70%
¥10 million	¥30 million	0.55%
¥30 million	¥50 million	0.40%
¥50 million	¥100 million	0.25%
¥100 million	¥1 billion	0.20%
¥1 billion	—	0.15%

Buyers have to pay accrued interest when they purchase convertible bonds on a date between two coupon payment periods. A 20% withholding tax is imposed on the coupon payments. The amount of accrued interest after taxes is conventionally calculated as follows:

1. Accrued interest after taxes per ¥100

$$= \ ¥100 \times \text{coupon rate} \ \times \ \frac{\text{lapsed days}}{365} \ \times \ (1 - 0.2)$$

2. Accrued interest on the total face value

= Accrued interest after tax per ¥100 ×
Total face value/100

In the calculation, figures after the eighth figure to the right of the decimal point are rounded down. Any figure less than ¥1 yen is rounded down.

To illustrate the calculation of accrued interest of a convertible bond, consider the following issue:

Trading amount = ¥10 million
Coupon rate = 2.0% or .02
Coupon payment dates: end of March and September
Trade date = May 7
Settlement date = May 10

Accrued interest after taxes per ¥100:

$$\text{¥100} \times .02 \times \frac{(30 + 10)}{365} \times .8 = \text{¥0.1753424}$$

Accrued interest on the total face value:

$$0.1753424 \times \text{¥10,000,000} / 100 = \text{¥1,754}$$

Participants in Secondary Market

More than 50% of the trades in convertible bonds are made by securities companies on their own behalf, as part of their portfolio investment activities; the rest of trading is for consignment sales and purchases on behalf of other investors. The following data show that consignment trading has steadily increased its share during the period 1985-1987:[12]

	1985	1986	1987
Consignment trading	41.27%	43.95%	45.37%

Exhibit 19 shows that banks and industrial corporations have been major market players. They account for more than 50% of the total amount of consignment trading. Compared to the previous year's level, banks have increased their share in fiscal year 1987, at the expense of industrial corporations. The exhibit also shows that

**EXHIBIT 19: INVESTORS IN THE SECONDARY MARKET FOR
CONVERTIBLE BONDS**

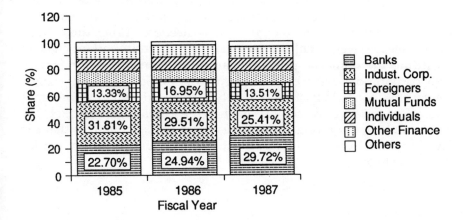

Source: *Koushasai Nenkan 1988 ed. (The Bond Yearbook of Fiscal Year 1988.)* The
Bond Underwriters Association of Japan.

foreign investors have been the third largest group, followed by mutual funds.

CONCLUSIONS

Progressive deregulation on the issuing side, and the growth of
many corporations have produced a large increase in bond issues,
not only in the Japanese domestic market but also overseas. Convertible bonds are currently the most popular in the domestic market,
while warrant bonds are almost exclusively issued overseas, particularly in the Euromarket. Access to the Euromarket for Japanese companies is more convenient because of the lower all-in costs of the
issues, the faster issuing procedures, and the fewer issuance standards required. Further deregulation is still needed, though, in order

to induce corporations to issue more bonds in the domestic market. The Japanese government has recently announced that the requirements for issuing warrant bonds will be relaxed. With this measure, the government intends to activate the domestic warrants market.

The convertible bond market has experienced more changes than any other domestic corporate bond market in the past few years. However further deregulation is needed. Along these lines, the Japanese government has recently announced important changes regarding the domestic primary market for convertible bonds. Foreign corporations have been allowed to issue Samurai and Shogun convertible bonds.[13] Factors other than financial deregulations may also affect the level of activity in the convertible bond market. Improvements in the rating system are one of the key changes that can favorably influence the development of the Japanese primary market for convertibles.

ENDNOTES

[1] The data were obtained from the Nikkei Data Base.

[2] Market quotes were obtained from *Nihon Keizai Shinbun [The Japanese Economy Newspaper]*, April 21, 1989.

[3] Takeshi Goto, *Tenkanshasai to Warantosai. [Convertible Bonds and Warrant Bonds.]* Tokyo: Tokyo Keizai. February 1989, p. 17.

[4] The Bond Underwriters Association of Japan. *Koushasai Nenkan 1988 ed. [The Bond Yearbook of Fiscal Year 1988.]* Tokyo: The Bond Underwriters Association of Japan.

[5] The C.B.Q. average is the market average price announced by Quick Inc. This is not a simple average price, but an adjusted average price modified by a certain index.

[6] Goto, p. 71.

[7] Goto, p. 29.

[8] Nomura Securities Co. Ltd. *Tenkanshasai Kyoushitsu [Convertible Bonds Lessons]* Tokyo: Nippon Keizai Shinbunsha. February 1989.

[9] The source of this information is the Yamaichi Data Base (IFS).

[10] The trading turnover ratio is defined as:

$$\frac{\text{Trading volume}}{\text{Total market value of all CBs listed on exchanges.}}$$

[11] Recall from Chapter 4 that the par or redemption value is ¥100.

[12] The Bond Underwriters Association of Japan. *Koushasai Nenkan 1988 ed. [The Bond Yearbook of Fiscal Year 1988.].*

[13] A Samurai convertible bond is a yen-denominated convertible bond issued in the Japanese market by a non-Japanese entity. A Shougun convertible bond is a foreign currency-denominated convertible bond issued in the Japanese market. Sumurai and Shougun bonds are discussed in Chapter 13.

CHAPTER 13

The Foreign Bond Market in Japan

Issen Sato
Tokyo, Japan

E.M. Kanovsky
Paris, France

In this chapter we will discuss the foreign bond market in Japan. Foreign bonds are yen and non-yen denominated. There are even bonds that have cash flows in more than one currency. The foreign bond market includes Samurai bonds, Daimyo bonds, Shibosai bonds, Shogun bonds and Geisha bonds. The last two bonds are denominated in foreign currencies. The Euroyen bond market is discussed in the next chapter.

SAMURAI BONDS

Samurai bonds are publicly-offered, yen-denominated bonds issued in Japan by foreign entities. The Samurai bond market expanded steadily due to the government's intentions to establish a foreign bond market similar to the Yankee bond market in the United States. There were, however, setbacks in its expansion due to the two oil crises in 1974 and in 1979–1980. (The 1974 crisis resulted in a temporary suspension of this market for 18 months.)

423

Samurai bonds reached their peak in 1985 with issues totalling 1,115 billion yen. The total issue amount of Samurai bonds has decreased since 1986, and a slight recovery in 1988 remained only marginal. The decline of the issue of Samurai bonds starting in 1986 has accompanied the dramatic shift in interest to the Euroyen bond. This latter trend followed the liberalization of Euroyen bonds in December 1984, after the Japan/U.S. Yen Dollar committee (see Exhibit 1).

The Issuers

Samurai bonds were first issued by supranational institutions, followed by sovereign governments. Only in 1979 were Samurai issues extended to the private sector.

The first Samurai bond was issued by the Asian Development Bank in 1970. This bond was officially publicly-offered. In practice, it was a private placement, since the amount issued was relatively small (6 billion yen), and 80% of these bonds were acquired by banks. The four subsequent issues, three by the World Bank in 1971 and the other by the Asian Development Bank in 1972, were more widely subscribed. These four issues were listed on the Tokyo and Osaka stock exchanges in 1973. About 30% of the issues were subscribed to by banks, 25% by medium-sized financial institutions, 35% to 40% by individuals, and the rest by nonfinancial corporations.

Following the supranational institutions, Samurai issues by sovereign governments, such as the Commonwealth of Australia, or by municipal governments such as Quebec, Canada, appeared in 1972. The first Samurai bonds by a nongovernmental entity were issued in 1979 by Sears Overseas Finance N.V. (guaranteed by Sears Roebuck Corporation).

Unlike corporate bonds issued by Japanese firms that were secured by collateral, the Sears issue was not. This issue made a strong impact in the domestic bond market and contributed to the relaxation of the domestic collateral practice, the "Yutan Gensoku," and to the introduction of the use of a rating system in its place.

While corporate bonds issued domestically by Japanese firms are callable, issuers typically do not exercise this option. In contrast, the prepayment of Samurai bonds (exercise of call option by the issuer) has been observed since 1983, and particularly in 1986 and

EXHIBIT 1: YEN BOND BY FOREIGNERS

(¥ 100 Million)

	Samurai		Tokyo Market Shibosai		Total		Euromarket Euroyen		Japanese Euroyen
	#	Amt.	#	Amt.	#	Amt.	#	Amt.	Amt.
1970	1	60	0	0	1	60			
1971	3	330	0	0	3	330			
1972	6	850	1	107	7	957			
1973	3	400	6	401	9	801			
1974	0	0	0	0	0	0			
1975	2	200	0	0	2	200			
1976	6	650	0	0	6	650			
1977	15	2,960	3	300	18	3,260	2	300	
1978	29	7,220	11	1,050	40	8,270	1	150	
1979	16	3,330	6	672	22	4,002	2	250	
1980	14	2,610	0	0	14	2,610	4	550	100
1981	27	4,950	13	1,175	40	6,125	5	800	100
1982	37	6,630	30	1,930	67	8,560	6	950	300
1983	41	7,200	32	1,790	73	8,990	4	700	0
1984	37	9,150	34	1,995	71	11,145	13	2,270	0
1985	35	11,150	24	1,575	59	12,725	66	14,457	1,000
1986	21	5,900	21	1,950	42	7,850	141	25,515	4,170
1987	15	4,200	10	775	25	4,975	151	29,940	5,200
1988	22	6,350	18	1,535	40	7,885	NA	NA	NA
Total	308	67,790	191	13,720	499	81,510	395	75,882	10,870

#: Number of issues per year
Amt.: Amount issued per year
Total: Excludes 1988

Source: Kokusai Kinyukyoku Nenpo (MOF) 1988; DKB International.

1987. In 1987, 43 issues were called (prepaid) to the amount of 620 billion yen, which is about 1.5 times more than that year's total Samurai bond issues. Issuers took advantage of refinancing at the historically low rate of interest.

Many of the Samurai bonds were refinanced with funds acquired through the issuance of new Euroyen bonds at lower rates, but some were refinanced within the Samurai market in order to maintain good relations with Japanese investors.

The first reaction by Japanese regulators and interested parties to the prepayment trend was to warn those issuers that prepaid that investors might not be willing to purchase future issues on the Japanese Samurai market, since it was not the custom to prepay. However, in 1986, when the governments of Denmark and Australia decided to prepay, and other issuers followed, the securities houses could not stop the trend and even competed to underwrite the reissues in the Samurai market.

The Investors

It has been estimated that around half of all outstanding Samurai issues were held by foreign investors, because foreigners are not subject to withholding tax on these bonds, as they are for JGBs.[1] However, experts from several Japanese banks have suggested that at least 90% of Samurai issues were held by Japanese investors. They believe that foreign investors are not as yet attracted to the domestic yen issues, preferring the more liquid Euroyen bonds that are also exempt from withholding tax.

Characteristics of Samurai Bonds

When the first Samurai bond was issued in 1970, the balance of payments was showing a cumulative surplus and the yen was appreciating. On the other hand, when the Samurai market was suspended in 1974, the balance of payments was showing a deficit following the oil crises. Thus it appears that Samurai issues were initially utilized to adjust the balance of payments.

A second aspect of the Samurai market is its dependence on supranational issuers. In 1987, 43% of the total issue volume was initiated by supranational entities. The World Bank was the most frequent issuer (37 issues by 1987), followed by the Asian Development Bank (19 issues), the European Investment Bank (15 issues) and the Inter-American Development Bank (14 issues). The share of less developed countries (LDC's) was about 11%.

If the issues of Samurai (publicly-offered) bonds are combined with those of the Shibosai (privately-offered) bonds, the share of supranationals in their combined issues from 1970 to 1987 was 30%, that of LDC's was 25% and that of developed countries was 45% (see Exhibit 2). According to OECD statistics, the corresponding issues by supranationals, LDC's and developed countries represented, respectively, a 4%, 2%, and 95% share in the total international bond market (see Exhibit 3). Since bonds issued by supranationals and LDC's are chiefly acquired by entities in the developed world and their proceeds are earmarked chiefly for the developing nations, we can observe that the Samurai and Shibosai markets are among the few capital markets for recycling funds from the developed North to the developing South.

A third aspect of the Samurai market is its comparative reliance on market conditions in fixing the terms of an issue as compared to the Japanese government bonds or domestic corporate bonds: these bonds are fully under the control of the Committee for Bond Issue ("Kisaikai") which gives less consideration to market conditions.

A fourth aspect of the Samurai bond market is its influence on the liberalization of the Japanese domestic bond market. For example, Samurai bonds contributed to the abolition of the collateral requirement for bonds issued by private corporations, as well as to the introduction of the bought-deal underwriting method in the primary market and of the market-making practices in the secondary market.

The standard structure of Samurai bonds, accounting for 74% of outstanding issue volume, has been 10 years to maturity and callable from the sixth year at a premium over par of around 3%. These premiums decline to reach par by the maturity date. In addition, there has been a mandatory redemption schedule of 10% annually starting from the sixth year,[2] which is applied to all the bonds in Japan except certain types of Japanese government bonds (JGBs). The purpose is to ensure redemption and to protect investors.

However investors find it very difficult to calculate the yields in this structure. This was one of the reasons for the introduction in

EXHIBIT 2: SAMURAI AND SHIBOSAI ISSUE DISTRIBUTION

(¥ 100 Million, %)

Year	LDC Country #	Amt.	%	Supranational #	Amt.	%	Developed #	Amt.	%	Total #	Amt.
1970	0	0	0	1	60	100	0	0	0	1	60
1971	0	0	0	3	330	100	0	0	0	3	330
1972	1	107	11	4	650	68	2	200	21	7	957
1973	6	471	59	3	330	41	0	0	0	9	801
1974	0	0	0	0	0	0	0	0	0	0	0
1975	0	0	0	0	0	0	2	200	100	2	200
1976	3	300	46	2	250	38	1	100	15	6	650
1977	7	1,100	34	4	1,100	34	7	1,060	33	18	3,260
1978	19	2,870	35	2	900	11	19	4,500	54	40	8,270
1979	10	1,570	39	4	700	17	8	1,732	43	22	4,002
1980	6	910	35	2	450	17	6	1,250	48	14	2,610
1981	9	950	16	9	1,900	31	22	3,275	53	40	6,125
1982	13	980	11	7	1,500	18	47	6,080	71	67	8,560
1983	19	1,440	16	14	2,700	30	40	4,850	54	73	8,990
1984	32	2,645	24	12	3,350	30	27	5,150	46	71	11,145
1985	29	3,375	27	13	5,050	40	17	4,300	34	59	12,725
1986	20	2,953	38	11	2,900	37	11	1,997	25	42	7,850
1987	9	995	20	7	2,000	40	9	1,980	40	25	4,975
*SA	3	450	11	5	1,750	43	7	1,900	46	15	4,100
*SHI	6	445	57	2	250	32	2	80	10	10	775
Total	183	20,666	25	98	24,170	30	218	36,674	45	499	81,510

*SA: Samurai
*SHI: Shibosai
#: Number of issues
LDC: Less developed country, DAC by OECD standard
Supranational: World Bank, ADB, AIDB, AFDB, EIB
Source: Derived from Kokusai Kinyukyoku Nempo (MOF) 1988.

EXHIBIT 3: INTERNATIONAL BOND DISTRIBUTION

($ Million, %)

Year	LDC Country #	LDC Country Amt.	%	Supranational #	Supranational Amt.	%	Developed #	Developed Amt.	%	Total #	Total Amt.
1982	NA	2,819	6	NA	2,267	5	NA	41,361	89	NA	46,447
1983	NA	1,997	4	NA	1,857	4	NA	46,244	92	NA	50,098
1984	NA	2,677	3	NA	2,460	3	NA	76,580	94	NA	81,717
1985	NA	6,370	5	NA	4,310	3	NA	124,750	92	NA	135,430
1986	NA	2,937	2	NA	3,955	2	NA	180,059	96	NA	186,951
1987	NA	2,261	2	NA	5,433	4	NA	132,787	95	NA	140,481

Source: OECD Financial Statistics.

July 1985 of "bullet repayment" for Samurai bonds. "Bullet repayment" means repayment is exercised in one lot at maturity.

Issuing Procedures

There are two important procedural aspects in issuing Samurai bonds, the "Mochiyori" and "Kisaikai" systems and government regulations.

The Mochiyori system refers to the adjustment of the number and volume of issues to avoid overflooding the market. Mochiyori is the name of a meeting held on the 20th of each month wherein banks and major securities houses confirm the identity of Samurai bond issuers and the amounts to be issued for the coming months. It is customary to disclose the name of the issuer at the meeting which takes place two months prior to the expected issue date. The Mochiyori system is becoming less important and more flexible, particularly since the introduction of shelf-registration in late 1988.

All the expected issues admitted by the Mochiyori are reported and confirmed at the Kisaikai meeting held at the end of each month.

The other important aspect of issuing Samurai bonds is a legal one. The Samurai bonds are governed by the Securities and Trading Act of 1948, and by the Foreign Exchange Law of 1980, the details of which are described later in this chapter.

Exhibit 4 shows the tentative time schedule for Samurai issues not subject to shelf registration procedures.

Guidelines for Issuing Bonds

The guidelines for Samurai bonds, which also apply to Shogun bonds, are set by the Kisaikai after consultation with the Ministry of Finance ("MOF") and govern the eligibility standards for bond issuers ("Tekisai Kijun") and the capital adequacy requirements ("Zaimu Seigen Jhoko") for nonsecured corporate bonds, as well as other related criteria. The eligibility standards were relaxed in April 1985 at the same time as those relating to Euroyen bonds issued by foreigners; they were replaced by the rating method in April 1986. The capital adequacy requirements were also relaxed in November of that same year.

EXHIBIT 4: TENTATIVE TIME SCHEDULE FOR ISSUANCE OF SAMURAI BONDS

Day-39	File registration statement with the Japanese Minister of Finance.
Day-30 to 40	Apply for approval of the payment for the bonds to the Japanese Minister of Finance through the Bank of Japan.
Day-20	Distribute preliminary prospectus to syndicate members.
Day-11 to 12	Pricing meeting in Tokyo to negotiate and determine final terms (such as coupon rate and issuing price) on the basis of market conditions.
Day-10	Signing of the Agreement with commissioned banks, underwriting agreements and others.
Day-8	Registration statement becomes effective.
Day-7	Offering commences.
Day-1	Offering ends.
Closing Day	Payment date.
Day+30 to 60	Deliver bond certificates.

The criteria for issuing Samurai bonds, as of October 1986, are described in Exhibit 5. The relationships among eligibility standards, ceilings for issue, maximum maturity and bullet repayments are described in Exhibit 6.

Legal Restrictions

Samurai bonds are now governed by two laws: the first, the Foreign Exchange Law of 1980 and the second, the Securities and Exchange Law of 1948. The first sets official disclosure requirements and the second regulates external capital transfers.

EXHIBIT 5: CRITERIA FOR ISSUING SAMURAI BONDS (AS OF OCTOBER 1986)

Samurai issuers are limited to:

- Supranational institutions, sovereign states, government agencies, municipal governments and municipal government agencies whose debts are rated A or better.
- Public entities guaranteed by the entities above.
- Entities that have already issued publicly-offered bonds in the Tokyo market.
- Private corporations whose debts are rated A or better, or, if not rated, that satisfy the eligibility standards described in Exhibit 6.

New Law and Old Law. The Foreign Exchange and Foreign Trade Control Law of 1933 (Old Law) was totally revised and integrated into the Revised Foreign Exchange Law of 1980 (New Law).

The Old Law was intended to control foreign exchange, foreign trade, and external transactions. Its aim was to achieve balanced international payments, a stabilized currency, and the most efficient usage of foreign currencies, as well as to reconstruct and develop the national economy. The objective of the Old Law was to insulate the Japanese economy from external interference by prohibiting all external transactions. All transactions required permission from the authorities. As the Japanese economy became stronger, the government relaxed the regulations on a piecemeal basis, resulting in a very complex and unwieldy Old Law.

The 1980 New Law totally changed the structure and framework of the Old Law. It has as its basic principle the liberalization of all external transactions without requiring permission. However, the New Law also maintained the Finance Minister's right to restrict capital movements in case of emergencies, such as unfavorable tendencies in the balance of payments, expected sharp fluctuations of the yen, or negative effects on the capital market in Japan.

Under the New Law, capital transactions are subject to one of four categories of procedures:

(a) Approval by the MOF is required. Example: Euroyen bonds issued by non-Japanese (New Law 21-1-2).

EXHIBIT 6: RELATIONSHIPS AMONG ELIGIBILITY STANDARDS, CEILINGS FOR ISSUE, MAXIMUM MATURITY AND BULLET REPAYMENT FOR SAMURAI BONDS

Issuer	Ceiling	Maturity	Bullet
Supranationals: Sovereign and Private Corporate Issuers:	No ceiling	15 yrs	15 yrs
AAA rated	No ceiling	15 yrs	15 yrs
AA rated	¥30 bil.	15 yrs	15 yrs
A rated	¥20 bil.	12 yrs	8 yrs
Nonrated	¥10 bil.	7 yrs	7 yrs

For sovereign borrowers, a 10-year or 12-year bullet can be discussed case-by-case. For private corporations, a 12-year bullet can be discussed if a company's net assets total more than 110 billion yen.

(The above rules for Samurai are applied correspondingly to issues of Shogun bonds.)

If a borrower wishes to issue Samurai bonds for an amount above the ceiling, an exception to the rule could be approved through negotiations between the lead commissioned bank and the Ministry of Finance.

For example AA and A rated borrowers may, subject to negotiation, issue up to 60 billion yen and 40 billion yen, respectively.

The authorized rating agencies are Standard & Poor, Moody's, Fitch, Nippon Investors Service, Nippon Koshasai Kenkyusho, and Nihon Kakuzuke Kenkyusho.

Source: *Public Offered Bond Primary Market (Koshasai Hakko Shijho)*, Tokyo, June 1987. Nihon Keizai Shimbun, Inc. & The Dai-Ichi Kangyo Bank, Ltd., Japan.

(b) Preliminary notification for authorization by the MOF is required. Example: issues and offerings of bonds by non-Japanese entities in Japan. (Samurai and Shogun bonds—New Law 22-1-6, 23); issues and offerings of foreign currency bonds in Japan by Japanese (New Law 22-1-5); issues and offerings of bonds outside Japan by Japanese (Sushi and Euroyen bonds—New Law 22-1-5).

(c) Preliminary notification is required (only for purposes of recording data, but automatically agreed to by MOF).

(d) No application and notification needed.

The Foreign Exchange and Foreign Trade Control Law of 1980.
This law defines Samurai issues as "sales and offerings of securities in Japan by foreign entities," and classifies such issues as capital investments, as opposed to trading transactions.

The issuer must submit the required information to the Minister of Finance prior to issue (Law 22-1-6, Law 23). Sales and offerings are prohibited for twenty days (called the "do nothing" period) following the submission of information. The Minister of Finance can recommend and/or order amendments and halt the issue during this period if he determines that the issue will negatively affect the Japanese financial and capital markets. In October 1988 the twenty day period was shortened to one day.

The Securities and Exchange Law of 1948. This law governs registration procedures for all bond issuers (as well as setting out in Article 65 the separation between banks and securities houses).

Article 4 requires a bond issuer to file a registration statement with the Minister of Finance for disclosure purposes prior to sales and offerings, except for exempt cases.

Article 3 states that registration is not required for those supranational institutions of which Japan is a member, such as the World Bank, Asian Development Bank, Inter-American Development Bank, and African Development Bank.

Secured corporate bonds (other than convertible bonds) and bank debentures are also exempt from registration.

Registration was required for all issuers at least 30 days prior to the public offering. In October 1988, the registration period was reduced to 15 days, except for first-time issuers, and the information needed for registration was simplified.

To encourage the development of the Samurai market, a shelf registration system was introduced. Under this system, an issuer can inform the Ministry of Finance, in advance, of the global planned issue amount, the classification of securities, and the effective issuing period (one or two years). After the filing is completed and approved, the issuer is only required to submit a "Supplemental Statement" before each public offering, and approval is given the same day.

Until 1988, the following were the principal disadvantages of the Samurai bonds as compared to Euroyen bonds for issuers:

- difficulty in swapping from yen to dollars,
- lack of flexibility in issuing due to disclosure requirements,
- lack of liquidity in secondary market,
- higher issuing cost due to the fee for a commissioned bank in Japan, and
- the lack of Samurai innovations due to strict regulations in the Japanese market.

The first two disadvantages were eliminated with the introduction of shelf registration.

Recent Developments in Primary and Secondary Markets

Primary Market. In the Samurai primary market, the "indication style" of underwriting prevailed. The Big Four securities houses (Nomura, Daiwa, Nikko, Yamaichi) took the role of lead manager in turn. Prices and coupon rates were negotiated prior to syndication and had to be agreed upon for each issue by at least one of the other Big Four.

The objective of this system was to prevent pricing competition among the Big Four underwriters. The disadvantage of the indication style is that it takes time to negotiate.

The thirty-fourth World Bank Samurai bond issue introduced the "bought deal style" in June 1986. In this more European underwriting style, the lead manager and the borrower alone determine the terms and conditions of the issue, and the manager initially purchases the entire issue amount. The lead manager has complete discretion in the allocation of this amount among the syndicate members.

Secondary Market. The secondary market for Samurai bonds is limited. Japanese investors hold Samurai bonds for long-term investment purposes. Trading volume on the Tokyo Stock Exchange is marginal, since most of these bonds trade over the counter, which is also a very limited market. In 1985 and 1986, Samurai bonds represented less than 1% of all publicly offered bond transactions.

In the Japanese "bought deal style," a lead manager is required to maintain the secondary market by being prepared to buy back all bonds presented to it. Traditionally, 25% of all issues are offered to the banking community, which retains the bonds for long-term investment.

Short sales were authorized in July 1987. This new measure should increase liquidity in the secondary market by providing a new hedging mechanism.

Daimyo Bonds

Daimyo bonds belong to the Samurai category but settlement is carried out through the Euro-clear or Cedel systems instead of in Japan. Such bonds were first issued by the World Bank in May 1987, with a total value of 130 billion yen in three issues. They represented 31% of all Samurai issues for that year. The Inter-American Development Bank and the African Development Bank followed with issues in 1988.

Daimyo bonds were introduced to increase the liquidity of the Samurai market (by using the European clearing systems) to attract foreign investors and to decrease issuing costs.

Representing a hybrid of Samurai and Euroyen bonds, Daimyo bonds are free from the 90 day "lock-up period" applied to Euroyen issues. (Samurai bonds are also not subject to this restriction.) They are listed in Luxembourg, not in Tokyo. Interest is paid annually on the Euro basis (calculated on a basis of 360 days a year; Samurai bonds are calculated semiannually on a basis of 365 days a year).

YENDATE SHIBOSAI (SHIBOSAI BOND)

Shibosai bonds are privately-placed, yen-denominated bonds issued by foreigners in Japan. The procedures are simpler than for Samurai bonds, but issuers are restricted to supranational institutions and sovereign entities. Before August 1983, when rules for issuing Shibosai bonds were introduced, private companies were also authorized to issue.[3]

Issuers

Shibosai bonds were first issued by Fairway Tankers Limited of Liberia in 1972. Between 1972 and 1988, 1,372 billion yen were raised through 191 issues. Sovereign entities which have no rating from authorized rating agencies cannot issue Samurai bonds, but they can apply to issue Shibosai bonds.

Less creditworthy entities which have no rating are frequent issuers in this market. In 1987, the share of less-developed countries in total Shibosai bond issues was 57%, while the corresponding figure in Samurai and in all international bonds was 11% and 2%, respectively. (See Exhibits 2 and 3.) Thus, Shibosai bonds play a more significant role than Samurai bonds in recycling funds from the developed North to the developing South.[4]

Since the abolition of the No-Return Rule explained below, an issuer eligible for Samurai bonds may also issue in the Shibosai market.

Restrictions Specific to Shibosai Bonds

Historically, Samurai bonds were given priority over the Shibosai bonds by the legislators just as in the domestic market where publicly-offered bonds were given priority over private placements.

Until 1986, there were two major restrictions in the Shibosai market. One is the "One-Third Rule" and the other is the "No Return Rule." The One-Third Rule was relaxed and the No Return Rule was abolished in 1986.

No Return Rule. The No Return Rule stipulated that an issuer which had, even once, issued Samurai bonds was prohibited from issuing in the Shibosai market. The abolition of this rule in February 1986 provided market alternatives to both Samurai and Shibosai issuers. The Samurai issuer was henceforth free to issue in the Shibosai market and to benefit from cost savings and simpler procedures. Three issuers returned to the Shibosai market in 1986 with a total issue amount of 54 billion yen.

One-Third Rule. The One-Third Rule provides that the total outstanding issue amount of Shibosai should be less than one-third of

Samurai amounts. The potential number of issuers of Shibosai bonds increased in 1986, following the above-mentioned abolition of the No Return Rule.

But because of the One-Third Rule, many Shibosai issues had to be postponed during that same year when Samurai bonds decreased following the major shift by issuers to the Euroyen market.

In November 1986, the One-Third Rule was relaxed to enable a greater issue volume of Shibosai bonds. Since that time, bonds denominated in foreign currencies, such as Shogun bonds and dual currency bonds, were included in the base calculation of this rule.

Characteristics of Shibosai Bonds

Shibosai bonds combine features of Samurai bonds and bank loans. While Samurai bonds can only be issued and lead managed by securities houses, banks and securities houses are equally qualified to be lead arrangers (quasi-underwriters) for Shibosai bonds. In addition to fees and other income, city banks have an added interest in this market which can provide them with experience and expertise in underwriting securities while awaiting reform of Article 65 that will allow them to compete in markets presently reserved for the securities houses.

The all-in-cost of Shibosai bond issues is less than for Samurai issues. They are also simpler in procedure than the traditional registration. It takes one or two months to finalize a Shibosai issue, compared to three or four months for the traditional Samurai operations (other than those using shelf registration).

Since these bonds are private placements, the Shibosai are exempt from the disclosure requirements of the Securities Act. There are restrictions as to their primary offering and resale in the secondary market. Shibosai bonds must be placed with fewer than 49 investors, and are usually placed with 15 to 30 institutions. Since limited information is available, certain nonprofessional investors, such as private corporations, individuals, religious entities, and schools that cannot analyze potential risks, are excluded as investors.

Since there is a two-year restriction on the resale of Shibosai bonds purchased in the primary market, they have no secondary market for that period. Sales after this period must be in one lot to only one buyer and authorized by the MOF. Partial resale is not allowed.

Issuing Procedures

A lead arranger acts not only as advisor to the issuer concerning terms and conditions of issue, but also as negotiator with the MOF on behalf of the issuer. Upon verbal approval from the MOF, the lead arranger initiates the issuing procedures according to the timetable described in Exhibit 7.

Qualified lead arrangers for Shibosai issues include three designated long-term credit banks, trust banks which have branches abroad, city banks, foreign banks that operate in Japan, securities houses that have subsidiaries abroad, and foreign securities houses located in Japan. Several arrangers are usually selected for each

EXHIBIT 7: TIMETABLE FOR ISSUING SHIBOSAI BONDS

Day-30 to 45	Decision to issue and designate a lead arranger.
Day-30	The lead arranger starts to organize the arranger group and form the investors' group.
Day-20	Documentation meeting between the issuer and the representative of the arrangers.
Day-17	Formal application to be submitted to MOF to confirm the prior notice for the issue.
Day-15	Pricing determined in Tokyo.
Day-12	Finalization of all documents and agreements.
Day-10	Placement completed.
Day-5	Signing.
Day-0	Closing (Payment Day).
Day+4	Filing of the report concerning the completion of the issue with the MOF.
Day+15	Delivery of certificates of recorded bonds by the lead arranger.

Source: The Dai-Ichi Kangyo Bank, Ltd., Japan.

issue. Manufacturers Hanover Trust Company became the first foreign lead arranger in November 1986.

Criteria for Issuance

Only public entities can issue Shibosai bonds. In April 1986, the eligibility standard was replaced by a rating system, as in Euroyen bonds and Samurai bonds.

The public entities which may issue Shibosai bonds are shown in Exhibit 8.

As of June 1987, the maximum issue amount and tenor was restricted to 10 billion yen and 10 years. But both restrictions were relaxed in 1986 at the same time that the No Return Rule was abolished. The World Bank and the Asian Development Bank issued 20-year bonds that year. The relationship of rating, pricing and coupon rates in Shibosai issues is described in Exhibit 9.

Shibosai vs. Samurai Bonds—Yield and Cost Spreads

In theory, the yield of a privately-placed bond should be higher than that of a publicly offered bond if the credit risk and the maturity of the bonds are the same. Investors expect higher yields for illiquid instruments. This principle is applicable to Samurai bonds (publicly-offered bonds) and Shibosai bonds (privately-placed bonds).

EXHIBIT 8: CRITERIA FOR ISSUING SHIBOSAI BONDS
(AS OF JUNE 1987)

- Supranational institutions, sovereign states, government agencies, municipal governments, and municipal government agencies whose debt are rated A or better, and public entities guaranteed by the entities above, or
- Public entities in a country of which the debt is rated AA or better, or
- Public entities, or entities guaranteed by them that borrowed through publicly-offered bonds or syndicated loans during the three preceding years in a major financial capital market.

EXHIBIT 9: RELATIONSHIPS AMONG RATING, CEILING, MATURITY, AND COUPON RATES FOR SHIBOSAI BONDS

Category	Ceiling	Maturity	Coupon
Supranational	¥30 bil.	5 yrs or more	BR+0.2%
AAA Sovereign	¥30 bil.	same	BR+0.3%
AA Sovereign	¥20 bil.	same	BR+0.4%
A Sovereign	¥10 bil.	same	BR+0.5%
Nonrated	same	same	same

NOTE:
BR (Base rate) is the yield to maturity of newly-issued government bonds + 0.3% (calculated to the second decimal point). However if the long-term prime rate (LTPR) is lower than the best rate (BR + 0.3%), this lower rate, the LTPR, can be applied as the best rate for AAA-rated entities (and LTPR+0.1% for AA-rated entities, LTPR+0.2% for those with a rating of A or less).

EXAMPLE:
Long-term government bond yield (newly issued) = 5.125%
Base Rate = 5.125+0.3 = 5.425% rounded to 5.43%
Coupon rate for AAA-rated issuers = BR+0.3% = 5.73%, for A-rated issuers >BR+0.5% = 5.93%

If the LTPR is reduced to 5.5% from 5.73%, the AAA-rated issuer can select a 5.5% coupon instead of a 5.73% one. The coupons for AA-rated and A-rated issuers could be 5.6% and 5.7%, respectively.

Source: *Public Offered Bond Primary market (Koshasai Hakko Shijho)*, Tokyo, June 1987. Nihon Keizai Shimbun, Inc. & The Dai-Ichi Kangyo Bank, Ltd., Japan.

However, the all-in-cost for issuers is not always clearly defined. It is generally observed in the U.S. that a private placement is cheaper for the issuer than a publicly-offered bond because of the difference in the initial costs (including fixed costs) such as legal fees, printing, listing, underwriting fees, advertising and the like, which are more expensive for publicly-placed offerings. The impact of the initial fixed-cost differs, therefore, according to the issue volume as well as to the term of the bond (the longer the maturity the less impact on cost).

As concerns the all-in-cost incurred by using these two types of bonds, we shall first discuss the relationhsip between the coupon rates of the Samurai and the Shibosai bonds. We shall then compare two hypothetical cases of a Shibosai and a Samurai bond.

In reality, the coupon rate of the Samurai bond is dependent on the long-term prime rate (LTPR). That is, the LTPR is equal to the five-year bank debenture coupon rate plus 0.9%; most Samurai coupons vary between the LTPR flat and LTPR plus 0.3%. On the other hand, the coupon of the Shibosai bond is dependent on the newly-issued government bond yields (see Exhibit 9). For AAA borrowers, the coupon rate is the lower of the LTPR or the rate of the newly-issued government bond yield plus 0.6% (which means that the coupon is less than the LTPR).

In general, the coupon of a publicly-offered bond (Samurai) is set lower than that of a privately-offered bond (Shibosai) in the case of the same borrower. However, in reality, it is not in the borrower's interest to set coupons with a wide differential for concurrent issues of both types of bonds.

For this reason, and since both coupons are directly dependent on the LTPR, the differential between the coupons is rarely greater than 0.2%. Therefore, we shall examine two cases, first, where the differential of the coupon is 0.1%, and second, where it is 0.2%.

In the first case, the coupon rate of the Shibosai bond is set at 5.5% and that of the Samurai bond is set at 5.4%. The all-in-cost of the Shibosai is 5.806%, that of the Samurai is 5.856% (see Exhibit 10). Therefore, the issuer will prefer Shibosai to Samurai bonds because of the cost benefits as well as the simpler procedures for issuance and fewer disclosure requirements.

In the second case, if the Samurai coupon is set at 5.3% instead of 5.4% when the Shibosai coupon is 5.5%, the cost for the Samurai bond is 5.751% (IRR annual base) and becomes less expensive than that for the Shibosai, which is 5.806%. In that case, the cost-sensitive issuer may prefer Samurai bonds.

SHOGUN BONDS

Shogun bonds are publicly-offered bonds issued by foreigners in Japan and denominated in foreign currencies. The preferred currency is the U.S. dollar. Privately-placed bonds with these features are referred to as *Geisha bonds*.

EXHIBIT 10: COST AND YIELD COMPARISON BETWEEN SHIBOSAI AND SAMURAI BONDS

		Shibosai	Samurai
Amount issued (yen)		10,000,000	20,000,000
Coupon rate		5.50%	5.40%
Price issued		100.00%	100.00%
Yield to maturity		5.50%	5.40%
Maturity		7 years	7 years
Redemption		Bullet	Bullet
Issuer's status		Sovereign	Sovereign
Amount issued (yen)		10,000,000	20,000,000
Arranging fee	1.000%	100,000	
Underwriting fee	1.500%		300,000
Commissioned fee	0.135%		27,000
Recording fee	0.080%	8,000	8,000
Stamp duty	@200		4,000
Legal fee		3,000	10,000
Printing fee		2,000	5,000
Tombstone			5,000
Other expenses		3,000	20,000
Total initial cost		116,000	379,000
Interest payment		3,850,000	7,560,000
Payment comm.	0.15%	5,775	
Payment comm.	0.10%		7,560
P. Payment comm.	0.30%	30,000	
P. Payment comm.	0.20%		40,000
Total running cost		3,885,775	7,607,560
All-in-cost	p/s.a.	5.724%	5.773%
All-in-cost	p/a.	5.806%	5.856%
Yield to maturity		5.500%	5.400%

Unit amount: Thousand yen
Arranging fee: Shibosai only, 1% of the principal amount
Underwriting fee: Up to 7 years; Supra 1.4%, Others 1.5%
Commiss. fee: Supra 0.09%, Sovereign 0.135%, Corporate 0.2%
Recording fee: Assuming that 100% of Shibosai and 50% of Samurai
 recorded
Stamp duty: 200 yen for each bearer bond
Legal fee: For issuer (Japan)
Tombstone: For advertising purposes (Nikkei Shimbun)
Other expenses: Reimbursement to the managers and commissioned banks,
 includes legal fee for managers
Payment Comm: Commission to the paying agent
P.Payment Comm: Payment commission for the principal

The first bond issued by foreigners and denominated in a foreign currency was placed in 1978 by the European Investment Bank (EIB). This bond was not a genuine Shogun issue, since it was mainly sold in Japan but issued in the Euromarket. It was listed in, and governed by the law of, Luxembourg.

The first true Shogun bonds were issued in August 1985 by the World Bank. The total borrowing of $300 million was listed, issued and sold in Tokyo, and was subject to Japanese law. This issue was underwritten in the "bought deal style," and led to the introduction of the same style in the Samurai market in 1986.

As of 1987, the annual issue amount of Shogun bonds was $848 million (see Exhibit 11). In comparison, that same year, Euroyen bonds issued by foreigners totaled 20.6 billion U.S. dollars, or 2,993 billion yen (see Exhibit 10 in Chapter 14).

Shogun bonds could potentially rival the two major U.S. dollar markets—the Yankee and Eurodollar bond markets. Because Tokyo is geographically situated between London and New York, increased efficiency and activity in the Tokyo market will benefit trading of dollar bonds worldwide.

However several critical problems involving taxation, recording and clearing systems, and further relaxation of eligibility standards must be resolved in order for Tokyo to compete with the other major international centers.

EXHIBIT 11: SHOGUN BONDS

($ Million)

	Public		Shibosai		Total	
	#	Amt.	#	Amt.	#	Amt.
1985	7	894	1	38	8	932
1986	10	956	0	0	10	956
1987	8	848	0	0	8	848
Total	25	2,698	1	38	26	2,736

Source: Kokusai Kinyukyoku Nenpo (MOF) 1988.

Taxation

Most of the bonds issued in Japan are recorded in order to avoid the withholding tax of 20% applied to bearer bonds. However, recorded bonds cannot be traded outside Japan, and the transfer within Japan from recorded (for Japanese tax reasons) to bearer status (for trading purposes) is a long procedure.

Such problems occurred, for example, in the $200 million Shogun issue in 1987 by the Federal National Mortgage Association ("Fannie Mae"). To circumscribe the transfer problem, this issue in Japan was to be exchanged with U.S. dollar denominated bonds issued by Fannie Mae in the United States under the same terms and conditions as the Japanese issue. This bond was not surprisingly called an "Exchangeable Shogun Bond."

Another example of taxation problems resulted from the "Equity And Fiscal Responsibility Act of 1982" in the U.S. Under this tax law, Shogun bonds may be subject to the U.S. withholding tax that, in effect, prevented American corporations from issuing Shogun bonds. In January 1987, this law was amended and Shogun bonds were no longer subject to the withholding tax. Shortly thereafter, in 1987 Standard Oil issued a $100 million Shogun bond in 1987.

Innovations were developed in the Japanese bond market, such as the dual-currency bond. The dual-currency bond combines two currencies in all combinations, for example, issuing currency and coupon payments in yen and redemption in U.S. dollars. The first of these bonds was issued by Fannie Mae and the Bank of China in April 1986.

In the Shogun market, it is customary for a lead manager to invite foreign securities firms to join the syndicates. SBCI Asia Securities became the first foreign lead manager in the Shogun market, placing a $50 million issue by Ciba-Geigy International Netherlands B.V. in February 1987.

Issuing Procedures and Criteria for Issuance

Since a Shogun bond issue is publicly offered, the same procedures as for Samurai bonds are applied.

Shogun issues, like Samurai issues, are governed by the Securities and Exchange Law and the Foreign Exchange and Foreign Trade Control Law. In November, 1985, it was ruled that Shogun bonds would be governed by the same rules and guidelines that are applied to the Samurai market. However, unlike Samurai bonds, the Shogun counterpart is not limited by a maximum amount. Terms and conditions of issues are determined purely by market conditions and issuers' credibility.

Secondary Market

The secondary market is in a primitive state. In order to attract investors as well as issuers, the growth of the secondary market is essential. Since this is a bond issued in currencies other than yen, market volume is limited if there are not foreign participants as final investors. As yet, due to liquidity problems, the Shogun is not as attractive an investment to the foreigner as Eurodollar or Yankee dollar bonds. It is interesting that the EIB structure for the first quasi-Shogun bond has focused the attention of market participants on these liquidity problems.

SUMMARY

In this chapter we have examined the foreign bond market in Japan. Samurai bonds are publicly-offered, yen-denominated bonds issued in Japan by foreign entities. These bonds reached their peak in 1985 and declined thereafter due to the increased popularity of Euroyen bonds. Samurai bonds contributed to the replacement of collateral requirements by a rating system on Japanese-issued bonds, the increased acceptance of prepayments, and the introduction of the shelf registration system.

Daimyo bonds are Samurai bonds that use the Euro-clear or Cedel systems for settlement. This feature was introduced to increase the liquidity of the Samurai market. Daimyo bonds are a hybrid of Samurai and Euroyen bonds.

Shibosai bonds are the privately-offered yen equivalent of the Samurai bond. These bonds, restricted to supranational and sovereign entities, attract less creditworthy issuers with no rating, such as many LDCs. Until 1986, Shibosai bonds were faced with legal restrictions (No Return Rule and One-Third Rule) not applicable to Samurai bonds.

Shogun bonds are publicly-offered bonds denominated in foreign currencies and issued by foreign entities in Japan. Geisha bonds are the privately-placed equivalent. A potential competitor to the Eurodollar and Yankee dollar bond markets, the Shogun bond development is still hampered by taxation and liquidity problems.

ENDNOTES

[1] Credit Suisse First Boston, *The Yen Bond Markets* (Chicago: Probus Publishing Company, 1988), p. 107.

[2] Ibid., p. 111.

[3] Eight long-term credit banks and trust banks, and the Big Four securities houses were involved in setting the rules.

[4] To stimulate this trend in 1987 for the Export Import Bank of Japan to purchase Shibosai bonds, the government raised the ceiling from 20% to 50% of each issue. That change was necessitated by the limits to risk exposure that participants were willing to undertake.

CHAPTER 14

Euroyen Bond Market

Issen Sato
Tokyo, Japan

E. M. Kanovsky
Paris, France

In this chapter, we shall examine Japanese participation in the Eurobond market, as borrower, investor, and trading partner, as well as foreign use of yen issues in that same international market.

EUROBOND MARKET

Eurobonds generally include bonds issued and subscribed outside the governing country of the issue currency, which are underwritten and sold by internationally syndicated groups in one or more capital markets in Europe. Typical examples are Eurodollar bonds, Euromark bonds, Euroyen bonds, and European Currency Unit (ECU) bonds.

In addition to issuing bonds on the Euromarket, firms can issue foreign currency bonds in national markets, such as Yankee bonds in the United States, Samurai bonds in Japan, Bulldogs in the UK, and foreign bonds in Switzerland (there is no Euroswiss bond).

Issuers of bonds denominated in foreign currencies generally choose the Euromarket over national markets. According to Morgan Guaranty, the annual issue volume of Eurobonds nearly tripled from

449

1983 to 1987, from $48.5 to $140.5 billion. Bonds denominated in foreign currencies in national markets increased only 32% during the same period.

According to DKB International, the U.S. dollar is the most favored currency but its share in the Eurobond market has decreased from 82% in 1982 to 40% in 1988. In contrast, the yen share of that bond market rapidly increased from 1% in 1982 to 16% in 1987, but decreased to 11% in 1988 (see Exhibit 1).

The increase of yen bonds was due partly to speculation on continuing re-evaluation of the yen after the Plaza agreement in September 1985, and partly to the deregulation of the international yen market and concurrent development of the swap market. The yen bond decreased its share in 1988 partly because of diminished expectations that the yen would continue to strengthen, and partly because of a liquidity problem in the secondary market of Euroyen bonds.

Exhibit 2 shows that, in the Eurobond market, the share of straight bonds issued in all currencies in 1988 was 71%, almost the same as its 1982 share of 72%. Straight bond share had decreased to 50% and 60% levels after 1982, parallel to the increase in popularity of floating rate notes (FRNs) (which reached a peak 41% share of the

EXHIBIT 1:   EUROBOND DISTRIBUTION BY CURRENCY

Currency	1982	1985	1986	1987	1988
US$	82%	70%	60%	41%	40%
DM	10	7	8	9	12
YEN	1	5	12	16	11
ECU	2	5	4	5	6
STG	2	4	5	10	13
A$	0	2	2	6	4
C$	3	2	3	4	7
DFL	0	1	1	2	2
FFR	0	1	2	2	1
NZ$	0	1	0	2	0
Others	0	1	2	3	4
Total	100%	100%	100%	100%	100%

Source: DKB International, London.

EXHIBIT 2:   EUROBOND DISTRIBUTION BY TYPE

Type	1982	1985	1986	1987	1988
Straight Bond	72%	53%	62%	66%	71%
Floating Rate Note	23	41	26	10	11
Convertible Bond	3	4	3	9	3
Bond with Warrants	1	2	9	15	15
Total	100%	100%	100%	100%	100%

Source: DKB International, London.

Eurobond market in 1985). Straight bonds regained market share starting in 1986, at the expense of floating rate notes (FRNs), which dropped to a 26% level in that same year.

Convertible bond share reached 9% in 1987 but fell to 3% in 1988, probably due to the effect of the stock crash in October 1987. It should be noted, however, that the share of equity warrant bonds, which gives investors the option to purchase the stocks at a preset price in exchange for the warrant and cash, increased dramatically from 1% in 1982 to 15% in 1987 and 1988.

The warrant bond share of Eurobonds was expected to increase in 1989. Recent data shows that the issue value of U.S. dollar-denominated equity warrant bonds, mainly issued by the Japanese, exceeded that of U.S. dollar-denominated straight bonds for the first time in the first quarter of 1989. In that period, $19.170 billion in equity warrant bonds were issued as compared to $16.013 billion in straight bonds. The corresponding annual issue volume in 1987 was $20.894 billion in equity warrant bonds and $28.401 billion in straight bonds; for 1988, $26.959 billion in equity warrant bonds and $44.050 billion in straight bonds.[1]

History of the Euromarket

The Eurodollar market dates back to the 1950s, when the "Cold War" between the U.S. and the Soviet Union reached its peak with the outbreak of the Korean War. The Russian authorities were afraid of their dollar assets being frozen by the U.S. government, and transferred their money to the Northern Commerce Bank in Paris, which was the largest foreign bank in France at that time. The bank lent the money to Italian banks for reconstruction following the Second World War.

The Northern Commerce Bank was also called Eurobank, therefore these funds were named Eurodollars. (The bank had been purchased by a rich Russian who escaped from the Russian revolution in 1925.) Other Eastern block countries also transferred their money to the Eurobank or to banks in London.[2]

There were several additional key factors which accelerated the development of the Eurodollar market.

In 1957, UK regulators restricted the use of pound sterling in the face of instability of that currency. Therefore, merchant banks in London had to use dollars instead of sterling for international business. In 1958, European currencies recovered free convertibility to dollars, further increasing dollar transactions among banks in London.

However, the most important impetus to the development of the Euromarket came from the U.S. government through three laws: "Regulation Q" in 1965, the "Interest Equalization Tax" (IET) in 1965, and the "Voluntary Foreign Currency Restriction" (VFCR) in 1968.

Regulation Q, which regulated the ceiling on interest rates that could be paid by depository institutions, caused the outflow of funds from the United States when market rates became higher than regulated rates. (The ceiling was abolished by 1985, under the Depository Institutions Deregulation and Monetary Control Act of 1980.)

The objective of the Interest Equalization Tax was to discourage foreign entities from raising funds in the U.S., thus improving the balance of payments. The IET was abolished in 1974, but it had already discouraged foreign investors and damaged the status of New York as an international capital market.

The Voluntary Foreign Currency Restriction restricted U.S. investment abroad in order to improve the U.S. balance of payments, which had deteriorated during the Vietnam War. This measure forced U.S. multinational corporations to raise funds in the Euromarket, thus once again contributing to the expansion of that market. In response to this situation, the London branches of U.S. banks nearly doubled, from 21 to 41, in the three years after 1967.

The oil crisis of 1974 further contributed to the expansion of the Eurodollar market, which recycled oil money, particularly to LDC countries. The establishment of a New York offshore center, the International Banking Facility (IBF) in 1981 resulted only in attracting offshore funds from the Cayman Islands and Panama, and did not detract from Euromarket development.

Recent Developments in the Eurobond Market

During the 1970s, most financing in the Euromarket was effected through syndicated loans by international banks and merchant banks in London. But, with the increase in securitization of debt instruments worldwide, issuers shifted their borrowing from loans to bonds. The share of loans in international markets decreased from 55% in 1982 to 16% in 1985, at the same time as the bond share increased from 42% in 1982 to 65% in 1985 (see Exhibit 3).

Floating Rate Notes. The expansion of the floating rate note (FRN) market preceded the expansion of the Eurobond market. The coupon of the FRN is reset periodically based on LIBOR.[3] The first FRN was issued in 1970 by ENEL, an Italian state-owned electric company.

FRNs became very popular both to issuers and to investors during the 1981 period of historically high U.S. interest rates for the following reasons:

(1) Issuers preferred to borrow at floating rather than fixed rates, not wanting to lock in high interest payments and speculating on a downturn in interest rates. They could raise funds more cheaply via the FRNs than through bank loans due to the fact that the FRN market has greater liquidity than loans.

(2) For investors, the advantage of FRNs compared to fixed-rate bonds is the relative price stability of the instrument and relative interest rate stability because the coupon is refixed periodically.

(3) The major buyers of FRNs, banks, were reluctant to have their own clients switch from loans to bonds. However, as an alternative to loans, these banks invested in FRNs due to their perceived high liquidity and their lack of a funding risk. This offset the disadvantage of the smaller margin on bond issues. As an extreme exam-

EXHIBIT 3:   INTERNATIONAL DEBT TREND BY CATEGORY

$ billion

	1982 Amt.	%	1983 Amt.	%	1984 Amt.	%	1985 Amt.	%	1986 Amt.	%
SY Loan	98.2	55	52.9	34	45.7	23	34.9	14	40.3	14
Res. Loan	0	0	14.3	9	11.3	6	7.2	3	0.0	0
Total Loans	98.2	55	67.2	44	57	29	42.1	16	40.3	14
Fixed	NA	NA	49.2	32	58.4	30	92.6	36	148.2	50
FRN	15.3	9	19.6	13	38.2	19	58.5	23	54.9	18
CB	NA	NA	8.1	5	10.8	5	11.5	4	23.0	8
Zero	NA	NA	0.3	0	4.1	2	5.1	2	6.0	2
Total Bonds	75.5	42	77.2	50	111.5	57	167.7	65	232.1	78
NIF	2.7	2	3.5	2	17.4	9	36.2	14	19.1	6
Others	2.7	2	6	4	11.4	6	10.5	4	6.8	2
Total Facility	5.4	3	9.5	6	28.8	15	46.7	18	25.9	9
Total	179.1	100	153.9	100	197.3	100	256.5	100	298.3	100

Notes:
Sy loan: Syndicated loan
Res. loan: Rescheduled loan
Fixed: Straight bond
FRN: Floating rate note
CB: Convertible bond
Zero: Zero coupon bond
NIF: Note issuance facility
Others: RUF, CPs

Source: OECD Financial Market Trends.

ple, the Kingdom of Denmark issued FRNs with a coupon rate of LIBOR minus 0.25%.

FRNs lost ground in late 1986, initiated by the collapse of the perpetual FRN market. (A perpetual financial instrument is one in which the principal has no maturity.) This collapse was due in part to rumors of forthcoming regulation of the capital/asset ratios for banks. Thereafter the market lost confidence in the liquidity of the FRN, which had previously enabled FRNs to be funded at a very tight margin.

The rumors concerning capital/asset ratios were in fact confirmed through the Bank for International Settlements (BIS) regulations of 1987. These resulted in the perpetual FRN becoming very expensive for banks to hold, because they had to deduct the face value of the perpetual bond from their capital base, thereby reducing their capital/asset ratio. As a result, the price of perpetual FRNs declined from above par (100) to the 85 level in a very short period of time.

The FRN market decreased from 41% of all Eurobonds in 1985, to 26% in 1986, to 10% in 1987 and 11% in 1988.

Euro Facilities. The second stage of securitization in the market was the introduction of Euro facilities such as Note Issuance Facilities (NIFs)[4] and Revolving Underwriting Facilities (RUFs).[5] The share of Euro facilities in the international debt market increased from 3% in 1982 to 18% in 1985, exceeding syndicated loans which held a 14% share in the market in 1985 (see Exhibit 3).

By using NIFs with a tender panel, prestigious borrowers can raise funds primarily by issuing Euro commercial paper notes ("ECP"), requesting bids from uncommitted tender panel members. Only if they cannot raise enough funds to reach a targeted level does the facility become effective. Syndicate members must lend or buy notes in accordance with the underwritten amount. Syndicate members receive commitment fees or facility fees for their contingent (off balance sheet) liabilities.

The Bank of England ruled that contingent liabilities such as NIFs should be included in the calculation of bank risk/asset ratios in 1985, and regulators in the U.S. and West Germany followed suit in 1986. Due to this regulation, whereby the risk portion would increase, the advantage of NIFs to the banks vanished and the share of NIFs decreased to 6% in 1986 from 14% in 1985. (See Exhibit 3.)

JAPANESE ACTIVITIES IN THE EUROBOND MARKET

According to OECD data, Japan had the largest share of borrowings in international capital markets in 1987. In that year, the Japanese share was 24.5% compared to 12.2% for the U.S. This represented issues by Japanese of $43.5 billion of bonds issued outside the country, more than any other nation. Two years prior, the U.S. and Japanese positions were reversed, the U.S. share being 23.7% while Japan's was 12.8%. Until 1986, the U.S. was the largest borrower. (For Euro-bond and foreign bond markets combined, see Exhibit 4. Specific Eu-robond country distribution is shown in Exhibit 5.)

EXHIBIT 4: BOND ISSUERS BY COUNTRY (INTERNATIONAL BONDS)

(U.S. $ billions)

Country	1985	(A) (%)	1986	(%)	1987	(B) (%)	(B)-(A) (%)
Australia	5.7	3.4	10.0	4.4	6.0	3.4	0.0
Austria	2.4	1.4	3.7	1.6	4.5	2.5	1.1
Belgium	2.5	1.5	4.3	1.9	4.0	2.3	0.8
Canada	9.7	5.7	16.8	7.4	8.7	4.9	-0.8
Denmark	2.9	1.7	9.1	4.0	4.1	2.3	0.6
Finland	1.4	0.8	3.3	1.4	3.0	1.7	0.9
France	11.6	6.9	13.6	6.0	8.9	5.0	-1.8
West Germany	3.1	1.8	11.8	5.2	10.5	5.9	4.1
Ireland	1.5	0.9	2.2	1.0	1.0	0.6	-0.3
Italy	5.4	3.2	5.3	2.3	7.2	4.1	0.9
Japan	21.6	12.8	34.4	15.1	43.5	24.5	11.8
Netherlands	1.4	0.8	3.0	1.3	3.2	1.8	1.0
New Zealand	1.6	0.9	4.8	2.1	3.4	1.9	1.0
Norway	2.3	1.4	5.8	2.5	4.0	2.3	0.9
Spain	1.4	0.8	1.7	0.7	0.6	0.3	-0.5
Sweden	6.2	3.7	5.8	2.5	4.6	2.6	-1.1
Switzerland	0.9	0.5	2.2	1.0	1.1	0.6	0.1
England	15.6	9.2	19.6	8.6	12.4	7.0	-2.2
USA	40.1	23.7	44.1	19.3	21.6	12.2	-11.5
EEC	6.5	3.8	7.8	3.4	6.3	3.6	-0.3
Others	4.4	2.6	4.0	1.8	5.6	3.2	0.6
OECD Total	148.2	87.6	213.3	93.5	164.2	92.6	5.0
Supranational	11.0	6.5	9.2	4.0	9.8	5.5	-1.0
Others	9.9	5.9	5.6	2.5	3.3	1.9	-4.0
Grand Total	169.1	100.0	228.1	100.0	177.3	100.0	-0.0

Source: Derived from OECD Financial Market Trends, Kokusai Kinyukyoku Nenpo, 1988 (MOF).

EXHIBIT 5: EUROBOND DISTRIBUTION BY COUNTRY

Issuer	1982	1985	1986	1987	1988
Europe	36%	41%	46%	40%	49%
US	32	27	20	14	10
Japan	5	11	12	26	22
Canada	16	5	8	4	5
Australia and New Zealand	3	4	6	5	5
Others	8	12	8	11	9
Total	100%	100%	100%	100%	100%
No. of issues	NA	1,357	1,926	1,678	1,891
Amount of total annual issue*	NA	133,133	202,355	158,322	197,788

*$ millions

Source: DKB International, London.

But the greatest international borrower is also among the world's richest nations. Japan's trade surplus in 1987 was more than 90 billion U.S. dollars (when Japan borrowed almost half that amount in international capital markets). Net investment in foreign bonds by the Japanese increased from $5.8 billion in 1981 to $93 billion in 1985 and to $72.9 billion in 1986. There is no doubt that Japan is the largest investor in the international bond market. According to the *International Finance Review*, Mrs. Watanabe, a wealthy middle class house wife in Tokyo, has now replaced the Belgian dentist as the typical Eurobond investor seeking high returns.[6]

The key to Japan's dual status as one of the world's leading investors and leading issuers, lies in the Gaisai market, and, in terms of type of issue, in equity warrant bonds, which hold a 15% share of the Eurobond market. Since 1986, there were large issues of equity-linked warrant bonds by Japanese corporations backed by the prosperous Tokyo stock market.

Gaisai

Gaisai (foreign bond) is ambiguous in Japanese. It generally refers to foreign currency bonds and/or bonds issued in foreign countries. For our purposes, Gaisai refers to all bonds issued by Japanese outside Japan. Gaisai include Euroyen bonds and Sushi bonds.

The first Gaisai was issued in 1959 by the Japanese government in the Yankee bond market. In 1987, 97% of Gaisai were issued by private corporations and 98% were issued in the Eurobond market.

Since 1985, Japanese corporations have borrowed more funds in the foreign market than in the domestic bond market, where the procedure is cumbersome and difficult when nonsecured bonds are to be issued. In addition, good swap opportunities, together with a strong Japanese equity market, enabled Japanese issuers to raise funds cheaply in international markets. For example, in June 1987, issuers could raise funds by issuing warrant bonds denominated in U.S. dollars with coupons of less than 2%, which enabled them to acquire funds at negative interest rates in yen terms (after swap operations). Even more recently, $7 billion in warrant bonds were issued by NKK in late 1988; in terms of yen, after swap, the interest rate was estimated at around 0.3%.[7]

Currencies. The Eurodollar is favored by Gaisai issuers, and its share in 1987 was 61% of Gaisai compared to 25% in 1980. The Swiss franc was favored in 1980, with a 53% share of Gaisai issues, but its share decreased to 21% in 1987. Euroyen bonds have been increasing since 1985, with an estimated share of about 10% of all Gaisai issues in 1987. (See Exhibits 6 and 7.)

Types of Bonds. Warrant bonds were approved in Japan only in June 1981, when the Commercial Code was revised. The share of warrant bonds in Gaisai increased from 13% in 1984 to 52% in 1987.[8]

Convertible bonds were once a leading choice among Gaisai issues, due to the absence of requirements for collateral, which was required for restricted domestic issues until 1984.[9] The share of convertible bonds in Gaisai decreased from 37% in 1984 to 16% in 1987. This was partly because of the deregulation of the domestic market in 1984 and partly because of the lower interest rates in Japan.

EXHIBIT 6: GAISAI DISTRIBUTION BY ISSUED MARKET

($ millions)

	N.Y. Market		Eurodollar Market		DM Market		SFR Market		Total	
	Amt.	%	Amt.	%	Amt.	%	Amt.	%	Amt.	%
1980	60	2	930	25	535	15	1,943	53	3,664	100
1981	350	7	2,060	43	120	3	1,831	39	4,750	100
1982	325	5	1,909	30	241	4	3,631	58	6,303	100
1983	52	0	3,924	35	491	4	6,544	58	11,235	100
1984	451	3	8,182	54	504	3	5,602	37	15,094	100
1985	200	1	11,425	55	759	4	6,079	29	20,712	100
1986	0	0	16,340	56	983	3	7,890	27	28,967	100
1987	712	2	25,817	61	781	2	8,994	21	42,191	100

Notes:
N.Y. Market: Yankee Bond Market.
Total: Total amount includes Asian and Arab dollar markets, and also includes bonds issued by overseas subsidiaries with parent company guarantees.

Source: Derived from Kokusai Kinyukyoku Nenpo, 1988 (MOF).

EXHIBIT 7: GAISAI DISTRIBUTION BY CURRENCY

($ millions)

	U.S. Dollar		DMark		SFR		Others		Total	
	Amt.	%	Amt.	%	Amt.	%	Amt.	%	Amt.	%
1980	990	27	535	15	1,943	53	196	5	3,664	100
1981	2,410	51	120	3	1,831	39	389	8	4,750	100
1982	2,234	35	241	4	3,631	58	197	3	6,303	100
1983	3,976	35	491	4	6,544	58	224	2	11,235	100
1984	8,633	57	504	3	5,602	37	355	2	15,094	100
1985	11,625	56	759	4	6,079	29	2,249	11	20,712	100
1986	16,340	56	983	3	7,890	27	3,754	13	28,967	100
1987	26,529	63	781	2	8,994	21	5,887	14	42.191	100

Notes:
Others: Mainly yen.
Total: Total amount includes Asian and Arab dollar markets, and also includes bonds issued by overseas subsidiaries with parent company guarantees.

Source: Derived from Kokusai Kinyukyoku Nenpo, 1988 (MOF).

Euroyen Bonds Issued by Japanese Entities

Japanese Euroyen bonds were first issued in 1980, in response to the Japanese current deficit, and were used to recycle petro-money.[10] The Ministry of Finance (MOF) authorized Euroyen issues only when they were private placements and issued in the Middle East. Five bonds were issued by 1982, four of them were convertible. Due to the gradual decrease in the oil producing countries' trade surplus, no additional Euroyen bonds were issued until 1985.

The issue of bonds by Japanese corporations in the Euroyen market was hindered by: eligibility requirements, withholding taxes, and other Japanese legal restrictions.

Eligibility Requirements. In April 1984, eligibility requirements were relaxed following the Takeshita/Reagan communiqué of November 1983. Forty Japanese corporations became eligible to issue nonsecured Euroyen bonds; 120 became eligible to issue convertible bonds. Prior to the relaxation, only Toyota and Matsushita fulfilled the eligibility requirements for issuing nonsecured straight bonds.

Since this market is an alternative to the issuer's domestic market, the relaxation of eligibility requirements on the Euromarket was preceded by the parallel relaxation in the domestic nonsecured bond market.

In July and October 1985, and February 1987, the eligibility requirements for Euroyen and convertible bonds were relaxed, and the number of corporations that could issue Euroyen bonds and Euroyen convertible bonds increased to approximately 170 and 320, respectively. Authorization was also given for issues in which the attached warrant could be sold separately.

Withholding Tax. Even after the relaxation of eligibility requirements, the withholding tax problem still was not resolved. During the discussion in the Yen/Dollar Committee, the MOF strictly opposed the abolition of the withholding tax for foreign bondholders, arguing that such a measure would have a severe effect on the total tax system in Japan. Therefore, the 1984 reform of eligibility requirements had no immediate consequences.

In April 1985, the withholding tax was abolished for foreign investors. (But Japanese investors were still liable for the withholding tax.) This change, together with the relaxation of eligibility requirements, resulted in the increased issue of Euroyen bonds by Japanese after 1985. (See Exhibit 1 in the previous chapter.)

Other Developments. In April 1986, floating rate bonds and currency conversion bonds were authorized. Restriction of sales to Japanese investors (the "lock-up period") was shortened to 90 days.

In June 1987, a rating system was introduced, which could replace the eligibility standard. The number of companies which could issue Euroyen bonds and Euroyen convertible bonds increased by 60 and 90, respectively.

Sushi Bonds

Sushi bonds appeared in the Eurobond market between 1985 and 1986. Sushi bonds are designed to meet the Japanese taste, although Sushi as a Japanese food is also becoming popular for Western people. Most Sushi bonds were eaten by Japanese life insurance companies. A Sushi bond is not a *Euroyen* bond, but a *foreign currency* bond issued by Japanese entities. Its coupon is higher than prevailing yen bonds.

Japanese life insurance companies are very active in investing in bonds issued in foreign currencies,[11] this is partly due to the frequency of earthquakes in Japan and the necessity of diversifying their portfolios abroad in order to be able to reimburse claims in the event of such a national catastrophe.

However, in order to understand the specific nature of Sushi bonds, we must examine the relevant accounting rules and MOF guidelines.

Accounting Rules. Accounting rules for Japanese insurance companies require that capital gains be entered in the capital reserve and only income gains be used as a source of dividends for policyholders. Insurance companies, therefore, compete for a return on investment based on income gains and eventually prefer high coupon bonds. They prefer foreign currencies to yen because yen rates have been lower than other major currencies.

MOF Guidelines. MOF guidelines require life insurance companies to limit their foreign currency bond holdings issued by foreign entities. This does not apply to bonds floated by Japanese issuers. Sushi bonds are therefore suitable for fund managers who have already reached this limit but who wish to further diversify the currencies represented in their portfolios.

MOF guidelines imposed a maximum ratio of 20% foreign bond investment to total assets. This ratio was relaxed to 30% in August 1986. Another requirement, limiting foreign bond investments to within 40% of the incremental increase of assets, was also abolished.

The insurance industry suffered huge foreign exchange losses from their high coupon bond holdings, especially from the appreciation of the yen after the Plaza agreement. The MOF warned the industry to restrict its investment in high coupon, high premium types of bonds as well as Sushi bonds in late 1986. This type of bond issue decreased thereafter.

The above-mentioned accounting rules are also under review.

Japanese Book Runners

Since 1987, Nomura has maintained a number one standing in all the rankings of Eurobond book runners, one of the most prestigious standings in the bond markets. Until 1986, Credit Suisse First Boston held this position. In 1988 there were five Japanese houses in the top ten ranking (Nomura, Daiwa, Yamaichi, Nikko—the "Big Four," and the Industrial Bank of Japan (IBJ)—see Exhibit 8). The Japanese Big Four achieved a 40% share in all Eurobonds and ranked in the top four issuers in the first quarter of 1989.[12]

The book runner position in Euroyen bonds is monopolized by Japanese securities firms, although there is no restriction for foreign book runners since 1984. In 1987, about 77% of Euroyen issues (including those issued by Japanese borrowers) were lead managed by the Big Four and the IBJ (see Exhibits 2 and 9b).

The active performance of Japanese securities firms in the Eurobond market can be explained by their dominant status in the Euroyen and Gaisai markets, especially in the equity warrant bond market.

EXHIBIT 8:   ALL EUROBOND BOOK RUNNER RANKING 1986–1988

1986 Ranking

	Managing Bank	No. of issues	Total amount ($M)	Share (%)
1	CSFB	102	19,639	10.7
2	Nomura	131	14,651	8.0
3	Deutsche Bank	92	12,414	6.8
4	Morgan Guaranty	65	9,843	5.4
5	Morgan Stanley	73	8,938	4.9
6	Daiwa	87	8,836	4.8
7	Salomon Brothers	56	8,438	4.6
8	Bank Paribas	71	7,245	3.9
9	Merrill Lynch	38	5,846	3.2
10	Nikko	54	5,113	2.8

1987 Ranking*

	Managing Bank	No. of issues	Total amount ($M)	Share (%)
1	Nomura	121	18,583	14.5
2	CSFB	75	9,368	7.3
3	Nikko	59	7,927	6.2
4	Yamaichi	71	7,249	5.7
5	Daiwa	69	6,624	5.2
6	Deutsche Bank	58	6,612	5.2
7	Morgan Stanley	35	5,045	3.9
8	Morgan Guaranty	44	4,684	3.7
9	Bank Paribas	43	4,415	3.4
10	Warburg Securities	37	3,965	3.1
	Others	643	53,722	41.9
	ALL ISSUES TOTAL	1,255	128,194	100.0

1988 Ranking**

	Managing Bank	No. of issues	Total amount ($M)	Share (%)
1	Nomura	135	17,679	10.3
2	CSFB	82	13,895	8.1
3	Deutsche Bank	84	12,230	7.1
4	Daiwa	80	9,432	5.5
5	Yamaichi	61	7,272	4.2
6	Nikko	61	6,867	4.0
7	Bankers Trust	50	6,022	3.5
8	Merrill Lynch	32	5,953	3.5
9	JP Morgan Securities	34	5,603	3.2
10	IBJ	49	5,589	3.2
	Others	816	81,928	47.5
	ALL ISSUES TOTAL	1,484	172,470	100.0

*International Financing Review, Issue 705 (Jan. 2, 1988).
**International Financing Review, Issue 757 (Jan. 7, 1989).

EXHIBIT 9:   BOOK RUNNER RANKING 1987

a. All Eurobond Book Runner Ranking 1987

Managing Bank		No. of issues	Total amount ($M)	Share (%)
1	Nomura	121	18,583	14.5
2	CSFB	75	9,368	7.3
3	Nikko	59	7,927	6.2
4	Yamaichi	71	7,249	5.7
5	Daiwa	69	6,624	5.2
6	Deutsche Bank	58	6,612	5.2
7	Morgan Stanley	35	5,045	3.9
8	Morgan Guaranty	44	4,684	3.7
9	Bank Paribas	43	4,415	3.4
10	Warburg Securities	37	3,965	3.1
	Others	643	53,722	41.9
	ALL ISSUES TOTAL	1,255	128,194	100.0

b. All Euroyen Bond Book Runner Ranking 1987

Managing Bank		No. of issues	Total amount ($M)	Share (%)	Total Amt. (¥ billion)
1	Nomura	41	8,832	39.0	1,281
2	IBJ	23	2,512	11.1	364
3	Daiwa	24	2,388	10.5	346
4	Nikko	12	2,182	9.6	316
5	Yamaichi	17	1,625	7.2	236
	Others	44	5,108	22.6	741
	ALL ISSUES TOTAL	161	22,647	100.0	3,284

c. All Equity Warrant Bond Book Runner Ranking 1987

Managing Bank		No. of issues	Total amount ($M)	Share (%)
1	Nomura	55	7,167	30.3
2	Nikko	36	4,573	19.3
3	Yamaichi	43	4,415	18.7
4	Daiwa	34	3,462	14.6
5	Deutsche Bank	9	1,622	6.9
	Others	33	2,401	10.2
	ALL ISSUES TOTAL	210	23,640	100.0

d. Share of Euroyen and Warrant Bonds by Number and Amount of Book Running by Japanese Big Four (b and c above)

Big Four		No. of issues	Total amount ($M)	Share in Numbers (%)	Share in Amount (%)
1	Nomura	96	15,999	79.3	86.1
2	Daiwa	58	5,850	84.1	88.3
3	Yamaichi	60	6,040	84.5	83.3
4	Nikko	48	6,755	81.4	85.2

Note: Calculations based on yen/$ = 145.

Source: *International Financing Review*, Issue 705 (Jan. 2, 1988).

Concurrently, as can be seen in Exhibits 2 and 9c, the share of equity warrant bonds in all Eurobonds increased to 15% in 1987 from 2% in 1985, and were mostly (about 83%) managed by the Big Four in 1987. Backed by strong performance in the Tokyo Stock Market, most equity warrant bonds were issued by Japanese companies and underwritten by Japanese securities firms. In the case of Nomura, the contribution of Euroyen and warrant bonds to the share in number and in amount of book running was 79% and 86%, respectively (see Exhibit 9d).

Japanese securities firms were in a good position to intermediate in swaps between Euroyen bonds issued by foreigners and warrant bonds issued by Japanese and denominated in a currency required by the foreigner. However in practice, Japanese banks are the frequent counterparts of swap transactions. Japanese city banks, which are not allowed to issue yen bonds, seek medium-term fixed-rate yen funds to finance their fixed-rate portfolios (e.g., mortgage loans, corporate loans based on long-term prime rate). They are often invited as counterparts in currency swap agreements in exchange for the co-lead manager status for the deals. Sometimes their swap rates are too aggressive and are referred to as "harakiri swaps" ("cut open the stomach" swaps).

It is estimated that about 90% of all Euroyen bonds have been swapped.[13]

EUROYEN BONDS ISSUED BY FOREIGNERS

The first Euroyen bond was issued by the European Investment Bank (EIB) in 1974, with an issue amount of 10 billion yen and a maturity of 7 years.

Euroyen bonds, as well as Euroyen loans, were strictly regulated by the Ministry of Finance. The MOF gave priority to Samurai over Euroyen bonds, since Japanese financial and monetary policy would be less affected if yen financing is originated in Tokyo. The total number of Euroyen issues was restricted to six or seven per year. The issuers were restricted to supranational institutions and the government, the maximum issue amount was 20 billion yen and the longest maturity was 10 years.

Following the Yen/Dollar Committee and the Action Program, guidelines for Euroyen bonds issued by foreigners were relaxed substantially. The annual issue amount increased from 227 billion yen in 1984, to 1,446 billion yen in 1985, and to 2,994 billion yen in 1987. (See Exhibit 1 in the previous chapter.) However Euroyen bond issues decreased in 1988 for the first time since deregulation started in 1984 (see Exhibit 1).

Decreasing volume caused liquidity problems in the Euroyen bond market and several market makers have withdrawn from the market. However it is estimated that the share of yen bonds will increase again because the huge trade surpluses in Japan will require the recycling of funds abroad.

Deregulation

In December 1984, the list of potential foreign issuers was extended to include foreign municipal governments, government agencies, private corporations (other than supranational institutions and sovereign states), and public entities with a single-A rating. Private entities must have a single-A rating or higher and must clear eligibility standards.

In addition, control over issue volume was abolished, and non-Japanese book runners for Euroyen bonds were authorized. In April 1985, further steps were taken to allow all private corporations to automatically qualify to issue if their rating was double-A. In case of a single-A rating, the entity was still required to clear eligibility standards. The entity guaranteed by an eligible guarantor also became eligible.

Two months later, innovative issues such as floating rate bonds, zero coupon bonds, deep discount bonds, currency conversion bonds, and dual currency bonds were authorized. (Currency conversion bonds allow for repayment of the principal in a different currency from that used at the time of issue, sometimes with options attached.)

In April 1986, the ratings system was fully introduced following the suggestion of the *Yen/Dollar Report*. All entities with single-A ratings, including private entities, were eligible to issue Euroyen bonds.

Five ratings agencies were authorized: Nippon Investors Service (established by banks and securities houses), Nihon Kakuzuke Kenkyusho (established by institutional investors), and Nihon Koshasai Kenkyusho (established by Nihon Keizai Shimbun Inc.) in addition to Standard & Poor's and Moody's in the U.S. Fitch was admitted as an eligible rating agency in 1987.

The reduction in the lock-up period to 90 days from 180 days was also applied to Euroyen bonds, except for dual currency bonds issued by the Japanese.

In June 1986, foreign banks were allowed to issue Euroyen bonds. They were requested not to bring the funds to Japan, since Japanese city banks were not allowed to issue yen bonds. (Only three long-term banks, Shokochukin, Norinchukin, and Bank of Tokyo are currently authorized to issue 5-year bank debentures in Japan.) Subordinated bonds were authorized for issue.

In June 1987, four-year bonds were authorized. Previously, the minimum maturity was five years. In practice, however, by attaching a call option and a put option, a bond with a shorter life is possible. For example, in January 1987, the Kingdom of Denmark issued a 5-year jumbo yen bond, with an issue amount of 130 billion yen, and with attached put and call options to be exercised three years from date of issue. It is widely expected that the MOF will abolish the minimum life restriction in the near future.

Following liberalization, Euroyen bonds issued by foreigners exceeded Samurai issues in 1985. The gap enlarged even further in 1986 and 1987. In 1987, foreign Euroyen issue amounts reached nearly 3 trillion yen compared with 0.4 trillion of Samurai (see Exhibit 1 in the previous chapter).

Primary Market

Euroyen bonds are underwritten in the "bought deal style" and syndicated like other Eurobonds by international securities firms. But MOF approval prior to issue is required under the Foreign Exchange and Foreign Trading Control Law 1980 (Article 21-1-2). In reality, approval is given promptly with little or no effect on the schedule.

Major issuers are sovereign borrowers (including supranational institutions), which accounted for 56% of the Euroyen market in 1986 and 71% in 1987. Foreign banks were allowed to issue only since June 1986, but accounted for 22% of the market in 1986 and 1987 (see Exhibit 10).

As can be seen in Exhibit 11, foreigners issue mainly plain vanilla Euroyen issues (68% in 1986 and 75% in 1987). Since many bonds are issued for specific investors such as Japanese life insurance companies or trust banks, innovative bonds such as index-linked bonds, step-up bonds and high coupon, high premium bonds have been developed. The share of dual-currency bonds has decreased from its peak of 48% in 1985 to 4% in 1987 (see Exhibit 11).

Secondary Market

As of January 1989, the market makers of Euroyen bonds included 19 Japanese and 15 foreign institutions. The peak was more than 40 in 1986.

Benchmark issues as of March 1989 were:

Kingdom of Norway,	coupon 5⅜%,	due 1991,
Republic of Italy,	coupon 5¾%,	due 1992,
Republic of Canada,	coupon 5⅝%,	due 1993,
The World Bank,	coupon 4⅞%,	due 1994,
The World Bank,	coupon 5¾%,	due 1996.

The annual compounded yield-to-maturity of the above bonds serve as benchmarks for other bond issues in the Euroyen bond market.

A two-way price is quoted, and the spread is ¼ of 1 point (e.g., 99.25-99.50) for liquid issues. The spread is widened to 1 or 2 points (e.g., 98 - 100) for issues that are more difficult to trade in the secondary market, like low volume issues or low credit issues. Although yen bonds are increasing their share in the international bond market, the secondary market is not active compared with other bonds. The above-mentioned withdrawal of several market makers from the Euroyen bond market was due mainly to the liquidity problem. The majority of Euroyen bonds are purchased by Japanese investors who keep bonds in their portfolio as long-term investments. Innovative bonds have the least liquidity.

EXHIBIT 10: NON-JAPANESE EUROYEN ISSUES BY ISSUER

(¥ 100 million)

Category	#	1986 Amount	%	#	1987 Amount	%
Supranational	13	2,115	8	15	3,100	10
Government	21	6,195	24	18	10,500	35
Local Government	5	630	2	2	500	2
Financial	28	4,639	18	38	5,730	19
Others	5	600	2	11	1,376	5
Sovereign Total	72	14,179	56	84	21,206	71
Banks	37	5,632	22	52	6,731	22
Enterprise (Private)	31	5,454	21	6	843	3
Others	1	250	1	9	1,160	4
Private Total	69	11,336	44	67	8,734	29
Total	141	25,515	100	151	29,940	100

EXHIBIT 11: NON-JAPANESE EUROYEN ISSUES BY TYPE

(¥ 100 million)

Type of Bond	#	1986 Amount	%	#	1987 Amount	%
Plain Vanilla	85	17,434	68	95	22,385	75
FRN	8	910	4	14	3,000	10
FRN (Long Prime)	0	0	0	9	2,360	8
Dual Currency	20	3,047	12	11	1,109	4
Currency Conversion	1	92	0	0	0	0
Zero Coupon	0	0	0	7	1,020	3
Equity Warrant	1	200	1	0	0	0
Debt Warrant	1	200	1	0	0	0
Index	7	700	3	4	385	1
Step-Up	3	280	1	11	980	3
High CPN, High Premium	15	2,652	10	3	251	1
Repackage	0	0	0	6	810	3
Total	141	25,515	100	151	29,940	100

Source: MOF Kokusai Kinyukyoku Nenpo, (MOF) 1988.

The interest of Japanese market makers is to increase market liquidity. However the view by Viner that the "Big Four" have not yet developed the trading skills characteristic of the leading U.S. and European banks seems to be a fair comment.[14]

Yield Spread between Eurobonds and Domestic Yen Bonds

There are several factors which can affect the yields of bonds, i.e., the liquidity, the credit risk, the time to maturity, taxes, and accounting rules in each country.

The yield of a bond increases with: a decrease in liquidity in the secondary market for the bond, an increase of credit risk of the issuer, the existence and relative importance of taxes (withholding taxes, transfer taxes), and with the time to maturity (the longer the time, the higher the yield—in a normal yield curve environment).

Below, we examine the yields of Euroyen bonds, Japanese government bonds and Samurai bonds, according to each of these factors.

Liquidity. The Japanese government bonds are the most liquid among these three bonds, the Euroyen next, and the Samurai the least. Therefore, the yields of these bonds should vary inversely to their liquidity (assuming that the issuers of Samurai and Euroyen bonds are supranationals or the equivalent highest rating, and that the time to maturity for all the bonds is ten years). However, the yield comparisons in Exhibit 12 between Samurai, Euroyen and JGB bonds do not always confirm these principles. Note that the yields of Samurai bonds are about 30 to 50 basis points higher than those for Japanese government bonds. However, the yield is sometimes lower than JGBs; for example, in 1982 it was about 30 basis points lower.

In the same exhibit, we also noted that the yields of JGBs were considerably higher than those of Euroyen bonds before 1980. Since that year, JGB yields have been considerably lower. The same phenomenon can be seen in the Samurai/Euroyen yield spread: for several years since 1980, the Euroyen yields were higher than those of the (theoretically less liquid) Samurai bonds.

There are two possible reasons for these reversals. First, Euroyen bond markets became very active only since 1984 or 1985 when liber-

EXHIBIT 12: YIELD COMPARISON: SAMURAI, EUROYEN, JGBS

	Samurai A	Euroyen B	JGBs C	Differentials A-C	B-C	A-B
1977	7.62%	6.58%	7.46%	16bp	-88bp	104bp
1977	6.80	5.57	6.40	40	-83	123
1978	6.71	5.37	6.27	44	-90	134
1978	6.87	5.77	6.40	47	-63	110
1979	8.75	7.74	8.81	-6	-107	101
1979	9.22	8.57	9.15	7	-58	65
1980	8.32	8.31	8.25	7	6	1
1980	8.86	9.34	8.86	0	48	-48
1981	8.47	8.75	8.00	47	75	-28
1981	8.46	8.55	8.12	34	43	-9
1982	8.20	8.95	8.52	-32	43	-75
1982	8.10	8.14	7.67	43	47	-4
1983	8.10	7.86	7.69	41	17	24
1983	7.80	7.74	7.37	43	37	6
1984	8.00	7.90	7.51	49	39	10
1984	7.09	NA	6.47	62	NA	NA
1985	6.75	NA	5.92	83	NA	NA
1986	5.81	NA	5.26	55	NA	NA
1987	6.22	5.18	4.87	135	31	104

Notes:
bp = basis points
Data: 2nd and 4th quarter, end of period, calendar year (–1984)
Data: 4th quarter, end of period, calendar year (1984–1987)
Simple Yield =

$$\text{Coupon Rate} + \frac{((\text{Redemption Value–Bond Price})/\text{No.Yrs. to Maturity}) \times 100}{\text{Bond Price}}$$

Source: Sally J. Staley, *International Bond Manual: Japanese Yen* (2nd ed). New
York, Salomon Brothers Inc (for 1973 to 1984, 2Q).
Karen S. Keegan, *Government of Japan Bond Futures*. London, First Boston,
November 1986 (for 1984 4Q, 1985 data).
MOF Securities Bureau Annual Report. Tokyo, Okurasho Shokenkyoku Nenpo,
1988 (for others).

alization started. Therefore, it may not be appropriate to compare the yields before that date. Second, the Foreign Exchange and Trade Control Law implemented in 1980 liberalized investments by foreigners in Japan. As a consequence, foreign investments in Samurai bonds and JGBs increased, leading to the decline of yields.

Interviews with securities firms in London reveal that it is not appropriate to conclude that the Euroyen is more liquid than the Samurai market (as of April 1989). It is generally agreed upon, however, that the yield spreads sometimes depend on the time to maturity. Most Eurobonds are issued with a term to maturity of five years, while most Samurai bonds are issued with terms of more than 10 years. Therefore, if we compare yields of both types of bonds with the same 10 years to maturity, yields of Samurai bonds are often lower than those of Euroyen bonds. This has been especially true after the introduction of shelf registration in October 1988.

Credit Risks. Interviews also reveal that the yield spread between the World Bank (supranational) and NTT (AAA-rated) in Euroyen bonds was approximately 20 basis points during the year 1988. Samurai bonds are less sensitive to the credit rating of the borrower than are yields on comparable bonds in international markets, partly because many of them are held by Japanese investors, not for trading, but for long-term investment purposes.

Benchmark. Euroyen bond yields fluctuate according to market conditions, but generally follow the JGB benchmark issue because swap terms are set in relation to JGBs, although not as closely as the Eurodollar issues are set to the U.S. Treasury.[15]

Accounting. High coupon yen bonds are traded with lower yields than low coupon bonds, because high coupon bonds are favored by Japanese investors (such as insurance companies) due to accounting reasons. For example, in May 1989, a JGB due June 1997 (#101) with a coupon of 3.9% traded at 5.63%, while a JGB due June 1997 (#97) with a coupon of 5% traded at 4.92%.

Taxation. JGBs are subject to a 20% withholding tax on interest payments to Japanese investors. Payments to foreigners are also subject to a withholding tax, according to the terms of the bilateral tax treaty between Japan and that nation. For a U.S. resident, a 10% withholding tax is applied. There is no such withholding tax for Samurai and Euroyen bonds. Theoretically this will result in higher yields for JGBs. However, in practice, taxes can be avoided by selling the bonds prior to the interest payments, for example, to nontaxable entities. Therefore, taxes should not affect the yield spreads.

JAPANESE BOND MARKET INNOVATIONS

After the liberalization of July 1985, many innovative products appeared. Since only plain vanilla issues are allowed for Samurai bonds, Euroyen issues were the focus of innovation. Tailor-made products were created to meet the needs of specific investors, such as Japanese life insurance companies and trust banks. Then potential issuers were sought for such new products.

Classification of Innovations

There are two types of innovation: "high risk, high return" and "tax oriented."

The "high risk, high return" (high yield) type is represented by dual currency bonds, which preceded the Euroyen bond. In the first six months after authorization of such bonds by the MOF in June 1985, there were 32 dual currency issues with a total issue amount of 736.7 billion yen. They represented nearly 50% of total Euroyen bonds issued by foreigners in 1985.

For "high risk, high return" bonds, the principal varies according to a risk-related index such as foreign exchange rates, interest rates, stock prices, the gold price, and/or oil prices. Examples include the "mini max bond"[16] by Yamaichi, the "Nikkei average index-linked bond" by Daiwa; in dollar terms, the "heaven and hell," or "Treasury index-linked bond," by Nomura and the "duet bond"[17] by DKB.[18]

The "tax oriented" type of innovation permits deferral of current profit to a future time and/or application of different tax rates on interest income and capital gains. Examples from this category of bonds are "deferred coupon bonds" by Daiwa and "high coupon, high premium bonds" by Yamaichi, and a bond invented by Nikko, where the coupon is paid every other year.

Another way to categorize these innovations is to divide them into "index bonds" and "arranged cash flow bonds."[19] Index bonds are characterized by a coupon and/or a redemption amount which varies according to a market index such as a foreign exchange rate or stock price. The final outcome for the investor, therefore, depends on the market price of the index.

The arranged cash flow bond transforms the cash flows artificially in order to meet investors' special requirements. For example, the timing of interest payments is varied or the bond is transformed from a straight to floating rate. Examples are floating rate bonds collateralized by Japanese ex-warrant bonds. (An ex-warrant bond is one in which the warrant has been detached.)

Exhibit 13 summarizes these innovations based on this classification.

The Structure of Major Innovations

Deferred Coupon Bond. A deferred coupon bond is a "tax oriented/arranged cash flow" type of bond.

As can be seen in the following example, interest payments are deferred until the fourth year.

Issuer	Sumitomo Corp (America)					
Amount	$50,000,000					
Term	5 years					
Price	99.00					
Coupon	8.00%	0.00%	0.00%	0.00%	32.00%	8.00%
		year 1	year 2	year 3	year 4	year 5
Investor	Japanese individual (tax shield)					

This bond is attractive to individual Japanese investors. If investors sell the bond just before interest is paid in year four, they will benefit because accrued interest is not subject to income tax in Japan. Issuers can raise funds more cheaply than the prevailing market rates when these tax benefits are shared.

EXHIBIT 13: CLASSIFICATION OF EUROYEN BOND INNOVATIONS

Arranged Cash Flow Bond

Repackaged bond	Synthetic FRN
Odd coupon bond	Step-up bond
	Step-down bond
	High coupon, high premium bond
	Deferred coupon bond

Index Bond

Foreign exchange index	Dual currency bond
	Mixed dual currency bond
	Heaven and hell bond
	Mini max bond
	Duet bond
	Higher yen merit bond
Bond price index	Treasury index bond
	JGBs index bond
Interest index	Survival bond
	Capped FRN
Stock price index	Average stock price index bond
Other mercantile index	Gold price linked bond
	Oil price Index bond

Dual Currency Bond. A dual currency bond is a "high risk, high return" "index" type of bond. The bond is issued in yen, interest is paid in yen, and the bond principal is repaid in U.S. dollars or in any other foreign currency. The coupon rate is higher than the prevailing yen market rate. Coupon gains for investors are theoretically offset by lower principal repayment amounts. Since the repayment is made at maturity in a foreign currency, the investor also has a foreign-exchange risk for the principal.

The bond is designed for specific Japanese investors seeking higher yen coupon income for the current accounting period, and who are less concerned about foreign exchange or capital losses. For example, the investor can receive 8% in yen interest, instead of the prevailing lower rate, for example, 5%.

Issuers can raise funds more cheaply than the prevailing market rate, because investors are willing to take foreign-exchange risks.

In a "reverse dual currency bond," the issue amount and interest are paid in U.S. dollars, and the bond is repaid in yen.

In a more complicated case, in the "mixed dual currency bond," (for example, yen and Australian dollars), a bond is issued in yen, the coupon is paid in Australian dollars, and the principal is repaid at maturity, for example, 80% in yen and 20% in Australian dollars. In this type of bond, the foreign-exchange risk is lower for the Japanese investor than it is in the dual currency bond, since the foreign-exchange risk is only 20%.

The following is an example of the terms of issue of a dual currency bond:

Issuer	Mitsui & Co.
Amount	¥20,000,000 (Units in thousands)
Term	5 years
Price	par
Repayment	$115,000,000 @173.49
Coupon	8.00% 8.00% 8.00% 8.00% 8.00% 8.00%
	year 1 year 2 year 3 year 4 year 5
Investor	Japanese insurance co., trust funds, mutual funds

High Coupon, High Premium Bond. A "high coupon, high premium bond" is an "arranged cash flow" bond. The coupon is set higher than prevailing rates to offset the issue price which is well above par, for example, 115⅝. The investor therefore receives high current income from the coupons, which are offset by the capital loss due to the high issue price and redemption at par. Theoretically, investors receive a part of the principal in each coupon payment, instead of the entire repayment at maturity. However, the realized yield is set lower than the theoretical yield, due to investors' special interest.

Investors such as Japanese insurance companies are interested in high coupon bonds, because only income gains such as those from coupons are allowed to be distributed as dividends to insurance policyholders. Such distributions are used by these companies to compete for clients. (According to Japanese accounting rules, capital and/or foreign exchange profits and losses are entered in the capital reserves account, and cannot be used for dividend payments.)

The all-in-cost of the bond for the issuers is lower than the market level. The MOF discourages this type of investment.

The following is an example of the issue terms of a high coupon high premium bond:

Issuer	Société Générale
Amount	¥16,000,000 (Units in thousands)
Term	5 years
Price	115⅝
Par	100
Repayment	100.00
Coupon	8.5% 8.5% 8.5% 8.5% 8.5% 8.5%
	year 1 year 2 year 3 year 4 year 5
Investor	Japanese insurance co., trust funds

Reverse Floater. The "reverse FRN" is a special type of floating rate note. Its coupon rate is reset semiannually (or quarterly), but the coupon rate moves in the reverse direction to the market rate; that is, when the market rate increases, the coupon rate decreases.

The coupon is set with a mixture of fixed rates (high) and floating rates, which enable the coupon to remain high when the market rate is low, and low when the market rate is high. When LIBOR is low, this bond becomes more popular.

The following are the terms of issue of a reverse floater:

Issuer	Kawasaki Steel
Amount	¥10,000,000 (Units in thousands)
Term	5 Years
Coupon	15.00% – 1.6 × six-month LIBOR
	float float float float float
	year 1 year 2 year 3 year 4 year 5
Investor	Trust funds

In our example, if LIBOR is 6%, the coupon rate is therefore 5.4%. If LIBOR is 9%, the coupon rate is 0.6%. If LIBOR is 4%, the coupon rate is 8.6%.

There can be no negative interest rate, and the floor is therefore 0% interest. There are no caps.

Investors can use this bond to make the average coupon rate of their total portfolio less volatile due to interest movements. Therefore, this bond is also called a "survival bond."

Step-up Bond. A step-up bond is a "tax-oriented/arranged cash flow" type of bond. Its coupon is set lower in the earlier period, and set higher in the later period to defer profits to the future.

The coupon can also be fixed or a combination of fixed and floating rates. For example, the State Bank of Victoria borrowed 20 billion yen in a five-year issue. For the first two years, the interest rate is fixed at 1.00%, and then, in years three to five, the rate is set at 7.5% plus 0.1 times six-month LIBOR.

Profitable companies that want to save current tax payments and retain profits as hidden reserves for future fluctuations of business are interested in investing in this type of bond. Issuers can raise funds more cheaply than the prevailing market rates, since these tax benefits may be shared.

A typical example of the terms of issue of this type of bond is as follows:

Issuer	PK Banken
Amount	$50,000,000
Term	5 years
Coupon	Six-month LIBOR – 5.00% for years 1 - 3
	Six-month LIBOR + 7.65% for years 4 - 5
Investor	Highly profitable corporations

Bull and Bear Bonds. A "bull and bear" bond is a "high risk, high return" "index linked" bond. The redemption price is linked to an index, for example, the Nikkei Dow Index of stocks in Japan. Many alternative indexes can be selected, such as bond futures or the market price of a specific bond or stock.

Bull tranches and bear tranches are issued at the same time with the same issue amount. Investors can select the orientation of the bond, bullish or bearish, according to their perspectives for the market and to their individual risk profiles. Issuers can raise funds more cheaply than the prevailing market rates, since investors take the index risks.

The key for a successful issue of this bond is to find two groups of investors who are willing to buy an equal amount of bull and bear investments.

The following is an example of the terms of a bull and bear issue:

Issuer	SEK
Amount	¥10,000,000 (Bull), ¥10,000,000 (Bear)
	(Units in thousands)
Term	5 years
Redemption	Bull = F1 × 100, F1 = 1 + (INDEX - 26,067)/22,720
	Bear = F2 × 100, F2 = 1 - (INDEX - 19,373)/22,720
Index =	Nikkei Dow average at time of redemption
Coupon	8.00% 8.00% 8.00% 8.00% 8.00% 8.00%
	year 1 year 2 year 3 year 4 year 5
Investor	Japanese insurance Co., trust funds

Analysis of Cash Flows—For Heaven and Hell Bonds

A "heaven and hell" bond is a "high risk, high return," foreign exchange "index linked" bond. It was invented by Nomura in October 1985 for IBM Credit Corporation and received the *International Finance Review's* award for "Deal of the Year."

We reviewed the structure of innovative instruments earlier. Here, we shall examine the cash flows of one such type of transaction. This case study is based on a simulation, and is not exactly the same transaction as the IBM issue. DKB coordinated the swap transactions in the IBM issue.

Our example involves two interest rate swaps, one currency swap, and one forward exchange transaction. (In general, more than one counterparty is needed to execute swap transactions in large volume and/or for periods longer than five years.) The final cost for the borrower in the example below is the U.S. one-month commercial paper rate minus 30 basis points.

The following are the terms and conditions of a heaven and hell bond which we are going to analyze:

Total Issued Amount: $100,000,000
Maturities: 10 years
Coupon rate: 8.3%
Issue price: 100
Commission: 2%
Redemption Ratio: $100 \times (1+ (F\text{-}105)/F)\%$
(F = spot exchange rate of Yen/$ at the time of redemption)

This is a typical foreign exchange index bond, in which the amount to be redeemed varies according to the foreign exchange rate at the time of redemption. The risk is fully transferred to investors. When the dollar strengthens against the yen, investors enjoy capital gains and are in heaven, but in a reverse situation they are in trouble falling to hell, hence, the name "heaven and hell."

In our analysis of the cash flows, we shall assume the following market conditions:

Yen/$ spot rate: 150/$
Yen/$ forward rate: 105/$ (10-year rate)
Yen/$ Currency Swap (10 years): Yen 4.80% s.a./$ 6-month LIBOR
$ Interest Swap (10 years):   8.78% s.a./$ 6-month LIBOR
$ Interest Swap (10 years):   8.14% s.a./$ 1-month CP rate
Average contract—forward
  exchange (10 years):   126.82 ¥/$

We shall now examine the cash flows of the instruments involved in this transaction: a bond, interest rate swaps 1 and 2, a currency swap and a forward exchange contract. The cash flows are summarized in Exhibit 14.

Bond Cash Flow (Units: 1000s). In year zero, the issuer receives net $98,000, which represents the issue amount of $100,000 minus a commission of $2,000. (We assume the commission includes all fees for underwriting, listing, printing, etc.)

In years 1 to 10, the annual coupon payment is $8,300 ($100,000 × 8.3%). At maturity, the redemption amount depends on the foreign exchange rate. The formula is:

$Y = \$100,000 + \$100,000 \times (1\text{-}105/F)$, where

EXHIBIT 14: HEAVEN AND HELL BOND CASH FLOW

Yr.	Bond Cash Flow	Interest Swap 1		Interest Swap 2	
		Rcvd.	Paid	Rcvd.	Paid
	$	$ Nominal	$100,000	$ Nominal	$ $70,000
0	$98,000				
1	($8,300)	$8,000	CP-30 bp.	$4,150	L-20 bp.
2	($8,300)	$8,000	CP-30 bp.	$4,150	L-20 bp.
3	($8,300)	$8,000	CP-30 bp.	$4,150	L-20 bp.
4	($8,300)	$8,000	CP-30 bp.	$4,150	L-20 bp.
5	($8,300)	$8,000	CP-30 bp.	$4,150	L-20 bp.
6	($8,300)	$8,000	CP-30 bp.	$4,150	L-20 bp.
7	($8,300)	$8,000	CP-30 bp.	$4,150	L-20 bp.
8	($8,300)	$8,000	CP-30 bp.	$4,150	L-20 bp.
9	($8,300)	$8,000	CP-30 bp.	$4,150	L-20 bp.
10	($8,300)	$8,000	CP-30 bp.	$34,150	L-20 bp.
10	-X				

$X=\$100,000+\$100,000 \times (1-105/F)$

	Final Cash Flow for the Issuer		Currency Swap 1		Ave. Forward FX	
	Rcvd.	Paid	Rcvd.	Paid	Rcvd.	Paid
			$ Nominal	Yen $70,000	Yen	$
0	$98,000.		—	—		
1		CP-30 bp.	L-20 bp.	¥488.25	¥488.25	$3,850
2		CP-30 bp.	L-20 bp.	¥488.25	¥488.25	$3,850
3		CP-30 bp.	L-20 bp.	¥488.25	¥488.25	$3,850
4		CP-30 bp.	L-20 bp.	¥488.25	¥488.25	$3,850
5		CP-30 bp.	L-20 bp.	¥488.25	¥488.25	$3,850
6		CP-30 bp.	L-20 bp.	¥488.25	¥488.25	$3,850
7		CP-30 bp.	L-20 bp.	¥488.25	¥488.25	$3,850
8		CP-30 bp.	L-20 bp.	¥488.25	¥488.25	$3,850
9		CP-30 bp.	L-20 bp.	¥488.25	¥488.25	$3,850
10		CP-30 bp.	L-20 bp.	¥488.25	¥488.25	$3,850
10		$100,000	$70,000	¥10,500		

Interest Swap 1: Nominal amount=$100 million. 10 years.
    Issuer receives fixed: 8.00% p.a. $8,000,000.
    Issuer pays floating: 1 month CP-30 b.p.

Interest Swap 2: Nominal amount=$70 million. 10 years.
    Issuer receives fixed: 8.78% p.a. However: Annually $4,150,000. After 10 yrs. $34,150,000.
    Issuer pays floating: 6 months $ LIBOR-20 b.p.

Currency Swap 1: Nominal amount=$70 million, ¥10.5 million. 10 years.
    Issuer receives floating $: 6 months $ LIBOR-20 b.p.
    Issuer pays fixed yen: 4.65% p.a. ¥488,250,000. @150 Yen/$.

Average Forward Exchange: 10 years
    Issuer buys ¥488.25 million, sells $3.85 million @126.82 ¥/$.

F = the spot rate of Yen/$ at the time of redemption.
Y = the amount to be redeemed.
If F = 105, Y = $100,000 and there is no capital gain or loss.
If F = 125, Y = $116,000 and there is a capital gain of $16,000.
If F = 85, Y = $76,471 and there is a capital loss of $23,529.

Investors take the risk of foreign exchange fluctuations. At the time of issuance, the forward exchange rate was close to Yen/$ = 105. Therefore, if an investor hedges the bond by a forward contract, he can get out of "hell" but he also loses "heaven," which means that the investor merely holds the 8.3% fixed dollar bond. However, investors may hedge when the foreign exchange rate is favorable to them during the ten-year period.

Of course, the price of the bond increases when the dollar increases, and the price of the bond decreases when the yen gets stronger.

Final Cash Flow for the Issuer. The final cost for an issuer equals the one-month commercial paper rate minus 30 basis points (excluding $2,000, which equals roughly 10 basis points in simple margin). This cash flow comes from the net cash flow of the bond and the swap and forward exchange contracts.

Interest Rate Swap 1 (Fixed $ Interest vs. CP Rate). Suppose the swap market is quoted (with no swap profit involved) as "8.14% s.a. = $ 1 month CP rate." This means that an 8.14% semiannual bond basis interest can be swapped to a one-month commercial paper rate. An 8.14% semiannual rate equals 8.30% annual rate. Therefore, an 8% annual rate equals one-month CP rate minus 30 basis points.

Interest Rate Swap 2 (Fixed $ vs. LIBOR). Suppose the swap market is quoted (with no swap profit involved) as "8.78% s.a. = $ six-month LIBOR." This means that an 8.78% semiannual bond basis interest can be swapped to a six-month LIBOR. An 8.78% semi-annual rate equals an 8.98% annual rate. Therefore, the 8.78% annual rate equals a six-month LIBOR minus 20 basis points. However the cash flow is adjusted to receive an additional $30,000 on maturity, which is the difference of $100,000 (principal of bond) and $70,000 (nominal amount of swap). The internal rate of return for this cash flow is 8.78%.

Currency Swap 1 (LIBOR$ vs. Fixed Yen). Suppose the swap market is quoted (with no swap profit involved) as "4.8% s.a. Yen = $ six-month LIBOR." This means that a 4.80% semiannual bond basis interest can be swapped to a six-month LIBOR. A 4.80% semiannual rate equals a 4.85% annual rate. Therefore, a 4.65% annual rate equals a six-month LIBOR minus 20 basis points.

The nominal amount of $70,000,000 is determined by the formula: (105/150) × $100,000,000 = $70,000,000. 105 is a forward exchange rate and 150 is the spot exchange rate of yen/dollar at the time of the initial transaction. Thus the nominal amount is $70,000,000, yen 10,500,000,000 and the conversion rate is 150 yen/dollar.

Average Forward Exchange. The forward exchange rate differs in accordance with the contract period. In theory, the higher interest currency is discounted against the lower currency in the forward exchange by the same percentage of interest differentials. For example, if the interest differential is 3.45% per annum (8.3% minus 4.85%), yen/$ forward is roughly 145, which is a 3.45% discount of 150. The longer the contract period the larger the discount rate. The average forward exchange is a package of forward exchange contracts that are artificially set at the same forward rate for cash flow purposes (in this case at 126.82). The IRR is set at the same (sometimes slightly better) rate as that calculated from the cash flows of the individual forward contracts.

SUMMARY

In this chapter, we first examined the stages in development of the Eurobond market in general, including the floating rate notes from about 1981 to late 1986, and the Euro Facilities, such as the NIF and RUF.

We then examined Japanese participation in this market through the issue of Gaisai. Gaisai are all bonds issued by Japanese entities outside the Japanese domestic bond market. They include Euroyen and Sushi bonds.

On the Euromarket, and in terms of currency, the Eurodollar is favored among Gaisai issues, and Euroyen bonds have been increasing. In terms of types of bonds, the share of warrant bonds has increased and that of convertible bonds has decreased.

Restrictions on Japanese eligibility requirements for Euroyen issues were relaxed starting in 1984. In 1985, the withholding tax was abolished for foreigners. More liberalization followed, including introduction of a rating system.

Sushi bonds are foreign currency bonds, and not Euroyen bonds, issued by Japanese entities. They are favored by Japanese life insurance companies, particularly for accounting reasons and because of MOF guidelines.

Third, we examined Euroyen bonds issued by foreigners. In 1984, the number of potential foreign issuers of Euroyen bonds increased and the control of issue volume was abolished following the Yen/Dollar Committee. The Japanese government had previously maintained strict control over all elements affecting monetary policy. Further liberalization included introduction of a ratings system and the appearance of innovative issues. By 1985, Euroyen bond issues surpassed Samurai issues. Euroyen bonds are chiefly purchased by Japanese for long-term investment, therefore, they are not concerned with liquidity. For other investors, liquidity is a problem.

Fourth, we examined the factors affecting the yield spread between Euroyen bonds and domestic yen bonds (JGBs and Samurai bonds), according to liquidity, credit risk, benchmark issues, accounting and taxation rules.

Finally, we examined the structure of major innovations in the Japanese bond market, chiefly in the Euroyen market. The two types of innovation are "high risk, high return" and "tax oriented." They may also be characterized as "index bonds" or "arranged bonds."

ENDNOTES

[1] *International Financing Review,* Issue 770, April 8, 1989, p. 33; Issue 757, Jan. 7, 1989, p. 38; Issue 705, Jan. 2, 1988, p. 31.

[2] Pierre Francois Champion and Jacques Trauman, *Euro Dollar Nyumon* (Mecanismes de change et marche des Euro-Dollars) (Tokyo: Nihon Keizai Shimbun, Inc., 1978).

[3] The London Interbank Offered Rate is a lending rate established by major banks in London. The interbank rate at 11:00 a.m. is used in rate fixing for most financial instruments based on LIBOR. Settlement is carried out two business days after trading. LIBOR is about 1/16% higher than the trading rate in the normal market. Other rates used as bases include: LIBID, which is 1/8% lower on the average than LIBOR, LI-MEAN, which is the midpoint between LIBOR and LIBID.

[4] This is a facility that guarantees the company the right to borrow from a group of banks up to some agreed maximum.

[5] This is a facility that guarantees the company the right to issue short-term Euronotes up to some agreed maximum.

[6] As cited in Aron Viner, *Inside Japanese Financial Markets* (Homewood, Ill.: Dow-Jones-Irwin, 1988), p. 174.

[7] *Nihon Keizai Shimbun* (Tokyo), January 19th, 1989.

[8] The holder of a warrant has a call option, the right to purchase a certain stock at the exercise price, which has been set at 102.5% of the closing price of the stock on the fixing day. The exercise price of the warrant is the same as that of all domestic issues in Japan.

[9] The holder of a convertible bond has a call option to exchange the bond for a certain stock at the conversion price, which is usually set at around 105% of the closing price of the stock on the fixing day. The foreign exchange rate for conversion is also fixed at the same time. The conversion price is the same as that of all domestic issues in Japan.

[10] In 1979, the current balance had changed to a deficit of $8.8 billion from a surplus of $16.6 billion in the previous year. In 1980, the deficit increased by almost $2 billion to $10.7 billion.

[11] Under the revised Foreign Exchange Law of 1980, investment in foreign bonds by Japanese residents is (in principle) liberalized. The direct purchase from nonresidents requires preliminary declaration to the MOF (Law 22-1), but if the purchase is done through designated securities houses, the transaction is free from regulation. Major insurance companies and investment trust companies are also designated as entities free from Law 22-1. However guidelines restrict their foreign investments.

[12] *International Financing Review,* Issue 769 (April 1, 1989), p. 32 and Issue 770 (April 8, 1989), p. 34.

[13] Interviews with Japanese securities houses in London.

[14] Viner, *Inside Japanese Financial Markets,* p. 185.

[15] Credit Suisse First Boston, *The CSFB Guide to the Yen Bond Markets.* (Chicago: Probus Publishing Company, 1988), p. 98.

[16] The redemption amount varies in accordance with the foreign exchange rate.

[17] This is an example of a foreign exchange "index" linked bonds. It was called a "duet" bond because not only the redemption amount (as in the dual currency bonds) but also the coupons vary in accordance with foreign exchange rates. The name "duet" is also derived from the dual potential for high profits (maybe losses)—high coupon income and capital gains.

[18] Nihon Keizai Shimbun, Inc., *Koshasai Ryutsu Shijo (Publicly-Offered Bonds: Secondary Market),* (Tokyo: Nihon Keizai Shimbun, Inc., 1987), p. 221. (This publication includes the first four examples of "high risk, high return" bonds, but does not include examples of duet bonds.)

[19] Takashi Ikuta and Katsunobu Katayama, *Shingata Saiken no Bunseki (The Analysis of Innovative Bonds)* (Tokyo: Kindai Sales-Sha Co., Ltd., 1988), p. 112.

CHAPTER 15

The Japanese Bond Futures Market

David H. Bessey
Associate, Portfolio Management Group
Prudential Insurance Company of America

Koji Kasai
Analyst
Daiwa Securities Company

Since its beginning in October 1985, the Japanese government bond (JGB) futures market has experienced tremendous growth. Its trading volume reached 4,000 trillion yen by March 1989, nearly 70% of that of the Japanese corporate, government, and municipal bond markets combined. Its yearly trading volume has surpassed the volume of the Chicago Board of Trade (CBOT) Treasury bond futures and the London International Financial Futures Exchange (LIFFE) gilt bond futures to become the largest futures market in the world.[1] The result has been improved liquidity and efficiency in one of the world's most important bond markets.

A futures transaction is a contract in which a party agrees to buy (or sell) a given instrument for a certain price at a predetermined future date. In the Japanese government bond (JGB) market, futures are traded on both the long-term government bond, with a maturity of 10 years, and the 20-year maturity super-long bond. Futures trading on the super-long bond began in July 1988 in Tokyo, and it is anticipated that these contracts will be listed on the Chicago Board of Trade in 1989.

Low margin requirements make the JGB futures markets attractive to both speculators and large bond-holding institutions. Speculators use the highly leveraged nature of futures contracts to profit from inefficiencies in the market and to make interest rate bets. Large institutions use the futures contracts as an inexpensive way to adjust the duration of their portfolios and to hedge against interest rate risk.

JGB futures are traded in a highly standardized system on the Tokyo Stock Exchange (TSE). Settlement or termination dates occur once per quarter. While investors can either hold contracts until the settlement date or trade them in the interim period, in practice over 99% of all positions are closed through trading prior to the settlement date.

PARTICIPANTS

By regulation, there are four classes of participants in the JGB futures market. Each class has different legal rights and obligations associated with it.[2]

The first class of participants are Tokyo Stock Exchange members. These organizations can invest in bond futures directly and can also act as brokers for futures customers. There were 92 member companies in August 1987.

The second class consists of securities companies that are not members of the TSE. While these companies can invest directly in bond futures contracts without the assistance of an exchange member, they can only broker futures contracts indirectly through member companies.

The third class is comprised of specific banks. These banks can also invest in bond futures directly, but they are prohibited from acting as brokers without permission. Participants in this class are also known as "special participants." There were 134 special participants in August 1987.

The fourth class of participants are investors. These are foreign and domestic corporations, individuals, investment trusts, insurance companies, etc., that can invest only through securities firms or specific participants who have brokerage rights.

Relative Importance of Classes

Since its inception, the futures market has been dominated by Japanese securities companies, banks, and other financial institutions. In aggregate, these investors have accounted for more than 90% of the trading volume since 1985. The relative importance of the players within this group has changed significantly over the past several years, however. Securities companies accounted for about 56% of all trading volume in 1985, but only 33% in 1988. Similarly, trading volume of corporations declined from 10% of total volume in 1985 to 2% in 1988. On the other hand, banks and insurance companies became increasingly important players in that period. Banks increased their share of trading volume from 24% in 1985 to 58% in 1988, while that of insurance companies increased from 0.1% to 0.9%.[3]

Although Japanese financial institutions have been the predominant players in the futures market, Japanese corporations have also had a large impact. In 1987, public attention was focused on "zaitech," the practice of speculating on the JGB bond and futures market with corporate funds.[4] Many corporations were placing large trades in the futures market, betting on a fall in interest rates and a rise in bond prices. The profits from this strategy were being used to augment faltering corporate incomes. This flow of funds contributed significantly to the high price-levels associated with the JGB cash and futures markets in early 1987. When the JGB market turned bearish in September of 1987, many corporations found themselves with substantial losses and fled the market. This steepened the already precipitous decline.

As of 1988, foreign investors accounted for only approximately 1% of the JGB futures trading volume.[5]

BENEFITS OF THE BOND FUTURES MARKET

The benefits of the introduction of the bond futures market can be split into three primary categories: 1) increased ease of portfolio management, 2) improved market liquidity, and 3) increased information available regarding price trends in the bond market.

The most prominent benefit of the introduction of the futures market is ease of portfolio management. By connecting investors who have opposing market positions and expectations, the futures market provides an inexpensive and efficient means of adjusting the interest risk exposure of currently held portfolios or the cost of future liabilities. Hedging in the futures market is also attractive because the bid/ask spreads are less than those found in the JGB market. Finally, the futures market provides an investor holding particular beliefs on the direction of interest rates with an inexpensive means of capitalizing on that view. This was particularly difficult to achieve prior to the introduction of the futures market due to problems associated with short selling in the JGB market.

A second advantage of the futures market has been increased liquidity of the JGB market. Initially, there was concern that the futures market would siphon funds away from JGBs, thereby making the bond market less liquid. Current research indicates that this fear was not substantiated. On the contrary, most researchers believe that by providing opportunities for arbitrage trading, the futures market has actually increased bond liquidity and reduced bid/ask spreads.[6] This view is further supported by the low margin required for futures contracts; it is difficult to see how this relatively small cash volume could result in a significant outflow of cash from the JGB market. It is also argued that the futures market increased the liquidity of the bond market by giving investors new channels for buying and selling bond positions.

The other often cited benefit of the futures market is that the price of each futures contract provides additional information to the market, thereby increasing market efficiency. Investors in the futures market are essentially betting on the price movement of bonds. Although individual expectations may vary widely, the price of the futures contract is the "best guess" of the aggregated market regarding future price movements. The availability of this information to all market participants increases market competition and helps to drive out excess profit.

TRADING MECHANICS

The JGB futures contracts are based upon fictional 10-year long-term or 20-year super-long term government bonds. These "standard" bonds each have a face value of 100 million yen and a coupon of 6%. Fictional rather than actual bonds were chosen to conform to the format used in other financial futures markets. This standardization made the contracts easier to understand and increased market acceptance and liquidity. Fictional bonds also had the advantage in terms of continuity of a term and coupon which did not change over time or issue.

The JGB was chosen as the underlying instrument for a number of reasons. First, these bonds are the most widely traded in Japan and had the broadest appeal for hedging and speculation. Second, these bonds are considered to be risk-free because they are issued by the Japanese government. Finally, high quality information regarding these bonds is available continually to a broad spectrum of investors.

Trading

Settlement days are the 20th of March, June, September, and December. The longest tradable term is one year and three months, giving an investor a choice between five potential delivery dates. The settlement dates are timed to coincide with the typical JGB coupon payment dates. The three month interval between settlement dates corresponds to the usual term of other Japanese short-term financial instruments, such as bond and interest rate forward contracts.

The schedule of delivery dates is quite different from that of the CBOT Treasury bond futures market. The longest tradable term at the CBOT is two years and nine months, considerably longer than that of the JGB futures. While the CBOT settlement dates fall in the same months as the JGB futures, CBOT short investors (i.e., investors who are short the futures) have the option of choosing any business day in those months as the settlement date. Finally, a CBOT short investor can also inform the exchange of his intent to deliver after the close of trading when the contract price has been fixed. (This is the so-called "wild card" option.) These delivery options make the timing of CBOT contract settlement much less predictable than that of the JGB futures market.

Orders at the TSE futures market are processed differently than the open outcry system at the CBOT. Investors at the TSE place their futures orders through exchange members, who then transfer these orders to the trading floor by telephone. On the trading floor, either trading clerks from the securities firm or independent intermediate clerks "marry" the outstanding orders. A contract is completed when bid and ask quotes are in accordance, and priority of completion is governed by a standard protocol. The first priority is based on price—the lowest price of selling and the highest price of buying have the first priority to be transacted. The second priority is according to the time that the order was placed. If there are several orders of the same price, the earliest placed order has priority.

Futures trading occurs from 9 a.m. to 11 a.m. and from 1 p.m. to 3 p.m. Tokyo time, with a trading unit of 100 million yen face value. The contracts trade on price ticks of 1/100 yen (one sen) per 100 yen face value. Daily price fluctuations for the 10-year contract are limited to plus or minus two yen per 100 yen face value from the previous day's closing price, or plus or minus three yen for the 20-year bond. In the event of particularly active trading, the Tokyo Stock Exchange has broad authority to regulate the market. This authority includes the ability to 1) advance the date to deposit additional margin money 2) increase the margin rate, 3) decrease the daily price limit, and, in extreme cases, 4) regulate or prohibit trading.

The last trading day for a JGB futures contract is nine business days before the settlement date. For example, an investor wanting to offset his position prior to the March 20, 1989 settlement date would need to perform the appropriate trade on or before March 7, 1989. Any open contract position remaining after the last trading day would be settled according to procedures described later in this section.

Margin Requirements and Marking-to-Market

In a futures contract, no money is exchanged between the buyer and seller at contract initiation. Any change in the contract value after this point, however, results in a gain for one party and an equivalent loss for the other. In both the TSE and the CBOT, the gain or loss is calculated daily in a process known as "marking to the market." In each market, payment must be made on a daily basis to settle these gains and losses. To ensure that the parties will be able to fulfill their obligations under the contract, each is required to deposit a given amount of "margin" with a broker.

The margin requirements for the JGB futures contract are significantly different than those for the CBOT Treasury bond futures contract. In the case of the CBOT contract, speculators must deposit an "initial margin" of $2,000 per contract with a securities company when opening a position.[7] These deposits can be in interest bearing securities. As long as the losses from marking to the market do not reduce the account balance below the $1,500 maintenance margin established by the exchange, no additional margin is required. If the losses reduce the margin below the maintenance margin, however, the investor must make cash deposits (variation margin) sufficient to restore the margin account to the initial margin level. Investors receive gains only when the value of those gains exceeds the initial margin.

In contrast, investors in a 10-year JGB futures contract are required to deposit with a broker an initial margin of either a) 3% of the contract face value, or b) six million yen, whichever is greater. This deposit must be made by noon of the third day after the contract is initiated. One percent or more of this margin (or at least 1 million yen) must be in cash, while the remainder may be in securities. The types of acceptable securities and their valuation rates are presented in Exhibit 1.

If losses exceed 1% of the face value of a JGB futures contract, additional margin, known as "Oisho," must be deposited with a securities broker. This additional margin must be deposited by noon of the third day after the shortage occurs. Oisho is roughly equivalent to variation margin in the CBOT Treasury bond futures contract, but there are some important differences. First of all, with the CBOT contract, the profit or loss is allocated immediately through a clearing corporation, and the three-day lag period for settlement does not exist. Secondly, unlike the situation with the CBOT contract, a JGB futures investor cannot receive any gains until he makes an offsetting trade. These untapped gains are not available to be used as margin.

EXHIBIT 1: REGULATIONS REGARDING USE OF SECURITIES FOR MARGIN REQUIREMENTS

Substitution Securities	Valuation Rate
Stock listed on a Japanese stock exchange	70%
Stock registered with the Japanese Securities Association	60%
Government Bond	95%
Municipal Bond (Public Issue)	85%
Bond issued by a corporation under special law	
Government guaranteed bond	90%
Other	85%
Bond issued by issuer of stock listed on a Japanese stock exchange (Public Issue)	
Convertible or Warrant bond	80%
Other bond	85%
Bond Issued by NTT	85%
Foreign government bond and foreign municipal bond listed on a Japanese stock exchange	85%
Yen denominated bonds issued by International Bank for Reconstruction and Development, and the Asian Development Bank	90%
Other yen denominated bonds listed on a Japanese stock exchange issued by foreign corporations	85%
Beneficial securities of securities investment trust	
Bond Investment Trust	85%
Other Investment Trust	70%

For the 20-year JGB contract, the initial margin requirement is 4.5% of the traded face value, and Oisho is due if losses exceed 1.5% of the face value. All other rules governing margin requirements are the same as for the 10-year bond contract.

Illustration of Margin Requirements. Suppose that an investor buys a 10-year JGB futures contract with a face value of 300 million yen for a contract price of 297. The investor would need to deposit margin equal to the greater of

$$3\% \times 300 \text{ million} = 9 \text{ million yen } or \text{ 6 million yen.}$$

Obviously, the required deposit would be nine million yen, and at least three million (1% of face value) of that would need to be in cash. Now, suppose that the next day, the contract price fell to 291 million yen. The investor would be forced to pay Oisho calculated as follows:

$$(6/300 - 1\%) \times 300 \text{ million yen} = 3 \text{ million yen.}$$

This would be due by noon of the third business day after the change occurred. Only one third of this must be in cash. The investor would not receive any gains until he makes an offsetting trade. Exhibit 2 provides a detailed explanation of margin requirement calculations.

Margins for Securities Firms. The margin requirements for securities houses are somewhat different from those for individual investors. First, initial margin of two million yen per 100 million yen face value is deposited with the exchange. Second, all losses and gains are settled on a daily basis, with no minimum threshold before profits or losses are incurred. Settlement occurs on the fourth business day after the change.

Settlement and Deliverable Bonds

As discussed earlier, a futures position can be settled by either taking an offsetting position, or by delivering or accepting securities on the settlement day.

In the case of an offsetting position, the investor will receive or pay the outstanding gains or losses on the fourth business day after the offsetting contract is completed. The investor's margin would also be returned on that day. As previously discussed, the last day to settle a contract is nine business days prior to the settlement date.

Example of Offsetting Settlement. A company bought 6-month bond futures whose face value was 2 billion yen at a price of 102.65 and sold them at a price of 103.77 20 days later. The profit from this transaction would be

$$(103.77 - 102.65) \times 2 \text{ billion yen} \times 1/100 = 22.400 \text{ million yen.}$$

EXHIBIT 2: MARGIN REQUIREMENT CALCULATION

Definitions

$F10$ = Face value of 10-year JGB
$F20$ = Face value of 20-year JGB
IC = Initial cash required for contract
IM = Initial margin required for contract
TC = Total cash as defined below
TM = Total margin as defined below

1) Let total cash and total margin be defined as:

$$TC = IC - \text{loss resulting from valuation of futures contract}$$
and
$$TM = IM - \text{loss resulting from valuation of futures contract}$$

Also let A and B be defined as follows:

$$A = (F10 \times 0.03) + (F20 \times 0.045) - TM$$
and
$$B = (F10 \times 0.01) + (F20 \times 0.015) - TC$$

2) Investors are required to deposit additional funds when either of the following cases occurs:

   a) $A \geq (F10 \times 0.01) + (F20 \times 0.015)$
   or
   b) $B \geq (F10 \times 0.01) + (F20 \times 0.015)$

3) If additional variation margin is required, the amount is determined by the following:

   a) If both 2(a) and 2(b) occur, additional required margin is:

   Cash = B   Securities = A – B

   b) If 2(a) occurs, the additional required margin is:

If B < 0	If B ≥ 0
Cash = 0	Cash = 0
Securities = A – B	Securities = A

   c) If 2(b) occurs, the additional required margin is:

If A < 0	If A ≥ 0
Cash = B	Cash = B
Should get back Securities = B – A if offset with trade	Should get back Securities = B if offset with trade

Delivery. If an investor holds his position for settlement, he must deliver bonds or money depending on whether the futures position is short or long, respectively. For the investor who is short a futures position, an acceptable bond must be chosen for delivery. For a 10-year JGB futures contract, the deliverable must be a Japanese government bond listed on the TSE with a face value of 100 million yen and a remaining life of between 7 and 11 years on the settlement day. The requirements are identical for the 20-year futures contract except the remaining life must be between 15 and 21 years. There is no limitation regarding the coupon rate.

The delivery price is adjusted for varying coupon rates and terms to maturity by using a conversion factor established by the exchange. This factor, which adjusts the price of the bond to correspond with a semiannual compound yield of 6% on the date of delivery, can be calculated from the following equation.[8]

$$CF = \frac{c/6 \times [(1 + 6/100 \times 1/2)^n - 1] + 1}{(1 + 6/100 \times 1/2)^{n - a/6}} - c/100 \times a/12$$

where
CF = conversion factor
c = coupon rate of the deliverable bond
n = number of coupon payments of the deliverable bond until maturity
a = number of months since the previous coupon payment.

Figures below the seventh decimal place are omitted. Tables of conversion factors for various issues and delivery dates may be obtained from securities dealers. A sample table is included in the appendix.

The delivery price for contracts between customers and member companies is based on the following formula:

$$\frac{\text{Delivery}}{\text{Price}} = (STD \times CF + \text{contract price} - STD) \times \frac{\text{bond}}{\text{face}} \times .01 \atop \text{value}$$
$$+ \text{accrued interest}$$

where

STD = the final settlement price of the standard bond on the last tradable day (9th business day prior to settlement date).

The reader is referred to the appendix for a more detailed explanation of the conversion factors and their use.

Accrued Interest. No accrued interest is paid by investors if they offset their futures position before the settlement date. If a contract is settled by delivery, however, the interest accrued since the previous coupon payment must accompany the deliverable bond. If the bond coupon date and the settlement date coincide, the bond is treated as ex-interest and no accrued interest is due. Taxation of accrued interest is described in a later section.

Illustration of Delivery Price Calculation. To illustrate the calculation of the delivery price, suppose that a tax-free corporation settled its position by delivering 7% coupon bonds with a value of 2 billion yen and a remaining life of 7 years and 3 months for the December 20th settlement date. The coupon payment date was 3 months prior to the settlement date, indicating that 3 months accrued coupon interest will be due to the seller. The contract price was 102.63 and the last settlement price was 102.67.

The first step is to calculate the conversion factor.

$$CF = \frac{7/6 \times [(1 + 6/100 \times 1/2)^{15} - 1] + 1}{(1 + 6/100 \times 1/2)^{15 - 3/6}} - 7/100 \times 3/12$$

$$= 1.057967$$

The investor will receive the following amount on December 20:

$$\begin{array}{c} \text{delivery} \\ \text{price} \end{array} = [102.67 \times 1.057967 + (102.63 - 102.67)] \\ \times 2 \text{ billion yen} \times 1/100$$

$$+ [(7 \times 90/365)] \times 2 \text{ billion yen} \times .01$$
$$= 2,206,148,547 \text{ yen}.$$

Cheapest to Deliver. At settlement, the seller of a futures contract has an incentive to choose for delivery the cheapest security that fulfills the exchange requirements. The cheapest to deliver is found by determining the bond that gives the minimum value to the following:

$$\begin{matrix} \text{cost to} \\ \text{deliver} \end{matrix} = \begin{matrix} \text{purchase price} \\ \text{of deliverable} \\ \text{bond} \end{matrix} - \begin{matrix} \text{futures} \\ \text{settlement} \\ \text{price} \end{matrix} \times \begin{matrix} \text{conversion} \\ \text{factor} \end{matrix}$$

In the CBOT futures market, the cheapest bond to deliver is almost always presented to fulfill the short position. There is greater uncertainty associated with the delivered bond in the JGB futures market, however. This is primarily due to the fact that over 90% of the trading in the JGB market is performed with a single bond, known as the benchmark. Other JGB issues are thinly traded and illiquid, and the theoretical cheapest bond to deliver may be unavailable or in short supply. For this reason, firms may be forced to settle with more expensive bonds that are currently in inventory. For many firms, this is a strong incentive to close short positions prior to the settlement date.[9]

Transactions and Income Taxes

Bourse Tax. JGB futures transactions that are settled prior to the delivery date are subject to a Bourse tax of 1/100,000 of the traded amount. This is paid by the buyer and seller of a position; thus, if an investor establishes a position and then offsets it later, a bourse tax of 2/100,000 will be levied. When a position is settled by delivery, however, the transaction is subject to the Securities Transaction Tax of 3/100,000 of the traded value.[10]

Income Tax. Profits realized from futures trading are taxed at the applicable rate for the corporation or individual. The profits taxed in this manner are the gains or losses associated with the change in the settlement price only; the accrued interest is taxed under a different method as described below.

Withholding Tax on Accrued Interest. Accrued interest gained by taxable investors with short futures positions is subject to a withholding tax of 20% at settlement. This withholding tax is constant for foreign investors regardless of any taxation treaties with Japan; the result is that accrued interest is taxed twice for most foreign investors settling JGB futures contracts.[11] Withholding tax may also be levied on nontaxable Japanese investors under certain circumstances detailed below. Exhibit 3 presents a summary of taxes on accrued interest for different bonds and investors.

To preserve their tax-free status, corporations and financial institutions legally specified to be free from withholding tax must deliver only registered or book entry bonds. Delivery of bearer bonds will always result in payment of withholding tax, regardless of the tax status of the holder. Taxable corporations and individuals have no restrictions regarding the types of bonds that they can deliver.

However, tax-free investors may be subject to withholding tax even with delivery of registered or book entry bonds. When the number of sellers and buyers with a given tax status do not coincide, the exchange must partition the benefits of being nontaxable. The process for doing this is as follows. Stock exchange members report buying and selling volumes to the exchange, separating the taxable and nontaxable elements of each. The exchange sums those positions,

EXHIBIT 3: TAXES ON ACCRUED INTEREST BASED ON TYPE OF INVESTOR AND FORM OF OWNERSHIP FOR JGB FUTURES CONTRACTS

	Form of ownership		
	Bearer	Registered	Book Entry
Corporation/ Individual	Withholding Tax	Withholding Tax	Withholding Tax
Tax-Free Corporation	Withholding Tax	No Withholding Tax	No Withholding Tax
Specified Financial Institution	Withholding Tax	No Withholding Tax	No Withholding Tax

and calculates for reporting purposes 1) the post-tax accrued interest that will be delivered to all taxable investors, and 2) the accrued interest to be delivered to all tax-free investors. If there is a mismatch between the number of sellers and buyers with tax-free situations, then there is in effect delivery of bonds between taxable and tax-free investors. The latter's transactions are subject to the withholding tax on accrued interest. The net effect is that some tax-free investors are treated as taxable; the unlucky groups are chosen in a lottery system.[12]

Process of Delivery

Immediately following the completion of trading, exchange members calculate and report the volume of unsettled positions (sorted by tax status) to the exchange. The exchange then draws lots to determine which tax-free positions will be treated as taxable. Once this has been accomplished, sellers choose the bonds to be transferred and complete the required paperwork to change ownership. Note that a tax-free investor whose settlement remained untaxed is likely to transfer a registered or book entry bond, while the same investor who became taxed as the result of the lottery may choose to deliver a bearer bond. The members report the types of bonds to be delivered to the exchange, and finally, on the settlement date, money or bonds are delivered to the customers.

Brokerage Fees

Brokerage fees on JGB futures trades are fixed. In 1989, these fees were as follows:

face value (yen million)	brokerage fee
face value ≤ 500	0.0150% × face value
500 < face value ≤ 1,000	0.0100% × face value + 25,000 yen
1,000 < face value ≤ 5,000	0.0050% × face value + 75,000 yen
face value > 5,000	0.0025% × face value + 200,000 yen

The above prices are for single trades and should be doubled to calculate round trip costs.[13]

DETERMINANTS OF BOND FUTURES PRICING

The theoretical price of a futures contract is a function of the cash market bond price and the cost of carry. The latter is equal to the difference between the cost of financing a position to the delivery date and the cash yield on the bond over the same period. In an ideal market, arbitrage should keep the actual futures price from deviating from the theoretical futures price. In the JGB and other futures markets, however, there is substantial deviation between actual and theoretical futures prices. In this section we will discuss the theoretical price of a futures contract and then explain the reasons for the divergence of actual JGB futures prices from their theoretical prices.

Theoretical Price

The payout characteristics of a futures position can be synthetically replicated using the cash market. The pricing of the futures market should therefore be governed by the arbitrage relationship between these two markets. This relationship is given by the following equation:[14]

$$F = C \times (1 + i - y)$$

where
F   =   theoretical futures price
C   =   cash price (price of deliverable bond ÷ conversion factor)
i   =   financing rate for the contract period
y   =   cash yield on bond during the contract period.

For example, assume that the cheapest bond to deliver on a futures contract with a delivery date in four months has a cash yield of 7%, a conversion factor of 1.076002, and is priced at 104.000 yen. Furthermore, assume that the bond purchaser can borrow at an interest rate of 5.5%. The theoretical price for this contract would be

$$F = 104.000 \div 1.076002 \times [1 + (0.055 \times 4/12) - (0.07 \times 4/12)]$$
$$= 99.170 \text{ yen}$$

If the actual futures price is greater than 99.170 yen, arbitrage profits could be earned by selling the futures contract, buying

104.000 × 1.076002 = 99.654 yen of deliverable bonds, and borrowing the purchase price. If the actual futures price is less than the theoretical futures price, the arbitrage would call for buying the futures, shorting the cash bond, and investing the proceeds from the short sale.

Reasons for the Divergence between Actual and Theoretical Futures Price

The divergence of the JGB futures price from its theoretical value occurs for a number of reasons, some of which are unique to the Japanese market and some of which are common to other futures markets.

The most important and predictable effect arises from the difficulty in shorting securities in the Japanese bond market. As a result of this difficulty, the futures market generally trades at a discount to its theoretical value. The underlying rationale for this can be found in the arbitrage relationships discussed above. If futures are selling at a premium to their theoretical value, an investor will sell futures and buy JGBs with borrowed money to lock in an arbitrage profit. The theoretical value therefore tends to act as an upper limit on futures pricing. If, however, the futures are selling at a discount to their theoretical value, an arbitrage profit can only be realized by shorting the JGB and buying futures. The transactions costs associated with shorting make this arbitrage quite difficult to perform. As a result, futures have traded at implied yields which have traditionally been 5 to 40 basis points higher than non-benchmark JGBs.[15] The only times when this relationship has broken down have been during periods of uncertainty associated with the changing of the benchmark bond. At these times, the liquidity of the JGB market decreased while that of the futures market was constant, resulting in futures briefly trading at a premium.[16]

Theoretical and market prices also diverge due to uncertainty regarding the deliverable bond. The choice of bond to be delivered at settlement is the prerogative of the seller. While the seller will typically try to choose the cheapest bond to deliver, the illiquidity of non-benchmark JGBs often makes acquisition and delivery of the cheapest bond difficult.[17] In addition, the cheapest to deliver may change over time.

Finally, transaction costs, margin requirements, and differences in borrowing and lending rates also drive the futures market from its theoretical value. The direction of these effects on price varies.[18]

INVESTMENT STRATEGIES EMPLOYING FUTURES

Participants in the JGB futures market typically use the contract for one of four purposes: arbitrage, spread or basis trading, hedging, or speculation.

Arbitrage

In a pure arbitrage, investors attempt to profit from imperfections in the pricing of futures contracts. A principal target of arbitrage trading is the discrepancy in pricing between the cash market and theoretical JGB futures prices. Examples of how this trade can be implemented are presented below. While these trades are identical in principle to those performed at the CBOT, there is one important difference: it is much more difficult in the Japanese market to derive arbitrage profits when futures are trading at a discount to their theoretical price. This will also be illustrated with the examples.

Suppose that there is a 10-year JGB with a cash yield of 6.1%, a conversion factor of 1.007154, and a current price of 100.000 yen. Further, assume that the next coupon date is four months from now, and that the current cost of borrowing and lending is 6%. The theoretical price of a futures contract with a four month delivery date is

$$F = 100.000 \div 1.0071549$$

$$\times [1 + (0.06 \times 4/12) - (0.061 \times 4/12)]$$

$$= 99.257 \text{ yen.}$$

But suppose that this contract is selling for 99.300 yen. To profit from this mispricing, the investor should (1) sell the futures contract for 99.300 yen (2) borrow 100.000 yen for four months at 6% per year and (3) use the borrowed money to purchase bonds in the cash market. Ignoring margin, no initial money would be required to complete this strategy since the futures contract does not require any funding and the purchase and borrowing exactly offset each other. Four months later, the bond would be delivered to settle the futures position and the loan would be paid off using the proceeds of the futures sale. The profit before transactions costs from this operation would be 0.043 yen per 100 yen as shown below:

Proceeds from settlement of
futures contract (delivering the bonds)
99.300 × 1.007154   100.010 yen

Accrued interest paid by
buyer at settlement
4/12 × 6.1% × 100.000   2.033 yen

Repayment of the principal
of the loan   −100.000 yen

Interest payment
4/12 × 6.0% × 100.000   −2.000 yen

Profit before transaction costs   0.043 yen

Now, assume that the conditions outlined above exist, except that the four month futures price is 99.200 yen. A strategy to capture arbitrage profit would be to (1) buy the futures contract at 99.222, (2) short 100.000 worth of bonds in the cash market, and (3) lend the proceeds at 6% (for simplicity assume equal lending and borrowing rates). The resulting profit before transactions costs will again be 0.058 yen per 100 yen, as shown below:

Proceeds from settlement of
futures contract (price paid
for purchase of bond)
99.200 × 1.007154   −99.909 yen

Accrued interest paid to
seller at settlement
4/12 × 6.1% × 100.614 million   −2.033 yen

Proceeds received from repayment of loan principal	100.000 yen
Interest earned 4/12 × 6% × 100.715 million	2.000 yen
Profit before transactions costs	0.058 yen

The second transaction has considerably more risk associated with it than the first for several reasons. The first reason is the previously discussed difficulty with shorting JGBs which makes this trade quite costly. Second, the seller of the futures contract has the right to choose the bonds delivered, and thus the shorted bonds may not be identical to those received at settlement. An investor's profit may turn into a loss due to the relative movement of the bond prices. For these reasons, arbitrage using long bonds and short futures contracts is much more prevalent in Japan than the second alternative.[19]

Basis and Spread Trading

Basis and spread trading are other techniques used by investors to take advantage of perceived imperfections in futures pricing. They are sometimes referred to as arbitrage transactions in the sense that they involve simultaneous long and short positions. However, unlike a pure arbitrage, no profit is locked-in.

Basis Trading. The basis of a futures contract is the difference between the price of a futures contract and the cash price of the deliverable bonds. If investors believe that the basis of a given contract is temporarily too high or low, they can attempt to profit by buying the cheaper security (bond or futures contract) and selling the other. This is known as a basis trade.

Unlike the situation at the CBOT where basis trades can be performed on numerous bonds, basis trading in the JGB futures market is confined to the heavily traded "benchmark" bond.[20] This situation arises from the illiquidity of other JGBs; even if investors were able to identify abnormal basis spreads in non-benchmark issues, the costs of accumulating and liquidating the bonds would wipe out any profit. Also, shorting the benchmark is dramatically less costly than shorting other issues.

While arbitrage and basis trading appear similar at first glance, they are really quite different. Investors in arbitrage focus on the differences between actual and theoretical futures prices, while basis traders look at the relative prices of bonds and futures. Whereas arbitrage trading involves nearly riskless exploitation of market imperfections, basis trading represents a riskier bet that the basis of an individual bond will change during the holding period. Another difference is that, unlike typical arbitrage trading, basis traders focus on the benchmark bond rather than on the cheapest to deliver.

To illustrate basis trading, suppose that on March 8th the price of the benchmark issue is 105.30 yen and the price of the futures is 101.90 yen. The basis is therefore 3.40 yen. If the average basis has historically been 2.90 yen, an investor might conclude that the current basis on the benchmark is too high. To profit from this belief, the investor would sell the bond of 100 million yen face value and buy a 100 million yen futures contract. If on March 14th, the bond price has changed to 105.10 yen and the futures price has become 102.2 yen, the basis has dropped to the 2.90 average. The investor would then buy back the bond and sell the futures contract. The result would be a profit, before transactions costs, of 0.5 million yen as shown below:

Proceeds from settlement of futures contract (102.2 - 101.90) × 100 million yen/100	0.3 million yen
Proceeds from trading of bonds (105.3 - 105.1) × 100 million yen/100	0.2 million yen
Profit before transactions costs	0.5 million yen

Calendar Spread Trading. This is a strategy for taking advantage of the difference between prices of futures with different settlement dates. It is particularly effective when the slope of the yield curve is expected to change significantly in a predictable direction. Calendar spread trading is not common in the JGB futures market because nearly all trading is in the near settlement date. Also, the yen money market is not sufficiently developed to efficiently carry out the necessary borrowing and lending.[21]

To illustrate the calendar spread strategy, assume that on March 8th the price of a futures contract with a June 20th settlement date is 102.90, while the same contract with a December 20th settlement date is 103.00. Further, assume that the yield curve is such that the theoretical spread between the prices of these two contracts is 0.20. It therefore appears that the June 20th contract is overpriced with respect to the December 20th contract, and a profit could potentially be made by purchasing the December contact and shorting the June contract, which is called a bull spread.

Now, suppose that on May 14th the spread between the December and June contracts has returned to the theoretical level of 0.20, with the June contract priced at 102.95 and the December at 103.15. The trade could be reversed and the following profit would result:

From June contract	102.90 – 102.95	= - 0.05
From December contract	- 103.00 + 103.15	= 0.15
Profit before transactions costs		0.10

Note that the above situation represents an expected steepening of the yield curve, or a bullish spread. Whenever this situation can be predicted, the investor will benefit from shorting the distant contract and purchasing the near term contract. When the yield curve steepens, the transaction can be reversed to lock in a profit. Conversely, if the spread between two futures prices is expected to become narrow (bear spread), the opposite strategy should be taken.

Spread trading is riskier than arbitrage or basis trading, as the transaction's profitability depends entirely upon correct forecasting of the yield curve. Furthermore, actual futures prices tend to vary from theoretical prices, especially when demand is high for futures with a particular settlement date. Thus, even if the yield curve is accurately forecasted, the futures price may not behave as expected. A final wrinkle associated with spread trading is that each contract is bought or sold twice. This results in double transactions costs as compared to arbitrage or basis trading.

Hedging

Hedging is a method of reducing the risk associated with bond price fluctuations by taking an offsetting position in the futures market. For example, an investor holding a long bond position scheduled for liquidation in two months can hedge the risk of a bond price decline (i.e., rise in interest rates) by selling futures contracts. Similarly, a corporation planning to issue bonds in six months can hedge against an interest rate rise by selling futures contracts.

Here we will present an overview of the mechanics of hedging in the JGB futures market. The hedge construction methods described below are common to both the JGB and CBOT futures markets.

Caution is required when hedging non-benchmark bonds in the Japanese market, however. Due to the illiquidity of non-benchmark issues, most traders use the difference in price between the benchmark bond and the futures market for basis calculations. The pricing of the futures and benchmark are therefore closely related. The volatility of the yield spread between the benchmark and non- benchmark bonds may be quite high, however, increasing the basis risk for the hedge.[22] Basis risk is discussed in more detail below.

Basis Risk and Cross Hedge Risk. A perfect hedge is impossible to achieve under most circumstances, because an economic event may affect the cash market and the futures market differently. This is known as *basis risk*.

To illustrate basis risk, suppose that an investor is planning to buy 100 million yen of the cheapest to deliver JGB in 2 months, and this investor is concerned that this bond will increase in price over that period. The investor might hedge the transaction by buying a bond futures contract. Assume that the cash price of the bond is 102.50 yen and the nearest futures contract is priced at 101.10, a basis of 1.4 yen. Also assume that the conversion factor for this JGB is one.

After two months, the bond and futures prices have risen to 103.10 and 101.60 yen, respectively. Note that the basis of the futures has risen from 1.40 to 1.50. To close out the position, the investor would now buy the bond and sell the futures contract, with the following result:

From the futures market

(101.60 − 101.10) × 100 million yen/100   = 500,000 yen

From the cash bond market

(102.50 − 103.10) × 100 million yen/100   = -600,000 yen

Total loss before transactions costs   -100,000 yen

The change in basis resulted in a loss of 100,000 yen. If the position had not been hedged, however, the loss would have been 600,000 yen. Thus hedging was beneficial even though it was imperfect.

Cross-hedge risk is another potential source of error in hedging with JGB futures. This risk results from the use of JGB futures to hedge either other types of securities (corporate bonds, etc.) or JGBs that are not the cheapest to deliver. If the cheapest to deliver and the security to be hedged do not move together, the hedge may experience additional losses over the basis loss. Samurai bonds (yen-denominated bonds issued by foreign borrowers) are a good example of a security that might be difficult to hedge for this reason; the yield spread between JGB and Samurai bonds has fluctuated from 0 to 120 basis points in the 1980s.[23]

Constructing the Hedge. Some of the hazards associated with hedging using JGB futures should be clear from the discussion above. Under perfect circumstances, cash positions in a given security would be hedged with futures contracts on the same security, and the futures contracts would expire on the date the hedge is to be lifted. Unfortunately, the expiration dates and types of securities underlying futures contracts are limited, and basis and cross hedge risk is sometimes difficult to avoid. The exposure to these risks can be mitigated, however, through careful construction of the hedge.[24]

An ideal hedge using futures would have the characteristic that the price change of the hedging vehicle (the futures contract) would be exactly the opposite of the cash market bond to be hedged. This is complicated by two factors. First, for a given change in yield, the price volatility of the cash bond to be hedged will not necessarily equal the price volatility of the deliverable bond underlying the futures contract. Second, the factors that result in a change in the yield of the security to be hedged may have a very different effect on the deliverable security. The following relationship takes these two factors into account:

price change of bond to be hedged =

price change of deliverable security ×

$$\frac{\text{price volatility of bond to be hedged}}{\text{price volatility of deliverable bond}}$$

The last ratio is called the hedge ratio (HR). Since the price value of a basis point (PVBP) is a measure of price volatility, the hedge ratio can be rewritten as follows:[25]

$$HR = \frac{\text{PVBP for bond to be hedged}}{\text{PVBP for deliverable bond}} \times$$

$$\frac{\text{Change in yield for bond to be hedged}}{\text{Change in yield for deliverable bond}} \times$$

Conversion Factor.

The first ratio corrects for the differences in price volatility of the two securities with respect to a given change in market yield. The second ratio, which is known as the *yield beta*, corrects for the change in the relative yield for each security. The yield beta can be obtained by estimating the following time series regression:

$$\begin{array}{l}\text{yield on} \\ \text{hedged} \\ \text{security}\end{array} = A + B \left(\begin{array}{l}\text{yield on} \\ \text{deliverable} \\ \text{security}\end{array}\right) + \text{error}$$

where B is the yield beta.

Another issue associated with implementing the hedge is choosing the appropriate contract month.[25]

Speculation

Speculators are investors who believe that they have superior information regarding future price movements of the market and use this
informational advantage to place bets on the market. Typically,
speculators base their information on fundamental and technical
analysis.

Fundamental analysis focuses on factors outside of the JGB futures market which are expected to have a significant impact on that
market. These factors include the domestic and world economy,
budgetary and monetary policies, balance of international payments,
exchange rates, etc. In the past, the primary subjects of fundamental
analysis have been the Japanese and US economies and their interrelationship. Factors such as domestic Japanese supply/demand for
money and volume of new bond issuing are becoming increasingly
important elements of fundamental analysis.[27]

Technical analysts believe that clues regarding future price
movements can be found from analysis of past price behavior in the
market. Although the validity of technical analysis is questioned in
the US, it remains a commonly used tool in Japan. The most often
cited rationale for this is that the JGB market is inefficient, rendering
fundamental analysis less effective in predicting price moves.[28]

OPTIONS ON JAPANESE GOVERNMENT BONDS

The over-the-counter market for JGB options began operation in
April 1989. Securities companies and financial institutions that are
dealers in the public bond market (JGB's, government-guaranteed
bonds, and publicly issued local government bonds) are allowed to
function as traders in this market. As of May 1989, there were 204
such eligible financial institutions.[29] Although the Ministry of Finance regulations allow trading in options on all Japanese domestic
and non-domestic sovereign yen-denominated bonds, market-making has concentrated in the 10-year benchmark bond.[30]

The unit of trade for these options is at least 100 million yen.
Both American and European style options are available, with exercise periods up to one year in length. The margin requirement for
option writers is the option price plus 5% of the face value of the

underlying security. Cash or substitute securities of this value must be deposited with the dealer before noon of the third business day after the contract issuance. Acceptable securities and their valuation rates are identical to those for margin on futures contracts (see Exhibit 1). Buyers must pay the option writer before the end of the fourth business day after the contract has been executed.

For an investor, each long or short option creates a contract with the participating broker. This contract is not transferable, and therefore a separate contract with the same broker is required to unwind the option position. Taking an offsetting position with a different dealer, therefore, will result in two unrelated positions.[31]

Securities companies, financial institutions, corporations listed on the securities exchanges, and corporations with stock traded over-the-counter are allowed to participate in the options market. In addition, securities companies may, at their discretion, allow other Japanese corporations, foreign corporations, and individuals to trade options provided that these corporations or individuals meet certain experience and portfolio requirements.

Dealers are not currently allowed to make markets in options on JGB futures contracts. The Ministry of Finance, however, is presently developing regulations for OTC options on a futures contract that would begin operation in mid-1990.

ENDNOTES

[1] Tetsuya Tashiro, *Bond Futures Market Two Years After Inception*, Shihonshijo, 1988, pp. 26-28. [In Japanese, title translated]

[2] Koichi Okuda, *Modern Bond Market*, Nipponhyoronsha, 1988, p. 337. [In Japanese, title translated]

[3] Tetsuya Tashiro, op. cit., p. 25 and Tokyo Stock Exchange data.

[4] Banque Paribas Capital Markets, *Japanese Bond Market—An Overview*, Banque Paribas Capital Markets, International Fixed Income Research, 1987, p. 26.

[5] Tetsuya Tashiro, op. cit., p. 25.

6 Seiji Noma; Toshio Haruki; and Noriyuki Hidema; *Swap, Bond Futures, and Currency Options*, Ginkokenshusha, 1987, p. 45. [In Japanese, title translated]

7 The level of margin requirements may be changed at any time by the exchange. The margin requirements used in the illustrations in this chapter are those specified at the time of this writing. Margin requirements are different for hedgers and spread traders.

8 Michisato Sakamoto, *Government Bonds*, Okurazaimukyokai, 1988, p. 211. [In Japanese, title translated]

9 Banque Paribas Capital Markets, op. cit., p. 29.

10 Daiwa Securities Co., Ltd, *Common Sense of Bonds*, 1989, p. 249. [In Japanese, title translated]

11 Credit Suisse First Boston, *The CSFB Guide to the Yen Bond Markets*, Chicago: Probus Publishing Company, 1988, p. 45.

12 Daiwa Securities Co., Ltd, op. cit., pp. 246-247.

13 Ibid., p. 249.

14 The relationship is derived in Frank J. Fabozzi and T. Dessa Fabozzi, *Bond Markets, Analysis and Strategies*, Englewood Cliffs, New Jersey: Prentice-Hall, Inc., 1989, pp. 240-242.

15 Credit Suisse First Boston, op. cit., p. 69.

16 Ibid., p. 70.

17 Banque Paribas Capital Markets, op. cit., p. 29

18 See Fabozzi and Fabozzi, op. cit., pp. 243-246.

19 Banque Paribas Capital Markets, op. cit., p. 30.

20 Ibid., p. 29.

21 Ibid., p. 31.

22 Karen S. Keegan, *Government of Japan Bond Futures*, London: First Boston Corporation, 1986, p. 11.

23 Ibid., p. 11.

24 See Fabozzi and Fabozzi, op. cit., pp. 252-254.

[25] The price value of a basis point is the change in price for a one basis point change in yield. Alternatively, the hedge ratio can be expressed in terms of dollar duration (i.e., modified duration times the bond price). See: Frank J. Fabozzi, *Fixed Income Mathematics*, Chicago, Illinois: Probus Publishing, 1988.

[26] For a more detailed discussion of how to implement a hedging strategy, see Mark Pitts and Frank J. Fabozzi, *Interest Rate Futures and Options*, Chicago: Probus Publishing, 1990, Chapter 9.

[27] Noma et al, op. cit., pp. 105-106.

[28] Ibid. p. 106.

[29] "Securities Industry's Role in Options," *Nikkei Newsletter on Bonds and Money*, November 21, 1988, p. 12.

[30] Daiwa Securities Company, Ltd., *The O.T.C. Market for Options on Japanese Government Bonds*, 1990, p. 4.

[30] Ibid. p. 12.

APPENDIX

The Derivation of the Conversion Factor for JGB Futures

Gerald G. Wisz, Ph.D.
President
The Cosmos Group, Inc.

This appendix will discuss conversion factors with regard to their derivation and the role they play in the delivery mechanism. The factors will also be compared to similar factors in the United States government bond and note markets.

The amount to be paid or received at the delivery of a Japanese futures contract is determined on the basis of the final delivery price. The delivery price is equal to the contract size multiplied by the futures contract settlement price (adjusted by the conversion factor) and the addition of accrued interest. The conversion factor is multiplied by the futures price. The conversion factor allows for the delivery of numerous Japanese cash bonds of varying coupon rates and different maturity dates (to that of the standard 6% coupon) against the 10- or 20-year notional bond specified in the two futures contracts. These conversion factors in effect provide a system of premiums and discounts to the invoiced futures price.

The formulas for determining the conversion factors can in essence be looked upon as a discounting of the remaining cash flows of the cash delivered bond from the first day of the delivery month to the final maturity date. The discount rate is the 6% yield for the Tokyo Stock Exchange (TSE) while it is 8% for the Chicago Board of Trade (CBOT) in the U.S. Both the TSE and the Financial Instrument Exchange (FINEX) in the U.S. require that the remaining maturity of each eligible cash bond be rounded down to the number of whole

The author wishes to thank the New York Research Office of the TSE for providing him with material on the Japanese Government Bond Futures and the conversion factor table for the 10-year bond futures contract.

months until the final actual maturity date. This is in contrast to the CBOT which requires rounding down to the nearest quarter. The cash flow however for all exchanges (TSE, CBOT, and FINEX) is calculated from the first day of the delivery month regardless of when the actual delivery is made during the month. Accrued interest is of course calculated to the actual date in the delivery month the bond is delivered.

To illustrate, we will compute the conversion factor for Japanese bond number 114 which has a coupon of 4.8% and matures on December 20, 1998. Let us assume a delivery month of June 1990. If we calculated the number of quarters from June 1, 1990 to December 20, 1998 we would arrive at a little over 34 quarters or eight years and a little over six months. In this case rounding down to the nearest quarter or month would yield the same results. When we are analyzing bonds which mature on the same month as the delivery month then rounding down to quarters or months provides identical results.

The conversion factor can now be calculated either by using the formula given in the body of this chapter or by using the formula with a coupon of 4.8%, 17 coupon payments to maturity, and 0 months since the last coupon payment yields a conversion factor of 0.921003.

Alternatively, we can simulate this time frame on any bond calculator by using a settlement date of June 1, 1990 (our delivery month), using a maturity date of December 1, 1998 (instead of December 20), to get our rounded down time frame and using a yield of 6%. Then our calculated price would be 92.100329 and dividing by 100 gives us our TSE conversion factor of .921003 (rounded to six places after the decimal point).

This factor is in essence the discount price for our bond. It is this factor multiplied by the futures price which adjusts the futures as part of the delivery invoice process. The TSE conversion factor has two more significant digits than the CBOT factor since the trading unit face value is 100 million yen versus the 100 thousand dollar face value for the U.S. bond and note futures.

One can also obtain these "factors" or prices from sets of tables provided by the Tokyo Stock Exchange. There are separate tables for the 10-year and the 20-year bond futures. The 10-year note table, shown as Exhibit 1, has columns which represent various coupon

EXHIBIT 1: CONVERSION FACTOR TABLE FOR THE 10-YEAR JGB FUTURES

（受渡適格銘柄の利率）

（受渡適格銘柄の残存期間）

年—月	4.000%	4.100%	4.200%	4.300%	4.400%	4.500%	4.600%	4.700%	4.800%	4.900%
7_0	0.887039	0.892687	0.898335	0.903983	0.909631	0.915279	0.920927	0.926575	0.932223	0.937871
7_1	0.885915	0.891616	0.897317	0.903018	0.908719	0.914420	0.920121	0.925823	0.931524	0.937225
7_2	0.884812	0.890567	0.896321	0.902076	0.907830	0.913584	0.919339	0.925093	0.930848	0.936602
7_3	0.883732	0.889540	0.895348	0.901155	0.906963	0.912771	0.918579	0.924387	0.930195	0.936002
7_4	0.882673	0.888534	0.894396	0.900257	0.906119	0.911980	0.917841	0.923703	0.929564	0.935426
7_5	0.881636	0.887551	0.893466	0.899381	0.905296	0.911211	0.917127	0.923042	0.928957	0.934872
7_6	0.880620	0.886589	0.892558	0.898527	0.904496	0.910465	0.916434	0.922403	0.928372	0.934341
7_7	0.879528	0.885548	0.891569	0.897589	0.903610	0.909630	0.915651	0.921671	0.927692	0.933712
7_8	0.878457	0.884529	0.890601	0.896673	0.902745	0.908818	0.914890	0.920962	0.927034	0.933107
7_9	0.877407	0.883531	0.889656	0.895780	0.901904	0.908028	0.914152	0.920276	0.926400	0.932524
7_10	0.876380	0.882556	0.888732	0.894908	0.901084	0.907260	0.913436	0.919612	0.925788	0.931964
7_11	0.875373	0.881602	0.887830	0.894058	0.900286	0.906515	0.912743	0.918971	0.925199	0.931428
8_0	0.874398	0.880669	0.886950	0.893230	0.899511	0.905791	0.912072	0.918352	0.924633	0.930913
8_1	0.873326	0.879657	0.885988	0.892318	0.898649	0.904979	0.911310	0.917640	0.923971	0.930302
8_2	0.872286	0.878667	0.885048	0.891428	0.897809	0.904190	0.910570	0.916951	0.923332	0.929713
8_3	0.871267	0.877698	0.884129	0.890560	0.896991	0.903423	0.909854	0.916285	0.922716	0.929147
8_4	0.870270	0.876751	0.883233	0.889714	0.896196	0.902677	0.909159	0.915641	0.922122	0.928604
8_5	0.869293	0.875826	0.882358	0.888890	0.895423	0.901955	0.908487	0.915019	0.921551	0.928084
8_6	0.868338	0.874921	0.881504	0.888087	0.894671	0.901254	0.907837	0.914420	0.921003	0.927586
8_7	0.867306	0.873938	0.880569	0.887201	0.893832	0.900464	0.907096	0.913727	0.920359	0.926990
8_8	0.866295	0.872975	0.879656	0.886336	0.893016	0.899697	0.906377	0.913057	0.919737	0.926418
8_9	0.865306	0.872035	0.878764	0.885493	0.892222	0.898951	0.905681	0.912410	0.919139	0.925868
8_10	0.864338	0.871116	0.877894	0.884672	0.891450	0.898228	0.905007	0.911785	0.918563	0.925341
8_11	0.863390	0.870218	0.877045	0.883873	0.890700	0.897527	0.904355	0.911182	0.918010	0.924837
9_0	0.862464	0.869341	0.876218	0.883095	0.889971	0.896848	0.903725	0.910602	0.917478	0.924355
9_1	0.861461	0.868385	0.875309	0.882232	0.889156	0.896080	0.903004	0.909928	0.916852	0.923776
9_2	0.860479	0.867450	0.874421	0.881392	0.888363	0.895334	0.902305	0.909277	0.916248	0.923219
9_3	0.859518	0.866537	0.873555	0.880574	0.887592	0.894611	0.901629	0.908648	0.915666	0.922685
9_4	0.858578	0.865644	0.872710	0.879777	0.886843	0.893909	0.900975	0.908041	0.915107	0.922174
9_5	0.857659	0.864773	0.871887	0.879001	0.886115	0.893229	0.900343	0.907457	0.914571	0.921685
9_6	0.856762	0.863923	0.871086	0.878247	0.885409	0.892571	0.899733	0.906895	0.914057	0.921219
9_7	0.855786	0.862994	0.870201	0.877409	0.884616	0.891824	0.899032	0.906239	0.913447	0.920654
9_8	0.854832	0.862085	0.869339	0.876592	0.883845	0.891099	0.898353	0.905606	0.912859	0.920113
9_9	0.853899	0.861198	0.868498	0.875797	0.883097	0.890396	0.897696	0.904995	0.912295	0.919594
9_10	0.852987	0.860332	0.867678	0.875024	0.882370	0.889715	0.897061	0.904407	0.911752	0.919098
9_11	0.852095	0.859487	0.866880	0.874272	0.881664	0.889056	0.896448	0.903840	0.911232	0.918625
10_0	0.851225	0.858663	0.866102	0.873541	0.880980	0.888418	0.895857	0.903296	0.910735	0.918173
10_1	0.850277	0.857760	0.865243	0.872726	0.880209	0.887692	0.895175	0.902658	0.910141	0.917624
10_2	0.849349	0.856877	0.864405	0.871932	0.879460	0.886987	0.894515	0.902042	0.909570	0.917098
10_3	0.848443	0.856016	0.863588	0.871160	0.878732	0.886305	0.893877	0.901449	0.909021	0.916594
10_4	0.847558	0.855175	0.862792	0.870409	0.878027	0.885644	0.893261	0.900878	0.908495	0.916112
10_5	0.846693	0.854356	0.862018	0.869680	0.877342	0.885004	0.892667	0.900329	0.907991	0.915653
10_6	0.845849	0.853557	0.861264	0.868972	0.876679	0.884387	0.892094	0.899802	0.907509	0.915217
10_7	0.844928	0.852678	0.860429	0.868179	0.875930	0.883680	0.891431	0.899181	0.906932	0.914682
10_8	0.844027	0.851820	0.859614	0.867408	0.875201	0.882995	0.890789	0.898583	0.906376	0.914170
10_9	0.843147	0.850984	0.858821	0.866658	0.874495	0.882332	0.890169	0.898006	0.905843	0.913681
10_10	0.842287	0.850168	0.858049	0.865929	0.873810	0.881691	0.889571	0.897452	0.905333	0.913214
10_11	0.841449	0.849373	0.857298	0.865222	0.873146	0.881071	0.888995	0.896920	0.904844	0.912769
11_0	0.840630	0.848599	0.856567	0.864536	0.872504	0.880473	0.888441	0.896410	0.904378	0.912346

（受渡適格銘柄の残存期間）

EXHIBIT 1: (continued)

（受渡適格銘柄の利率）

（受渡適格銘柄の残存期間）

年-月	5.000X	5.100X	5.200X	5.300X	5.400X	5.500X	5.600X	5.700X	5.800X	5.900X
7- 0	0.943519	0.949167	0.954815	0.960463	0.966111	0.971759	0.977407	0.983055	0.988703	0.994351
7- 1	0.942926	0.948627	0.954328	0.960030	0.965731	0.971432	0.977133	0.982834	0.988535	0.994237
7- 2	0.942357	0.948111	0.953865	0.959620	0.965374	0.971129	0.976883	0.982638	0.988392	0.994146
7- 3	0.941810	0.947618	0.953426	0.959234	0.965042	0.970849	0.976657	0.982465	0.988273	0.994081
7- 4	0.941287	0.947149	0.953010	0.958871	0.964733	0.970594	0.976456	0.982317	0.988178	0.994040
7- 5	0.940787	0.946702	0.952617	0.958532	0.964447	0.970363	0.976278	0.982193	0.988108	0.994023
7- 6	0.940310	0.946279	0.952248	0.958217	0.964186	0.970155	0.976124	0.982093	0.988062	0.994031
7- 7	0.939733	0.945753	0.951774	0.957794	0.963815	0.969835	0.975856	0.981876	0.987897	0.993917
7- 8	0.939179	0.945251	0.951323	0.957395	0.963468	0.969540	0.975612	0.981684	0.987756	0.993829
7- 9	0.938648	0.944772	0.950896	0.957020	0.963144	0.969268	0.975392	0.981516	0.987641	0.993765
7-10	0.938140	0.944316	0.950493	0.956669	0.962845	0.969021	0.975197	0.981373	0.987549	0.993725
7-11	0.937656	0.943884	0.950112	0.956340	0.962569	0.968797	0.975025	0.981253	0.987482	0.993710
8- 0	0.937194	0.943475	0.949755	0.956036	0.962316	0.968597	0.974877	0.981158	0.987438	0.993719
8- 1	0.936632	0.942963	0.949293	0.955624	0.961954	0.968285	0.974615	0.980944	0.987277	0.993607
8- 2	0.936093	0.942474	0.948855	0.955236	0.961616	0.967997	0.974378	0.980759	0.987139	0.993520
8- 3	0.935578	0.942009	0.948440	0.954871	0.961302	0.967733	0.974164	0.980595	0.987027	0.993458
8- 4	0.935085	0.941567	0.948049	0.954530	0.961012	0.967493	0.973975	0.980456	0.986938	0.993420
8- 5	0.934616	0.941148	0.947680	0.954212	0.960745	0.967277	0.973809	0.980341	0.986874	0.993406
8- 6	0.934169	0.940752	0.947335	0.953918	0.960501	0.967084	0.973667	0.980250	0.986833	0.993416
8- 7	0.933622	0.940253	0.946885	0.953517	0.960148	0.966780	0.973411	0.980043	0.986675	0.993306
8- 8	0.933098	0.939778	0.946459	0.953139	0.959818	0.966499	0.973180	0.979860	0.986540	0.993221
8- 9	0.932597	0.939326	0.946055	0.952785	0.959514	0.966243	0.972972	0.979701	0.986430	0.993160
8-10	0.932119	0.938898	0.945676	0.952454	0.959232	0.966010	0.972788	0.979567	0.986345	0.993123
8-11	0.931664	0.938492	0.945319	0.952146	0.958974	0.965801	0.972629	0.979456	0.986283	0.993111
9- 0	0.931232	0.938109	0.944985	0.951862	0.958739	0.965616	0.972492	0.979369	0.986246	0.993123
9- 1	0.930699	0.937623	0.944547	0.951471	0.958395	0.965319	0.972242	0.979166	0.986090	0.993014
9- 2	0.930190	0.937161	0.944132	0.951103	0.958074	0.965045	0.972016	0.978988	0.985959	0.992930
9- 3	0.929703	0.936722	0.943740	0.950739	0.957777	0.964796	0.971815	0.978833	0.985852	0.992870
9- 4	0.929240	0.936306	0.943372	0.950438	0.957504	0.964570	0.971637	0.978703	0.985769	0.992835
9- 5	0.928799	0.935913	0.943027	0.950141	0.957255	0.964368	0.971482	0.978596	0.985710	0.992824
9- 6	0.928381	0.935542	0.942704	0.949866	0.957028	0.964190	0.971352	0.978514	0.985676	0.992838
9- 7	0.927862	0.935070	0.942277	0.949485	0.956692	0.963900	0.971107	0.978315	0.985523	0.992730
9- 8	0.927366	0.934620	0.941873	0.949127	0.956380	0.963634	0.970887	0.978140	0.985394	0.992647
9- 9	0.926894	0.934193	0.941493	0.948792	0.956092	0.963391	0.970691	0.977990	0.985290	0.992589
9-10	0.926444	0.933790	0.941135	0.948481	0.955827	0.963173	0.970518	0.977864	0.985210	0.992555
9-11	0.926017	0.933409	0.940801	0.948193	0.955585	0.962977	0.970370	0.977762	0.985154	0.992546
10- 0	0.925612	0.933051	0.940490	0.947928	0.955367	0.962806	0.970245	0.977683	0.985122	0.992561
10- 1	0.925107	0.932590	0.940073	0.947556	0.955039	0.962523	0.970005	0.977489	0.984972	0.992455
10- 2	0.924625	0.932153	0.939680	0.947208	0.954735	0.962263	0.969791	0.977318	0.984846	0.992373
10- 3	0.924166	0.931738	0.939310	0.946883	0.954455	0.962027	0.969600	0.977172	0.984744	0.992316
10- 4	0.923730	0.931347	0.938964	0.946581	0.954198	0.961815	0.969432	0.977050	0.984667	0.992284
10- 5	0.923316	0.930978	0.938640	0.946302	0.953965	0.961627	0.969289	0.976951	0.984614	0.992276
10- 6	0.922924	0.930632	0.938339	0.946047	0.953754	0.961462	0.969169	0.976877	0.984584	0.992292
10- 7	0.922433	0.930183	0.937934	0.945684	0.953435	0.961185	0.968936	0.976686	0.984437	0.992187
10- 8	0.921964	0.929757	0.937551	0.945345	0.953139	0.960932	0.968728	0.976520	0.984313	0.992107
10- 9	0.921518	0.929355	0.937192	0.945029	0.952866	0.960703	0.968540	0.976377	0.984214	0.992052
10-10	0.921094	0.928975	0.936856	0.944736	0.952617	0.960498	0.968378	0.976259	0.984140	0.992020
10-11	0.920693	0.928618	0.936542	0.944467	0.952391	0.960316	0.968240	0.976165	0.984089	0.992014
11- 0	0.920315	0.928283	0.936252	0.944220	0.952189	0.960157	0.968126	0.976094	0.984063	0.992031

（受渡適格銘柄の残存期間）

rates on the cash bonds, namely from 4.000% to 9.900%. The rows represent the time to maturity from the first of the delivery month to the actual maturity date rounded to the nearest month. The table has a time range from seven years and zero months to eleven years and zero months. This time range corresponds to the eligibility range for deliverability of a cash bond against the standardized 6%, 10-year Japanese government bond. So for our example, if we look at the 8–6 row and the intersection of the 4.800% column we obtain 0.921003 which is the same factor we can obtain with our bond calculator.

For the June 1990 10-year government bond futures there were ten cash bonds eligible for delivery and for the 20-year bond futures there were 30 cash bonds eligible for delivery. The maturity date of all these bonds corresponds to a delivery month so one needs to round down only to the nearest quarter when calculating the conversion factors. In the past, for the 10-year bond futures there were seven cash bonds whose maturity dates did not coincide with the four delivery months (March, June, September, December). These were bond numbers 77, 78, 81, 82, 87, 90, 98. So for bond number 98 with a 5% coupon and maturing on January 20, 1997 being delivered for the December 1988 futures contract, the time frame of 8 years, 1 month and 20 days would be rounded down to 8 years and 1 month with a resultant factor of 0.936632 as can be seen from the second page of Exhibit 1.

As we have seen so far, the conversion factors have all been scaled to be less than one since we have shown coupon rates less than our assumed yield of 6%. If the coupon rates are above the 6% mark as in bonds #128 and #129 which have rates of 6.2% and 6.4%, respectively, then our factors were greater than one (1.014488 and 1.029087) for the June 1990 10-year futures contract.

The conversion factor plays another important role in addition to providing proper invoicing. Of all the issues eligible for delivery one must determine which is the "cheapest" to deliver. This is determined as the issue which has the smallest "basis." Basis is calculated as the difference between the cash market bond price and its futures invoice price. The futures invoice price is the closing futures price multiplied by the relevant conversion factor. Hence, suppose we have a futures price of 90.91 and a conversion factor of 0.967403, then the result of multiplying these two quantities together would be 87.947. If we now subtract this amount from a cash price of 87.761

we would obtain a negative 0.186 which in 32nds corresponds to a negative basis of 5.95. The cheapest to deliver issue would then be the cash bond with the smallest basis calculated as shown above.

The focus in this appendix has been on the derivation of the conversion factor utilized by the TSE. Conversion factor tables or a bond calculator could be used to determine the proper factors.

Index